PRACTICAL COUNSELLING AND HELPING SKILLS

PRACTICAL COUNSELLING AND HELPING SKILLS

How to Use the Lifeskills Helping Model

Third edition

Richard Nelson-Jones

CASSELL

Cassell Educational Limited
Villiers House, 41/47 Strand, London WC2N 5JE
387 Park Avenue South, New York, NY 10016–8810

First edition, entitled *Practical Counselling Skills*, 1983
Second edition 1988
Third edition first published 1993, reprinted 1994

British Library Cataloguing-in-Publication Data

A catalogue record for this book is available from the British Library.

ISBN 0-304-32543-0

Typeset by Litho Link Ltd., Welshpool, Powys, Wales.
Printed and bound in Great Britain by Page Bros., Norwich.

PART TWO: STAGES AND SKILLS OF THE LIFESKILLS HELPING MODEL

Stage 1: Develop the Relationship, Identify and Clarify Problem(s)

CONTENTS

Preface

Practical Counselling and Helping Skills: How to Use the Lifeskills Helping Model presents a systematic people-centred approach not only for managing immediate problems, but also for altering the skills weaknesses, or problematic skills, that sustain problems. The focus of lifeskills helping is not just the present. Helpers can assist clients to learn self-helping skills to prevent and manage future problems. I describe a five-stage model for helping clients develop specific lifeskills for assuming responsibility for how they feel, think and act.

This book is a basic text for trainers and students in the counselling and helping service areas. Courses for which the book might be suitable include those in counselling, psychotherapy, psychology, social work, probation work, nursing, rehabilitation, education, career work, youth work, correctional work, welfare work, community relations, pastoral care and personnel management. I also intend the book to support trainers and students in voluntary agencies, for instance in marital counselling, immigrant counselling, or gay and lesbian counselling.

A number of assumptions underlie the lifeskills helping approach. First, to live effectively clients need to learn and then maintain good lifeskills. Second, though external factors contribute, clients sustain problems because of weaknesses in one or more lifeskills. Third, after helping, clients often repeat problematic behaviours when faced with the same or similar problems to those that brought them to helping. Helpers have insufficiently assisted them to learn and maintain relevant lifeskills. Fourth, the aim of helping is to provide clients with self-helping skills for managing not only current, but future problems. People-centredness involves showing clients how to become their own best helpers.

Part One consists of three introductory chapters. Chapter 1 defines terms and presents a psychological education theoretical framework for the lifeskills helping model. In Chapter 2 I overview the model. Chapter 3 looks at what students and helpers bring to their helping work. The book's second part systematically presents the lifeskills helping model's five stages. Chapters 4 and 5 focus on the component skills of stage 1: develop the relationship, identify and clarify problem(s). Chapter 6 presents skills for stage 2: assess problem(s) and redefine in skills terms. Chapters 7 and 8 describe skills for stage 3: state working goals and plan interventions. The next four chapters present skills for stage 4: intervene to develop self-helping skills. Chapter 9 describes central training skills for delivering interventions. Chapters 10, 11 and 12 review interventions focused on thinking skills, action skills and feelings, respectively. Chapter 13 presents skills for stage 5: end and consolidate self-helping skills. A separate *Training Manual* of exercises and experiments is available to supplement the text and encourage learning-by-doing.

This book differs from its predecessor, *Practical Counselling and Helping Skills* (2nd edn) in many significant ways. First, this book is based on a more coherent psychological education theoretical framework. Second, I more clearly articulate the five-stage model of helping, including structuring the book around it. Third, I have put the exercises in a separate training manual. This is partly because a single large volume is too unwieldy, for instance in skills classes. Fourth, the book has new chapters entitled 'Framework and goals', 'What you bring to training and helping', 'How to assess problems and redefine in skills terms', 'How to state working goals', 'How to plan interventions', 'How to use training skills to deliver interventions', and 'How to end and consolidate self-helping skills'. Fifth, I have deleted the previous book's chapters on group counselling and lifeskills training. This is because I cover such topics in detail in *Lifeskills: A Handbook*, also published by Cassell (1991).

The lifeskills helping approach uses a simple meta-language that frees you to draw from existing theoretical positions without becoming trapped in their separate languages. Also, I emphasize that helpers and clients should think about problems in the same simple language. The lifeskills helping approach owes much to others' work. For example, the emphasis on the importance of supportive helping relationships and on sensitively attending to clients' feelings shows the influence of Carl Rogers' person-centred therapy. The emphasis on thinking skills is derived from the writing of Albert Ellis, Aaron Beck and Donald Meichenbaum, among others. The emphasis on action skills represents the influence of the behaviourists. The emphasis on personal responsibility and choice has origins in the work of Viktor Frankl, Irvin Yalom, Abraham Maslow, William Glasser, Hobart Mowrer and the theologian Paul Tillich. In addition, Harry Stack Sullivan, Gerard Egan and Robert Carkhuff were forerunners in presenting stage models of helping sessions and the helping process. I express appreciation to all these writers and to the many others whose names are referenced in the bibliography.

I also thank the following people who assisted in the book's production: my friends Maggie and John Phelan, for providing a sanctuary where I could recharge batteries; Erica Hallebone, for her understanding administrative support at the Royal Melbourne Institute of Technology; and at Cassell, Naomi Roth for commissioning the book and Sandra Margolies for overseeing its production.

I hope that *Practical Counselling and Helping Skills: How to Use the Lifeskills Helping Model* challenges you to think somewhat differently about how you work and live. I also hope it offers you the choice of a language, model and skills to become a more effective helper.

PART ONE

Introduction

ONE
Framework and Goals

Everything should be made as simple as possible, but not simpler.

Albert Einstein

CHAPTER QUESTIONS

What is lifeskills helping?

How is lifeskills helping a people-centred approach?

What are lifeskills?

What is a psychological education theoretical framework?

How do people acquire and maintain lifeskills?

How can people change and develop lifeskills?

What are the ultimate and mediating goals of lifeskills helping?

What are some characteristics of lifeskills helpers?

This is a helping skills textbook based on a psychological education or lifeskills model. Lifeskills helping is a people-centred approach for assisting clients and others to develop self-helping skills. This approach spurns psychological jargon in favour of a simple, direct educational framework. Geared to the needs of the vast majority of ordinary people, lifeskills helping assumes that *all people* have acquired and sustain lifeskills strengths and weaknesses. People's ineffective feeling, thinking and acting represent one or more lifeskills weaknesses rather than sickness or disease. Lifeskills helpers collaborate with clients to detect the lifeskills weaknesses that sustain difficulties and then, within supportive relationships, educate them in relevant self-helping skills.

Lifeskills helping always entails learning. As Corsini observes of psychotherapy, lifeskills helping 'may be learning something new or relearning something one has forgotten; it may be learning how to learn or it may be unlearning; paradoxically, it may even be learning what one already knows' (Corsini, 1989, p.5). Below are some common concerns presented to helpers.

- 'Our marriage seems to be heading for the rocks.'

- 'I feel depressed and apathetic.'

- 'I find it difficult to make up my mind about my career.'

- 'I get very tense and anxious over exams.'

- 'I'm having difficulty adjusting to my new surroundings.'

- 'I feel lonely and find it difficult to make friends.'

- 'I'm full of anger much of the time.'

- My life seems to lack purpose.'

- 'I find it difficult to stand up for myself.'

- I feel over-stressed and don't know what to do about it.'

- I feel guilty about being a mother and having a career.'

- 'Our sex life is practically non-existent.'

- I can't break loose from the hold my parents have on me.'

For all the above statements, the basic starting-point for lifeskills helpers is that they are learning problems. However, if relevant, medical considerations are also taken into account. Nevertheless, almost by definition, educational considerations are paramount for explaining most psychological problems.

Lifeskills helping is nothing new. Without necessarily using the same language, most helpers attempt to help clients develop skills of productive living. Furthermore, most parents attempt to help their children develop skills of living happily. Lifeskills helping aims to articulate the 'common sense' of effective helping. I do not require an originality complex to present the approach. Lifeskills helping builds upon the work of numerous theorists, researchers, helper trainers and practitioners. Why reinvent the wheel rather than help the wheel to run more smoothly?

A PEOPLE-CENTRED APPROACH

When the term people-centred is applied to lifeskills helping what does it mean? Below are some dimensions of people-centredness.

Goals

The basic theoretical, research and practical question of lifeskills helping is: 'How can counsellors and lifeskills trainers become more efficient personal responsibility educators?' The goals of lifeskills helping emphasize helping people to help themselves. The goal of any helping encounter, however brief, is not just to help clients either to feel better or to cope better with an immediate problem. Rather lifeskills helpers aim for clients to take away some skills for living. In this 'take-away' respect, lifeskills helping resembles McDonald's or Kentucky Fried Chicken, though hopefully with longer-lasting results! People are viewed as personally responsible for making the most of their lives. The goal of lifeskills helping is to provide them with the confidence and skills for assuming rather than avoiding this responsibility. Lifeskills helping aims to empower people not only now but in future. The approach seeks to develop clients' self-helping skills so that they become their own best helpers.

Language

Since the goal of lifeskills helping is self-help for afterwards, the language of helping must lend itself to client self-instruction. In any helping contact, there are at least four possible languages operative: helper and client inner and outer speech (Nelson-Jones, 1986). Lifeskills helping is based on an educational theoretical framework that helpers can use for both inner and outer speech. Helpers do not need to talk one language to themselves and another to clients. Lifeskills helpers use their own and their clients' outer speech to develop clients' inner speech so that they can understand their problems and instruct themselves through sequences of choices to cope with them.

Contrast the above idea of people-centred language with the language of so-called person-centred therapy. Person-centred helpers operate out of a theoretical framework that is rarely, if ever, explicitly communicated to clients (Raskin & Rogers, 1989; Rogers, 1951, 1959). Consequently, to a certain extent at least, person-centred helpers may be talking one language to themselves and another to clients. The process of person-centred helping involves helpers empathically reflecting in their outer responses the outer statements of their clients. No attempt is made directly to influence clients' inner speech so that they can instruct themselves in relevant learnings for afterwards. Person-centred helping is based on an unfolding of potential rather than a systematic development of competencies model. Both models are necessary for effective helping. Because of this lopsidedness, person-centred helping falls short of people-centred helping. Approaches like rational-emotive therapy and transactional analysis both more closely match helper inner and outer speech and also attempt to train clients in self-instruction (Berne, 1961, 1964, 1972; Dusay & Dusay, 1989; Ellis, 1962, 1980, 1989).

Figure 1.1 provides an illustration of public and private talk in counselling and lifeskills training. Much counselling and training is educationally inefficient. It focuses insufficiently on moving beyond helper and client public talk at B and C. In lifeskills helping, counsellors and group leaders use public talk at B and C not just to develop a helping relationship, but actively to work from helper private self-talk at A to influence client private self-talk at D. By communicating from an educational framework expressed in relatively simple language, counsellors and group leaders can help clients acquire relevant private self-talk to monitor, maintain and develop skills. Hence, the language of lifeskills helping becomes the people-centred language of self-helping and self-instruction.

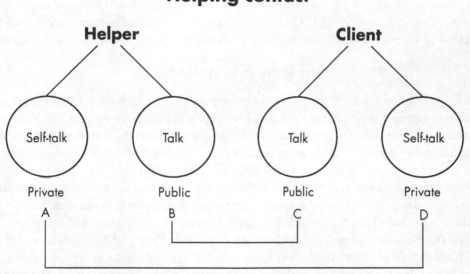

Figure 1.1 *Public and private talk in counselling and lifeskills training*

Clienteles

A lifeskills approach takes acquiring and maintaining psychological wellness rather than psychological disturbance as its starting-point. Lifeskills helping is people-centred in that all people may benefit at some stage of their lives from contact with skilled helpers. You do not have to be sick or fit into a *Diagnostic and Statistical Manual of Mental Disorders* – revised category (*DSM-111-R;* American Psychiatric Association, 1987) to benefit from helping. Problems of living are widespread. As Ellis quips, a way to spell life is H-A-S-S-L-E (Ellis, 1977). When growing up, the fortunate acquire many of the requisite lifeskills in developmental and preventive ways. Such acquisitions may include individual and group contact with lifeskills helpers. Those less fortunate may require considerable remedial help to develop good lifeskills. Even those more fortunate may later wish to work on specific problems and to become more skilled in various areas.

The statistics on marital breakdown provide one indication of the pervasiveness of human problems. The number of divorces in England and Wales during 1990 is estimated to have been 153,000, about 2 per cent more than in 1989 and the highest total since 1986 (Office of Population Censuses and Surveys, 1991a). Even at the lower 1987 divorce rate level, 37 per cent of marriages in England and Wales are predicted to end in divorce (Office of Population Censuses and Surveys, 1991b). These figures partly reflect the fact that obtaining a divorce has become easier than for earlier generations. Also, divorce is less socially stigmatized. Nevertheless, the figures underestimate the extent of marital breakdown. If the figures for the separated population were added to those of the divorced population to form a 'dissolution index', the statistics for marital breakdown would be considerably higher. In addition, many couples, neither separated nor divorced, are deeply unhappy. Marital breakdown and distress involve children. In 1990, there were 153,000 children affected by divorce in England and Wales. If the 1988–89 divorce rate remains unchanged, it is estimated that one-quarter of all children will, before the age of 16, experience divorce in their families (Office of Population Censuses and Surveys, 1991b). There is much pain in Britain, as in the rest of the world. Furthermore, poor lifeskills are probably transmitted from generation to generation.

Problems and potentials

Lifeskills helping not only focuses on helping people cope with their problems, it also focuses on freeing their potentials. Lifeskills helping is people-centred in that it focuses on the range of competencies that all people require for their survival, maintenance and enhancement. It is an egalitarian approach that assumes that everyone, regardless of age, sex, race, colour or creed, has the 'potential for growth and the right to personal maximization of competence' (Albee, 1984, p.230). Problems for which people require adaptive feelings, thoughts and actions to maximize their potentials can occur at all ages of the life-span and in all areas of life (Egan & Cowan, 1979; Erikson, 1963; Havighurst, 1972; Kohlberg & Gilligan, 1971; Masterpasqua, 1989; Perry, 1970; Sugarman, 1986).

The kinds of problem and potential for which lifeskills helping is appropriate range from basic thinking and action skills for all stages of the lifespan to developmental competencies that are more life-stage specific: for example, learning intimacy and sexual relating skills for young adults and coping with ageing and dying skills for the old. Lifeskills helping can focus on problems and potentials in all major areas of life: for example, partner relationships, sex, parenting, occupational choice, work, study and test taking, leisure and health. Furthermore, lifeskills helpers work with many symptoms often more indicative of dis-ease than disease: for example, depression, acute and chronic anxiety, phobias, delinquent behaviour, substance abuse and aggression.

Helping process

The process of lifeskills helping is people-centred. Helpers and clients collaborate in such activities as clarifying problems, redefining problems in skills terms, setting goals, choosing interventions, setting session agendas and evaluating progress. Lifeskills helpers require both good training and good helping relationship skills. They can hide behind neither a facade of phoney expertness nor the mystique of a medical model. The process of lifeskills helping entails much client participation in decision making. If helpers want clients to redefine problems in skills terms, they have to offer clear explanations and negotiate such redefinitions with them. After all, it is their clients' lives they seek to influence and clients ultimately implement treatment recommendations on their own. At all times helpers attempt to be psychologically present in interviews as genuine and caring people (May & Yalom, 1989). However, they do not have to accept everything that clients tell them. Frequently, lifeskills helpers are more people-centred if they confront and expand upon clients' perceptions rather than only reflectively respond. In addition, clients may feel more understood by helpers who expand their awareness than by those who stay closely to their view of themselves and their problems. Lifeskills helpers are educators who offer training expertise within the context of democratic supportive relationships. Another way of looking at the client role is that of trainee. This trainee role reflects Mosak's comment about Adlerian psychotherapy: 'Although assuming the role of student, the patient is still an active learner responsible for contributing to his or her own education' (Mosak, 1989, p.85).

Helpers

Lifeskills helping is people-centred in that many different categories of people are helpers. Earlier the point was made that clients need to develop the competencies of becoming their own helpers in targeted skills areas. Formal helping provides one arena for lifeskills helping. Such helpers are likely to be helping service professionals and para-professionals: counsellors, psychologists, social workers, probation officers, nurses and personnel officers among others. Many can use the lifeskills helping framework and skills in their jobs: for example, ministers of religion, teachers, sports coaches, managers and supervisors. Even more people can use lifeskills helping skills as partners, parents and friends. Helpers apply the same lifeskills framework to themselves as to their clients. Though helpers may be of differing levels of competence and sophistication, the more widely distributed that lifeskills helping becomes the better.

DEFINING LIFESKILLS HELPING
What are skills?

Whether referring to client or to helper skills, meanings of the word skill include proficiency, competence and expertise. The essential element of any skill is the ability to make and implement sequences of choices to achieve objectives. For instance, if clients are to be good at asserting themselves or managing stress, they have to make and implement effective choices in these lifeskills areas. Similarly, if you are to be good lifeskills helpers, you have to make and implement effective choices in such helper skills as facilitating clients, assessing lifeskills strengths and weaknesses, redefining problems in skills terms, offering appropriate interventions, and assisting clients to consolidate trained skills as self-helping skills.

The concept of skill is best viewed not as an either/or matter in which you either possess or do not possess a skill. It is preferable to think of yourselves and clients as possessing *skills strengths* or *skills weaknesses* or a mixture of the two. Good choices in skills areas are skills strengths. Poor choices are skills weaknesses. Put simply, the criterion for good or poor client choices is whether they help or hinder clients in assuming personal responsibility for happiness and fulfilment. The criterion for good or poor helper choices is whether they best help clients assume personal responsibility.

In all lifeskills and helping skills areas people are likely to possess skills strengths and weaknesses in varying degrees. For instance, in the skills area of listening, you may be good at understanding talkers, but poor at showing your understanding. The object of lifeskills helping is to help clients, in one or more skills areas, move more in the direction of skills strengths than skills weaknesses. The object of helper training is the same, but in regard to helping skills rather than lifeskills. In both instances, those being trained are helped to affirm themselves and others by becoming *better choosers*.

What are lifeskills?

A number of dimensions of a positive definition of lifeskills are explored below.

Lifeskills entail *personally responsible choices*. When people are being personally responsible they are in the process of making the choices that maximize their happiness and fulfilment (Frankl, 1959; May & Yalom, 1989; Nelson-Jones, 1984; Yalom, 1980). Personal responsibility is a positive concept whereby people are responsible for their well-being and making their own choices within the givens of their existences. Lifeskills are the component skills through which people assume rather than avoid personal responsibility for their lives. Lifeskills are *self-helping skills* or competencies that enable people to help themselves. As such they empower rather than depower or weaken people (Hopson & Scally, 1981; Masterpasqua, 1989).

Lifeskills are conducive to *mental wellness*. People who possess inadequate lifeskills are less able to fulfil their potential and meet their needs than those more skilled. Psychological distress both reflects and results from deficiencies in lifeskills. However, this is less true for biologically influenced conditions, for instance schizophrenia and bipolar depressive disorders (Lazarus, 1989). Lifeskills possess a *psychological component*. Virtually any skill, for instance cooking, might be viewed as a lifeskill. However, all the lifeskills mentioned in this book have a large 'mind' component in them. Thus, even though many lifeskills are stated as specific observable actions, they usually heavily involve people's thoughts and feelings as well.

Lifeskills are *processes*. People lead their lives into the future and are always in process of becoming (Allport, 1955). Throughout their lives people are choosers who can never escape the mandate to choose between possibilities (Frankl, 1969). People possessing a lifeskill choose to make, and hopefully continue making, the choices involved in implementing that lifeskill. To attain their full humanness, people require a *repertoire of lifeskills* in a number of different areas. These lifeskills need to be appropriate both to their developmental tasks and also to any special problems of living, challenges and transitions they may face.

Below some of the above dimensions are drawn together into a definition of lifeskills for this book.

> Lifeskills are personally responsible sequences of self-helping choices in specific psychological skills areas conducive to mental wellness. People require a repertoire of lifeskills according to their developmental tasks and specific problems of living.

What is lifeskills helping?

Lifeskills helping involves helpers in making choices that assist clients to develop lifeskills. Many of these helping choices are made in one-to-one interviews. However, lifeskills helpers may also work with couples and families. In addition, lifeskills helpers frequently lead structured groups to train participants in one or more specific skills. Elsewhere I review helper skills for leading lifeskills groups (Nelson-Jones, 1991). In Part Two of this book I present skills for individual lifeskills helping.

Attitude, knowledge and skills

Specific lifeskills can be viewed as comprising three dimensions: attitude, knowledge and skills. Helping skills comprise the same three dimensions.

Attitude. An appropriate attitude to any lifeskill or helping skill is that you assume personal responsibility for acquiring, maintaining, using and developing it. You may lose some or all of a skill if you fail to work at maintaining it. A personally responsible attitude is the motivational or 'wanting to do it' dimension of both a lifeskill and a helping skill.

Knowledge. Each lifeskill and helping skill involves knowledge concerning what are the correct choices to make. People who have been exposed to good examples, for instance by parental behaviour, may acquire much knowledge implicitly rather than explicitly. People with skills weaknesses often need the requisite knowledge clearly spelled out so that they can instruct themselves. Knowledge is the 'knowing how to do it' dimension of a lifeskill or a helping skill.

Skills. The skills dimension of a lifeskill or a helping skill entails the application of attitude and knowledge to practice. Skills can be either inner, focusing on feeling and thinking, or outer, focusing on observable actions, or a combination of inner and outer. In appropriate circumstances, you translate your 'wanting to do it' and 'knowing how to do it' into 'actually doing it'.

A PSYCHOLOGICAL EDUCATION THEORETICAL FRAMEWORK

The word education has a double derivation from its Latin origins. Education is derived from the verb *educare*, 'to nurture, rear'. However, the verb *educare* is a variant of the verb *educere*, 'to lead out' (Jones, 1990). A psychological education theoretical framework encompasses both meanings of the word education. On the one hand, the framework acknowledges the importance of nurturing and facilitation. On the other hand, it also stresses the need for instruction to lead people out to develop better lifeskills.

The term psychoeducation has been popularized by writers like Ivey (1976). Ivey acknowledges his debt to Guerney in stressing the educator model of helping (Guerney et al., 1971). Ivey and his colleagues observe: 'In the psychoeducation model the counselor or therapist becomes a "teacher"' (Ivey et al., 1987, p.360). The theoretical framework presented here acknowledges that helping, be it parental or professional, requires a combination of nurturing and teaching. In most instances, it is insufficient to be solely a teacher in the narrow didactic sense.

Helping practice rests on conceptual or theoretical frameworks. Models of the person guide models of practice. The psychological education framework underlying the helping skills described in this book attempts to integrate concepts from the existential, humanistic, cognitive and behavioural theoretical positions. Due to the applied nature of this book, I present only an illustrative overview or 'thumbnail sketch' of its psychological education framework. Elsewhere I provide fuller statements of the framework (Nelson-Jones, 1984, 1991).

Assumptions

Underling assumptions or basic concepts of the lifeskills approach include the following.

LIFESKILLS Apart from such obviously biological functions as breathing, virtually all human behaviour is viewed in terms of learned lifeskills. The term lifeskills in itself is a neutral concept. Lifeskills may be strengths or weaknesses depending on whether or not they help people both to survive and to maintain and develop potentials. As mentioned earlier, lifeskills are viewed as sequences of choices that may be well or poorly made.

INTERRELATIONSHIP OF THINKING, FEELING AND ACTION In varying degrees most lifeskills comprise thinking, feeling and action elements. Thinking, feeling and action influence each other. Thinking often accompanies or results from feelings at various levels of awareness. Conversely, people may choose to regulate feelings by altering the way they think about themselves, others and the environment. The connection between thinking and action is also two-way: thinking influences action and action influences thinking. Likewise, as with Beck's depressed patients, feelings and actions influence each other (Beck et al., 1979). Figure 1.2 depicts the interrelationships of feeling, thinking and acting.

ENERGIZING DRIVE Ordinary people may have difficulty understanding terms like 'the organism's actualizing tendency' (Raskin & Rogers, 1989, p.169) or self-realizing. All people possess an energizing drive towards surviving, maintaining and developing themselves. However, humans possess weak instinctual remnants (Maslow, 1970).

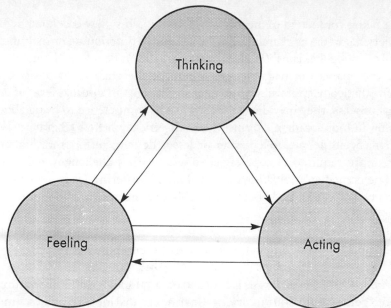

Figure 1.2 *Interrelationships of thinking, feeling and acting*

Consequently, to the degree to which people have fortunate or unfortunate experiences in both acquiring and learning how to maintain and develop lifeskills, so they harness their energizing drive to work for or against them.

The goals of the energizing drive may be viewed on at least three dimensions: the basic animal survival dimension; the pleasure dimension or what Ellis terms 'short-range hedonism' (Ellis, 1989, p.209); and the dimension of higher-level and often more socially oriented involvements and commitments. Terms like self-actualizing (Maslow, 1962, 1970) and propriate striving have been used to describe 'the integrity that comes only from maintaining major directions of striving' (Allport, 1955, p.51). Lifeskills are required for each of the above three ways of expending energy. However, most humans are probably driven more by survival and short-range hedonism than by longer-term and higher-level strivings.

The energizing drive is neither good nor bad: nature does not operate in such terms. Humans are animals first and people second. If anything, instinctually people are more likely to operate in ways that protect themselves and the species than not. However, the long human learning process and humans' ability for symbolic thought offer much scope for acquiring and maintaining lifeskills weaknesses as well as strengths. Biologically, both as individuals and as a species, humans have predispositions towards both adaptive and maladaptive behaviours. Human fallibility is a biological as well as psychological fact of life.

SURVIVAL ANXIETY To the existential psychologists, the fear of death, non-being or destruction is the underlying fear from which all other fears are derived (May & Yalom, 1989; Yalom, 1980). The term survival anxiety seems preferable to that of death anxiety. The notion of survival anxiety focuses more than death anxiety on the continual fears of the living. Survival anxiety relates both to people's fear of death itself and also to their fear of not being competent to meet survival needs. This view is echoed by Beck, who views anxiety disorders as characterized by 'excessive functioning or malfunctioning of normal survival mechanisms' (Beck & Weishaar, 1989). People with anxiety disorders maximize the chances of negative and minimize the chances of positive outcomes instead of realistically appraising situations and having an optimal level of anxiety. As part of this process, they may distort their sense of competence to bring about desired outcomes or, in more academic terms, their self-efficacy beliefs (Bandura, 1977, 1986, 1989). Virtually all people, to a greater or lesser degree, suffer from higher levels of anxiety than are required to cope effectively with life's challenges, either general or specific. The comedian Mel Brooks is not alone in suffering from high anxiety! High anxiety can be both cause and effect of lifeskills weaknesses.

THREEFOLD VIEW OF SELF A person's self is what they call 'I' or 'me'. It is the centre of their personal universe. The self has three major components.

- *The Natural Self.* Each person has a fundamental biological inner nature, or inner core of genetic aptitudes, drives, instincts, instinct remnants and human potentialities. This is their animal nature. Some of this animal nature is shared by the entire human species; for instance, the need for food, shelter, physical safety, belonging and love. Some of this animal nature is unique to each person; their individual aptitudes, inner valuing process and energizing drive. This inner nature or biological core of personhood is the Natural Self.

- *The Learned Self.* The Learned Self is the product of the individual's social learning experiences. It reflects the way people have been taught to perceive themselves and their lifeskills strengths and weaknesses. In an ideal world, people's Learned Selves would be in accord with their Natural Selves. Their Learned Selves would provide them with lifeskills to fulfil their animal natures within the constraints of reality. However, in the real world, most people have acquired misperceptions and lifeskills weaknesses that block attainment of human potential. The Learned Self can be for good or ill, usually for both.

- *The Choosing Self.* Whereas people's Natural Self represents their biological endowment and their Learned Self reflects their past learning history, their Choosing Self represents their capacity to *make* their lives through their choices in the present and future. Thus people not only have selves but also continuously create selves. The Choosing Self provides a means whereby people can discard the misperceptions and skills weaknesses of their Learned Selves that block the fulfilment of their Natural Selves. Another advantage is that people can choose aspects of their multipotential Natural Selves that they wish to develop. This is particularly important in lifeskills helping where clients choose to develop specific skills to attain personal goals.

PERSONAL RESPONSIBILITY Focusing on personal responsibility is almost like focusing on one's nose. Though right in front of the face, the concept is not always easy to observe (Nelson-Jones, 1984). Lifeskills helping adopts the existential notion of people as responsible for the authorship of their lives (Sartre, 1956; May & Yalom, 1989; Yalom, 1980). Another metaphor is that people are responsible for inventing their lives. Authorship or invention requires a continuous process of choosing. Maslow wrote of this process in terms of a series of two-sided choices. One side represented safety, defence, being afraid and regression; the other progression or growth (Maslow, 1962, 1971).

Personal responsibility is an inner process in which people work from 'inside to outside'. This process starts with people's thoughts and feelings and leads to their observable actions. Furthermore, especially as people grow older, many if not most of the significant barriers to assuming responsibility are internal rather than external. However, both inside and outside of helping, people 'differ enormously in the degree of responsibility they are willing to accept for their life situation and in their modes of denying responsibility' (May & Yalom, 1989, p.377). Assuming personal responsibility involves acquiring, maintaining and developing effective lifeskills. Such lifeskills enable people to affirm their existences despite all inner and outer barriers, threats and fears.

Acquiring lifeskills

Suggested below are some factors influencing how people initially learn lifeskills strengths and weaknesses.

SUPPORTIVE RELATIONSHIPS Children require supportive relationships. Bowlby (1979) talks of the concept of a secure base, otherwise referred to as an attachment figure. He notes accumulating evidence that humans of all ages are happiest and most effective when they feel that standing behind them is a trusted person who will come to their aid should difficulties arise. Rogers has also stressed the need for supportive parent–child relationships characterized by high degrees of respect, genuineness and empathic understanding whereby children can feel sensitively and accurately understood (Rogers, 1951, 1959). Supportive relationships can be provided by many people other than parents, for instance, by relatives and teachers. When growing up, most people seem to need at least one primary supportive relationship.

There are many reasons why the presence of supportive and absence of unsupportive or hostile relationships can help children to develop lifeskills. First, supportive relationships provide children with the security to engage in exploratory behaviour and risk trial-and-error learning. Such exploratory behaviour represents a series of personal experiments in which children collect information about themselves and their environments. Second, supportive relationships help children listen better to themselves. By feeling prized and accurately understood, children can get more in touch with their wants, wishes and personal meanings. Third, children may feel freer to manifest emerging lifeskills without risk of ridicule. Fourth, instruction in specific skills is frequently best conducted in the context of supportive relationships in which the anxiety attached to learning is diminished. Fifth, the presence or absence of supportive relationships can either affirm or disconfirm children's sense of worth. They may either be helped to become confident to face life's challenges or they may become inhibited, withdrawn, and afraid to take risks. Alternatively, they may mask their insecurity by excessive attention seeking.

LEARNING FROM EXAMPLE Learning from example is a major way in which people acquire lifeskills strengths and weaknesses. How to think, feel and act can be learned from others' examples. Frequently people remain unaware of behaviours they demonstrate to children. If either or both parents are emotionally inexpressive, children miss opportunities for observing how to express emotions. If parents and others use ineffective thinking skills, for example blaming and overgeneralizing, children may be quick to do likewise. In addition, children may acquire from parents' examples poor action skills for relationships, work, leisure and health care. The converse is also true in that lifeskills strengths in how to feel, think and act may be acquired from the role modelling of parents and significant others. Significant others may include peers, teachers, siblings, other relatives and even the media.

Bandura considers that an observer is more likely to adopt another's example if the demonstrated behaviour is valued by the observer and also brings rewards to the person being observed (Bandura, 1977). However, just as teaching by example is often unintentional, so is learning by example. For instance, the effects of modelling are less direct when thinking skills rather than action skills are involved. Not only are thinking skills not visual in the sense that action skills are, they are seldom clearly verbalized. People may absorb from example deficient skills for thinking, feeling and action and then possess the added barrier of remaining unaware that this has happened.

LEARNING FROM CONSEQUENCES Lifeskills learning from observing role models is frequently intermingled with learning from rewarding or unrewarding consequences. For example, parents poor at showing emotions may also be poor at receiving children's emotions. Rewarding consequences can be either primary or secondary. Primary rewarding consequences people find rewarding independent of their learning histories: for instance, food, shelter, sex and human warmth. Skinner considers that all rewards eventually derive their power from evolutionary selection and that it is part of human nature to be rewarded by particular things (Skinner, 1971). However, only a small part of behaviour is immediately reinforced by rewards of evident biological significance. Most behaviour is emitted in response to secondary rewards, such as approval or money, that have become associated with or conditioned to primary rewards.

People receive consequences in two main ways. First, there is *classical conditioning* where consequences are independent of the conditioned person first operating on the environment. For example, a person who has been in a serious car accident may feel anxious either about being in a car or about other characteristics of the accident, for instance its location. Many aversions appear to result from classical conditioning (Lazarus, 1989). Second, there is *operant conditioning* where consequences result from behaviours that operate on the environment. For example, the behaviour of asking someone out may lead to acceptance or rejection.

Rewarding consequences play a large part in helping or hindering people from acquiring lifeskills. Virtually from birth, humans receive messages about how 'good' or 'bad' their actions are. Usually, with the best of intentions, adults try to reward children for developing the skills necessary to cope with the world. However, adults often provide rewards in deficient ways. For example, most people learn their relationship skills and thinking skills from a mixture of observing others, unsystematic feedback and trial and error. Rarely, either inside or outside the home, are people systematically rewarded as they develop these lifeskills. Furthermore, children are sometimes rewarded for exhibiting skills weaknesses rather than strengths. For instance, they may find that they are more likely to get their way if they shout aggressively rather than take a more reasonable approach. In addition skills weaknesses can be acquired by people becoming too dependent on the need for external rewards rather than trusting their own judgement and skills. Skills weaknesses can also be developed by people receiving the message that their whole personhood is bad rather than that a specific behaviour is insufficiently skilled. Last but not least, many people acquire skills weaknesses through receiving negative consequences because of their biological sex, race, social class or culture.

INSTRUCTION AND SELF-INSTRUCTION Psychologists researching animal behaviour stress the importance of learning from example and consequences. However, humans possess the capacity for symbolic thought and communication. Consequently, instruction is a major transmitter of lifeskills. Much lifeskills instruction takes place informally in the home. Some of this is very basic: for instance asking children to say 'please' and 'thank you'. Children are frequently told by their parents how to relate, how to study, how to look after their health and so on. Relatives and peers are other providers of instruction outside educational settings.

Much informal lifeskills instruction takes place in schools and colleges, but systematic attempts to train children in a range of relationship skills are probably still more the exception than the rule (Hatch & Guerney, 1975; Morgan, 1984; Sprinthall, 1980). Nevertheless, lifeskills programmes are run in many schools in such areas as career education (Amatea *et al.*, 1984; Roessler, 1988) and drug and alcohol education (Dorn & South, 1986). In addition, a range of lifeskills programmes may be offered in colleges and universities inside or outside the formal curriculum. The lifeskills targeted include relationship skills; study skills, managing test anxiety; career development skills (Swain, 1984); anxiety and stress management skills (Romano, 1984); and effective thinking skills (Barrow & Moore, 1984; Heppner *et al.*, 1984a). Participation in such programmes is usually voluntary.

Instruction can be for better or worse: skills weaknesses as well as strengths can be imparted. For various reasons, those instructed may resist instructors. Sometimes instructors are poor at drawing out learners rather than just telling them what to do. Frequently instruction contains sex bias: for instance teaching only girls parenting skills. In addition, lifeskills may not be communicated clearly enough for learners to instruct themselves afterwards. If learners are unable to talk themselves through the relevant sequences of choices, many lifeskills have been inadequately imparted and learned. Much instruction falls far short of this self-instructional objective.

INFORMATION AND OPPORTUNITY People require adequate information to develop lifeskills. For example, keeping children in ignorance about basic facts of sexuality and death impedes self-awareness and emotional responsiveness. Intentionally or unintentionally, adults often relate to their children on the basis of lies, omissions of truth and partial truths (Steiner, 1974). Furthermore, necessary information may not be readily available outside the home. For instance, schools differ greatly in the adequacy of the career information they provide.

Children, adolescents and adults alike need opportunities to test out and develop lifeskills. Ideally such opportunities are in line with their maturation and state of readiness. People may have different opportunities on account of their sex, race, culture, social class, financial position and schooling, to mention just some barriers. Furthermore, people can be fortunate or unfortunate in having parents who open up rather than restrict learning opportunities. Children and adults also have a role in seeking out information and opportunities. Some have better skills at this than others.

ANXIETY AND CONFIDENCE Children grow up having both helpful and harmful experiences for developing self-esteem. The fortunate acquire a level of anxiety that both protects against actual dangers and also motivates them towards realistic achievements. Those less fortunate may acquire debilitating anxieties through role modelling, instruction and provision of faulty consequences. Even parents who communicate carefully can bruise children's fragile self-esteem. Far worse are hostile and defensive parents. Here children's feelings and perceptions are doubly discounted: first by the initial aggression and second by being subjected to further aggression when they react. Deficient behaviours resulting from as well as manifesting anxiety include unwillingness to take realistic risks; tense and nervous rather than relaxed learning; a heightened tendency to say and do the wrong things; unnecessary aggression; excessive approval seeking; and underachieving, with or without overstriving. Inadequate performance in different skills may further raise anxiety and make future lifeskills learning even more difficult. However, people who are helped or who help themselves to acquire anxiety management skills may learn lifeskills more easily than those without such skills.

Maintaining lifeskills

People can maintain both lifeskills strengths and weaknesses. This section focuses only on how people maintain lifeskills weaknesses. Especially for children, *acquiring* lifeskills strengths and weaknesses is more a matter of 'what the environment does to me' than 'what I do to myself'. Young people are frequently at the mercy of their elders. *Maintaining* lifeskills strengths and weaknesses is a different matter. Here, partly because lifeskills are maintained into adulthood, cause shifts more in the direction of 'what I do to myself' than 'what the environment has done or does to me'. The following are processes that maintain lifeskills weaknesses.

THINKING SKILLS WEAKNESSES Thinking skills weaknesses are a major reason why people maintain poor lifeskills. Too much anxiety tends to be a common theme in faulty thinking. Below are some thinking skills weaknesses.

- *Attributional deficiencies.* How people assign cause influences the degree to which they maintain lifeskills weaknesses. Attributions of responsibility and cause are explanations that people tell themselves to make sense of what happens in their lives. Faulty attributions explain responsibility and cause inaccurately. People who avoid rather than assume responsibility for their lives are poor candidates for initiating desirable behaviour changes. The following are possible attributional errors that may sustain lifeskills weaknesses. A common theme is that these attributional deficiencies tend to convert partial truths into whole truths by missing out relevant aspects of personal responsibility.

  'It's my nature.' Such an attribution inadequately acknowledges the large learned component in most lifeskills weaknesses.

  'It's my unfortunate past.' For people who have left home, attributions of inadequate pasts are largely irrelevant to how they maintain their skills weaknesses in the present.

  'It's my bad luck.' People often make their luck by developing relevant skills.

  'It's my poor environment.' Many people have learned to overcome the skills weaknesses contributed to by their poor environments.

  'It's all your fault.' Why bother to change when negative events are someone else's fault?

  'It's all my fault.' Quite apart from being inaccurate, overinternalizing cause may erode the confidence people require to deal with difficulties in their lives.

- *Unrealistic personal rules.* Personal rules are the 'do's' and 'don'ts' by which people lead their lives. Each person has an inner rulebook of standards for themselves and for others. Sometimes these standards are realistic and appropriately flexible. On other occasions the standards may be unrealistic and inappropriately rigid. Ellis has coined the term 'mustabation' to refer to rigid internal rules characterized by 'musts', 'oughts' and 'shoulds' (Ellis, 1980, 1989). These unrealistic rules are not only lifeskills weaknesses in themselves, but may help maintain other lifeskills weaknesses. Below are illustrations of mustabatory personal rules in different lifeskills areas.

  Feeling: 'I must never get angry.'

  Sex: 'I must always perform at a high level.'

  Thinking: 'Women are less smart than men.'

  Relationships: 'I must always win an argument.'

Study: 'I must write the perfect essay.'

Work: 'I must always be stimulated by my job.'

Leisure: 'I must not enjoy myself too much.'

Health: 'I must always push myself to the limit of my endurance.'

- *Perceiving inaccurately.* A Chinese proverb states: 'Two-thirds of what we see is behind our eyes.' People erroneously maintain lifeskills weaknesses if they rigidly perceive their skills to be either better or worse than they are. They may find it difficult to accept contrary feedback if they overestimate how intelligent, affectionate, competent at work or good in bed they are. People may also misperceive positive feedback to sustain a negative self-picture as well as negative feedback to sustain a positive self-picture (Rogers, 1959). In both instances, the faulty perceiving contributes to maintaining lifeskills weaknesses as well as being a lifeskills weakness in itself.

  'Defence mechanisms', 'defences' or 'security operations' are terms for the ways that people operate on incoming information that differs from their existing self-pictures (Arlow, 1989; Clark, 1991; Freud, 1936; Maslow, 1962, 1970; Sullivan, 1953). Defensive processes involve people diminishing awareness for short-term psychological comfort. Defensive processes range from denying incoming information to distorting it in various ways: for example, rationalizing, making excuses when your behaviour causes you anxiety, or projecting: externalizing thoughts and feelings on to others rather than owning them.

- *Negative self-talk.* Negative self-talk may be contrasted with coping self-talk (Meichenbaum, 1977, 1983, 1985, 1986; Meichenbaum & Deffenbacher, 1988). Coping self-talk has two main functions: calming and coaching. A sample calming self-instruction might be 'Keep calm.' A sample coaching self-instruction might be 'Break the task down.' Frequently, calming and coaching statements appear together: 'Keep calm. Break the task down.' Negative self-talk statements inhibit people from working on a range of lifeskills weaknesses. Such negative statements include: 'I'm never going to be able to do it', 'I'm starting to feel anxious and this is a signal that things may get out of control', and 'The future is hopeless'.

- *Fear of change.* Once acquired, lifeskills weaknesses can become well-established habits resistant to change (Ellis, 1985, 1987; Grieger, 1989). Dimensions of fear of change include the following.

  fear of the unknown;

  fear of the discomfort in making the effort to change;

  fear of losing the payoffs from existing behaviours;

fear of inner conflict between the old and the emerging self;

fear of conflict with others arising from changing;

fear of failure;

fear of the consequences of success.

All learning involves giving up the safety of the known to develop new or different skills. Some people are better able to confront fears about change than others. Some of the thinking skills mentioned earlier – for example perceiving accurately and using coping self-talk – help people manage rather than avoid change.

UNCHANGED ENVIRONMENTAL CIRCUMSTANCES Lifeskills weaknesses are usually maintained both by how people think and also by what the environment keeps doing to them. Most factors mentioned in the section on how people acquire lifeskills can help maintain lifeskills weaknesses. People may continue to have insufficiently supportive relationships. They may still be exposed to examples of poor thinking and action skills. They may continue to receive inappropriate rewarding consequences. They may fail to receive or find adequate lifeskills instruction and also continue instructing themselves in their weaknesses. In addition, they may still be exposed to insufficient or faulty information and lack suitable opportunities to develop their skills and human potential.

Change and self-development

Change in lifeskills helping may entail acquiring new skills strengths, releasing and developing existing skills strengths, relearning previously acquired skills strengths, unlearning and possibly extinguishing skills weaknesses, and learning how to maintain and develop skills after helping. In addition, wherever possible lifeskills helpers attempt to strengthen people's general level of self-esteem. Here, rather than outlining specific helping skills, mention is made of some mechanisms of change within a psychological education framework.

LEARNING BY SUPPORTIVE RELATIONSHIPS People do not always require supportive relationships to develop lifeskills – for example they may learn from skills manuals or computers. Nevertheless, change is usually more likely to occur if lifeskills learning takes place within the context of supportive relationships. Earlier, mention was made of some reasons why children learn best in supportive relationships where they are understood and prized. They feel confident to engage in exploratory behaviour. They are better able to listen to themselves and get in touch with wants and wishes. They are better able to take the risks involved in learning new skills. All of these reasons apply to offering supportive relationships to clients both individually and in groups.

In addition, supportive relationships help clients drop some defences and assume rather than avoid personal responsibility for life and behaviour. Sometimes clients arrive at such insights on their own. On other occasions, they may be assisted by helper challenges and confrontations. However, such challenges are best made within the context of supportive relationships or else they risk doing more harm than good. A further reason for offering supportive helping relationships is that many clients require reaffirmation of their faith in human relating. Some clients need a gentle, sensitive, nurturing and healing relationship prior to a more active skills focus. In their contacts with clients, lifeskills helpers provide rewarding consequences both for relating in general and for developing specific targeted skills.

LEARNING BY INSTRUCTION While helpers can encourage clients to do their own work, clients often require instruction as well. Lifeskills helpers are both facilitators and trainers. Conversely, clients are both persons whose potential is unfolding and also students requiring specific knowledge and skills to function more effectively. Instruction within helping relationships is not only a matter of initial presentation of concepts and ideas; much lifeskills instruction takes place as people rework and practise the original concepts and skills. Furthermore, good lifeskills helpers are always on the lookout for ways of presenting material so clearly that clients learn to instruct themselves. Where relevant, lifeskills helpers instruct clients in the skills of information seeking and opportunity creation. Helpers are far from the only sources of instruction. Books, training manuals, self-help cassettes and videos, computer-assisted learning packages, other helpers and lifeskills group participants can all be additional instructional sources.

LEARNING BY OBSERVING Areas for observational learning include feelings, thinking skills, action skills, and action skills with accompanying self-talk. In lifeskills helping observational learning can take place in many ways. First, helpers are role models of competent helping relationships. Second, helpers may demonstrate specific skills: for example, the verbal, voice and body messages to make assertive behaviour change requests. Third, helpers may arrange that clients observe pre-recorded audio-cassette or videotape demonstrations. Such material may have been developed by the helper or purchased from commercial sources. Fourth, thinking skills in particular may be demonstrated in writing: for instance in self-help manuals. Fifth, helpers may encourage clients between sessions to identify and observe role models who demonstrate targeted skills. Sixth, helpers may encourage visualized demonstration. Here clients imagine themselves or a third party performing the targeted skills competently. Seventh, in lifeskills groups, participants are likely to demonstrate both skills strengths and weaknesses for each other.

Where possible helpers try to increase the attention level of clients. Strategies for this include demonstrating skills that clients want to learn, choosing demonstrators with whom clients can identify, and telling clients what to look out for either in advance or as the demonstration unfolds.

LEARNING BY DOING Lifeskills helping lays heavy stress on active learning. Supportive helping relationships enable clients to develop the skills of talking about themselves and of breaking down and clarifying problems. Where appropriate, within-session instruction and demonstration of skills is either accompanied by or followed by coached practice. Further behaviour rehearsals may then take place, possibly incorporating video feedback. Learning by doing is often accompanied by teaching clients how to verbalize, and then sub-vocalize, appropriate self-instructions. Frequently clients are given between-session homework. At the end of sessions they play active roles in choosing assignments. At the start of subsequent sessions both clients and helpers review progress: successes are acknowledged and difficulties and setbacks analysed. Homework assignments include self-monitoring forms, exercises, thinksheets, games, conducting personal experiments in which behaviour changes are tried out and evaluated, and practice, practice, practice.

LEARNING BY CONSOLIDATING TRAINED SKILLS AS SELF-HELPING SKILLS Lifeskills helpers do not rely on the 'Train and Hope' approach to whether or not clients work to maintain their treatment gains (Goldstein & Keller, 1987; Stokes & Osnes, 1989). On the assumption that it is not what happens in helping that counts but what happens afterwards, lifeskills helping always pays attention to consolidating trained skills as self-helping skills. From the start, with each client helpers pay attention to issues of transfer, generalization, maintenance and development of skills. Helper strategies for consolidating self-helping skills include providing rationales for helping that emphasize self-helping; developing clients' self-assessment and goal-setting skills; regular homework tasks; rehearsing coping with difficulties and setbacks; helping clients identify and use supports; working with significant others who can help clients in their home or work environments; arranging for follow-up contact with the helper or other appropriate people; identifying peer self-help groups; providing information on further skills-building opportunities; and suggesting further reading and audiovisual material. In addition, helpers can pay attention to thinking skills for maintaining change: for example, attributing cause accurately, knowing how to self-instruct, using self-reward, accurately perceiving feedback, and acknowledging rather than discounting the rewards from maintaining change.

LEARNING BY SELF-DEVELOPMENT Ideally, former clients can go beyond maintaining existing skills to develop them to higher levels. They may become self-motivated learners who know and apply the principles of developing lifeskills strengths on their own. Such people are committed to personal development either in specific skills areas or across a range of skills. Clients and people in general need to learn to become their own best helpers. A distinction may be made between difficulties and problems. Problems arise when attempted solutions to difficulties are unsuccessful. Thus the attempts at solving the difficulty become part of the problem. People who have learned the skills of psychological self-helping are much less likely to allow themselves to stay stuck in chronic problems than are those who do not possess self-helping skills. Well-functioning people are capable of sustaining their own development. However, where appropriate, they use others as resources both for support and for building up specific skills strengths.

GOALS FOR LIFESKILLS HELPING

Parloff (1967) suggests that the goals of counselling and therapy can be better understood if they are divided into two categories: mediating and ultimate. Ellis makes the distinction between inelegant and elegant changes as goals for Rational-Emotive Therapy (RET) (Ellis, 1980). Whereas inelegant change focuses on symptom removal, elegant change: 'goes much beyond this kind of symptom removal, and aims at a significant lessening (rather than a complete removal) of clients' *disturbability*' (Ellis, 1980, p.13). In lifeskills helping a distinction can also be made between ultimate or elegant goals and mediating or inelegant goals. In addition lifeskills helping emphasizes preventive goals. For example, attending a friendship skills training programme in elementary school may prevent the development of skills weaknesses.

Ultimate goal: Personal excellence

Lifeskills helping is a positive and optimistic approach whose goals need to be stated positively. The ultimate goal of lifeskills helping is people who assume responsibility for personal excellence. Other terms for personal excellence are high-level competence, psychological wellness, self-actualizing (Maslow, 1970), and assuming personal responsibility (Nelson-Jones, 1984). The term personal excellence has been chosen because of its clearly educational connotations. Top educational institutions strive not only to be excellent in themselves but to impart to students the skills with which they will continue to strive for excellence once they leave. Similarly, at the elegant end of lifeskills helping, clients work towards broader, higher and longer-lasting levels of skills that go well beyond 'just getting by'.

Personal excellence is both state and process. The state of personal excellence is that of attaining a high level of competence across a range of skills areas. However, lifeskills are not static, but have to be reclaimed daily. The process of personal excellence is that of assuming effective personal responsibility for making the choices that maintain and develop the positive aspects of one's human potential. Personal excellence requires the ability consistently to make and implement life-affirming choices.

Mediating goals: Specific lifeskills

Mediating goals in lifeskills helping entail helping clients acquire the processes of effective choosing in specific skills areas. Terms like symptom removal are not used because of their medical rather than educational connotations. Elsewhere lifeskills have been grouped according to the four Rs of psychological well-being: responsiveness, realism, relatedness and rewarding activity (Nelson-Jones, 1984). Another way to view lifeskills is in terms of thinking skills, action skills and feelings-related skills.

THINKING SKILLS Effective people think realistically (Ellis & Harper, 1975; Emery, 1982; Nelson-Jones, 1989). Thinking skills include possessing a realistic conceptual and linguistic framework; assuming responsibility for one's choices; coping self-talk; choosing realistic personal rules; perceiving accurately; attributing cause accurately;

predicting risk and reward realistically; setting personal goals; visualizing skills; decision-making skills; and managing problems skills.

ACTION SKILLS Action skills are observable behaviours. They are what you do and how you do it rather than what and how you feel and think. Action skills vary by area of application. Below are some applied areas, albeit an incomplete listing, with illustrative action skills.

- *Relationships*. Skills include: making initial contact, conversing, disclosing, listening, showing caring, assertion, and managing anger and conflict.

- *Parenting*. Skills include the above with special reference to rearing children; also skills like sexual and moral education.

- *Study*. Skills include: managing time effectively, meeting deadlines, effective reading, writing essays and theses, managing achievement and test anxiety, test taking, group participation and public speaking.

- *Work*. Skills include: job seeking, interviewing, supervising, managing, teamwork, negotiating, handling transitions, making the most of a work setting, and giving and receiving feedback.

- *Leisure*. Skills include: seeking out rewarding pastimes, willingness to develop skills in specific activities, ability for passive relaxation, and having adequate and enjoyable holidays.

- *Health*. Skills include: eating nutritionally and in moderation, moderating alcohol consumption, avoiding smoking, avoiding addictive drugs, keeping physically fit, managing stress well, and observing a good balance between work, relationship, family and recreational activities.

- *Social participation*. Skills include: being a good neighbour, identifying and participating in community activities, and working for desirable social changes.

FEELINGS-RELATED SKILLS Effective people are responsive to their underlying animal natures, and emotionally literate. Feelings-related skills include: acknowledging the importance of feelings; awareness of and openness to feelings; awareness of wants and wishes; inner empathy or the ability to 'tune into' and explore feelings; awareness of bodily sensations; the capacity to experience sensuality; the capacity to experience loving and pro-social feelings; and a full awareness of existential limitations, for instance death. Feelings-related skills can be extended to include such composite feeling, thinking and action skills as relaxation, anxiety management and stress management. Feelings-related skills can also be viewed in more general terms, such as confidence, self-acceptance (Ellis, 1989), and a broadly based sense of self-efficacy (Bandura, 1977, 1986, 1989).

THE LIFESKILLS HELPER

What lifeskills helpers are

Lifeskills helpers hold humanistic values either outside of or within religious frameworks. These values include respect for each individual; acknowledgement of human fallibility; belief in human educability; belief in the human potential for reason and social living; and a sincere desire for a better world. Lifeskills helpers subscribe to a psychological education theoretical framework, an outline of which was provided earlier. This theoretical framework integrates elements of existential-humanistic and cognitive-behavioural psychology. In both their helping and personal lives, lifeskills helpers are always choosers.

Lifeskills helpers are practitioner-researchers who constantly make, implement and evaluate behaviour change hypotheses. At least four sources of knowledge enlighten their helping. First, they pay attention to theoretical knowledge. The psychological education theoretical framework requires continuous updating in light of new knowledge about human development. Second, they endeavour to keep abreast of relevant research findings into the processes and outcomes of helping. When they work in a specialized area, for example vocational counselling or marriage and family counselling, they need to keep up with pertinent research findings. Third, they learn from professional experience. They are active seekers for ways of operating more effectively. They evaluate their work and, if necessary, modify their helping skills accordingly. Fourth, lifeskills helpers are alive and vibrant human beings who learn from their personal experience outside formal helping. This kind of reflective learning is especially important for helpers operating within a psychological education framework in which they and their clients require the same lifeskills. If you can acquire, maintain and develop your own lifeskills, you should be better placed to help clients.

Lifeskills helpers are educators. Taking into account the state of readiness, expectations and skills levels of each client, they flexibly use both helping relationship and training skills. The focus of helping includes nurturing and healing vulnerable clients; assisting clients with specific problems and decisions; crisis management work; and preventive and developmental lifeskills training. The clientele for helping may be an individual, a group or an institution. Lifeskills helpers are always conscious of ways to 'seed' or disseminate helping skills to others. Furthermore, they recognize that sometimes 'upstream' helping focusing on organizational policies and practices that create problems may be necessary either instead of or in addition to 'downstream' helping with individuals or groups of clients (Egan & Cowan, 1979).

Within an educational framework, lifeskills helpers use a variety of training interventions focusing on feeling, thinking and action. In individual work, lifeskills helpers tend not to be archaeologists or historians: instead they mainly focus on clients' presents and futures. In particular helpers collaborate with clients to identify skills weaknesses that currently sustain difficulties. Helpers then assist clients in shifting the balance of the relevant skills weaknesses and strengths more in the direction of strengths. Lifeskills helpers always heavily emphasize that clients should consolidate trained skills as self-helping skills. They always encourage people to become their own best helpers.

What lifeskills helpers are not

Another way of presenting what lifeskills helpers are is to indicate what they are not. First, they are no different from other people except that they possess better helping skills. They still have their own struggles, imperfections and difficulties in affirming their positive rather than negative potentials. Second, they are not superficial manipulators. They genuinely care for the growth and development of their clients and collaborate with them to choose working goals and methods. Where clients require gentle and sensitive nurturing, they attempt to provide it pending more skills-focused training approaches. Third, lifeskills helpers are neither magicians nor witch doctors promising instant cures. People usually come to helping with long-established skills weaknesses as well as strengths. Helpers emphasize that initial behaviour change usually requires hard work. Clients require continuing effort and practice to maintain and develop skills.

Fourth, lifeskills helpers cannot do clients' work. They do not encourage dependent relationships: they quietly and sometimes more forcefully confront clients with their responsibility for making their own lives. At best they can only influence clients to develop better lifeskills. If clients are going to change, they have to demonstrate their own commitment. Fifth, lifeskills helpers do not encourage conformity. Each client is assisted to think through which choices are best in his or her unique life circumstances. Sixth, lifeskills helpers do not view themselves as having a monopoly on helping skills. Many helping skills are similar to skills needed for other roles – for example, being a partner, a friend, parent or supervisor. In addition, many helping skills can be used for self-help. The more people who possess good helping skills the better.

CHAPTER HIGHLIGHTS

- Lifeskills helping is a people-centred approach for assisting clients and others to develop self-helping skills.

- The language of lifeskills helping is democratic and lends itself to client self-instruction.

- Lifeskills helping focuses on the problems and potentials of people in general. It takes psychological wellness rather than psychological disturbance as its starting-point.

- Lifeskills are personally responsible sequences of self-helping choices in specific psychological skills areas conducive to mental wellness. People require a repertoire of lifeskills according to their developmental tasks and specific problems of living.

- Lifeskills helping aims to shift the balance of clients' skills strengths and weaknesses more in the direction of strengths.

- The underlying assumptions of a lifeskills psychological education framework incorporate the following basic concepts: lifeskills; interrelationship of thinking, feeling and action; energizing drive; survival anxiety, Natural, Learned and Choosing Selves; and personal responsibility.

- Lifeskills strengths and weaknesses are acquired by supportive relationships; learning from example; learning from consequences; instruction and self-instruction; information and opportunity; and anxiety and confidence.

- Lifeskills weaknesses are maintained by thinking skills weaknesses and by unchanged environmental circumstances.

- Change and self-development take place through learning by supportive relationships, instruction, observing, doing, consolidating trained skills as self-helping skills, and assuming personal responsibility for self-development.

- The ultimate goal of lifeskills helping is personal excellence: attaining a high level of competence across a range of skills areas and consistently making and implementing life-affirming choices.

- The mediating goals of lifeskills helping are specific lifeskills in the areas of thinking, action and feelings. Applied areas for lifeskills include relationships, parenting, study, work, leisure, health, and social participation.

- Lifeskills helpers hold humanistic values either outside of or within religious frameworks. They are practitioner-researchers who constantly make, implement and evaluate behaviour change hypotheses. Within an educational framework, they use a variety of interventions focusing on feeling, thinking and action.

- Lifeskills helpers always encourage people to become their own best helpers.

TWO
Overview of the Lifeskills Helping Model

You're either part of the solution or part of the problem.
Eldridge Cleaver

CHAPTER QUESTIONS

What are the inner and outer games of lifeskills helping?

Why is it important for both helpers and clients to focus on both inner and outer games?

What is the difference between managing problems and altering problematic skills?

What is DASIE, the five-stage model for managing problems and altering problematic lifeskills?

What helper skills and client behaviours illustrate each stage of DASIE?

What are issues in applying the lifeskills helping model?

THE INNER AND OUTER GAMES OF HELPING

The cognitive-behavioural approach to helping emphasizes cognitions and behaviours. However, terms like cognitions and behaviours are not everyday language, let alone the language of self-helping. Borrowing and adapting terms from Gallwey's book *The Inner Game of Tennis* (Gallwey, 1974), often the lifeskills approach uses the terms inner game skills and outer game skills. Inner games skills are thinking skills or how you think. Thinking skills comprise such areas as perceiving accurately, using coping self-talk, possessing realistic personal rules, and attributing cause accurately, among others

(Beck, 1976; Ellis, 1989; Nelson-Jones, 1989). Thinking skills can be used to influence feelings as well as to guide actions. Outer game skills are action skills, or how you act. Unlike thinking skills which are mostly covert, action skills are by definition overt. The appropriateness of action skills differs across areas of living: for example relationships, sex, work, study or leisure.

You do not ignore feelings if you focus on thinking and action skills. People feel how they feel. Though feelings, thoughts and actions are interrelated, people cannot alter how they feel unless they alter how they either think and act or both think and act. If they consciously wish to alter how they feel, they must make thinking and action skills choices. Even if unintended, such choices influence feelings.

Lifeskills helping takes a two-pronged approach to viewing both helper and client skills. Effective helpers and clients make effective inner and outer game choices. If I am maximally to help you become an effective helper, I need to work not only with your action skills choices, but also with your thinking skills choices. If you are maximally to help your clients become more effective, you also need to work with not only their action skills, but also their thinking skills. After formal helping ends, if clients are maximally to help themselves they need to work on both their thinking and action skills. You may find the inner and outer game analogy useful for communicating to clients what I try to communicate to you now. The inner and outer game distinction is basic to the lifeskills model of helping.

Clients' inner and outer games

INNER GAME Clients' inner games comprise their thinking skills strengths and weaknesses. Clients possess profiles of thinking skills strengths and weaknesses. Sometimes, if fortunate, people can get by in life without significant thinking skills weaknesses being activated. However, when people come to helpers as clients the probability is that they have activated their thinking skills fault lines. Both inside and outside of helping, clients cannot avoid the inner game. There is no taking time out on the touchline. Just close your eyes for thirty seconds and try to think of nothing. Probably you found that all the time you conducted an inner dialogue. You cannot avoid thinking and, consequently, making implicit and explicit thinking skills choices. Often these choices are the 'under-choices' that position clients for self-defeating feelings and actions.

When it comes to managing and preventing personal problems, clients tend not to think of themselves as possessing thinking skills, let alone thinking skills strengths and weaknesses. At best most clients have only a partial awareness of their inner games skills and of how they can use these to support rather than to oppress themselves. Being insufficiently aware both of the concept of thinking skills and of their own thinking skills strengths and weaknesses leaves clients vulnerable to maintaining problems. They may want to change, but not have insight into the thinking under-choices that hinder change. Unwittingly, by making poor thinking choices, clients may become their own worst enemies. Also, during helping sessions, clients may remain unaware that some of their thinking skills weaknesss, for example an unrealistic rule about the need for helper approval, may hinder rather than assist change.

OUTER GAME Clients' outer games comprise their action skills strengths and weaknesses. As with thinking skills, clients possess profiles of action skills strengths and weaknesses. Continuously, both inside and outside helping, clients act on the environment with varying degrees of success. Both inside and outside of helping clients send verbal, voice, body, touch and action messages (Nelson-Jones, 1990). Clients are more likely to use skills language when describing actions rather than thoughts. Nevertheless, most clients probably do not conceptualize what they do in important areas of their lives, such as relationships or parenting, in skills terms. For example, while a client might talk of the need to become more assertive, few would go the next step to talk about assertion skills. Fewer clients still, if any, would go further to break assertion skills down into their verbal, voice, body, touch and action message components.

Helpers' inner and outer games

INNER GAME Helpers' inner games comprise their thinking skills strengths and weaknesses and how they use them. Like clients, helpers cannot avoid using thinking skills. They cannot not think. Helpers use their thinking skills strengths and weaknesses in their private and working lives. The use of thinking and action skills weaknesses in helpers' private lives may affect how they perform with clients. For example, helpers may bring unfinished private business into helping. Helpers can also exhibit thinking skills strengths and weaknesses in regard to helping. For example, helpers who are unclear about the theoretical and research basis for their work may communicate confusion to clients. Helpers either consciously or unconsciously wishing to create dependence may exhibit one or more thinking skills weaknesses: possibly, unrealistic needs for approval or power and failure to attribute to clients sufficient responsibility for change. Helpers may also misperceive clients and their problems: for example, either projecting their own difficulties on to clients or exaggerating the degree to which clients have sexual problems. How well you play your inner game constitutes a central part of your ability to help. Helper thinking skills represent the 'under-choices' that position them for good or poor action skills choices with clients.

OUTER GAME Helpers are senders of observable messages in both their private and working lives. To date most counselling and helping skills textbooks have been much stronger on training helpers in action skills than in thinking skills. The basic helper action skills 'tools of the trade' include attending – for example, eye contact, using openers and continuation messages, reflecting, helpful questioning, challenging and confronting, and summarizing, to mention but some. Additional action skills with a clearer educational focus include assessing, redefining problems in skills terms, stating working goals, instructing, demonstrating, arranging structured activities and setting homework. Each stage of helping challenges helpers to use both thinking skills and action skills.

Helpers and clients use inner game and outer game skills both in their outside lives and during helping. To the extent that helpers use good thinking and action skills in their outside lives, they are effective people; to the extent that they use such skills in helping they are effective helpers. Effective helpers work to develop clients' thinking and action skills during helping for use outside. Clients exhibit different levels of thinking and action skills both at the start of and during their helping sessions. Frequently, the thinking and action skills that clients exhibit in helping offer helpers valuable clues to how they think and act outside.

DASIE: THE FIVE-STAGE MODEL
Problems and problematic skills

Lifeskills helping has preventive and developmental as well as problem management goals. Being an educational approach, lifeskills helping lends itself to both individual and group training interventions. As far as possible, in addition to managing presenting problems, lifeskills helpers assist clients to alter underlying patterns of problematic skills. Beyond the immediate problem, skills weaknesses can manifest themselves both *horizontally* across a range of current situations, and *vertically* in future similar situations. Many problems occur in repetitive cycles. For example, individuals may not only require assistance in finding employment, but also in identifying and developing job-seeking skills for future use. A further example is that of people relating poorly to work colleagues in one setting often having similar troubles in future work settings. Indeed such people's relationship problems may extend far beyond work. Helping clients deal with relationship difficulties in one work setting is laudable. Helping the same clients develop skills to prevent and contain future difficulties with work colleagues is even more laudable. Still better, if appropriate, is to help these clients develop relationship skills for use across a range of settings, both now and in the future.

> Mary was a middle-aged divorcée with custody of her 15-year-old son Richard. For just over a year she had been seeing George, a divorcé with custody of two boys, aged 8 and 10. For some months Mary had been planning a camping holiday. Repeatedly she had tried to talk Richard into having George and his two children on the holiday. Richard adamantly refused. Mary was very reluctant to bring Richard's refusal to the attention of George because he might be hurt and react angrily. The date for the proposed holiday was getting nearer and nearer. When asked, Mary told the counsellor that she found it hard to bring up difficult issues across a range of relationships and that she disliked any form of conflict. The counsellor pointed out to Mary the difference between managing a problem, discussing Richard's refusal with George, and using this problem to build skills for raising and working through future difficult issues in relationships. Mary agreed that she needed to develop her skills both for now and for the future.

> This would help her not only with George but also
> with others, for instance Richard.

Table 2.1 depicts the relationship between working to manage a problem and working to manage an underlying predisposing pattern of skills weaknesses. Ideally the object is to avoid repetitive cycles of the same problems. Practical considerations often limit helper contact with individual clients: for example, heavy helper caseloads and clients being content with short-term problem amelioration. However, helpers who only aim to help clients manage immediate and specific problems, when they could work more thoroughly with them to alter problematic skills, do clients a disservice. Where possible, the focus in lifeskills helping is on developing skills for life and not just for the immediate present. In reality, helpers and clients often compromise on the amount of time and effort they address to underlying patterns of skills weaknesses.

Table 2.1 Outline of the ideal relationship between managing problems and changing problematic skills weaknesses into self-helping skills strengths

PERIOD	EVENT
Period 1 Pre-helping	Problematic skills pattern(s) is either inadequately attended to or goes unrecognized by client
Period 2 Request for helping	Recognition by client of problem(s) in coping with one or more aspects of living, and willingness to seek help
Period 3 During helping	Helper and client develop client's self-helping skills for not only immediate problem(s), but also future similar problem(s)
Period 4 Post-helping, short-term	Client uses self-helping skills to manage immediate problem(s) and other similar problem(s) better
Period 5 Post-helping, longer term	Client maintains and consolidates self-helping skills strengths both to prevent recurrences of problematic skills weaknesses and also to manage future problems better

Overview of DASIE

At risk of over-simplification, I present DASIE, a five-stage model for helping clients manage problems and alter problematic lifeskills. The model provides a framework or set of guidelines for helper choices. The use of the acronym is deliberate; it is intended to assist beginning helping service trainees to remember the five stages when faced with the anxiety of working with clients for the first time. As depicted in Figure 2.1, DASIE's five stages are

D   DEVELOP the relationship, identify and clarify problem(s)
A   ASSESS problem(s) and redefine in skills terms
S   STATE working goals and plan interventions
I   INTERVENE to develop self-helping skills
E   END and consolidate self-helping skills

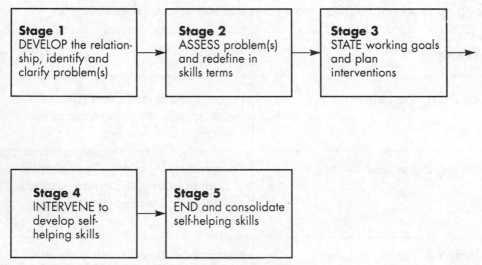

Figure 2.1 *DASIE: the five-stage lifeskills helping model*

DASIE is not only a five-stage model for managing problems. The model also assumes that where possible helpers work with underlying skills weaknesses that predispose and position clients for further problems. Thus, DASIE is a model of managing problems and altering problematic lifeskills.

Table 2.2 overviews the central task, illustrative helper thinking and action skills and desired client behaviours for each stage of the model.

STAGE 1: DEVELOP THE RELATIONSHIP, IDENTIFY AND CLARIFY PROBLEM(S)

Stage 1 extends to various pre-helping contacts by clients. Even though helpers may not be directly involved, making appointments to see helpers and being greeted at

Table 2.2 DASIE: A five-stage model for managing problems and altering problematic lifeskills patterns

Task	Illustrative helper skills	Client behaviours
Stage 1 DEVELOP the relationship, identify and clarify problem(s)		
Build rapport and help clients to reveal, identify and describe problem(s)	*Thinking skills:* coping self-talk, perceiving accurately *Action skills:* Structuring, permission to talk, continuation messages, empathic responses, establishing agendas, helpful questioning, encouraging self-talk, confronting appropriately, summarizing	Identify problem areas, specify details, share, thoughts, feelings and personal meanings
Stage 2 ASSESS problem(s) and redefine in skills terms		
Elicit relevant information to define problem(s) in skills terms	*Thinking skills:* accurately perceiving, accurately attributing cause, forming explanatory hypotheses, analysing and evaluating information *Action skills:* relationship skills plus active empathy, focused information gathering, formulating and discussing working definitions	Collaborate to identify skills weaknesses, develop 'handles' for working on problems and problematic skills
Stage 3 STATE working goals and plan interventions		
State working goals and negotiate self-helping interventions to attain them	*Thinking skills:* realistic rules, predicting, goal setting *Action skills:* Translating skills redefinitions into goal statements, choosing and discussing educational interventions, answering questions, designing programmes to attain goals	Collaborate in setting goals, acknowledge need to work actively on problems and problematic skills patterns, collaborate in discussing interventions and plans

Stage 4 INTERVENE to develop self-helping skills

Work to develop self-helping skills strengths in problem areas	*Thinking skills:* making realistic rules, accurately attributing cause, accurately perceiving, evaluating and possibly reformulating change hypotheses *Action skills:* relationship skills plus implementing self-helping interventions; establishing session agendas; instructing; demonstrating; arranging structured activities; setting homework; discussing and evaluating progress; encouraging and supporting self-helping; reverting to earlier stages of model as necessary	Work to acquire thinking and action self-helping skills strengths, develop self-instruction skills, do homework, review progress, work through difficulties and setbacks

Stage 5 END and consolidate self-helping skills

Terminate helping contact and consolidate self-helping skills	*Thinking skills:* predicting realistically, accurately attributing cause, goal setting, developing managing problem strategies *Action skills* anticipatory structuring for termination, reviewing progress and goal attainment, consolidating learnings, developing maintenance and relapse prevention strategies, getting feedback, handling affective and relationship issues, saying goodbye	Share in reviewing progress, anticipate difficulties, develop coping strategies summarize learnings, work on problem(s) and problematic skills

reception desks are two important preliminaries that can be handled well or poorly. If initial phone enquiries are fumbled, no further contacts may transpire. If clients perceive they are mechanistically treated at reception desks, such perceptions create a negative climate for meeting helpers. A further important preliminary is how helpers meet, greet and seat clients. Developing the helping relationship starts from the moment of first contact. When you meet clients in waiting areas, they may perceive you as more friendly and competent if, as well as calling out their names, you go over to them and show them into your office rather than just stand at the door. Clients often feel threatened by the prospect of meeting helpers and you need to show empathy to feelings of vulnerability. Furthermore, initial impressions are important. Early negative judgements about helpers are hard to retrieve.

On re-entering your office you should politely show clients to their seats and help them to feel safe. At an appropriate moment, possibly even in waiting areas, you may greet them along the lines of: 'Hello, I'm . . . a (helper) here.' The issue of what you and your clients call each other can be handled during the initial or subsequent sessions according to the wishes of both parties and the rules of the social context in which helping occurs. Always pay attention to your voice and body as well as to your verbal messages. The old saying 'It ain't what you say, but how you say it' applies for both helpers and clients. Helpers can override good verbal messages (what they say) by sloppy voice and body messages (how they say it). From the start, you observe and listen to clients' verbal, voice and body messages so that you can respond appropriately. In addition, you start formulating your working model about what clients' problems really are and what thinking and action skills weaknesses sustain them.

Stage 1 has two main overlapping functions: developing helping relationships with clients and working with them to identify and obtain fuller descriptions of problems. Lifeskills helping places heavy emphasis on building supportive working relationships with clients. Such relationships go beyond helpers showing empathy, non-possessive warmth and genuiness (Rogers, 1957) to the more active fostering of client self-support. Helpers support clients emotionally and technically. Emotionally, they support clients as they tell their stories, gain insight into their patterns of skills strengths and weaknesses and strive to manage problems and develop skills strengths. Technically, helpers support clients in analysing their skills strengths and weaknesses, setting realistic goals, planning for change, and in implementing interventions. The nature of the supportive relationship differs according to the stage of the lifeskills helping model. In stage 1 the primary emphasis is on providing emotional support as clients tell their stories and share their frames of reference. In subsequent stages, whilst still offering emotional support, helpers support clients by offering specific expertise as psychological educators.

When clients are seated, you may perform some initial structuring regarding such matters as how much time you have together, any limitations on confidentiality, and how you work. At this stage the sorts of question that helpers seek to answer are, 'Why is the client here?', 'What is going on that causes and sustains the problems?' and 'Am I going to be able to work with this client?' The sorts of question that clients seek to answer are, 'Can I trust this helper not to hurt me?', 'Will I get relief from my distressing feelings?', 'Is my problem solvable?' and 'Can this helper do anything for me?' If clients have had previous unsuccessful contacts with other helpers, a further question may be, 'In what way is this helper different from the others?'

You end your initial structuring by giving clients permission to talk and tell their stories. You encourage them to share their frames of reference concerning their problem areas. At first you give clients space to tell their stories in their own way. Many of your early questions may be open-ended. You do not wish to curtail prematurely their response options. Often it is helpful and less jarring if your questions build on what clients have just said rather than seeming to come from 'outer space'. You can request examples, greater specificity, and elaboration of feelings and personal meanings. If you intersperse empathic reflections with questions, clients are less likely to feel interrogated. Together you and your clients build fuller descriptive pictures of problem areas. Sometimes you may need to refrain from exploring a problem area more fully to check that there are not other more important agendas. If unclear, you can also ask your clients what areas are important for them to work on.

What of the inner game of helping? For each stage of the model, how helpers think influences how they behave. Helpers subscribing to the psychological education theoretical framework advocated for this book can still possess thinking skills weaknesses that significantly intervene with effectiveness. Helpers need to acknowledge that throughout the helping process they are always choosers. How helpers send verbal, voice and body messages is one area of choosing. How they choose to think about their clients is another area. Ideally helpers are practitioner-researchers who make sound hypotheses both about how to respond to clients' communications and about how to form working definitions and interventions. Helping is a continuous process of hypothesis making and testing on the part of both helpers and clients (Kelly, 1955). Part of being a practitioner-researcher entails awareness of relevant research literature. However, a large part of a research or scientific approach rests in how helpers make moment-by-moment and case-by-case decisions. Helpers require sensitivity to the processes of 'clinical' hypothesis making and testing, and also to how they can invalidate these processes.

The following is a cautionary tale about being practitioner-researchers and resisting impulses to label clients prematurely. Judy is a 20-year-old student client. In the following highly hypothetical excerpt, each time Judy says something more about herself, the helper labels her problem differently – all within the first five minutes of the initial session! Imagine a cartoon format, with each 'client says' and 'helper thinks' pair being represented by 'thinks' balloons.

Judy: I'm very tense about my upcoming exams.

Helper thinks: This is an exam anxiety problem.

Judy: I have not been studying efficiently for some time now.

Helper thinks: Aha. Her test anxiety is consequent upon poor study skills. Judy has a study skills problem.

Judy: I wonder if I'm doing the right subject.

Helper thinks: Perhaps this is really an educational choice problem.

Judy: My parents are always pressurizing me to achieve on their terms. I just want to be my own person.

Helper thinks: Judy has a young adult identity problem. Also, she needs to assert herself more with her parents.

Judy: I was doing all right until my relationship with Bill broke up. Since then I've been feeling very depressed.

Helper thinks: Judy must have a reactive depression problem.

Judy: I think I drove Bill away through being too aggressive. Now I regret my behaviour.

Helper thinks: This is now a managing anger and conflict problem. Help, I've got a problem too. I'm confused!

The message in this tongue-in-cheek excerpt is the same that porcupine parents give to their offspring when advising them on how to make love: 'proceed carefully'. Especially at the start of stage 1, helpers need to remember that they are practitioner-researchers. Practitioner-researchers base their hypotheses on careful collaboration and assessment of information.

Helpers' thinking skills are also related to their ability to listen and respond with understanding to clients. For example, beginning helpers are often very anxious. Even experienced helpers may be too anxious with new clients. When anxiety gets above a certain level it debilitates rather than facilitates (Alpert & Haber, 1960). Helpers may contribute to their anxiety by negative self-talk, where they focus on their shortcomings, and catastrophic predictions, where they overemphasize what might go wrong. Excessive helper anxiety interferes with both inner listening (helpers' capacity to listen to what goes on in themselves), and outer listening (helpers' capacity to listen to and understand clients). Helpers may also bring unrealistic personal rules regarding need for approval and achievement to their work. Such rules distort listening if helpers focus too much on themselves rather than their clients.

Inaccurately attributing responsibility for clients' lives and for change is another potential weakness in helper thinking skills. Helpers may be unclear about the boundaries of their own and their clients' responsibilities. Consciously or unconsciously, helpers may create dependency and fail to build client self-helping skills adequately. For instance, they may selectively listen for evidence of client weakness and need for help rather than for evidence of client strength and ability for self-support. Also, helpers may leap in with suggestions for how clients might behave rather than help clients to make their own choices.

Helpers can misperceive clients in numerous ways. You may find it hard to perceive accurately clients who either exhibit certain emotions, for instance anger or self-pity, or who remind you of significant others in your past or present life, or who are skilled at manipulating you, for instance through flattery. In addition, there may be basic differences between helpers and clients, for example in age, sex, social class or culture, contributing to misperceptions. Helpers and clients relate to each other on the basis of 'personifications' (Sullivan, 1953, 1954). Personifications are mental constructions that people make of each other. An important helper task of stage 1 is to start making accurate personifications of clients. However, a poor base for effective helping is when 'my picture of me' needs to distort 'my picture of you' to stay intact. All helpers possess anxieties and defences that interfere with their effectiveness to a greater or lesser degree. Will observes in his introduction to Sullivan's *The Psychiatric Interview:* 'Thus both psychiatrist and patient, while strongly motivated to meet, are also driven by anxiety to withdraw from each other. This interplay of movements – multiple variations of advance and retreat – is characteristic of the field of the interview' (Sullivan, 1954, p.xii). Stage 1 of lifeskills helping, where both parties have the anxiety of meeting for the first time and helpers have the added anxiety of the expectation that they will help clients, is a particularly fertile breeding ground for distorted personifications and communications, for advances and retreats.

A short illustrative summary of the same case is provided to end the description of each stage of the lifeskills helping model. Only the bare bones of the case are presented. Not all cases fit so neatly into the five-stage lifeskills helping model as this one.

> Rob, a married man in his mid-forties decides to see a counsellor, Sue Clark, because he is afraid his marriage may break up because of his temper outbursts. Sue starts the initial session by telling Rob that this is an exploratory interview to find out what concerns him and to see if together they can identify possible options and skills for dealing with his problems. Sue encourages Rob to say why he has come and to describe his concerns more fully. Sue's verbal, voice and body messages convey both person orientation and task orientation. Within the context of a supportive relationship, this is a working session. Early on Rob reveals that his wife Betty knows he has come for counselling and approves, but does not wish to come herself. Rob and Betty are the parents of three girls, aged 15, 13, and 11. The precipitating crisis was that Rob struck his oldest daughter, Ruth, whom he has always found hard to handle. Rob cares deeply for family life and is scared that the family may disintegrate unless he gets on top of his temper. Sue encourages Rob to describe how he and Ruth relate, including focusing on the recent physical violence. Rob also shares his perceptions of how he and the other family members relate. He

expresses mixed feelings about his wife, who dislikes trouble at home and does not always support his discipline attempts. Rob has a short fuse; people stir him. He has had trouble outside the home too, for instance rows with employers and colleagues. Rob recalls that his father was very strict and had a bad temper. Sue facilitates Rob's description of his problem and of how he and others think and behave. Sue is alert for clues concerning Rob's thinking and action skills weaknesses. For instance, when Rob says that people stir him, he gives the impression that he has no choice over how he reacts. As the initial stage proceeds, Rob feels that Sue is helping him to develop a fuller picture of his problem. After a series of exploratory questions, interspersed with empathic reflections, Sue summarizes the content of the interview so far and checks out Rob's reactions to the summary. By now not only does Sue have a greater knowledge of Rob and his problem, but Rob has broadened his perspective too. Nevertheless, Sue is aware that further work remains to be done in moving beyond a descriptive to a skills definition of Rob's problem.

STAGE 2: ASSESS PROBLEM(S) AND REDEFINE IN SKILLS TERMS

The object of this stage is to build a definitional bridge between *describing* and *actively working* on a problem and its underlying skills weaknesses. In stage 1, problems have been described, amplified and clarified largely in everyday language. The description of clients' problems represents an expansion of their internal viewpoints rather than providing them with different insights. In stage 2, helpers build upon information collected in stage 1 to explore hypotheses about how clients think and act that sustains difficulties. Helpers add to and go beyond clients' present perceptions to look for 'handles' on how to work for change. They collaborate in the detective work of breaking down clients' problems into their component skills weaknesses. Whereas stage 1 might end with descriptive summaries of problems in everyday terms, stage 2 ends with redefinitions of problems in skills terms.

Helpers offer clients supportive relationships in stage 2. In stage 1, helpers support clients in telling their stories in their own terms. In stage 2 helpers support clients in making sense of their stories. A distinction can be made between *reflective* empathy and *active* empathy, each of which may help clients to expand their perceptions. In reflective empathy helpers understand clients' existing perceptions. Clients are provided with psychological space to explore and experience their thoughts, feelings and personal meanings. Helpers are mirrors that allow clients to see their reflections and then, when ready, to go further in self-understanding. In active empathy, helpers use their psychological skills and insights not only to understand where clients are, but to provide insights on how clients can get to where they want to be. Clients who come for initial interviews may feel better understood by helpers who give them handles with which to work on problems than by helpers just offering reflective empathy. Reflective and active empathy are not different ends on a continuum. Skilled helpers offer both reflective and active empathy. The explanations they offer as part of active empathy are likely to be better if based on information clients shared because of the quality of their reflective empathy.

A critical ingredient of stage 2 is for helpers to maintain a skills focus. This does not mean that helpers immediately translate everything clients say into skills language. However, the question at the back of helpers' minds in stage 2 is always: 'What skills weaknesses sustain clients' problems?' Especially for beginning helpers, another question is: 'If I identify skills weaknesses, do I possess the interventions to deal with them?' Many neophyte helpers possess very restricted repertoires of practical interventions, thus limiting their capacity both to formulate working definitions and to follow through on them. Most clients do not think of their problems in skills language, so helpers require sensitivity in when and how they convey the view that clients may have specific thinking and action skills weaknesses.

What are helper action skills for assessing problems and redefining them in skills terms? Fundamental is the ability to maintain supportive relationships. Basic facilitation skills of attentive body messages, reflective responding, and sending verbal, voice and body continuation messages are very important. Helper facilitation skills help maintain the emotional aspect of supportive relationships.

Supportive relationships also have more technical or task-oriented aspects. The emphasis in helpers' questions differ in stage 2 from that in stage 1. In stage 1, helpers ask questions to clarify clients' existing frames of reference. In stage 2 helpers are likely to question as much from their own as from their clients' frames of reference. Much of their questioning is based on information provided wittingly or unwittingly by clients, clues, hunches, how things are said, what is left unsaid, and on overt and subtle indications of what underlying thought patterns might be. While the major focus is on pinpointing skills weaknesses, attention is also paid to identifying skills strengths and resources. Strength reviews or what Ivey and his colleagues call 'positive asset search' (Ivey *et al.*, 1987) both identify skills for coping with problems and prevent the tone of assessments from becoming too negative.

A distinction exists between clients acknowledging that that they have problems and acknowledging that certain of their behaviours may sustain them. In stage 2, helpers go beyond helping clients own that they have problems to assisting them in acknowledging personal responsibility for what they do or fail to do that perpetuates them. Clients can err in the direction of overexternalizing or overinternalizing the causes of their problems. Accurate attribution of cause and responsibility is desirable. For example, Stephen externalizes his marriage problems. He plays the victim and launches into a long description of what Mary does to him without mentioning how he behaves toward Mary. Sometimes getting clients like Stephen to provide information about their own behaviour helps them to acknowledge responsibility more accurately. Within the context of supportive relationships, helpers may need to confront such clients with challenges of varying degrees of strength to their existing perceptions. Sometimes helpers ask personal responsibility questions that help clients confront themselves with their roles in sustaining problems. Such questions include: 'How is your behaviour helping you?' and 'Is there anything you could be doing in the situation different to what you are doing now?'

Kate is an example of someone who attributes too much responsibility to herself. She contributes to her anxiety and depression by thinking that everything that goes wrong is her fault. She is just as much in need of help as Stephen in learning how to attribute responsibility accurately for her problems. Some clients need help in overcoming a passive stance to life. Tania, a bored housewife in her mid-forties whose children have grown up, has been waiting for change to come from outside herself rather than acknowledging her own responsibility for making changes occur. This observation might be shared with her. In stage 2, helpers not only assist clients in pinpointing skills weaknesses, but also encourage them to have the motivation and commitment to acknowledge their own roles in sustaining problems, and to change.

Helpers need to develop good skills in redefining problems in skills terms and in communicating these working definitions to clients. A good redefinition succinctly suggests clients' main skills weaknesses that are sustaining problems. Helpers need to distinguish important from less important material. Redefinitions that are too comprehensive confuse. If not already done, helpers can say it is valuable to break problems down into the component skills weaknesses sustaining them. Furthermore, they may introduce clients to the distinction between thinking skills and action skills, possibly using the analogy of the inner and outer games.

Problem

Thinking skills weaknesses	Action skills weaknesses
1.	1.
2.	2.
3.	3.
4.	4.

Figure 2.2 *Simple T diagram for presenting redefinitions of problems in skills terms*

Often it helps to write redefinitions in skills terms on whiteboards. Visual communication makes it easier for clients to retain what you say and, if necessary, suggest alterations. Helpers may use a simple T diagram to present thinking and action skills weaknesses for sustaining each problem (see Figure 2.2). Redefinitions of problems in skills terms, otherwise known as T redefinitions, need to be negotiated with clients. Helpers require good questioning and facilitation skills when checking redefinitions with clients. If helpers, in stages 1 and 2, have competently gathered information, skills redefinitions should flow reasonably logically from this material. Clients who share their helpers' conceptualizations of problems are more likely to commit themselves to developing needed self-helping skills than clients who are resisting helpers' conceptualizations. Redefinitions of problems in skills terms are essentially hypotheses, based on careful analysis of available information, about clients' thinking and action skills weaknesses. As hypotheses they are open to modification in light of further or better information.

Redefining problems in skills terms can be difficult. Mistakes in redefinition not only lead to time and effort being wasted, but may contribute to clients being even less able to manage problems.

> Lee was a Chinese-Malaysian foreign student repeating the first year of a university production engineering course that he was obviously going to fail. Lee was afraid of how his parents would react to his failure and also undecided about whether or not he wanted to be a production engineer. Instead of helping Lee develop skills to handle these areas, his helper, a beginning counsellor trainee, defined his problem as lack of assertive skills in seeking help from faculty members. Lee himself had reservations about this way of viewing his situation. Despite this feedback, the helper persisted in spending time in trying to build up Lee's academic help-seeking skills. Thus, the helper's faulty working definition blocked Lee from working on more pertinent skills weaknesses.

What thinking skills weaknesses can block helper effectiveness in stage 2? Helpers require good memories and powers of reasoning to analyse and evaluate relevant information. The process of formulating redefinitions in skills terms may create anxiety in some helpers over and above the anxiety of relating to new clients. Helpers need to tolerate ambiguity as they search for handles on clients' problems. Especially for beginning helpers, the combination of their own lack of experience and lack of clarity as they strive to formulate client problems in skills terms may be daunting. Coping self-talk, possessing realistic rules and expectations, and being clear about the boundaries of their own and their clients' responsibilities may ease their anxieties. Additional helper thinking skills weaknesses are that the helper may not perceive clients' communications accurately, and may have a tendency to fit clients to pet explanatory hypotheses, despite contradictory evidence.

Below is an illustrative summary of how the counsellor and Rob proceeded in stage 2 of their helping contact.

The counsellor, Sue Clark, after checking her descriptive summary with Rob, said she would now like to explore some specific areas of how Rob thought and acted to see if they could find ways for him to improve his situation. Sue observed that some things Rob said indicated that he thought he had little choice over how he behaved. Rob agreed that he had little control over his temper. As far as he was concerned he had always been that way and wondered if it were his nature. Sue also explored what Rob said to himself when faced with provocations, for example his daughter Ruth coming home later than agreed after being out with her boyfriend. Rob's self-talk appeared to fire him up rather than calm him down. The realism of his rules concerning family behaviour was another thinking skills area that, in an initial way, Sue explored with Rob. Because the action skills of how Rob communicated to his family had already been covered in stage 1, Sue did not repeat this exploration. Using the whiteboard, she then suggested a tentative T redefinition of Rob's anger problem in skills terms. Sue's T redefinition included the following *thinking* skills weaknesses: (1) inadequately acknowledging that he was always a chooser and responsible for his thoughts, feelings and actions; (2) using anger-engendering self-talk when faced with provocations; and (3) possibly having rigid and unrealistic personal rules concerning standards of behaviour in the family. *Action* skills weaknesses included (1) poor listening skills, especially when angry; (2) poor assertion skills, for instance in how he stated his wishes about his daughter's behaviour; and (3) poor skills at working through conflicts with others. Sue checked each part of this working definition with Rob both to see whether he understood it and whether he agreed with it. Rob expressed relief when the redefinition in skills terms was explained to him since, for the first time, he thought he could do something about his temper.

STAGE 3: STATE WORKING GOALS AND PLAN INTERVENTIONS

In stages 1 and 2, you and your clients moved from *descriptive definitions* to *skills redefinitions* of problems. In these early stages, you attempted to answer the questions: 'What is or are the problems?' and 'What thinking and action skills weaknesses sustain them?' Stage 3 builds on your redefinitions in skills terms to focus on the question 'What is the best way to manage problems and develop requisite skills?' Stage 3 consists of two phases: stating goals and planning interventions.

Stating goals

Goals can be stated at different levels of specificity. First, they can be stated in overall terms such as: 'I want to feel less depressed', 'I want to improve my marriage', or 'I want to come to terms with my disability and get back into life'. Such statements have value in giving clients visions about what they want out of helping. However, overall goal statements refer more to ends than to means.

Second, goals can be stated in terms of the broad skills required to attain ends. This is the level of specificity required for stage 3. Assuming you succeed in redefining problems in skills terms, stating goals becomes a relatively simple matter. Working goals are the flip-side of your redefinitions: positive statements of skills strengths to replace existing skills weaknesses. For instance, if part of the skills redefinition of Shahid's problem is that he has poor job-seeking skills, developing job-seeking skills becomes his working goal.

Third, goals can be stated still more specifically. For example, Shahid's job-seeking skills could be broken down into such subskills as how to telephone prospective employers, develop a résumé, conduct newspaper searches, handle interviews, deal with being turned down, and so on. Helpers have to decide the level of detail with which to share goals in early sessions. Each case needs to be treated on its merits; clients can only cope with so much information at any one time. A risk of getting into too much detail in an initial session is that clients retain little, if anything.

If necessary, restate and check clients' overall goals. State working goals clearly and succinctly. If using whiteboards, you can alter skills redefinitions to become working goals. T redefinitions of skills weaknesses become T statements of goals. Check with clients that they understand and agree that working goals truly represent skills required to manage problems better.

How helpers think influences how well they set working goals. Goals need to be stated clearly, realistically and, where appropriate, with a time frame. Helpers require realism concerning what is attainable. Helpers' own needs for achievement and for results may interfere with such realism. Stating goals realistically implies predicting how attainable they are for clients. Risks are attached to stating goals that are either too high or too low.

Planning interventions

Having stated goals, helpers' next set of choices concerns how best to help clients attain them. Interventions are actions on the part of helpers designed to help clients attain goals. Helpers tend to state goals in terms of their repertoire of interventions. For example, helpers knowledgeable about thinking skills tend to include thinking skills in statements of working goals. Consequently, when stating goals, you already have ideas about how to attain them.

There is no single best way to plan interventions, since clients' problems and underlying problematic skills vary so much. Try to involve clients as much as possible. For example you might say, 'Given that these are your goals , how might you best attain them?' You can still add to clients' suggestions. You can outline ways of attaining each skills goal, but remain flexible as to when and how to use different interventions. For example, you might schedule interventions to build on current specific issues that clients bring to helping. Then, at different stages of helping, you can negotiate with clients what goals and interventions are important. Another approach is to design more formal plans focused on one or more specific skills. Here helpers and clients trade off flexibility for programme clarity. Still another approach is to use a standard treatment package: for example, a cognitive–behavioural programme for insomnia (Morawetz, 1989).

Two final points concerning plans. First, even though plans may entail helpers offering interventions, for example teaching relaxation skills, their purpose is always that these become self–helping interventions. Second, plans are hypotheses about how to attain working goals. Both working goals and plans are open to modification in light of feedback.

The following is a summary of how the helper handled stating working goals and planned interventions in stage 3 of the case study about Rob.

> The counsellor, Sue Clark, clarified with Rob that his overall goal was to improve his relationship with Ruth and hence improve his marriage. Now Sue turned the previously agreed redefinition of Rob's anger problem in skills terms into a T statement of working goals. Rob's *thinking* skills goals were: (1) to acknowledge that he was a chooser and responsible for his thoughts, feelings and actions; (2) to use coping self-talk when faced with provocations; and (3) to develop realistic personal rules concerning standards of family behaviour. Rob's *action* skills goals included developing (1) good listening skills; (2) assertion skills with specific reference to how he stated his wishes about his daughter's behaviour; and (3) conflict negotiation skills. Sue realized that Rob's objective was to develop some skills as quickly as possible rather than to have a long-term helping relationship. Instead of designing a step-by-step training plan, Sue suggested that the best way to proceed was to help Rob develop thinking and action skills in relation to material brought into each session.

Sue required homework, including listening to audio cassettes of sessions. She asked Rob to monitor how he communicated to Ruth and other family members and to report back next session. She also requested that Rob keep a log of his thoughts and feelings before, during and after specific anger provocations.

STAGE 4: INTERVENE TO DEVELOP SELF-HELPING SKILLS

The interventions stage has two objectives: to help clients manage their presenting problems better; and to assist clients in working on their problematic skills patterns and developing skills strengths. The emotional climate throughout the intervention stage is collaborative. Within the context of supportive relationships, helpers assist clients in assuming responsibility for managing problems and altering problematic skills. Good helping relationship skills are important during this stage. One use of facilitation skills is to understand clients both for their sake and for yours. Clients feel more supported if they think that helpers understand what they go through both in having problems and in trying to cope with them. Good helping relationship skills also enable you to understand clients better and, if necessary, to adjust your working definitions and goals accordingly. Another use of facilitation skills is to support didactic interventions. You may need to process clients' thoughts and feelings about engaging in specific interventions: for instance role plays or muscular relaxation. Helpers require relationships skills for clients to learn maximally from skills demonstrations: for instance, checking out their learning and showing understanding as they try out demonstrated skills.

Throughout lifeskills helping there is a tension between helpers being person oriented and task oriented. A risk in the intervention stage is that helpers become too task oriented. For instance, with clients coming to sessions after very difficult weeks, helpers may decide it is premature to work directly on problems and problematic skills until clients have had the opportunity to share and process their thoughts and feelings concerning what currently bothers them. Of course, there are risks in the other direction: namely, becoming so person oriented that the training focus of sessions is lost.

Sometimes another tension in lifeskills helping is that between focusing on problems and focusing on problematic skills. Realistically, what many clients want is to deal with problems as quickly as possible rather than focus on underlying problematic skills. For instance, what bothers Erica is containing her anxiety sufficiently to pass a test in two weeks' time rather than developing anxiety management skills for future tests. Another example is that of Rafiq, who wants to cope with a forthcoming job interview rather than subsequent job interviews. Helpers too may operate under time and resource limitations, which militate against their intervening as thoroughly as they might like. Furthermore, both helpers and clients work within an overall culture that is more problem oriented than problematic skills oriented. Skills are for fixing motor cars and playing sports rather than for managing psychological problems. Even though the focus may not be as thorough as desirable, helpers require creativity in maintaining a skills focus in all helping contacts.

What are some helper action skills for the intervention stage? When helpers provide rationales for interventions, they emphasize both skills language and also client responsibility for skills development. Clients are clearly encouraged to own both problems and problematic skills. Helpers need to develop a repertoire of interventions encompassing both thinking skills and action skills. Thinking skills interventions tend to be generic across most problem areas. Action skills interventions are more specific to problem areas, though not always. Helpers need to develop a repertoire of action skills interventions most relevant to the problems of their target populations: for example career choice helpers require interventions that support clients acquiring career decision-making, job-seeking and interviewing skills; and marital and family helpers require interventions that support relationships skills such as listening, self-disclosing and managing anger and conflict. Helpers should keep abreast of relevant theoretical and research literature on how best to intervene for specific problems and skills weaknesses.

Helpers are psychological educators: they require good training as well as good assessment and helping relationship skills to intervene effectively. It is insufficient to know *what* interventions to offer without also being skilled in *how* to offer them. Table 2.3 depicts modes of psychological education or training and modes of learning in lifeskills helping. Helpers work much of the time with the three training modes of 'tell', 'show' and 'do'. They require special skills for each. 'Tell' entails giving clients clear instructions concerning the skills they wish to develop. 'Show' means offering demonstrations of how to implement skills. 'Do' means arranging for clients to perform structured activities and homework tasks.

Table 2.3 Modes of psychological education or training, and of learning

Psychological education or training mode	Learning mode
Facilitate	Learning from self-exploring and from experiencing self more fully
Assess	Learning from self-evaluating and from self-monitoring
Tell	Learning from hearing
Show	Learning from observing
Do	Learning from doing structured activities and homework tasks
Consolidate	Learning from developing self-helping skills in all the above modes

Table 2.3 incorporates the notion of consolidation, thus highlighting the importance throughout helping of focusing on issues of transfer, development and maintenance of skills. As far as possible, helpers train skills as self-helping skills. For example, helpers can train relaxation skills in either helper-centred or people-centred ways. The main difference is that people-centred training emphasizes more how clients can relax themselves through self-instruction and also how they can use relaxation as a coping skill. In this vein, Goldfried and Davison have advocated teaching systematic desensitization, which incorporates relaxation skills, as a self-control procedure (Goldfried, 1971; Goldfried & Davison, 1976).

Like overall helping contacts, individual sessions in the intervention stage may be viewed in four phases: preparatory, initial, working and ending. These session phases overlap. The preparatory phase entails helpers thinking in advance how best to assist clients. Helpers ensure that, if appropriate, they have available session plans; training materials, for instance handouts; and audiovisual aids, for instance whiteboards and audio–cassette recorders.

The initial phase consists of meeting, greeting and seating, then giving permission to talk. Though a skill not restricted to the initial phase, early on helpers may wish to establish session agendas. These can be both explicit and implicit. For instance, without verbalizing session agendas, helpers may go from checking how clients feel, to reviewing the past week's homework, to focusing on one or more problematic skills and/or problems in clients' lives. On other occasions, helpers and clients may openly negotiate session agendas. Once you establish session agendas, you may alter them if more pressing business arises.

The working phase focuses on specific interventions designed to help clients manage problems and develop lifeskills. While being sensitive to clients' needs to focus on describing problems, helpers should maintain a skills focus. Basically there are three main approaches to the working phase. First, you may adapt your skills training to material clients bring into sessions. Second, you may follow prearranged skills training plans. Third, you may both work with clients' material and also complete specific training plans. During the working phase you use helping relationship skills to encourage self-disclosure and self-exploration and to support specific didactic activities.

The ending phase lasts from towards the end of one session to the beginning of the next. This phase focuses on summarizing the major session learnings, negotiating homework, strengthening commitment to between-session work, and rehearsing and practising skills outside helping. Consolidating learned skills as self-helping skills takes place at the end of sessions and between each session. Frequently clients are asked to write down what their homework assignments are. This serves the following purposes: giving a message that homework is important, clarifying what is required, helping clients' memories, and providing something in writing that can be posted as a reminder.

What thinking skills can help or hinder the intervention stage? Helpers require accurate perception and, where necessary, flexibility in being able to discard or reformulate working goals and definitions. Highly rigid and defensive helpers may deny or insufficiently acknowledge the ineffectiveness of certain interventions. Helpers require the ability to attribute responsibility and cause accurately. For instance, helpers need to help clients to own both their problems and their responsibility for developing skills strengths. However, helpers have responsibilities too: for instance, to perform competently. They need to beware of falsely attributing the cause of slow or non-existent progress to clients without examining the adequacy of their helping behaviours. As always, helpers' unrealistic personal rules regarding such matters as making mistakes, needing clients' approval, and getting quick and impressive results may interfere with effective performance. Furthermore, helpers can use self-talk for good or ill: for example, calming themselves down and staying task oriented when faced with angry and manipulative clients rather than giving way to negative self-talk about themselves and their clients.

Below is a continuation of the case study of Rob in regard to stage 4, intervene and develop client self-helping skills.

> The counsellor, Sue Clark, saw Rob for a total of seven sessions over a two and a half month period. The intervention stage lasted from the second to the sixth session. At the start of each session, Sue checked whether Rob had any pressing concerns, and how he had progressed with homework. Sue approached each session flexibly within the context of the agreed skills redefinition and working goals. Her considerations in establishing session agendas included both where Rob wanted to focus and how best to develop Rob's self-helping skills. Sue trained Rob in the thinking skills goal that he was a chooser partly by articulating this as a skill, partly by encouraging Rob to become more aware of the consequences of his choices, partly by reframing his language – for example, 'Ruth made me so angry' was reformulated into 'I chose to get very angry with Ruth' – and partly by reflective responses that continuously and unobtrusively emphasized personal responsibility. Sue trained Rob in coping self-talk skills by spending part of an early session directly teaching him by instruction, demonstration and coached practice. In subsequent sessions, Sue checked how well Rob had used his coping self-talk skills outside counselling. She trained the skill of choosing realistic personal rules by getting Rob to identify and examine his rules regarding his own and Ruth's behaviour in relation to specific situations that Rob brought into helping. Sue then helped Rob dispute and reformulate inappropriate rules. In regard to attaining action skills goals, Sue taught Rob some simple listening skills: for instance not interrupting, and checking how well he understood

his daughter's position. Sue trained Rob in action skills for being more assertive in stating wants and wishes and negotiating conflicts. She reviewed with him different ways of acting in specific family situations and their consequences. She paid attention to voice and body as well as verbal messages when rehearsing Rob in assertion and negotiating conflict skills. Sue made extensive use of the whiteboard for working on both thinking and action skills, and ended each session by summarizing the main learning points and negotiating homework assignments. Rob listened to the cassettes of preceding sessions as part of his homework. Since Rob was surrounded by his family, Sue encouraged him to start using his skills at home and to 'learn on the job'. His wife and daughters appreciated Rob's efforts to work on his temper. Even early on, his efforts were rewarded by less family tension.

STAGE 5: END AND CONSOLIDATE SELF-HELPING SKILLS

The ending of lifeskills helping is built into its beginning. From start to finish, helpers and clients develop skills for self-helping. Though longer contact may be warranted, much lifeskills helping is relatively short term, say up to ten sessions. Sometimes helpers have to work in even tighter time frames such as one or two sessions. Reasons for very brief helping include clients' personal deadlines, for instance upcoming meetings with estranged spouses, or imminent tests. Also, even if seeing skilled helpers, some people do not like the client role. Reluctance to continue with helping may be heightened where either clients or third parties pay for it. Sometimes ending is formalized into fixed-term contracts. In most instances ending helping is more open-ended. Ideally, ending is based on both parties perceiving that clients have made appreciable gains in their ability to manage their problems, and that they have also consolidated their gains into self-helping skills for use afterwards.

Most often either helpers or clients bring up the topic of ending before the final session. This allows both parties to work through the various task and relationship issues connected with ending the contact. A useful option is to fade contact with some clients by seeing them progressively less often. Certain clients may appreciate the opportunity for booster sessions, say one, two, three or even six months later. Booster sessions provide both clients and helpers with the chance to review progress and consolidate self-helping skills. Scheduling follow-up telephone calls can perform some of these functions too.

Lifeskills helping seeks to avoid the 'Train and Hope' approach (Goldstein & Keller, 1987; Stokes & Osnes, 1989). For instance, prior to the ending stage, helpers structure realistic expectations when discussing working definitions and goals with clients. Helpers also attempt to build client self-observation and assessment skills. Transfer and maintenance of skills is encouraged by such means as developing clients' self-instructional abilities, working with real-life situations during helping, and using between-session time productively to rehearse and practise skills.

Strategies that helpers may use during the ending and consolidating self-helping skills stage include encouraging clients to assume the primary responsibility for reviewing their progress (Ward, 1984). Clients can summarize their managing problem skills. These summaries may be audio-recorded for later playback and revision purposes. A strategy for clients who experience difficulty in acknowledging gains is to listen to a recording of an early session, if it exists. Helpers can work with clients to identify difficulties and setbacks, then together they can develop and rehearse coping strategies for dealing with them. Sometimes clients require help in identifying people to support their efforts to maintain skills. Helpers may also provide clients with information about further skills-building opportunities.

Helper thinking skills are relevant to conducting the ending and consolidating self-helping skills stage. For instance, as much as possible, helpers must accurately perceive their clients' progress in acquiring skills. Assuming clients do not make the decision for you, knowing when to end entails predicting realistically how well clients will use skills on their own. Helping may either be ended prematurely or allowed to drag on too long. When ending, you may attribute cause and responsibility inaccurately: for instance you may overestimate your responsibility for clients' lives and be reluctant to let go of them. Helpers can use their skills in formulating realistic goals to assist clients in maintaining and developing skills. In addition, helpers can use their skills in managing problems to assist clients to develop managing problems strategies to maintain skills.

Below is a summary of stage 5, end and consolidate self-helping skills, in the case study of Rob.

> Throughout helping, the counsellor, Sue Clark, worked to consolidate Rob's managing anger skills as self-helping skills. During the sixth session, Sue and Rob decided that they would probably have one more session in four weeks' time when Sue came back from an overseas trip. In this session, Rob mentioned that he felt he had lost some of his influence in the family by adopting a more reasonable approach to provocations. Using the whiteboard, Sue developed with Rob a balance sheet of positive and negative consequences of using his skills. As a result, Rob perceived the balance to be heavily in favour of maintaining them. He started the seventh and final session by stating that his life was going much better. Sue helped Rob to provide specific evidence for this assertion. Together they explored each of Rob's main relationships to see how

well Rob was using his skills and with what consequences. Rob was definitely attaining his initial goal of an improved relationship with his oldest daughter, Ruth. Rob affirmed his decision to end counselling. Sue helped him to review his learnings from the sessions. Rob mentioned how he was more prepared to think first, talk things over, and play the game of life more with his head. He thought that there were still problems in his marriage, but did not wish to work on them at present. Sue Clark left it open for Rob to return for helping if necessary.

APPLYING THE MODEL

Below are some considerations in applying the lifeskills helping model. The underlying theme is that helpers, in the best interests of clients, need to apply the model flexibly.

Sequencing

DASIE (develop relationship – assess – state goals – intervene – end) is intended to provide some guidelines rather than be a straightjacket. Though your roles differ, the model assumes a degree of collaboration between you and your clients. Managing problems and altering problematic skills rarely proceed according to neatly ordered stages. The stages tend to overlap: for instance your clients' descriptions of problems contribute to how you jointly assess them. Also, there may be reversion to earlier stages: for example as more information or new problems arise during the intervention stage, working definitions and goals may be refined. Helping can be messy. You operate on the basis of hypotheses about yourself, your clients and the helping process. You require flexibility to incorporate either new or previously overlooked information into your hypotheses making and testing. A further point is that the five-stage model requires adjusting not only to individual clients, but also to the setting and social context in which you work. For example, a priest helping a parishioner is likely to operate in a much more informal way than a counselling psychologist in private practice.

Brief helping

The following assumptions underlie the DASIE model: first, much helping is relatively short term, say three to ten sessions: and second, it tends to be focused on one or two major problems or problematic skills areas. As such DASIE is a model of central tendency. However, helping can also be very brief, say one or two sessions, or more extended, say ten to twenty sessions or more. Often very brief helping contacts take place because clients have immediate agendas that require attention: for example a test, a job interview or an unexpected crisis. In such instances, helpers require flexibility in choosing how person oriented or task oriented to be. An early skills focus may be inappropriate with recently bereaved clients needing space to tell their stories and experience their feelings, but it may be highly appropriate with clients anxious about imminent job interviews. Here, based on tailor-made T definitions, helpers may provide clients with 'crash training courses' in anxiety management and job interview skills.

Extended helping

Even with competent helpers, numerous reasons exist why helping may last longer than ten sessions. For example, clients may come from very emotionally deprived backgrounds in which, along with learning poor lifeskills, their confidence has been badly undermined. Clients may have multiple problems and skills weaknesses. Or they may differ in the severity with which they possess the same problem, for instance shyness or tendencies to irrational thinking. In addition, clients may possess resistances to change (Ellis, 1987) or feel that change is being forced upon them by others. Furthermore, some clients' personal and social environments may not support change.

Since different reasons exist for extended helping, there are no simple answers for how best to go about it. With highly vulnerable clients, helpers may need to spend more time establishing trusting relationships. Vulnerable clients may also require more gentle and nurturing relationships than more robust clients. Such clients may take longer to get to the point where they possess insight into how they sustain problems. However, it is possible to overgeneralize. Some vulnerable clients may benefit from helpers' confronting their skills weaknesses. Also, right from the initial session, some vulnerable clients may appreciate working on one or two specific skills.

Helping may go more slowly where clients' starting-off points are low in specific skills areas. Helpers may have to break down skills more, spend more time on instruction and demonstration, and offer clients more support as they rehearse and practise skills. In extended helping, much session time is spent on working through the application of targeted skills to specific issues in clients' lives, including their fears about using the skills. Where clients have multiple problems and skills weaknesses, helpers and clients face the issue of prioritizing those skills most in need of attention. In extended contacts, helpers and clients also have to prioritize between initial and emerging problems and problematic skills areas. Emerging problems may arise through clients themselves changing, or through changes in their environment. Working definitions and goals may require reformulation. Clients' progress may be slowed down by others in their environment, for example teachers, parents or spouses. If so, helpers need to consider whether it is worth broadening helping to include them.

CONCLUDING COMMENT

Beginning helpers are likely to find that it takes time to become proficient in the lifeskills helping model. This training model requires helpers to go beyond offering good helping relationship skills to offering good assessment and didactic skills. The model also requires helpers to possess effective inner game or thinking skills as well as effective outer game or action skills. Many beginning helpers experience difficulty in making the transition from *talking* relationships, based on good facilitation skills, to *training* relationships, based on assessment and specific interventions designed to assist clients manage problems and problematic skills patterns. The lifeskills helping model requires helpers to step outside their everyday language to conceptualize problems in skills terms. Some beginning helpers do not find this congenial and take a great deal of time to make the transition, if at all. The lifeskills helping model requires helpers to develop a range of specific interventions related to clients' problem and problematic skills; again, it takes time to build up a repertoire of interventions. In fact, there is always room for improvement. It is a lifetime challenge to stay proficient in and to develop your lifeskills helping skills still further.

CHAPTER HIGHLIGHTS

- Lifeskills helping focuses on both client and helper inner games, or thinking skills, and outer games, or action skills.

- A distinction exists between problems and the problematic skills that sustain problems. Lifeskills helping focuses on both problems and problematic skills.

- Beyond a presenting problem, problematic skills can manifest themselves both horizontally, across a range of similar current situations, and vertically, in future similar situations.

- DASIE is a five-stage model for helping clients manage problems and alter problematic lifeskills patterns.

- In stage 1 helpers develop supportive relationships with clients and work with them to identify and clarify problems.

- In stage 2, assess problem(s) and redefine in skills terms, helpers and clients collaborate to build definitional bridges between describing and actively working on problems and problematic skills.

- In stage 3 helpers translate skills redefinitions into working goals and plan interventions to attain them.

- In stage 4, within the context of supportive relationships helpers intervene to develop clients' self-helping skills. Helpers require a repertoire of thinking skills and action skills interventions about which they are knowledgeable, and which they are skilled in applying.

- In stage 5 the helping contact ends with further attention to consolidating clients' self-helping skills.

- Helpers should apply the DASIE lifeskills helping model flexibly: for instance the sequencing of stages may overlap.

- Helpers also require flexibility in adapting DASIE to very brief and to extended helping contacts.

- Beginning helpers are likely to take time to become proficient in the lifeskills helping model. It is a lifetime challenge to stay proficient in and to develop your lifeskills helping skills still further.

THREE

What You Bring to Training and Helping

I am simply a human being, more or less.

Saul Bellow

CHAPTER QUESTIONS

What are your motives for helping?

What helping skills have you learned?

How do you think about helping?

How emotionally responsive are you?

How confident are you?

What anxieties and fears do you have about helping?

How might your sexuality influence helping?

What sex-role identity and expectations do you possess?

What are your values?

What are your ethics?

What culture and cross-cultural skills do you bring?

What race are you and what racial attitudes do you possess?

To what social class do you bring?

INTRODUCTION

Nobody starts helper training from scratch. Each of you brings various skills, characteristics and attributes to the task. Lifeskills helping is not the mechanistic application of a set of techniques. Helpers work within the context of person-to-person relationships to develop clients' self-helping skills. The personhood of both helpers and clients is central to the approach. This chapter focuses on *you*, what you bring to helper training and to helping. Some characteristics, for instance your biological sex, you cannot change. Other characteristics, for instance cross-cultural sensitivity, you can improve. In all instances, your personal characteristics influence how you help.

Helping differs from most other occupants in that the tools are *people* who use various *people* skills to help *people* help themselves. Contrast this with dentists who use tools, such as drills, to work on teeth or with car mechanics who use tools, such as spanners, to work on cars. In helping, the self is the main instrument or tool. The lifeskill model of helping is not independent of the people who apply it. The self that you bring to helper training possesses both strengths and weaknesses. Skilled helpers both enhance their strengths and try to overcome personal blocks. Helpers and clients are made from the same human clay. Yalom (1989), in his book of case studies entitled *Love's Executioner*, provides excellent illustrations of how helper humanity can permeate helping.

Just as helper characteristics influence helping, so student characteristics influence helper training. Below is an illustration.

Sandra was a highly sensitive M.A. in Counselling student in her late thirties. She successfully completed a first-term practical course focused on helping relationship skills. The second-term practical course, in addition to helping relationship skills, focused on assessing and redefining clients' problems, identifying at least one thinking skill weakness and one action skill weakness. Sandra was one of ten students in a practical taught by the course leader who used instruction, modelling and coaching. In addition students received three individual supervisions by another experienced counselling psychologist using interview cassettes made with volunteer undergraduate 'clients'. At the end of the term, the course leader failed Sandra's assessment cassette because she had listened inadequately to her client. She kept jumping in, offering explanations and interpretations from an external viewpoint. She had panicked when requested to go beyond helping relationship skills to formulate a working definition of her client's problem. Sandra became highly anxious at failing her assessment at the first attempt. She considered dropping out of the course and suing her supervisor. Given the discrepancy between her performance and his perceptions of her counselling potential, the course leader offered Sandra some individual coaching to bring her up to passing standard. In the first coaching session the supervisor suggested that he and Sandra take turns in offering each other 15-minute counselling sessions emphasizing basic facilitation skills. Sandra used her 15 minutes to explore why she became so controlling when interviewing. She started by attributing this to her earlier social work training. Then she acknowledged that she put herself under tremendous pressure to get quick results, especially when assessed. She became aware of feeling highly anxious and vulnerable when interviewing. She put this in the context of being one of two daughters who, when her father died when she was six, was brought up by a single parent. Sandra's mother always encouraged her sister, but actively discouraged all Sandra's scholastic and professional endeavours. Sandra hated this side of her mother and was terrified that any lack of performance on her part would prove that her mother was right all along in disparaging her. In her assessment cassette, Sandra did not just work with the client, but also fought an inner struggle against her mother's 'voices in her head'. The mental tapes Sandra brought to helper training helped neither her nor her clients. Sandra needed to work on her inner game, her thinking skills weaknesses, as well as on her outer game, how she related to clients.

The case of Sandra illustrates many points in helper training. First, students are influenced by their past and not just by their current training. Second, trainers need to take into account the individual circumstances of each student. Third, an important paradox exists in helper training and helping. Qualities like sensitivity and vulnerability that can be huge assets in helping can also be huge liabilities unless students and helpers use them for rather than against clients. The personal characteristics that make students good can make them bad. A less sensitive and vulnerable person than Sandra might not have 'screwed up' so badly, yet would have lacked her helping potential.

Some starting-points for helping

Helping interviews are ever-changing processes between two people who influence each other. Helpers and clients bring many characteristics into interviews and experience many thoughts and feelings during interviews. What helpers and clients bring to interviews are not just matters of fact, but also matters of perception. For example, helpers may perceive their race positively, but their clients may perceive it negatively. Figure 3.1 shows some of the characteristics that both helpers and clients bring to interviews. Though this chapter focuses on helper characteristics, part of their significance lies in the ways such characteristics may be perceived by clients. In turn, part of the significance of clients' characteristics rests in how they are perceived by helpers.

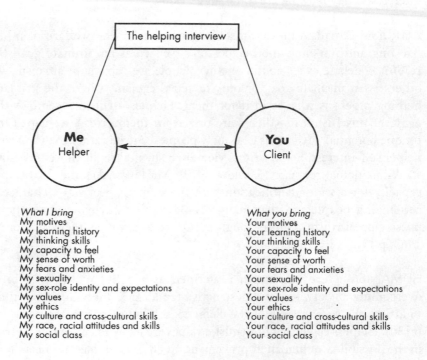

Figure 3.1 *Some characteristics both helpers and clients bring to helping*

The remainder of this chapter encourages you to become more aware of and explore the significance of personal characteristics you bring to helper training and helping.

YOUR MOTIVES

The area of people's motives for helping is both complex and also provides fertile soil for self-deception. Apart from the obvious requirements for professional recognition, many applicants give vague reasons for wanting to join helper training courses. Such reasons include, 'I like helping people' and 'People find me a good person with whom to talk over problems'. Beginning students can hardly be expected to have the diamond-hard commitment of effective and experienced helpers. Nevertheless, some soul searching concerning reasons for entering helping may highlight beneficial motives and unearth harmful motives. The criterion for a beneficial motive is whether its consequences are in the best interests of clients. Needless to say, the categories of beneficial and harmful motives overlap: specific motives may be both beneficial and harmful. Helpers possess profiles of both beneficial and damaging motives. These profiles of motives can change over time and also between individual clients.

Possible beneficial motives

What are some of the rewards and values that motivate helpers to pursue clients' best interests? The following are some suggestions.

ALTRUISM Altruism means unselfish concern for the welfare of others. It entails 'viewing and pursuing another person's welfare as an ultimate goal' (Batson, 1990, p.336). A debate exists about whether people are capable of altruism, where helping others is an ultimate goal, or only of social egoism, where the primary purpose of helping others is what is in it for them. Helper altruism resembles the concept of *agape* or unselfish love. Clients are prized for themselves and helped to unfold their unique potential. Helping is genuinely people-centred rather than a means of pursuing helper self-interest. Some writers view altruism as a fragile flower (Batson, 1990) and a weak instinctual remnant (Maslow, 1970). Maslow makes the further points that the capacity for a wide identification with the human species is a characteristic of self-actualizing people and that many people repress altruistic instincts. Even helpers possessing altruism require 'tough minds' to accompany their 'tender hearts' (King, 1963, p.13).

HUMANISM Here humanism is defined as a belief in the possibility of reason overcoming anxiety, fear and destructive tendencies. Individuals can find the courage to affirm the self 'in spite of the elements of nonbeing threatening it' (Tillich, 1952, p.120). Helpers espousing humanistic values are likely to gain strength from their belief in the possibility of human improvement. Such a belief does not mean ignoring human fallibility and destructiveness. Instead humanism allows helpers to commit themselves to the struggle to make themselves and others better people for the sake of a better world. Many helpers find that religious faith provides strength to strive for personal improvement and others' welfare.

PEOPLE ORIENTATION Holland's theory of personality types asserts that the special heredity and experiences of people lead to the characteristics of six main personality types: realistic, investigative, artistic, social, enterprising and conventional (Holland, 1973). The social personality type in particular is found in the helping professions. Illustrative characteristics of this type are: responsible, helpful, friendly, idealistic, feminine, insightful and kind. People may be attracted to helping by a good matching between the demands of the role and their personality type. Holland acknowledges that a simple six-category scheme of personality types is unrealistic and talks in terms of profiles of personality types. Nevertheless, the social personality type is still likely to predominate in helpers' profiles.

INTELLECTUAL CURIOSITY Effective helpers tend to have a great interest in 'what makes people tick'. They enjoy the challenge of making and testing hypotheses about human behaviour. They are in a constant process of revising their models of the person and of helping practice. They are creative people who continue learning. As such, they acknowledge mistakes. Effective helpers experience excitement in developing their knowledge and competence. Yalom observes that ideological schools of therapy tend to assuage the therapist's rather than the patients' anxiety. He states that: 'The creative members of an orthodoxy, any orthodoxy, ultimately outgrow their disciplines' (Yalom, 1989, p.36).

WORKED-THROUGH EMOTIONAL PAIN Many people enter helping having experienced significant emotional pain. This pain may be associated with relationships in their families of origin or regarding any one or more of a number of specific circumstances: divorce, sexual abuse, racial discrimination or physical disability, to mention some. Emotional pain can be for good or ill. Helpers who have worked through their pain and attained some distance from it may have extra sensitivity to the needs of others. In addition, they may have acquired some useful helping skills and insights from being in the client role.

COMMITMENT TO COMPETENCE Effective helpers like to do things well and are prepared to work at it. They take pride in their work and resist taking short cuts that are not in clients' best interests. Egan observes: 'Competence in helping is not a goal to be achieved: it is a lifelong pursuit' (1990, p.63). Both helper trainees and trained helpers differ in the extent to which they are prepared to work at *being* as contrasted with *seeming* competent. Helper competence has many dimensions: honestly evaluating your helping processes and outcomes; keeping abreast of the literature; being prepared to work on professional and personal problems; and, where necessary, obtaining and learning from supervision. Professional integrity is another term for a commitment to competence.

The above are only some potentially beneficial helper motives. You may be able to think of others. Some motives, for instance money and client goodwill, may help or hinder, depending on how pursued.

Possible harmful motives

Harmful motives have the common thread that, in varying degrees, they lead to clients being treated as objects for helpers' gratification rather than respected as unique human beings. Helpers make inadequate distinctions between 'me' and 'you'. Emotional boundaries get blurred to clients' detriment. Though the issues are rarely black and white, potentially harmful motives include the following.

UNRESOLVED EMOTIONAL PAIN Many helpers require counselling themselves before they can be fully effective. Without acknowledging it, some enter helping as a way of working on their own concerns at one remove. Their underlying agenda is seeking help rather than providing it. Their sensitivity toward nurturing others stems from their own need to be nurtured. A possible consequence of unresolved emotional pain is that helpers provide clients with the kinds of help that they rather than their clients need. The attraction of helping for people with problems seem widespread. For instance Yeo observes: 'When the Samaritans of Singapore first started advertising they had an overwhelming response. Soon after the selection and screening process was complete, it was discovered that about half the people who volunteered actually needed help with their problems' (Yeo, 1981, p.24).

DO-GOODING Do-gooding may be contrasted with altruism. With altruism, the ultimate agenda is another's welfare. With do-gooding, the ultimate agenda is my own feelings of satisfaction at what a good guy or gal I am. Do-gooders need others in dependent roles. They may wish to take charge and, by so doing, treat clients as objects and infantilize them. Though not alone in this tendency, do-gooders may over-concern themselves with obtaining clients' approval and appreciation for their good works.

SEEKING INTIMACY Some are attracted to helping because it provides opportunities for psychological closeness they find difficult to obtain otherwise. Afraid to take the risks of authentic living, the limited nature of the helping role attracts. In addition, some see helping as a way of spending time with sexually attractive people, even though they may stop short of meeting them outside helping or having sexual relations with them.

TRUE BELIEVERISM True believers are those who enter helping rigidly committed to causes. True believerism implies lack of openness to conflicting evidence and to the specific needs of individual clients. For example, true believers in the rights of minority groups may view individual clients in terms of larger political agendas, for instance gay rights, rather than as individuals. Once in helping, some become true believers in theoretical positions, for example, hard-line rational-emotive or Gestalt therapy advocates. Then, whether appropriate or not, clients risk getting pigeon-holed in terms of the concepts of the theoretical position.

EXPEDIENCY Some people enter helping out of expedience rather than from genuine commitment. An example might be physical education teachers who are tempted to become school counsellors once their joints start aching. Some are motivated towards helping as an easy way of making a living. Unfortunately, some helper trainers fall into this category too. In addition, some people may be thrust by managers into helping roles because they have underperformed in positions regarded as more sensitive.

As with beneficial motives, the suggestions for possible harmful motives are not exhaustive. You may be able to think of others. What are your motives for entering or being in helping? Which beneficial and harmful motives apply to you? Are you satisfied that your motives for helping will always work for rather than against your clients' best interests?

YOUR HELPING SKILLS LEARNING HISTORY

Because helping skills are broken down in much greater detail elsewhere, this discussion is brief. People entering helper training all have learning histories of observing others trying to help. In addition, you have all learned from the consequences of both your own and others' helping behaviours.

Learning from observing

Throughout your life, you have observed a variety of helping relationships. Without always being aware, you have acquired helping skills strengths and weaknesses from observing others. Your parents or surrogate parents provided you with your primary helping relationships. They were important models of both how to and how not to help. Some of this modelling related to how they acted, their outer game or verbal, voice, body and touch messages. For instance, either or both of them may have used good or poor verbal and nonverbal skills when trying to understand what upset you. In addition, your parents modelled how they thought, their inner game. Either or both of them may have thought that it showed weakness to admit problems and that people should be able to stand on their own two feet. Others too have demonstrated various kinds of helping behaviours, including brothers and sisters, grandparents, aunts and uncles, friends, teachers, supervisors, sporting coaches, doctors, church ministers and community leaders. Some of you may have learned as counselling clients from how your helpers behaved. Also, once you enter helper training, the modelling provided by your trainers can be powerful. What do you think has been the influence of others' modelling on the skills strengths and weaknesses that you bring to helping?

Learning from consequences

You learn from the consequences both of others' and of your own helping behaviours. At different stages in life you have been the recipient of others' attempts to help you. You may be able to recall specific examples of people providing helpful or harmful responses to your help-seeking behaviours. For instance, when Luke, aged 18, mentioned to his uncle his feelings of depression he was told not to be such a wimp. Jane, aged 14, was more fortunate. When she told her school counsellor how upset she was by her parents splitting up, she met with a warm, interested and accepting response. You may also be aware of others' responses to your help-offering behaviours. Which of your helping behaviours do you think have been useful or harmful, and how do you know?

YOUR THINKING SKILLS

Already I have emphasized the importance of the inner game of helping. As a helper you do not just help others, you also think about how to help and always think when you help. However, you may remain unaware of some of your underlying assumptions and thinking skills strengths and weaknesses. Though not covered here, helpers also use thinking skills in their outside lives in ways that later have an impact on their helping effectiveness.

Important thinking skills for helping include the following.

Using coping self-talk

People bring their styles of self-talk into helping. Beginning helpers are especially inclined to make anxiety-engendering and task-irrelevant self-statements (Kendall & Hollon, 1989; Meichenbaum, 1977; Meichenbaum & Deffenbacher, 1988). They may make remarks to themselves like: 'I can't cope', 'I'm inadequate', 'What's going to happen next?', and 'The client knows I'm no good'. Helpers need to develop the skills of coping self-talk. This consists of the ability to make calming and coaching self-statements (Nelson-Jones, 1989). Examples of calming self-statements are: 'Relax', 'Calm down', 'Take it easy' and 'Breath slowly and regularly'. Examples of coaching self-statements are: 'I must make sure I arrive on time so I do not feel rushed at the start of a session', 'I need to concentrate on what the client is trying to tell me', and 'I need to speak at a moderate rate and be clearly audible'. Often calming and coaching self-statements can be joined: for example 'Calm down. I need to concentrate on what the client is trying to tell me.'

Choosing realistic helping rules

Each person has a rulebook of personal rules for living. Your personal rules are the standards and beliefs by which you live (Beck, 1976; Ellis, 1989). You bring to helping a chapter in your rulebook entitled 'My rules for helping'. These rules can either blight your helping through their rigidity and irrationality or provide you with realistic and flexible guidelines for behaviour. The skill of choosing realistic helping rules includes becoming aware of when your rules may oppress rather than support you and clients. In such instances you need to discard the unrealistic rules altogether or reformulate them into more rational standards. In general, unrealistic helping rules are overgeneralizations that convert partial truths into false whole truths. Below are examples of unrealistic helping rules that may be held both by beginning and by more experienced helpers.

- 'I *must* be the sole source of wisdom and expertise in my helping relationships.'

- 'I *must* be in control of my interviews at all times.'

- 'I *must* never make mistakes.'

- 'I *must* always have my clients' approval.'

- 'I *must* always maintain a professional facade.'

- 'I *must* pressurize clients to self-disclose whether they want to or not.'

- 'I *must* always have an explanation and interpretation for everything.'

- 'My clients *must* always improve.'

- 'I *must* always get quick results.'

In addition, some students possess unrealistic training rules, including the following:

- 'Learning *must* always be easy and effortless.'

- 'Mistakes and setbacks *must* be avoided at all costs.'

- 'I *must* develop effective helping skills immediately or else I will never be any good.'

Attributing responsibility accurately

Beginning helpers bring their attributional styles to helping. Often they experience difficulty in accurately attributing responsibility. If anything, beginning helpers attribute to themselves too much rather than too little responsibility. Some helpers have difficulty in accepting clients' responsibility for their own lives. At best helpers can only influence clients. Ways in which helpers take too much responsibility for helping processes and outcomes include: asking too many questions and allowing clients insufficient space to tell their stories; making premature suggestions rather than collaborating with clients to formulate working definitions of problems that have meaning for them; insufficiently helping clients to develop self-helping skills; and engaging in excessive self-blame when progress is slow. Conversely, both beginning and experienced helpers sometimes attribute too little responsibility to themselves. They attribute difficulties they experience with clients to 'resistances', and fail to acknowledge the contribution of their own poor helping skills.

Perceiving yourself and clients accurately

Two people in a helping relationship do not just relate to each other. Instead, they relate to their perceptions of themselves, each other and the relationship. These perceptions may be of varying degrees of accuracy. In Chapter 2 I mentioned that in helping relationships each person develops a *personification* of themselves and of the other person (Sullivan, 1953). These personifications – literally, making up or constructing a person – are mental maps of self and others.

You bring to helper training and helping your skills of perceiving yourself and your clients accurately. Central to this is the ability to distinguish fact from inference. Your perceptions are your subjective facts; they are not necessarily objective acts. They may contain many inferences of varying degrees of realism in terms of the available facts. Furthermore, you bring to helping the extent of and nature of your defensive processes (Clark, 1991). Defensive processes are *security operations* (Sullivan, 1953) by means of which you may deny and distort information contradicting your self-picture.

Other thinking skills are important for your helping effectiveness. Fundamental is the skill of assuming responsibility for acquiring, maintaining and developing your helping skills. Related to this you need a conceptual framework that allows you to think of helping in skills terms and identifies which skills are important. The challenge to work on your helping skills requires specifying them. Other important thinking skills include assessing clients' problems and redefining them in skills terms; setting clear and realistic goals; predicting consequences; using visualizing; making plans; assisting clients' decision making and making realistic decisions yourself.

YOUR CAPACITY TO FEEL

You bring to helping your capacity to experience your feelings. Dictionary definitions of feelings tend to use words like 'physical sensation', 'emotions' and 'awareness'. All three words illustrate dimensions of feelings. Feelings as *physical sensations* represent your underlying animal nature. The word *emotions* implies movement. Feelings are processes. You are subject to a continual flow of biological experiencing. *Awareness* implies you can be conscious of your feelings. However, you may also deny and distort some of them, and you may have learned some unexamined personal rules with their related feelings from your parents and others. Thus some of your feelings may be based more on *their* standards than on *your own* valuing process. To the extent that you are out of touch with your feelings you are alienated from the core of your personhood. Rogers, in particular, stressed that a feature of modern life is that all people, in varying degrees, are out of touch with their inner valuing process (Rogers, 1961, 1980).

There are many reasons why it is important for helpers to be responsive to their flow of feelings. These reasons include being genuine, spontaneous, and able to resonate and respond appropriately to clients' feelings. In helping you are continuously required to listen to your own as well as to clients' feelings. Your feelings are a good guide to issues in your relationships with clients that may be similar to issues they experience outside helping. For instance, if you feel bored and distant from clients, they may have the same effect on others. You then have the opportunity to analyse the skills weaknesses creating distance.

YOUR SENSE OF WORTH AND ANXIETIES

To helping you bring your feelings of security and insecurity, your pain and unfinished business, and your fears and anxieties. Vulnerability can be an attractive quality in helping relationships. Acknowledging your vulnerability to yourself can make you more understanding of clients' vulnerabilities. Furthermore, appropriate disclosure of vulnerability to clients may be viewed as a token of caring and that you too are a part of the human race.

Your sense of worth

Confidence and self-esteem are general traits, and also vary across specific situations that people face. Some people find difficulty in acknowledging that they lack confidence; others admit it all too readily. Sometimes, by disclosing underconfidence, they seek to manipulate the environment to look after them. Insecurities and fears, if not confronted and managed, can be the breeding ground for distorted communication. Nobody's upbringing is perfect. In varying degrees you have learned to feel 'Not Okay' as well as

'Okay', even though sometimes these 'Not Okay' feelings are difficult to acknowledge.

Intentionally or unintentionally, when people communicate they send two broad categories of messages. One set is specific, having to do with the ostensible purpose of the communication. The other set of messages may be more general and less intentional. These messages send information to receivers pertaining to their worth as persons as well as revealing how high or low the senders value themselves. Children need the security of positive messages about their unique lovableness. Unfortunately, many parents fail to realize that they often send messages that undermine the tender self-esteem of those they love. Even though their need for understanding may be much greater, the pain of children whose parents often send damaging messages is less likely to be heard than that of children whose parents mostly send positive messages.

In varying degrees, all helpers possess some unresolved pain and unfinished business from their families of origin. Many have overcome significant obstacles to become more confident and effective people. As a helper, related to how confident you feel, you may send to clients either positive and affirming or negative and damaging messages. Effective helpers send many more affirming messages than ineffective helpers. Were you helped to feel confident when you were growing up? How confident a person are you now? How do you think your level of confidence influences the messages you send to clients about their worth?

Your fears and anxieties

Both helper and client anxiety is always present in helping encounters (Sullivan, 1954). Part of it comes from being human, part from starting as strangers, part from clients admitting problems, and part from work undertaken in helping. The words anxiety and fear are interchangeable. Anxiety may be defined as your fears about your capacity to cope adequately with the future. Anxiety may be viewed either as a general *trait* or as a *state* that applies to specific situations. There is a close connection between your sense of worth and feelings of anxiety. Insecurity both manifests and engenders anxiety. People who feel worthwhile are relatively free from debilitating anxieties.

Beginning helpers bring their general level of anxiety to helping as well as their specific fears and anxieties about it. Helper anxiety may be facilitating, debilitating or both (Alpert & Haber, 1960). Excessive levels of debilitating anxiety tend to be associated with unrealistic helping rules. For example, the rule 'I must always have my clients' approval' leads to oversensitivity to cues of rejection.

SPECIFIC FEARS AND ANXIETIES Below is an illustrative list of just a few of the fears and anxieties that people bring to helping. These fears represent subjective rather than objective reality, yet they are often exaggerated and result in unhelpful feelings and actions. Sometimes you may be more afraid of getting what you want than of not getting it. Consequently, I group fears into three categories, fear of failure, success and change.

Fear of failure
   Fear or rejection
   Fear of losing clients

Fear of being incompetent
Fear of being seen through
Fear of silences
Fear of not formulating a satisfactory skills redefinition of a problem
Fear of not knowing what to do next
Fear of clients making no progress
Fear of certain client feelings, for instance anger
Fears about coping with certain kinds of client, for instance clients in crisis
Fears that certain clients may highlight unfulfilled areas in your life
Fear of what your supervisor thinks

Fear of success
Fears about attaining psychological closeness
Fear of not being able to maintain success
Fears about dealing with expressions of gratitude and appreciation

Fear of change
Fear that you may be touched deeply by clients and forced to re-examine how you live
Fear that you may have to change how you help
Fear of practical changes, for example the consequences of building up a caseload

SOME CONSEQUENCES OF HELPER ANXIETY Anxiety can have positive and negative consequences. Helpers able to experience and cope with their own anxieties may be more sensitive to clients' anxieties. A certain degree of anxiety is necessary to tone helpers up and motivate them to give skilled performances. When helpers feel anxious in relation to specific clients or helping events, this anxiety can serve as a signal that issues regarding themselves, their clients or their helping relationships merit exploration.

Many negative consequences flow when helper anxiety becomes debilitating rather than facilitating. Helpers may cease to listen accurately. They may perceive and relate to clients in terms of their own needs and fail to keep adequate psychological boundaries between 'me' and 'you'. The psychoanalysts call this phenomenon countertransference. Helpers may assume too much responsibility both for the content of helping sessions and for their clients' lives. In addition, helpers may use their defensive processes both to distort feedback from clients and to misperceive the extent of client progress. Some specific behaviours that may result from excessive helper anxiety include asking too many questions, offering superficial reassurance, and being too directive in telling clients how to behave.

PERSONAL COUNSELLING How can helping students become more aware of their levels and cues of anxiety and of what might be the consequences for clients? What can students do to overcome debilitating anxieties? Some of the anxiety may dissipate with experience, practice and good supervision. In addition, the lifeskills approach to training includes, where possible, teaching skills in self-referent ways. For instance, a good way to learn how to use thinking skills with clients is to use them with yourself. However, the question remains whether students still require the more intense focus on their skills and anxieties provided by personal counselling. Debilitating anxieties affect beginning helpers to varying levels of intensity and in many different ways. Assuming the availability of skilled counsellors, most students probably profit from individual work on their sense of worth, anxieties and lifeskills weaknesses. Lifeskills helping does not assume that a single course of helping is necessarily enough. During their careers, helpers may supplement their self-helping by focused work with other helpers on problematic issues and skills. There is also much to be said for seeking peer support, possibly in support groups.

YOUR SEXUALITY

All helpers are sexual beings, but you have a choice as to how much of your sexuality you bring into helping. Despite the strength of their sexual urges, people differ in the extent to which they experience themselves as sexual beings. While genetic differences undoubtedly exist for libido strength, much of the variation in ability to experience sexuality reflects learned inhibitions and prohibitions. Helpers possess thoughts and feelings about their own and their clients' sexuality. Hopefully your attitude to your sexuality is healthy and loving and, where appropriate, this gets transmitted to clients. However, sexual ignorance and poor thinking skills may interfere with helpers' effectiveness in their personal and 'professional' lives. Furthermore, many helpers experience great difficulty avoiding dual relationships and sexual intimacy with clients (Corey *et al.*, 1988; Egan, 1990; Yalom, 1989). Professional codes for psychologists and counsellors clearly state that such relationships are unethical (American Psychological Association, 1990; Australian Psychological Society, 1986; British Association for Counselling, 1990).

Helpers have differing sexual preferences: the world is not divided into heterosexuals and homosexuals. Pioneering studies on sexual behaviour were conducted in America in the late 1940s and early 1950s by Kinsey and his colleagues (Kinsey *et al.*, 1948; Kinsey *et al.*, 1953). They found that in the large, predominantly white middle-class population that they surveyed, 4 per cent of males and between 1 and 3 per cent of females were exclusively homosexual. However, by the age of 45, half the males and about a quarter of the females had responded homosexually by either arousal or orgasm, at some point during their lives. The Kinsey studies are outdated and based on an unrepresentative sample. Nevertheless, they indicate that many helpers are confronted with choices in their personal lives about how to handle homosexual feelings, whether to engage in homosexual sex, and whether openly to admit to homosexual feelings. Kinsey and his colleagues considered that, if social constraints had not been so strong, there would have been a much higher incidence of homosexual response.

Helpers have attitudes about clients' sexual preferences, whether they are the same or different to their own. Furthermore, they possess varying degrees of knowledge about the psychology and behaviour of people with different sexual preferences. Especially if you plan to work in such areas as marital counselling, sexual dysfunction counselling or counselling gay and bisexual people, you need to review the adequacy of your knowledge and attitudes about sexuality and sexual preference.

YOUR SEX-ROLE IDENTITY AND EXPECTATIONS

The following are stipulated definitions of terms relevant to exploring the sex-role identity and expectations that you bring to helper training and helping.

- *Sex* In this context sex refers to biological differences between males and females: for instance, differences in genitals, reproductive functions, bone structure and size.

- *Gender.* Gender refers to the social and cultural classification of attributes, attitudes and behaviours as 'feminine' or 'masculine.'

- *Sex-role identity.* Your sex-role identity is how you view yourself and behave on the dimensions of 'masculinity' and 'femininity'.

- *Sex-role expectations.* These are your thoughts and feelings about how you and others should think, feel and behave on account of differences in biological sex.

- *Gender awareness.* Gender awareness relates to how aware you are of the processes and consequences of gender scripting on both males and females.

- *Sexism.* Individual sexism relates to any feelings, thoughts and actions that assume the superiority of one sex over the other. Institutional sexism relates to institutional structures that discriminate and devalue a person on the grounds of sex.

Masculinity, femininity and androgyny

In Western societies, certain psychological characteristics have traditionally been viewed as either 'feminine' or 'masculine.' Feminine characteristics have included being affectionate, gentle, sensitive to the needs of others, tender and warm. Masculine characteristics have included being aggressive, ambitious, assertive, analytical and dominant (Bem, 1974). Sex roles based on gender learning influence social behaviour. Argyle (1984) states that the research evidence suggests that there are a number of areas where females may be more socially competent than males. These areas include being better at sending and receiving body language; being more rewarding and polite; and disclosing more and forming closer relationships. However, he notes that assertion is an area in which women appear to have more problems than men. Both masculine and feminine gender roles may have costs. The traditional feminine sex role has created problems for many women in such areas as expressing anger, being autonomous and obtaining power and status (DeVoe, 1990). The traditional masculine role has created problems for many men through over-concern with success, power and competition, emotional restriction, and restricted affectionate behaviour between men (Good *et al.*, 1989).

Underlying the 'femininity–masculinity' discussion is the issue of nature versus nurture. The consensus among social scientists increasingly seems to be that humans have weak instinctual remnants toward either a male or female sex-role identity and that such biological predispositions may easily be overwhelmed by the strength of their learning experiences (Oakley, 1972). Related to the importance of nurture over nature has been the growing popularity of the concept of psychological androgyny. The androgynous male or female 'is flexibly masculine or feminine as circumstances warrant' (Bem, 1981, p.362). Thus, females and males can be brought up to express a range of characteristics independently of whether they have traditionally been viewed as 'masculine' or 'feminine'. Possibly in time masculinity and femininity may become outmoded concepts.

The ways in which you learned your current sex-role identity are many and varied. Your gender scripting started at the cradle with pink for a girl and blue for a boy. You may have observed your parents undertaking different household tasks: for instance, mending clothes and looking after the car. Probably your parents and significant others gave you different toys according to your sex and rewarded different behaviours and characteristics. The books you read showed boys and girls in different roles as did the films and television programmes you watched. When you went to school, you may have been treated differently according to your sex. Furthermore, the subjects you were encouraged to study and the occupations thought appropriate for you also varied by sex. Though not all ways of scripting apply to everyone, nobody can grow up in Western society without a considerable amount of gender brainwashing. Your current sex-role identity is the internalized sum of this brainwashing plus any modifications from countervailing experiences and from thinking for yourself.

Your sex-role expectations

Based on your gender socialization and sex-role identity, you bring sex-role expectations to helping. Your sex-role identity also influences behaviour. For example, a consistent research finding is that female therapists are more oriented towards their clients' affect than are male therapists (Mintz & O'Neil, 1990). Female therapists experience and express more feelings in interactions with clients than do male therapists (Maracek & Johnson, 1980). Sex-role identity and its associated behaviours can also provide a way of categorizing helpers, for example non-sexist/humanist, liberal feminist, or radical feminist (Enns & Hackett, 1990). Good and his colleagues have proposed gender-aware therapy. They state 'Counsellors must not only be nonsexist in their work with clients, but they must also understand clients' difficulties within a gender perspective' (Good et al., 1990, p. 377).

Sex-role expectations can permeate helping in a number of ways. You may assess clients differently according to whether or not they fit into traditional sex roles (Robertson & Fitzgerald, 1990). You may bring to helping inflexible and sexist assumptions about appropriate behaviour in dating, marital and partner relationships, and parenting. Your attitudes to sexual harassment, rape and domestic psychological and physical violence may be sexist. You may also possess unexamined sexist assumptions about the place of males and females in the home or workforce and about jobs and careers appropriate for each sex. In addition, you may engage in simplistic overgeneralizations about the characteristics of males and females and insufficiently acknowledge within-group differences. Some students bring to helping such strong feelings about sex-role and gender issues that these interfere with their ability to formulate accurate working definitions of clients' problems.

YOUR VALUES

The earlier section on motives explored some values underlying your decision to be a helper. However, you bring many other values too. Your values influence how you work with clients, and in helping you may be subject to value conflicts both within your own values and between your clients' values.

Perhaps the most prominent American measure of values is the Rokeach Value Survey (Rokeach, 1967). Rokeach was influenced by Kluckhohn's definition of values as 'conceptions of the desirable means and ends of action' (1951, p. 395). The Rokeach Value Survey makes a distinction between terminal values, or the ultimate end-goals of existence, and instrumental values, or the behavioural means of achieving such end goals. Between 1968 and 1981 there was a high degree of stability in Amercan terminal values (Rokeach & Ball-Rokeach, 1989). In 1981 the six most highly ranked terminal values were a world at peace, family security, freedom, happiness, self-esteem and wisdom. Rokeach last surveyed instrumental values in 1971, with the six most highly ranked values then being honesty, ambition, responsibility, forgiveness, broadmindedness and courage (Rokeach & Ball-Rokeach, 1989).

The Rokeach Value Survey data relate to national values. However, you bring your individual values to helping. For instance, you may place a low value on materialism, yet be working with a highly materialistic client. Helpers need to be aware of significant values they bring to helping; then they can be in a position to choose how to handle them: for instance by consciously trying not to influence clients' values or by disclosing your values. One way of viewing your values is, like Rokeach, to place them in a hierarchy rank-ordered by importance. Another way is to view yourself as possessing a profile of values. This profile is composed of your values and the weight you attach to them. Below are some values that people consider, consciously or otherwise, when forming a philosophy of life (Allport *et al.*, 1960; Holland, 1973; Maslow, 1970).

- *Survival:* the primary instinctual value, though other values sometimes override it, for example patriotism or religious belief;

- *Love:* loving and being loved; appreciating others for what they are and not just for what they do;

- *Friendship:* being joined to others outside your family by mutual intimacy and interests;

- *Family life:* having and being part of a family; valuing parenthood;

- *Religion:* acknowledging the need for connectedness to some ultimate and superhuman power;

- *Materialism:* valuing the accumulation and control of money;

- *Aesthetics:* appreciating beauty and good taste, with special reference to arts such as music, literature and painting;

- *Intellect:* valuing analytical and rational pursuits;

- *Social consciousness:* helping others, showing social concern;

- *Hedonism:* valuing fun, pleasure, and having a good time;

- *Career:* valuing having a career and the work entailed;

- *Practical orientation:* valuing practical pursuits and, where practical matters are concerned, self-reliance;

- *Nature:* appreciating and valuing being outdoors and in communion with nature;

- *Autonomy:* valuing independence, thinking for yourself, and personal enterprise;

- *Convention:* appreciating tradition, valuing obedience and conformity to the status quo;

- *Self-actualization:* being committed to personal growth and development.

Value conflicts

Helpers bring their value conflicts to helping. For instance, a helper may feel conflicted about wanting to help others and at the same time charging fees. Helpers experience many value conflicts similar to those of clients: for instance between home and career and between religious teachings and liberal-pragmatic values, for example regarding abortion.

The values you bring to helping may put you in conflict with clients. Sexual behaviour constitutes a potential area of value conflict (Corey *et al.*, 1988). What are your attitudes to pre-marital sex; extra-marital sex; casual sex; group sex; teenage sex; and homosexuality? For Catholic helpers, issues of contraception, abortion, divorce and intentional single parenting create value conflicts. Value conflicts are not restricted to personal counselling. For instance, in academic counselling, how might you feel about clients consciously choosing not to try hard when their parents make sacrifices to keep them in college? In vocational counselling, how might you feel about clients drawing unemployment benefit for as long as possible?

You may bring to helping a style of handling value conflicts. For instance, some helpers may want to 'push' their values irrespective of their clients' wishes. Other helpers may consider that the way to handle severe value conflicts is to refer clients to helpers with more similar values. Yet another option is to keep quiet about your values. A further option is to declare your values as your own and, possibly, use this as a springboard for helping clients to clarify their values.

Questioning your values

There are many questions you may ask about your values. When I interview applicants for helper training, many experience difficulty answering the question, 'What are your core values?' How might you answer that question? Would you find it helpful to formulate either a hierarchy or a profile of your values, or both? Other questions that you might ask yourself are: 'How did I acquire my values and to what degree do they represent my inner valuing process rather than being "hand-me-downs" of others' values?'; 'What are my key areas of value conflict?'; 'In what areas, if any, do I anticipate I might have significant value conflicts with clients?'; and 'To what degree are my values open to modification, and how might they influence my work with clients?'

YOUR ETHICS

Your ethics and values are interrelated. Numerous ethical issues are connected with helping. Such issues include confidentiality, putting undue pressure on clients, false advertising, financial exploitation and sexual relationships. Here the emphasis is not on dealing with such important issues of helper practice. Rather I focus on the ethical orientation you bring to helper training in two overlapping areas: learning helping skills and personal integrity.

Learning helping skills

Ethical issues abound in learning helping skills. Though not an either–or matter, students differ in the extent to which they approach helper training with high ethical standards. Probably most students would say that their approach to learning helping skills was highly ethical. Unfortunately students have varying degrees of commitment to competence as well as varying abilities to explore the adequacy of their learning behaviours. Below are a few examples of less than ethical student behaviour.

> As part of the contract in a counselling skills course, Ken is required to confirm that he has done 30 hours of independent interview practice. Ken does only 10 hours, but confirms that he has done 30 hours.

> Janet is required to read up on different approaches to working with depressed clients, prior to having such clients referred to her. Janet fails to do most of her reading homework.

Julie has been told by her supervisor that she intrudes too much by 'pushing' her own values on to her clients. Julie thinks that she knows better than her supervisor and just becomes more subtle as to how she goes about altering her clients' values.

In a practical helping skills course, there is a clear requirement that students attend all sessions. Paul misses a number of sessions and each time makes excuses claiming pressure of other business.

Just as a commitment to competence is the hallmark of an ethical helping practitioner, so a genuine commitment to becoming competent is essential for helping students. Issues of professional ethics start with practitioner training. Though obtaining helping degrees and certificates is important, acquiring the knowledge and skills that go with the qualifications is even more important. To what extent are you open to learning and working on your helping skills? How committed to helping competence are you?

Personal integrity

Allied to working on helping skills is the area of working on potentially damaging aspects of yourself that you bring to helping. Helping students vary in the degree to which they acknowledge that their own fears, insecurities, anxieties and lifeskills weaknesses interfere with effectiveness. They also vary in the extent to which they realistically acknowledge their strengths and assets. An ethical commitment to helping entails not just working on your outer game or action skills, but also having the courage to confront your inner game or thinking skills weaknesses. As mentioned earlier, methods of confronting personal deficiencies range from learning helping skills in self-referent ways, self-helping, good supervision and personal counselling. An ethical commitment to helping entails dealing with specific tendencies you have towards non-ethical helping behaviour: be it breaking confidentiality for the sake of telling a good story or taking a purient interest in clients' sexual lives. Awareness of areas of fallibility is the first step in preventing ethical lapses.

YOUR CULTURE AND CROSS-CULTURAL SKILLS

You bring your cultural rules and assumptions to helping. Culture pervades every aspect of living: values, ethics, language, food, table manners, music, religion, attitudes towards politics, sporting activities, family structures and relations, social relations, and body language, to mention only some aspects. Examples of cultural differences abound. Ho (1985) observes that important Western values include emphasis on youth, assertiveness, independence and competition, whereas the corresponding Eastern values are emphasis on maturity, compliance, interdependence and cooperation. Argyle studied common rules in twenty-two social relationships in four different cultures: Britain, Hong Kong, Japan and Italy. He found: 'In Japan virtually all highly endorsed rules were conflict-regulating ones. In contrast, Italy endorsed intimacy-reward rules more, especially compared to Japan' (1986, p.313). Cultures differed on both verbal and nonverbal dimensions. Addressing the other person by first name was highly endorsed in only three Japanese relationships, a much lower figure than in the other three cultures. Looking the other person in the eye during conversation was highly endorsed in virtually all British and Italian relationships, but in under half of Japanese and Hong Kong relationships. Yet another example is that eye contact by young people is a sign of disrespect among some Native American groups (Ivey, 1988).

Your cultural and ancestral roots

What are your cultural and ancestral roots? Are you English, Irish, Scottish or Welsh, or some mixture of these? Alternatively, you may come from one of the many ethnic minority groups. During the 1987–89 period, the total ethnic minority population of Great Britain formed 2.57 million or 4.7 per cent of the overall population (Office of Population Censuses and Surveys, 1991a). Of this ethnic minority total Indians comprised 30 per cent; West Indians, 19 per cent; Pakistanis, 17 per cent; mixed, 11 per cent; Chinese, 5 per cent; Africans, 5 per cent; Bangladeshis, 4 per cent; Arabs, 3 per cent; and others, 6 per cent.

Your cross-cultural awareness, sensitivity and skills

You bring your degree of cultural awareness to helping. Helpers differ to the extent to which they are aware that how they think, feel and behave has been conditioned by their cultural upbringing. You may possess cultural tunnel vision without knowing it. Some helpers gain knowledge of other cultures by having relatives, friends and acquaintances from them. Overseas travel may also have heightened your awareness of cultural differences and increased your sensitivity to immigrants who experience culture shock and disorientation.

You also bring your cultural assumptions to helping. A useful distinction is that between culture-deficit and culture-sensitive assumptions. The culture-deficit helping model assumes that the rules and values of the dominant or mainstream culture are normal. Variations observed in minorities are deficits (Rogoff & Morelli, 1989). The culture-deficit helping model incorporates oppression even by those 'trying to help' minorities. For example, patronizing attitudes and 'missionary zeal' are two kinds of majority group helper insensitivity experienced by many American Indians (LaFromboise et al., 1990). The culture-sensitive helping model avoids the assumption that dominant group practices are proper and superior. Respect is shown for cultural differences and positive features of cultural variation may be emphasized. Furthermore, helpers show sensitivity to minority group members' differing levels of and wishes for acculturation (LaFromboise et al., 1990).

You also bring your cross-cultural skills to helping. How good are you at helping people from different cultures share their cultural differences with you? For instance, if you show interest and give people from different cultures permission to talk about the role of culture in their problems you may be perceived as more empathic (Poon et al., 1991) and culturally competent (Pomales et al., 1986) than if you are culture neutral or culture blind. Such culture-sensitive behaviours also help you to get more within the frames of reference of clients culturally dissimilar to you. Ivey has been a prominent advocate of the need for helpers to develop cultural empathy (Ivey, 1987, 1988; Ivey *et al.*, 1987). Cultural empathy consists of various components: knowledge about clients' cultures, yet acknowledgement of individual differences within them; understanding the cultural meaning of verbal, voice and body messages; allowing clients to reveal the cultural context of problems; helping clients work through cross-cultural mistrust; and responding in ways appropiate to clients' cultures, for instance by varying amount of eye contact. Both beginning helping students and experienced helpers vary in their degree of cultural empathy with clients.

YOUR RACE, RACIAL ATTITUDES AND SKILLS

You also bring your race to helping – whether you are white, black, Asian, or of another racial grouping. Axelson observes: 'Race as a subdivision of a species simply implies a degree of inbreeding among the ancestors of the group during their evolution within a specified region of the world. It also implies the ability to adapt to the surrounding physical environment' (1985, p.132). In Britain, approximately 95 per cent of the population is white (Office of Population Censuses and Surveys, 1991a).

Your racial attitudes and skills

You bring your attitudes towards your own and other races to helping. Ideally, all helpers subscribe to the fundamental value of racial equality. However, helpers have racial learning histories in which they may have acquired negative thoughts and feelings about either their own or other races, or both. In Western societies, the main kind of racism is the belief in white genetic superiority over other racial groups. White stereotypes of other races abound, for instance, black sexual prowess and Asian cleverness. Helpers from minority races are especially likely to have been the victim of racism on both individual and institutional levels. Racist assumptions and behaviours by members of the white majority can lead to second-order racism whereby members of oppressed minority groups react with simplistic racial stereotypes of whites. Racial differences are often highlighted by cultural differences. Much behaviour labelled racist stems from cultural and socioeconomic rather than solely from racial differences.

Whether members of racial majority or minority groups, helpers possess different levels of awareness about the impact of race on their own and others' identity and life chances (Christensen, 1989). Furthermore, they possess different levels of racial mistrust and attraction, and different skills in demonstrating racial empathy. In multiracial societies, it is important that you possess race-sensitive as well as culture-sensitive skills: for instance, giving clients permission to comment both on seeing a racially different helper and also on the racial context of their problems.

YOUR SOCIAL CLASS

Income, educational attainment and occupational status are three of the main ways social class is measured in Britain. Other indicators of social class include how you speak, your table manners, how you dress, the area in which you live, and what schools and colleges you attended. The social class in which you were born and raised influences your chances of surviving at birth, your educational and occupational opportunities, whom you are likely to meet and to marry, how much money you are likely to make, how well your health is looked after, and the quality of your funeral. The same holds true for your clients.

Each of you brings your social class to helping. A common stereotype is a middle-class helper who lacks the language, life experience and skills to relate to lower-class clients. You also bring your sensitivity to the effects of others' social class on you and your social class on them. Furthermore, you bring your skills at understanding people from different social classes and of forming helping relationships with them. One skill may be handling resistances and negative messages resulting from others' social class insecurities. Another skill is that of using language appropriate to your client group. If you possess feelings of inferiority or superiority on account of your social class, you should work to eliminate them. Being an effective helper is difficult enough without the intrusion of avoidable social class agendas.

CHAPTER HIGHLIGHTS

- Helping differs from most other occupations in that its main tools are people.

- Your motives for helping can be beneficial or harmful. Beneficial motives include altruism, humanism, people orientation, intellectual curiousity, worked-through emotional pain, and commitment to competence. Harmful motives include unresolved emotional pain, do-gooding, seeking intimacy, true believerism, and expediency.

- You are influenced by your learning helping skills history, including observing others and learning from the consequences of your own and others' attempts to help.

- You bring thinking skills strengths and weaknesses to helping in such areas as coping self-talk, choosing realistic helping rules, attributing responsibility accurately, and perceiving yourself and your clients accurately.

- You bring to helping your capacity to feel, be emotionally responsive and spontaneous.

- Depending on your sense of worth, you may send either negative or positive messages to clients about their worth.

- You may lessen your helping effectiveness through debilitating fears and anxieties. Most helping students can benefit from personal counselling.

- Your sexuality and sexual preference influence how you help.

- Your sex-role identity may be 'feminine', 'masculine' or 'androgynous'.

- Your sex-role expectations may liberate or restrict clients' identity and choices.

- You need to become aware of your values in order to clarify and deal with value issues and conflicts in helping.

- Commitment to competence and personal integrity are ethical issues for helping students.

- You bring your culture, cultural awareness, sensitivity and skills to helping. In multicultural societies, helpers require cultural empathy.

- You bring to helping your race, experiences of racism, attitudes to race and skills at relating to racially different people.

- Your social class may make it hard for you to understand and work with clients whose life experiences are very different to yours. In addition, you may have to cope with your own and your clients' social class insecurities.

PART TWO

Stages and Skills of the Lifeskills Helping Model

STAGE 1

DEVELOP THE RELATIONSHIP, IDENTIFY AND CLARIFY PROBLEM(S)

Chapters 4 and 5 present some skills for stage 1 of the lifeskills helping model. Chapter 4 focuses on using rewarding listening skills to develop the helping relationship. Chapter 5 presents a range of skills for assisting clients in identifying and clarifying their problems.

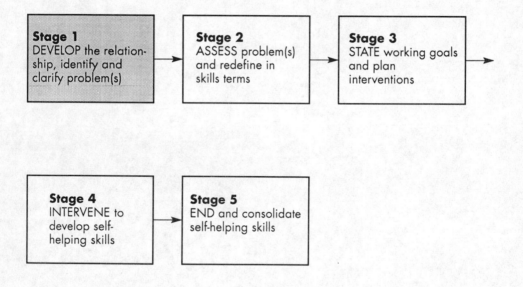

FOUR

How to Develop Helping Relationships

It is as though he [she] listened
and such listening as his [hers] enfolds us in a silence
in which at last we begin to hear
what we are meant to be.

Lao–Tse

CHAPTER QUESTIONS

What is a helping relationship?

What messages do helpers and clients send and receive?

Why are perceptions of messages important?

What is rewarding listening?

Why is rewarding listening important?

What are the component skills of rewarding listening?

Clients come to helping in pain, with problems, with decisions, in crisis and in need of support. They need to relate to or become connected to helpers as a means of working on their concerns. Throughout all five stages, the lifeskills helping model heavily emphasizes the quality of the helper–client relationship. However, unlike in the person-centred approach where the helping relationship is considered both necessary and sufficient for client change to occur (Rogers, 1957), I consider it necessary, but for the most part insufficient.

Though a simplification, there is a useful distinction in helping between a relationship orientation and a task orientation. But relationship and task orientations are not opposite ends of a continuum. Effective helpers focus both on the relationship and also on the task of helping clients develop lifeskills. They go beyond establishing *talking* relationships, where the relationship overshadows the task, to forming supportive *working* relationships, where the relationship facilitates the task. Though overstating the point, an analogy may be made with school teaching, where good teacher–student relationships should not be viewed as a substitute for teaching and learning. In stage 1 of the lifeskills model, helpers use relationship skills to form bonds with clients and to elicit information to clarify problems. Throughout DASIE's five stages, helpers use relationship skills both to support helper–client bonding and to support the tasks of each stage. Helping relationships are tools to support clients as they learn self-support. As such, they contain the seeds of their own destruction.

HELPERS AND CLIENTS AS SENDERS AND RECEIVERS OF MESSAGES

Messages are encoded by senders and decoded by receivers (Argyle, 1983). There are five important ways in which helpers and clients send messages.

- *Verbal messages.* These are messages expressed in words – for example what you say when you respond to clients.

- *Voice messages.* These messages relate to how you talk – for example loudly or softly.

- *Body messages.* Sometimes called body language, these are the messages you send with your face and other parts of your body.

- *Touch messages.* Touch is a special kind of body message involving physical contact with another.

- *Action messages.* Action messages are what you do as contrasted with what you say or how you say it: for example, keeping your appointments and starting on time.

Helpers and clients are not only senders of messages, they are perceivers of how they send messages. For instance, helpers may rightly or wrongly perceive that they send supportive messages to clients. Furthermore, they are perceivers of each other's reactions to their messages; for instance, helpers may consider that clients misunderstand their supportive messages. Since helpers and clients can send messages in so many different ways, genuineness is important. How something is said needs to be congruent with what is said.

Helpers and clients are also receivers of each other's messages and they perceive the messages they receive with varying degrees of accuracy. The focus of this chapter is on how to develop relationships by receiving and showing that you have received your clients' messages accurately. Good listening skills are at the heart of developing effective helping relationships.

Effective listening entails helpers' both receiving and sending messages. On the surface, a client communicates/helper responds unit of interaction may seem simple. However, this is not the case. As depicted in Figure 4.1, at each of the four points of the cycle – client sends, helper receives, helper sends, client receives – communication difficulties, which impede effective helping relationships, can arise.

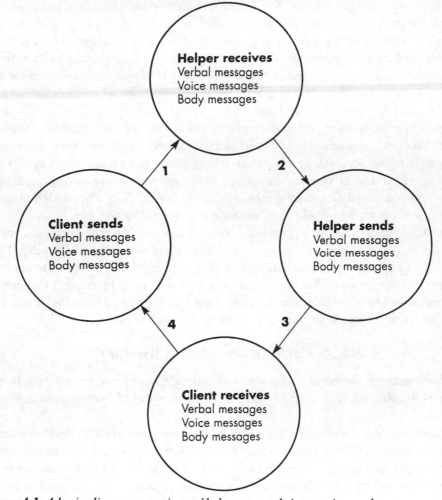

Figure 4.1 *A basic client communicates/helper responds interaction cycle*

REWARDING LISTENING AND DEVELOPING HELPING RELATIONSHIPS
Defining rewarding listening

A distinction may be made between hearing and listening. *Hearing* involves the capacity to be aware of and to receive sound. *Listening* involves not only receiving sounds but, as much as possible, accurately understanding their meaning. As such it entails hearing and memorizing words, being sensitive to vocal cues, observing body language, and taking into account the personal and social context of communications. However, you can listen accurately without being a rewarding listener. *Rewarding listening* entails not only accurately understanding speakers' communications, but being rewarding for them by also showing that you have understood. Rewarding listening involves receiver and sender skills.

You may wonder why rewarding listening is so important when there are so many opportunities for people to be listened to in everday life. Here, it is possible to distinguish between social and helping conversations. *Social* conversations are geared towards meeting the needs of both participants; they have facetiously been described as between 'two people, both of whom are taking turns to exercise their ego.' Often listening, let alone rewarding listening, becomes lost along the way. *Helping* conversations primarily emphasize meeting clients' needs. They place a high premium on rewarding clients by listening and showing understanding to them.

Four kinds of listening take place in any helping relationship. Listening does not just take place between helper and client, it also takes place within each (Gendlin, 1981). Indeed the quality of your *inner* listening, or being appropriately sensitive to your own thoughts and feelings, may be vital to the quality of your *outer* listening. Furthermore, if you listen well to others, this may help the quality of their inner listening; if you listen either poorly or too much to yourself, you listen less well to others.

Importance of rewarding listening

Rewarding listening is probably the central skill in developing and maintaining helping relationships. Rewarding listening by helpers has a number of important consequences.

ESTABLISHING AND MAINTAINING RAPPORT You are more likely to develop effective working relationships with clients if they feel understood by you. For example, a study of helpful and non-helpful events in brief counselling identified eight kinds of events perceived as helpful by clients (Elliott, 1985). These were grouped into two superclusters corresponding to interpersonal and task aspects of counselling. Understanding was the predominant cluster in the interpersonal grouping.

HELPING CLIENTS TO DISCLOSE Clients are often shy and anxious. They may be divulging highly sensitive information. Trust and disclosure may not come easily because previously clients may have received much overt and subtle rejection for disclosing. Helpers usually need to establish their human credentials. Good listening helps clients to feel accepted, safe and understood. This in turn helps clients choose to reveal their inner world to you.

HELPING CLIENTS TO EXPERIENCE AND EXPRESS THEIR FEELINGS Many clients have been inadequately listened to in the past. Consequently, they may have relinquished, temporarily at least, some of their capacity for emotional responsiveness (Rogers, 1959, 1961, 1975). Rewarding listening can help clients acknowledge more the inner flow of their emotions. The message some clients may require is that it is okay to experience and express feelings.

CREATING A KNOWLEDGE BASE A facetious remark about a psychologist colleague was that he had to ask everyone whether they were male or female since he was incapable of gathering information without asking questions. If you listen well, most clients collaborate in providing relevant information about themselves; you do not have to interrogate them. Together you build a working model of their problems and problematic skills patterns. At later stages of helping, clients will also provide you with knowledge about how they use self–helping interventions and about other important life events. Many beginning helpers use questions too much and rewarding listening too little. Some students, however, have the reverse problem.

CREATING AN INFLUENCE BASE The lifeskills helper is a psychological educator actively influencing clients to develop self–helping skills. Rewarding listening is one way you can build your influence base so that clients are more likely to listen to you. It contributes to clients perceiving you as competent, trustworthy and attractive (Strong, 1968, 1978). Showing understanding to clients from different cultural groups contributes to your ascribed status and credibility (Sue & Zane, 1987).

HELPING CLIENTS TO ASSUME RESPONSIBILITY Clients who are listened to sharply and sensitively are more likely to assume responsibility for working on their problems and problematic skills than those who are not. Rewarding listening may reduce defensiveness and provide a base for offering well–timed confrontations that encourage clients to assume rather than to avoid responsibility.

REWARDING LISTENING: A TEN-SKILLS APPROACH

The remainder of this chapter describes ten key skills of rewarding listening. Each of these entails choices on the part of helpers. How well you implement these skills has consequences for both you and your clients. As a practitioner-researcher you need to become aware of your rewarding listening choices and to evaluate their consequences. Many of the following skills overlap.

Skills of Rewarding Listening

Skill 1   Know the difference between me and you.

Skill 2   Possess an attitude of respect and acceptance.

Skill 3   Send good body messages.

Skill 4   Send good voice messages.

Skill 5   Use openers, small rewards and open-ended questions.

Skill 6   Reword.

Skill 7   Reflect feelings.

Skill 8   Reflect feelings and reasons.

Skill 9   Avoid unrewarding 'don'ts'.

Skill 10 Avoid poor thinking skills.

SKILL 1: KNOW THE DIFFERENCE BETWEEN ME AND YOU

Don't judge any person until you have walked two moons in their moccasins.

Native American proverb

If clients are to feel you receive them loud and clear, you need to develop the ability to 'walk in their moccasins', 'get inside their skins' and 'see the world through their eyes'. At the heart of rewarding listening is a basic distinction between 'you' and 'me', between 'your view of you' and 'my view of you', and between 'your view of me' and 'my view of me'. Your view of you and my view of me are both inside or internal viewpoints, whereas your view of me and my view of you are both outside or external viewpoints. The skill of listening to and understanding another person is based on your choosing to acknowledge the separateness between 'me' and 'you' by getting inside the other's internal viewpoint rather than remaining in your own external viewpoint.

If you respond to what clients say in ways that show accurate understanding of their viewpoints, you respond as if inside their internal viewpoints. Such responses do not mean you agree with them, rather that you acknowledge that what they say is their subjective reality. If, however, you choose not to show understanding of your clients' viewpoints or lack the skills to understand them, you respond from your external viewpoint. In short, if you respond to clients as if inside their internal viewpoints, you respond to them from where they are. If you step outside your clients' internal viewpoints, you respond more from where you are, or from where you think they should be.

Here are some helper comments from an external viewpoint:

'What can I do for you?'
'I think you should always respect your parents.'

'Why don't you drop him/her? He/she is not helping you get better.'
'You are going to be all right.'
'I think you have paranoid tendencies.'
'You should consider taking tranquillizers over your exam period.'

Responding as if in your clients' internal viewpoint entails understanding what they say on their terms. Such understanding requires careful listening and allowing clients the psychological space to tell their own stories. Understanding their internal viewpoint entails decoding clients' messages, especially when these are not clearly sent. The following are examples of internal viewpoint comments by helpers:

'You're elated at passing your maths test.'
'You feel that often people don't look beyond your blindness to discover what sort of a person you are.'
'You find getting fired in a recession a terrifying prospect.'
'You have mixed feelings about your parents-in-law.'
'You've found immigration a much bigger adjustment than anticipated.'
'You feel really good that your daughter phoned on your birthday.'

Think of a three-link chain: client statement – helper response – client statement. If helpers respond from clients' internal viewpoints, they allow them either to continue on the same path or to choose to change direction. However, if helpers respond from the external viewpoint, they influence clients to take a diversion from paths they would have chosen on their own. Sometimes such external influence is desirable, but frequently it is not. In all instances helpers need to make conscious choices whether or not to respond as if inside clients' internal viewpoints.

SKILL 2: POSSESS AN ATTITUDE OF RESPECT AND ACCEPTANCE

An accepting attitude means respecting clients as separate and unique human beings with rights to their own thoughts and feelings independent of yours. Carl Rogers, the founder of person-centred therapy, which heavily emphasizes that helpers should be accepting, grew up afraid that if he said anything significant to his mother she would judge it negatively (Heppner *et al.*, 1984b). An accepting attitude entails suspending moral judgement. All humans are fallible and possess lifeskills strengths and weaknesses that may have good or bad consequences for themselves and others.

Barriers to an accepting attitude

As a helper you need to be psychologically present to clients. This entails absence of defensiveness and a willingness to allow clients' expressions and experiencing to affect you. Ideally, you should be 'all there' – with your body, your thoughts, your senses and your emotions. Psychological accessibility entails your possessing an accepting attitude not only to clients, but to yourself. Put simply, a confident person's acceptance of self translates into acceptance of others, and the reverse is also true.

Barriers to an accepting attitude manifest themselves in both how you think and how you act. They manifest themselves internally in that you may operate on, distort and filter out certain parts of clients' messages. At worst you deny or block out the whole of an incoming message. Barriers operate externally in subtle and not so subtle verbal, voice and body cues to clients indicating that they should edit what they say. The following are some barriers likely to influence how you listen.

ANXIETY-EVOKING FEELINGS Clients can express feelings that helpers find hard to handle: for instance feeling very depressed or even very happy. Helpers may feel threatened by feelings directed towards them, for instance hostility or liking. Alternatively, helper anxiety may be evoked by the intensity of clients' feelings about others, for instance, envy of a sibling or grief over a bereavement.

> Tina, 25, a beginning helper, listened to Stan pour out his resentment over his girlfriend Eva's behaviour. Tina was uncomfortable when people became angry in her outside helping life. Even though none of Stan's anger was directed at her, she started feeling very anxious and wondered whether the interview would get out of control.

ANXIETY-EVOKING CLIENTS Helpers may find themselves feeling threatened by certain categories of clients: for example, clients of the opposite sex, seriously disturbed clients, highly successful clients, very intelligent clients, and clients who hold strong feelings with which the helper disagrees.

> Penny, 29, a trainee counsellor, became uncomfortable when faced with Frank, a sexually active homosexual client. Her discomfort stemmed not from prejudice about gays, but because she felt out of her depth in being unable to relate to his life experiences. She was aware that her anxiety about coping made it even harder to empathize with Frank.

ANXIETY-EVOKING SITUATIONS Anxiety and threat are present in all helping situations. The following are some common situations where helpers may feel vulnerable, and so their own agendas may preclude their fully listening to clients:

the first few minutes of an initial session;
concentrating on developing new skills as well as on their clients;
finding difficulty formulating a working definition of a problem;
feeling that progress is too slow;
a client coming late for an appointment;
recording an interview for supervision.

TRIGGER WORDS, PHRASES AND ATTITUDES Trigger words, phrases and attitudes raise a 'red flag' for you. Each helper has his or her own emotionally charged triggers. For example, some helpers are triggered by sexist comments, some by prejudice against gays, some by cross-cultural put-downs, and some by racist comments. Trigger phrases can also be 'You' messages from clients to helpers – for example, 'You screwed up', 'You don't understand', or 'You're not helping me enough.'

> Abe, 31, a Jewish helper, has to work hard to listen to anyone who expresses racist attitudes. Recently Abe had a client, Wayne, who started using the term 'nigger'. Abe became so angry that, for some moments, he lost sight of his client's vulnerability.

> Sarah, a trainee group therapist who had been raped, allowed herself to be triggered by Carlos, an advanced cancer patient who was a new entrant to her group. Carlos belittled the experiences of rape victims and ended by saying he would welcome a rape attempt by any woman in the group. At this last remark, Sarah said, 'If you believe that, you're fucking ignorant!' (Yalom, 1989, p.70)

Positive words and phrases can also trigger feelings that interfere with your listening: for example, flattery like 'Gee, you're wonderful, Ms Murgatroyd.'

BEING PREJUDICED Helpers are not immune to varying degrees of prejudice. For reasons connected with your upbringing, you may tune out to people different to you because of their age, sex, sexual preference, culture, race, social class, physical disability or intelligence level, among other possible differences.

> Dale, 27, dislikes working with elderly clients. He not only tries to avoid seeing them, but also withdraws from forming close helping relationships with them. He rationalizes his behaviour by saying that he is much more used to spending time with younger clients.

CURRENT UNFINISHED BUSINESS Unfinished business can interfere with your being open to clients. For instance, if you have just come from a heated staff meeting, you may be less ready to listen and accept your next client. If you have just rushed to get to a session, you may not listen adequately until you have calmed down. You may think about something said in an earlier helping session and fail to attend to the present. In addition, you may have intrusive personal worries that you bring to helping.

PRESENTING A PROFESSIONAL FACADE Genuineness is an important characteristic for helpers (Rogers, 1957, 1975). A difference exists between being genuine and seeming genuine. Some helpers are too concerned with maintaining a smooth professional facade. Their concern with how clients perceive them may interfere with perceiving their clients accurately. Such helpers are too busy listening to their own needs to accept clients fully. Maintaining a professional facade is especially difficult when clients directly challenge your professional adequacy.

> Danny, 26, a counselling psychology student on placement at his university's student counselling service, worries that clients will see that he is not yet fully competent. He puts on an act, being too friendly and trying to appear too expert. He takes control rather than forming collaborative working alliances with clients.

EMOTIONAL EXHAUSTION AND BURNOUT Helpers often possess a combination of difficult environments, demanding clients, and poor skills at setting limits on their involvement. Freudenberger defines burnout: 'To deplete oneself. To exhaust one's physical and mental resources. To wear oneself out by excessively striving to reach some unrealistic expectation imposed by one's self or by the values of society' (1980, p.17). Emotionally exhausted helpers may be less accepting of clients than when they feel well. Their energy level and sense of personal accomplishment is low. Helping relationships, instead of being positive challenges, can become endurance tests.

> Patricia, 43, is a social worker with a heavy caseload. She is highly conscientious and worries a lot about what happens to her clients. Recently she has been feeling depressed, irritable and very tired. Patricia has to drag herself to work and feels anxious much of the time. She is not doing her best work.

INSUFFICIENT ADMINISTRATIVE SUPPORT Helpers in institutions may spend much time securing budgets, ensuring their role is understood, and dealing with other administrative matters. Frequently, they lack adequate secretarial support. Insufficient administrative support can undermine morale, increase caseloads, and involve helpers in routine secretarial and administrative chores. A casualty can be how accepting helpers are of clients.

PHYSICAL BARRIERS Physical barriers may contribute to your being less accepting of clients than desirable. For example, you may be too hot or too cold, you may lack privacy, your room may be dreary, your chair may be uncomfortable, the lighting may be poor, or there may be too much noise.

> Helen is a counselling trainee who is required to interview secondary school 'clients' assigned to her. There is a shortage of suitable interview rooms. On

some occasions the only room available is one that
has glass windows facing the corridor. Though the
room is quiet, Helen feels distracted by the lack of
privacy for herself and her clients.

So far we have discussed ten barriers and filters to your adopting an attitude of respect
and acceptance for your clients. Some of the barriers are created solely by you. Some
originate in the environment. In both cases, helpers can choose how to react. The list is
far from exhaustive. You may think of other barriers and filters applicable to you.

SKILL 3: SEND GOOD BODY MESSAGES

Helpers always send messages to clients. Your body messages as a listener are important
both when clients and you speak. Here the emphasis is on the former. To be a rewarding
person with whom to talk you need physically to convey your receptiveness and interest.
Often this is referred to as attending behaviour (Ivey, 1988; Ivey *et al.*, 1987). Body
messages are the main helper responses *during* clients' verbal utterances. A simple
example may highlight the point. Imagine a helper looking out of the window at the
start of a session when the client describes a sensitive personal problem. Congruence,
both within your body messages and between your verbal, voice and body messages,
increases the chances of your being perceived as a rewarding listener.

The following are some of the main body messages that demonstrate interest and
attention. In varying degrees they provide non-verbal rewards for talking.

AVAILABILITY It may seem obvious, but helpers may sometimes rightly or wrongly be
perceived as insufficiently available to help. You may be overworked. You may be poor
at letting your availability be known. Intentionally or unintentionally you may send
messages that create distance. For instance, teachers may physically edge away from
pupils wishing to discuss personal concerns. You need to be clear about messages you
convey to clients and others about availability and access.

RELAXED BODY POSTURE A relaxed body posture, without slumping or slouching,
contributes to the message that you are receptive. If you sit in a tense and uptight
fashion, your clients may consciously or intuitively feel that you are too bound up in
your personal agendas and unfinished business to be fully accessible to them.

PHYSICAL OPENNESS Physical openness means facing speakers with both your face and
body. Trainers such as Carkhuff and Egan recommend sitting square to clients – your
left shoulder opposite their right shoulder (Carkuff, 1983; Egan, 1990). Another option
is to sit at a slight angle to clients. Here, both of you can still receive all of each other's
significant facial and bodily messages. The advantage of this is that it provides each of
you with more discretion in varying the directness of your contact than when sitting
opposite each other. Highly vulnerable clients may especially appreciate this seating
arrangement.

SLIGHT FORWARD LEAN Whether you lean forwards, backwards or sideways is another aspect of your body posture. If you lean too far forward you look odd and clients may feel that you invade their personal space. If you lean too far back, clients may find this distancing. Especially at the start of helping, a slight forward lean can encourage clients, without threatening them.

GOOD USE OF GAZE AND EYE CONTACT *Gaze*, or looking at people in the area of their faces, is a way both to show interest and to receive facial messages. Women are usually more attentive than men on all measures of gaze (Henley, 1977; Argyle, 1983). Gaze can give you cues about when to stop listening and start responding. However, the main cues used in synchronizing conversation are verbal and voice messages rather than body messages (Argyle, 1983). *Eye contact* means meeting your clients' eyes. Good eye contact entails arriving at a comfortable level of contact for each client. Staring threatens clients: they may feel dominated or seen through. Some clients even feel threatened by seeing their reflections in shop windows! Clients may perceive you as tense or bored if you look down or away too often.

APPROPRIATE FACIAL EXPRESSIONS Your face is perhaps your main vehicle for sending body messages. Ekman, Friesen and Ellsworth identified seven main expressions of emotion: happiness, interest, surprise, fear, sadness, anger, and disgust or contempt (Ekman *et al.*, 1972). Much facial information is conveyed through the mouth and eyebrows. A friendly, relaxed facial expression, including a smile, usually demonstrates interest. However, during clients' communications, you need to vary your face to show that you understand their emotions: for example, looking concerned at bad news.

APPROPRIATE GESTURES Perhaps the most common gesture in helping is the nod. Each nod can be viewed as a reward to clients, signifying interest. On the negative side, selective nodding can also control clients. Unconditional acceptance becomes conditional. Arm and hand gestures can also be used to demonstrate responsiveness. However, helpers using expressive arm gestures too much or too little can be off-putting. Other negative gestures include tightly crossing your arms and legs as barriers, clenching your hands together, drumming fingers, fiddling with your hair or glasses, keeping your hand over your mouth, tugging an ear, and scratching yourself.

SENSITIVITY TO PHYSICAL PROXIMITY AND HEIGHT Rewarding listening entails respecting clients' personal space. Helpers can be too close or too far away. Perhaps a comfortable physical distance for helpers and clients is sitting with their heads about five feet apart. In Western cultures clients might perceive any less distance as too personal (Hall, 1966; Pease, 1981). On the other hand, if helpers are physically too far away not only do clients have to talk louder, but they may perceive you as emotionally distant. The most comfortable height for helping conversations is with heads at the same level. This fact is forgotten by some helpers who sit in higher and more elaborate chairs than clients.

APPROPRIATE USE OF TOUCH Use of touch may be appropriate in helping, though care needs to be taken that it is not an unwanted invasion of personal space (Bacorn & Dixon, 1984). For example, demonstration of concern may include touching a client's hands, arms, shoulders and upper back. The intensity and duration of touch should be sufficient to establish contact yet avoid discomfort or any hint of sexual interest. Touch is an area in which helpers need to proceed with great caution.

CLOTHING AND GROOMING Helpers' clothes send messages which may influence how much and in which areas clients reveal themselves. These messages include social and occupational standing, sex-role identity, ethnicity, conformity to peer group norms, rebelliousness and how outgoing you are. While maintaining your individuality, you need to dress appropriately for your clienteles: for example, delinquent teenagers probably respond better to informally dressed helpers than do stressed business executives. Your personal grooming also provides important information about how well you take care of yourself; for instance, you may be clean or dirty, neat or tidy. In addition, the length and styling of your hair send messages about you.

The concept of rules is very important for understanding the appropriateness of body messages (Argyle & Henderson, 1985: Argyle, 1986). Mention has been of differing physical proximity rules depending on whether you are in a personal or helping relationship. Relationship rules also differ across cultures. For instance, Arabs and Latin Americans stand very close, by Western standards. You require sensitivity to the body message rules of the social and cultural contexts in which you work as well as to your own and to clients' individual needs.

Helpers require flexibility in making rewarding listening choices. As your helping relationship develops, clients get to know whether and when you are receptive to them. For instance, clients may know from past experience that when you lean back you still attend. Sometimes it is better to withdraw sending message cues of interest and attention. Occasions where such withdrawal may be desirable include needing to check out your understanding of clients' messages, keeping clients focused on agendas relevant to their problems, and when you think it is important that clients receive input from you.

SKILL 4: SEND GOOD VOICE MESSAGES

Your voice messages can greatly enhance the emotional atmosphere when you listen. When supervising beginning counselling students, I pay great attention to how they use their voice to frame verbal responses to clients. The two most common faults are speaking too quickly and too softly; both indicate anxiety. Your voice can speak volumes about what you truly feel and how emotionally responsive you are to clients' feelings. Helpers may use voice messages little during clients' verbal utterances, perhaps restricting them to 'uh-hmms'. However, voice messages always accompany verbal responses. As such, they are an integral part of rewarding listening.

The following are five dimensions of voice messages. They form the acronym VAPER – volume, articulation, pitch, emphasis and rate.

VOLUME Volume refers to loudness or quietness. You need to respond at a level of audibility that is comfortable and easy to hear. Some helpers have the bad habit of fading, letting their voices trail away at the end of sentences. Sometimes helpers unnecessarily quieten their voices to match those of clients. While a booming voice overwhelms, speaking in too quiet a voice may make you appear weak.

ARTICULATION Articulation refers to the distinctness and clarity of speech. Helpers may speak with adequate loudness, but still be difficult to understand. You must enunciate words clearly. Helpers possessing excessively nasal, guttural or throaty voices might consider speech therapy. Some helpers need to modify strong regional or overseas accents.

PITCH Pitch refers to the highness or lowness of voice. An optimum pitch range includes all the levels at which a pleasing voice can be produced without strain (Kruger, 1970). Errors of pitch include being either too high-pitched or too low-pitched. Helpers' voices may be higher pitched when anxious than when calmer.

EMPHASIS It is important that your voice is expressive in picking up the major feelings and feeling nuances of speakers. Helpers may use emphasis in the wrong places. Additionally, you may use too much emphasis, and seem melodramatic, or too little emphasis, and seem wooden.

RATE Often measured in words per minute, speech rate depends both on how quickly words are spoken and also on the frequency and duration of pauses between them. A rapid helper speech rate may contribute to keeping clients anxious rather than calming them down. Often it is a good idea for beginning helping students to speak more slowly. This helps them appear less nervous and also provides more time to think of what to say.

Your use of pauses and silences can also enhance your capacity to be a rewarding listener. If you want to make it easier for clients to tell their stories, you can pause each time they cease speaking before responding, to see if they wish to continue. Good use of silences can also allow speakers more psychological space to think things through before speaking and to get more in touch with feelings. Some helping students find silences threatening: they have to work on tendencies to speak too soon.

SKILL 5: USE OPENERS, SMALL REWARDS AND OPEN-ENDED QUESTIONS

Openers, small rewards and open-ended questions tend to require using a few words as well as sending voice and body messages. They make it easier for clients to talk.

Openers

Lifeskills helping always starts with checking 'where the client is at'. Helpers are not all-knowing. Openers, or permissions to talk, are brief statements indicating that helpers are prepared to listen. Often helpers start initial sessions with a brief opener that encourages clients to share and explain why they have come. Helpers may leave until later in the session a fuller statement of how they work. Openers are 'door openers' that give clients the message 'I'm interested and prepared to listen. Please share with me your internal viewpoint.' Examples of openers that might be used in initial helping sessions include:

> 'Hello, I'm . . . . Please
>   tell me why you've come?
>   tell me why you're here?
>   tell me what's concerning you?
>   tell me what's the problem?
>   put me in the picture?
> 'You've been referred by . . . . Now how do you see
>   your situation?'

Sometimes helpers make opening statements in response to client body messages:

> 'You seem upset. Would you care to say what's bothering you?'
> 'You seem very nervous.'

The statement 'You seem very nervous' gives clients the opportunity to talk about a problem they bring to helping, or about how they feel here and now in the interview. Helpers can sometimes give permission to talk by body messages alone: for instance a look, possibly accompanied by an arm gesture.

Some helpers have contacts with clients outside formal interviews, for instance prison officers in youth custody centres; residential staff in half-way houses for former drug addicts; or nurses in hospitals. Here you may use permission to talk when you sense that someone has a personal agenda that bothers them, but requires that extra bit of encouragement to share it. Openers for use in informal helping include:

> 'Is there something on your mind?'
> 'You seem tense today?'
> 'I'm available if you want to talk.'

Small rewards

Small rewards are brief verbal and nonverbal expressions of interest designed to encourage clients to continue speaking. The message they convey is, 'I'm with you. Please go on.' Wrongly used small rewards can encourage clients to respond to their helpers rather than to themselves. For instance, you may say 'Tell me more' whenever clients talk about topics of interest to you. Many small rewards are body rather than verbal messages: for example, facial expressions, nods, and good eye contact. The following are examples of verbal small rewards, though perhaps the most frequently used 'Uh-hmm' is more a voice than a verbal message.

'Uh-hmm.'	'Sure.'
'Please continue.'	'Indeed.'
'Tell me more.'	'And . . .'
'Go on.'	So . . .'
'I see.'	'Really.'
'Oh?'	'Right.'
'Then . . .'	'Yes.'
'I hear you.'	'You're not kidding.'

Another kind of small reward is to repeat the last word a client has said:

Client: 'I'm feeling nervous.'
Helper: 'Nervous.'

Open-ended questions

Helpers may use questions in ways that either help clients to elaborate their internal viewpoints or lead them out of their viewpoints and possibly into yours. Open-ended questions allow clients to share their internal viewpoints without curtailing their options. A good use of open-ended questions is when, in the initial session, you wish to assist clients to tell their stories. In subsequent sessions too, you are likely to find open-ended questions useful. These include: 'Tell me about it?'; 'Please elaborate?'; and, slightly less open-ended, 'How do you feel about that?' Open-ended questions may be contrasted with closed-ended questions that curtail speakers' options: for example, 'Tell me whether or not you like your boss?' Open-ended questions may also be contrasted with leading questions that put answers into clients' mouths: for example, 'How do you feel about her? She's a great person, isn't she?'

REFLECTIVE RESPONDING

Rewarding listening requires helpers not only to understand clients' communications accurately, but to make verbal responses showing accurate understanding. Helpers provide the gift of their listening so that clients genuinely feel understood. Sometimes responding as if within clients' internal viewpoints is called empathy (Rogers, 1957, 1962, 1975, 1980). Rogers describes empathy likewise: 'To sense the client's inner world of private personal meanings as if it were your own, but without ever losing the "as if" quality, this is empathy' (1962, p.419). Rogers emphasizes the importance of helpers' 'communicating your sensings of his/her world as you look with fresh and unfrightened eyes at elements of which the individual is fearful' (1975, p.4). Furthermore, clients need to perceive that helpers empathically understand them or at the very least communicate the intent to understand (Barrett-Lennard, 1962, 1981; Rogers, 1962).

In Rogers' person-centred helping, empathic reflections are the helper's major tool. Rogers' use of empathy particularly focuses on the construct of experiencing (Gendlin, 1962). He attempts to improve the quantity and quality of his clients' inner listening to the ongoing flow of experiencing within them. This flow is a referent to which clients can repeatedly turn to discover the meaning of their experience so that they can move forward in it. One study showed that over 53 per cent of Rogers' verbal responses fell in the reflection/restatement category, whereas Lazarus, a more eclectic and task-oriented helper, had only 10 per cent of responses in this category (Lee & Uhlemann, 1984).

In lifeskills helping the term *reflective responding* is shorthand for 'responding with understanding as if in the client's internal viewpoint'. Reflective responding entails tuning in to and 'mirroring' with your verbal, voice and body messages the crux of the meaning contained in your clients' verbal, voice and body messages. In lifeskills helping reflective responding is just one of the skills, albeit an extremely important one, that helpers use to help clients manage problems and problematic skill patterns. Helpers use reflective responding not just to build relationships, but also when developing clients' specific skills. The term reflective responding is preferred to empathy or empathic responding for two main reasons. First, the word reflection more closely describes the process involved than empathy. Second, the term avoids confusion with Rogers' use of empathy. Rogers preferred not to think of empathy as a skill, but as an attitude (Rogers, 1951) or way of being (Rogers, 1975). Rogers' therapeutic goal was to help people become more in touch with their inner valuing process rather than to develop specific lifeskills. Before discussing some component skills of reflective responding, here are a few examples.

Patient to nurse

Patient: 'When I first heard I had terminal cancer, my world fell apart. I'm still reeling and frightened at the thought of death.'

Nurse: 'You still feel shaken and scared by the diagnosis of terminal cancer.'

Woman to career counsellor

Woman: 'With the children nearing the end of their education I want to build more of a life for myself. I don't want to hang around the house all the time.'

Career counsellor: 'You're determined to carve something outside the home for yourself and not keep brooding over an empty nest.'

When helping students are first introduced to the skill of reflective responding, many express reservations.

'It's so unnatural.'
'Clients will just think I'm repeating everything they say.'
'It gets in the way of my being spontaneous.'
'It makes me too self-conscious.'

When learning any new skill, for instance driving a car or swimming, at first you have to concentrate extra hard to make the correct sequence of choices that constitute the skill. Ultimately, if you work and practise at reflective responding, you are likely to gain fluency in it. Then reflective responding will both appear and feel 'natural'.

Reflective responding should not be something you use all the time: you should flexibly incorporate such responses into your helping skills repertoire. Reflective responses may help on many occasions.

- when creating a safe emotional climate for clients to tell their stories;

- when you need to show that you have understood;

- when you need to check that you have understood;

- when clients struggle to get in touch with thoughts and feelings;

- when clients need to experience their thoughts and feelings as valid;

- when you want to ensure that clients assume responsibility for their thoughts and feelings independent of what you may think;

- when clients need a reward or emotional stepping-stone to continue talking;

- when you check clients' understanding of specific points you make.

SKILL 6: REWORDING

Visualize a helping session between a client and a parrot. The parrot repeats precisely everything the client says. It is important for helpers to reword or paraphrase, because you drive speakers crazy if you parrot them. Rewording just focuses on the verbal content of what clients say. Sometimes rewording is termed reflection of content. Focusing only on the verbal content of clients' messages is a first step in learning to respond to their combined voice, body and verbal messages. When you reword, you may sometimes use the client's words, but sparingly. You try to stay close to the kind of language they use. Here are a few basic examples.

Patient to speech therapist
Patient: 'I'm finding swallowing difficult.'
Speech therapist: 'You're having trouble swallowing.'

Parishioner to priest
Parishioner: 'I'm delighted that you've come back to our church.'
Priest: 'You're very pleased to have me back in the parish.'

Parent to family counsellor
Parent: 'I told my kids to go to hell.'
Family counsellor: 'You were really angry with them.'

> Employee to manager
> *Employee:* 'Some of the time I like working here, but some of the time I'm less positive.'
> *Manager:* 'You have mixed feelings about what you do here.'

A good rewording of verbal content can provide mirror reflections that are clearer and more succinct than the original statements. Clients may show appreciation with comments such as 'That's right' or 'You've got me'. A simple tip for rewording is to start your responses with the personal pronoun 'you' to indicate that you reflect clients' internal viewpoints. Another tip is to slow your speech rate down to give you more time to think. You need a good memory and a good command of vocabulary to reword. To become confident, flexible and fluent in the skill requires much practice.

SKILL 7: REFLECTING FEELINGS

Skilled helpers are very sharp at picking up clients' feelings. Reflecting feelings is both similar to, yet different from, rewording. Both reflecting feelings and rewording involve mirroring. Also, reflecting feelings usually involves rewording. However, the language of feelings is not words. Feelings are bodily sensations which may then have word labels attached to them. Consequently, rewording alone has distinct limitations. For example, clients may send voice and body messages that qualify or negate verbal messages. Paul says 'I'm okay', yet speaks softly and has tearful eyes. A good reflection of feelings picks up these other messages as well. Reflecting feelings entails responding to clients' music and not just to their words. To do this, helper responses incorporate appropriate voice and body messages.

Reflecting feelings may be viewed as feeling with a client's flow of emotions and experiencing and being able to communicate this back. Helping students often have trouble with the notion of reflecting feelings. They may just talk about feelings rather than offer an expressive emotional companionship. Inadequately distinguishing between thoughts and feelings can be another problem for both clients and helpers. For example, 'I feel that equality between the sexes is essential' describes a thought rather than a feeling. On the other hand, 'I feel angry when I see sex discrimination' labels a feeling. This distinction is important both in reflecting feelings and also when helping clients to influence how they feel by altering how they think. Constant reflective responding focusing on feelings runs the risk of encouraging clients to wallow in feelings rather than to move on to how best to deal with them.

Reflecting feelings involves both receiver and sender skills.

Receiver skills

understanding clients' face and body messages;
understanding clients' voice messages;
understanding clients' verbal messages;
tuning into the flow of your own emotional reactions;
taking into account the context of clients' messages;
sensing the surface and underlying meanings of clients' messages.

Sender skills

responding in ways that pick up clients' feelings words and phrases;
rewording feelings appropriately, using expressive rather than wooden language;
using voice and body messages that neither add to nor subtract from the emotions
  conveyed;
checking the accuracy of your understanding.

Picking up feelings words and phrases

A good, but not infallible way to find out what clients feel is to listen to their feelings words and phrases. Picking up feelings words and phrases is similar to rewording, but with a heightened focus on feelings rather than informational content. Sometimes helping students ask, 'Well, what did you feel?' after clients have just told them. They need to discipline their listening more. Feelings phrases are colloquial expressions used to describe feelings words. For example 'I've got the blues' is a feelings phrase describing the word depressed. Table 4.1 provides a list of feelings words. Incidentally, it is cumbersome, when reflecting feelings, always to put 'You feel' before feelings words: sometimes 'You're' is sufficient: for example, 'You're sad' instead of 'You feel sad.'

Table 4.1 List of feelings words

accepted	dependent	involved	supported
adventurous	depressed	irresponsible	suspicious
affectionate	discontented	jealous	tense
aggressive	embarrassed	joyful	tired
ambitious	energetic	lonely	trusting
angry	envious	loved	unambitious
anxious	excited	loving	unappreciated
apathetic	fit	optimistic	unassertive
appreciated	free	outgoing	unattractive
assertive	friendly	pessimistic	underconfident
attractive	frightened	powerful	uneasy
bored	grieving	powerless	unfit
carefree	guilt-free	rejected	unfriendly
cautious	guilty	relaxed	unloved
cheerful	happy	resentful	unsafe
competitive	humiliated	responsible	unsupported
confident	hurt	sad	unwanted
confused	indecisive	secure	uptight
contented	independent	shy	vulnerable
cooperative	inferior	stressed	wanted
daring	insecure	strong	weak
decisive	interested	superior	worried

The following are some dimensions of reflecting feelings words and phrases.

INTENSITY. You should try to mirror the intensity of clients' feelings and words in rewordings. For example, Imran has just had a negative experience about which he might feel either 'devastated' (strong intensity), 'upset' (moderate intensity) or 'slightly upset' (weak intensity). Corresponding helper rewordings might be either 'sent reeling' (strong intensity), or 'distressed' (moderate intensity), or 'a little distressed' (weak intensity). You may err on the side of either adding or subtracting intensity.

MULTIPLE AND MIXED FEELINGS. Sometimes clients use many words to describe their feelings. The words may form a cluster around the same theme, in which case you may choose only to reword the crux of the feeling. Alternatively, clients may have varying degrees of mixed feelings ranging from simple opposites, for instance, 'happy/sad', to more complex combinations, for instance, 'hurt/angry'. Good rewordings pick up all key elements of feelings messages. For instance:

> *Client:* 'I'm sorry, but relieved, not to have got the promotion.'
> *Helper:* 'You're upset, but feel that a weight's been taken off your shoulders, at not being promoted.'

> *Client:* 'I both like being with her, yet also like being on my own.'
> *Helper:* 'You appreciate her companionship, but enjoy your own too.'

ASSISTING LABELLING OF FEELINGS. Sometimes helpers assist clients in finding the right feelings words. Here reflecting feelings goes beyond rewording feelings to helping choose feelings words that resonate for clients:

> *Client:* 'I don't quite know how to express my reaction to losing my job . . . possibly angry . . . upset, no that's not quite it . . . bewildered . . .'
> *Helper:* 'Hurt, anxious, confused . . . are any of those words appropiate?'

Picking up voice and body messages

Much information about clients' feelings does not come from what they say, but from how they say it. Sometimes the verbal, voice and body messages clients send are congruent. In such instances, it is relatively easy to label feelings and intensity accurately. However, clients' messages are often heavily encoded. Clients may struggle to express what they *truly* feel in face of their conditioning about what they *should* feel. It also takes time for clients to trust helpers. Consequently many emotional messages 'come out sideways' rather than loud and clear. Effective helpers are skilled at listening with the 'third ear' to clients' voice and body messages and to what is left unsaid or camouflaged. They realize that certain clients take time to develop skills of clearly identifying and articulating feelings. You need to be sensitive to the pace at which clients can work. Clients may require patience rather than pressure.

Helpers unclear about clients' real or underlying feelings can check with them. For instance, you may make comments like 'I think I hear you saying [state feelings tentatively] . . . Am I right?' or 'I would like to understand what you're feeling, but I'm still not altogether clear. Can you help me?' Another option is to say, 'I'm getting a mixed message from you. On the one hand you are saying you do not mind. On the other hand you seem tearful?' After a pause, you might add, 'I'm wondering if you are putting on a brave face?'

A further consideration in picking up feelings is to understand whether and to what extent clients possess insight into their feelings. For instance, as a helper you may infer that a parent is absolutely furious with a child, but the parent may not be able to handle such an observation since it clashes with his or her self-image of being a loving parent. Consequently, you may need to pick up three feelings: the parent's stated feeling of unconditional love for the child; the underlying anger with the child; and the feeling of threat were the parent's self-picture to be challenged by your reflecting how intensely angry he or she was.

Sender skills of reflecting feelings

When reflecting feelings, you may wonder how best to respond to the numerous verbal, voice and body messages you have received. There are no simple answers. What you try to do is (1) decode the overall message accurately; and (2) formulate an emotionally expressive reflective response that communicates back the crux of the client's feelings. Here are a few guidelines for sending reflecting feelings messages.

SEND BACK THE CRUX OF THE CLIENT'S MESSAGE Where possible show that you have understood the client's main message or messages. Whatever else you do, communicate back the core feeling.

> *Client:* We just argue and argue and don't seem to get anywhere. I don't know what to do. It's so frustrating. I wish I knew the answer. I don't seem to be able to handle our relationship.
> *Helper:* You're extremely frustrated with constant unproductive arguments and not knowing how to improve matters.

BE SENSITIVE TO CLIENTS' UNDERLYING FEELINGS AND AGENDAS Sometimes there are no hidden agendas in what clients communicate. On other occasions you may help them to articulate underlying feelings. However, sometimes you may intentionally not respond to underlying feelings and agendas. For example, clients may require more space to acknowledge the feelings on their own, or they may not be ready for a deeper reflection. When making deeper reflections you run a greater risk of being wrong than when making surface reflections.

KEEP YOUR RESPONSE APPROPRIATELY SIMPLE Use simple and clear language. Avoid unnecessary words and qualifications. However, be prepared to state different parts of multiple and mixed messages.

USE VOICE AND BODY MESSAGES TO ADD EXPRESSIVENESS TO YOUR VERBAL MESSAGE(S) You are not just talking about feelings, you are reflecting feelings. For instance, if a suicidal client says 'I feel terrible', you can adjust your voice and facial expression to mirror, to some extent, a sense of desperation. Congruence between your verbal, voice and body messages is important. If you send mixed messages you may be perceived as insincere.

STATE THE CLIENT'S MAIN FEELING AT THE START OF YOUR RESPONSE Even though the clients may not start with their main feeling, they may feel better understood by you if you reflect their main feeling at the start of your response than if you reflect information first:

> *Client:* I've failed my statistics exam and have to repeat it. I'm so disappointed.
> *Helper:* You're bitterly disappointed at failing.

In this example the helper has tuned into feelings immediately. However, imagine that the helper had replied: 'You failed your stats test and are bitterly disappointed.' The helper has started by responding from the head to the client's head. By the time the helper reflects the feeling of disappointment, it may be too late for the client to experience being emotionally understood.

CHECK YOUR UNDERSTANDING You respond to client statements with different degrees of tentativeness depending on how clearly they have communicated and how confident you are about receiving their messages accurately. However, all reflective responses should contain an element of checking whether you accurately understand your client's internal viewpoint. Sometimes checking may be achieved by slight voice inflections. On other occasions you check more explicitly.

SKILL 8: REFLECTING FEELINGS AND REASONS

A useful variation of reflective responding is to reflect both feelings and the reasons for them. Reflecting back reasons does not mean that you make an interpretation or offer an explanation from your external viewpoint. Instead where clients have already provided reasons for a feeling, you reflect these feelings back in a 'You feel . . . because . . .' statement that mirrors the other's internal viewpoint. Here is an example:

> *Mark:* I've struggled so hard to get to the end of the course and now I'm afraid I'm going to fail the last term's assessment.
> *Helper:* You're worried because you might fail after

all that effort.
Mark: Yes. I get anxious just thinking of all the time I
may have wasted.

Here the helper's 'You feel . . . because . . .' response showed more understanding of Mark's predicament than if the response had stopped after 'You're worried'. Mark was able to emphasize that the meaning of passing was not only getting through the course, but avoiding wasting so much time and effort. Put another way, the because part of the helper's response identified the thinking contributing to Mark's feeling. Thus, 'You feel . . . because . . .' reflections are useful not only for helping clients tell their stories, but also for assessing how clients' thinking contributes to unwanted feelings.

SKILL 9: AVOID UNREWARDING 'DON'TS'

If clients are going to self-disclose, explore problems and problematic skills areas, and experience their feelings more fully, they require psychological safety and space. Here the emphasis is on how not to spoil your listening by sending clumsy verbal messages. Psychological safety and space are both quantitative and qualitative. If you are rarely physically accessible, or if when present, you monopolize or keep interrupting, you scarcely give clients the quantity of psychological safety and space they need. Helpers can also deprive clients of the quality of safety and space they need by responding in ways that show lack of respect for their internal viewpoints. Showing such lack of respect not only makes it more difficult for clients to talk to you, it also interferes with their inner listening. Clients may block material from awareness and be more inclined to edit what they disclose for fear of disapproval.

Below are some ways that helpers communicate to clients that they are not totally safe and free to talk. Avoiding these 'don'ts' does not mean you should never use any of them. You simply need to be aware of their possible negative consequences before choosing to use them.

- *Directing and leading:* Taking control of what the client can talk about: for example, 'I would like you to start with what happened to you when you were a child.'

- *Judging and evaluating:* Making evaluative statements, especially ones implying that the client does not live up to your own standards: for example, 'You are overpossessive of your children.'

- *Blaming:* Assigning responsibility for what happens to clients in a finger-pointing way: for example, 'It's all your fault.'

- *Moralizing, preaching and being patronizing:* Telling clients how they should be leading their lives: for example, 'People who help others are usually happier than those who live for themselves.'

- *Labelling and diagnosing:* Placing superficial diagnostic categories on clients and their behaviour: for example, 'You're paranoid', or 'You have an inferiority complex.'

- *Reassuring and humouring:* Trying to make clients feel better, yet not acknowledging their true feelings: for example, 'You'll be all right . . . Don't worry.'

- *Not accepting clients' feelings:* Telling clients that their positive or negative feelings should be different to what they are: for example, 'You've got no reason to be so depressed.'

- *Advising and teaching:* Not giving clients the space to arrive at their own solutions: for example, 'Why don't you go round to see her and try to make things up?'

- *Interrogating:* Using questions in ways that threaten clients with unwanted probing: 'Tell me about your weaknesses. Be specific.'

- *Overinterpreting:* Offering explanations that come from your internal viewpoint and that bear little similarity to what clients might have thought: for example, 'Your indecision about choosing a career is related to your fear of failing to live up to your father's perfectionist standards.'

- *Inappropriately self-disclosing:* Talking about yourself in ways that interfere with clients' disclosures: for example, 'You have troubles. Let me tell you mine.'

- *Putting on a professional facade:* Trying to make yourself seem an expert and thereby communicating in a defensive or otherwise inauthentic way: for example, 'I've had a lot of training and experience with problems such as yours.'

- *Faking attention:* Insincerely pretending to be more interested and involved in what is being said than you are: for example, 'That's so interesting.'

- *Placing time pressures:* Letting clients know that your availability for listening is limited: for example, 'You had better be brief.'

A major 'don't' not mentioned above is breaking confidences. Quite apart from damaging specific helping relationships, breaking confidences represents a serious breach of ethics. All the above 'don'ts' focus on verbal responses, but as mentioned earlier, helpers' voice and body messages can also create a lack of psychological safety.

SKILL 10: AVOID POOR THINKING SKILLS

You bring your thinking skills strengths and weaknesses to listening. All of the verbal 'don'ts' just mentioned that restrict clients' psychological space and freedom reflect poor thinking skills. You may talk to yourself in ways that create anxiety or calm you down. You may possess helpful or harmful rules about yourself, others and the helping process. You may attribute responsibility for what happens in helping in ways that strengthen or weaken clients' capacities to develop self-helping skills. You may possess ways of perceiving clients and their reactions to your responses that make for accuracy or inaccuracy. The need for effective thinking skills on the part of both helpers and clients pervades this book. Despite its importance, the topic is only mentioned in passing here.

CONCLUDING COMMENT

Rewarding listening is the fundamental skill of developing supportive helping relationships. Without this basic skill of getting inside clients' internal viewpoints and showing that you understand and care about what they say, you severely, if not fatally, limit your capacity to help. Furthermore, you may even add to clients' pain and distress by sending negative messages. In lifeskills helping, rewarding listening is central to assisting clients in managing problems and overcoming problematic skills patterns. Beginning students need to work and practise to develop the sensitive fluency of skilled helpers. Experienced helpers should also pay close attention to whether they maintain high listening standards or let bad habits interfere. In most instances, rewarding listening needs to be accompanied by other helper skills. We turn to these additional skills in the next chapter.

CHAPTER HIGHLIGHTS

- Lifeskills helping heavily emphasizes the importance of the helper–client relationship.

- Five ways that helpers and clients send and receive messages are: verbal, voice, body, touch and action messages.

- Rewarding listening is the central skill in developing supportive helping relationships.

- Functions of rewarding listening include: establishing and maintaining rapport; helping clients disclose; helping clients experience and express feelings; creating a knowledge base; creating an influence base; and helping clients to assume responsibility.

- Helpers always need to be aware of whether they respond inside or outside their clients' internal viewpoints.

- Barriers to possessing an attitude of respect and acceptance include: anxiety-evoking feelings, clients, and situations; trigger words, phrases and attitudes; being prejudiced; current unfinished business; needing to present a professional facade; emotional exhaustion and burnout; insufficient administrative support; and physical barriers.

- Helper body messages are important for demonstrating interest and attention, showing responsiveness as clients talk, and framing verbal messages.

- Five dimensions of sending good voice messages are volume, articulation, pitch, emphasis and rate (VAPER).

- Openers are permissions for clients to talk. Small rewards are brief verbal and nonverbal expressions of interest that help clients keep talking. Open-ended questions help clients elaborate their internal viewpoints.

- Reflective responding entails tuning in to and 'mirroring' with your verbal, voice and body messages the crux of the meaning contained in your clients' verbal, voice and body messages.

- Rewording involves paraphrasing clients' key words. Good rewordings can be clearer and more succinct than clients' original statements.

- The language of feelings is not verbal. Consequently good reflections of feelings both pick up and communicate back nonverbal as well as verbal messages. Helpers require good skills at picking up feelings messages including their intensity and whether they are multiple or mixed feelings. Helpers sometimes assist clients in labelling feelings.

- A variant of reflective responding is to reflect back feelings and the reasons for them. Reflecting feelings and reasons identifies thoughts contributing to feelings.

- You create unsafe emotional climates for clients by sending clumsy verbal messages. 'Don'ts' to avoid include: directing and leading; judging and evaluating; blaming; moralizing; preaching and being patronizing; labelling and diagnosing; reassuring and humouring; not accepting clients' feelings; advising and teaching; interrogating; overinterpreting; inappropriately self-disclosing; putting on a professional facade; faking attention; and putting unnecessary time pressures on clients.

- Poor helper thinking skills can impede rewarding listening: for example, anxiety-engendering self-talk, unrealistic helping rules, and inaccurately perceiving what clients say and do.

- For most clients, rewarding listening needs to be accompanied by other helper skills focused on managing problems and developing lifeskills.

FIVE

How to Identify and Clarify Problems

A matter that becomes clear ceases to concern us.
Friedrich Nietzsche

CHAPTER QUESTIONS

What are some of the main objectives of initial helping sessions?

What is the nature of the helper–client relationship?

What action skills are important for identifying and clarifying problems?

What thinking skills are important for identifying and clarifying problems?

INTRODUCTION

Below are concerns that people might bring to helpers.

'I'm feeling depressed and apathetic.'

'I wish I could relate better and have more social life.'

'Our marriage is heading for the rocks.'

'I feel stressed all the time.'

'I've had a heart attack and want to look after my health better in future.'

'I'm having hassles with my boss and don't know what to do.'

'I'm unemployed and want to rejoin the workforce.'

'I can't concentrate on my studies.'

'I carry my parents round in my head all the time and find difficulty deciding what I
  want to do.'

Clients bringing such problems to helpers want to move beyond their stuckness, but are
unclear how best to proceed. In stage 1 of the lifeskills model, helpers go beyond
developing the relationship to identifying and clarifying clients' problems. The previous
chapter on rewarding listening skills heavily emphasized staying within clients' internal
viewpoints. This chapter emphasizes using a range of skills to elaborate and clarify
clients' internal viewpoints. In reality, the identifying and clarifying work of stage 1
frequently overlaps with the stage 2 work of assessing and redefining problems in skills
terms. Helpers use many identifying and clarifying skills both when intervening and
when ending and consolidating clients' self-helping skills, stages 4 and 5 of the model.

OBJECTIVES FOR INITIAL SESSIONS

Below the first three stages of the lifeskills helping models are restated in terms of four
main objectives for the initial helping session or sessions. These objectives apply to
clients as well as to helpers.

DEVELOP A SUPPORTIVE WORKING RELATIONSHIP Both helpers and clients need to
feel that they can work together. Clients wish to be understood by helpers and to have
some expectation of benefit from helping contacts. Though limited by ethical and
professional considerations, a personal bond can develop between helpers and clients
(Bordin, 1979; Kokotovic & Tracey, 1990). Helpers and clients are partners in
developing the clients' skills resources. From the start, helpers convey understanding
and support as a basis for developing clients' skills. The relationship in lifeskills helping
is rarely an end in itself; it is a vehicle for assisting clients to work on problems and
problematic skills. There may be some healthy dependency on helpers. However, this
dependency is transitional as clients develop self-helping skills.

DEVELOP A WORKING MODEL Clients tend to be stuck at their present level of
understanding problems. Both helpers and clients collaborate to develop working models.
A working model consists of a set of hypotheses about how clients function in problem
areas. Working models are statements of how individual clients feel, think and act.
    There are many advantages to helpers and clients working together in the detective
work of developing working models. First, clients can provide valuable insights if
allowed to do much of the work themselves; their contributions are greater when they
are treated as active rather than passive partners. Second, clients as well as helpers are
hypothesis makers and testers. Collaborating with helpers improves both parties' skills

as practitioner-researchers. Third, clients are more likely to own responsibility for possessing and altering skills weaknesses that they have played some part in discovering. Fourth, collaborating to understand clients' problems can develop the helping relationship more than rewarding listening alone. Helpers may be perceived as more empathic when active than when passive.

DEVELOP A WORKING DEFINITION Helpers assist clients to identify not only problems, but also the component parts of problems. For example, a client who starts by saying 'I am depressed. Help me', may then reveal contributing problems in the areas of relating poorly to spouse, having a difficult parent, being short of friends, not having adequate recreational outlets, and getting little satisfaction from work. The plot thickens. However, it is insufficient to leave clients hanging; helpers need to assist clients to redefine their problems in skills terms so that they then have 'handles' for working on them. Here the earlier distinction between *descriptive* and *skills* definitions of problems becomes important. Descriptive definitions clarify problems, but do not move much outside clients' existing concepts and internal viewpoints. Skills definitions identify the specific action and thinking skills weaknesses sustaining problems. Where possible, helpers should reach agreement with clients on skills definitions.

DEVELOP WORKING GOALS AND INTERVENTIONS By the end of the initial session, or if necessary initial sessions, helpers and clients should agree on preliminary statements of working goals to guide future work. Furthermore, helpers need to indicate how goals might be attained. As part of this process, they may discuss the appropriateness of different interventions. Bordin (1979) has suggested that there are three main elements that determine the quality and strength of the helper–client working alliance. In addition to the development of a personal bond (relationship), helpers and clients require agreement on treatment goals (goals) and on the tasks to achieve these goals (tasks). Helpers and clients who achieve each of these three elements in the initial session or sessions have a strong foundation for continuing to develop the working alliance. A final word: sometimes it is appropriate to start implementing interventions during as well as at the end of initial sessions. Helpers make such decisions in the light of progress made in sessions and individual clients' needs.

SKILLS FOR IDENTIFYING AND CLARIFYING PROBLEMS

In addition to rewarding listening skills, effective helpers use all the skills discussed in this chapter. Skills in identifying and clarifying problems contain elements of stepping outside or going beyond clients' internal viewpoints. Nevertheless, these skills help clients elaborate and therefore more fully understand their internal viewpoints. Put another way, rewarding listening focuses on helping clients share their internal viewpoints concerning problems with relatively little input from helpers' external viewpoints. The skills covered in this chapter focus on helping clients expand their internal viewpoints by means of greater input from helpers' viewpoints.

STRUCTURING SKILLS
Objectives of structuring

Structuring is a term used to describe the behaviours by which helpers let their clients know their respective roles at various stages of the helping process. Cormier and Cormier state: *'Structuring* refers to an interactional process between counselors and clients in which they arrive at similar perceptions of the role of the counselor, an understanding of what occurs in counseling, and an agreement on which outcome goals will be achieved' (1985, p.53). Structuring occurs throughout helping and even prior to helping: for example through the publicity, image and reputation of helpers and helping agencies. Here the focus is on structuring skills for initial sessions.

Effective structuring both leads to positive outcomes and prevents or minimizes the chance of negative outcomes. The functions of structuring in initial sessions include establishing expectancies conducive to clients' working on rather than just talking about problems; outlining the initial session; providing an introductory rationale for working within the lifeskills helping framework; establishing the expectancy that change may be possible; and, if necessary, communicating limitations concerning the helping relationship, for instance restrictions on confidentiality.

Too much and too little structure

Helpers may provide both too much and too little structure (Osipow *et al.*, 1984). If you provide too much structuring, clients may feel stifled by your agendas and reluctant or unable to reveal their own. You may establish a 'teacher knows best' emotional climate that is conducive to dependency and resistances. Clients may perceive you as too set on fitting them into your way of working, whether it suits them or not. Furthermore, if you talk too much at the beginning of sessions, not only do you make it difficult for clients to talk, but you may structure the helping process in too intellectual a way. Too little structuring also has dangers. Clients may feel anxious and confused. You may be anxious and confused too. In addition, clients may perceive that you have nothing of value to offer.

Helpers' voice and body messages may enhance or impede structuring. Again, negative outcomes may arise if helpers come on either too strong or too weak. For instance, clients may feel overwhelmed and put off by helpers who structure in loud voices and gesticulate too much. On the other hand, helpers who structure in diffident voices, with minimal use of gesture and eye contact, may convey insufficient commitment.

Some structuring skills

The objective of initial structuring is to initiate the process of client self-helping. You attempt to establish working alliances in which you collaborate with clients as partners in developing their skills rather than doing things either to or for them. In a medical model of helping, doctors might say: 'What can I do to cure my patients?' In the lifeskills model, helpers say: 'How can I best collaborate with clients to develop their self-helping skills?'

VERBAL MESSAGE SKILLS A choice that helpers face is how much to structure at the start of sessions. Already, I've mentioned that lifeskills helping always starts with checking 'where the client is at'. You may perform initial session structuring with at least two statements. The first statement gets the session started and allows clients to introduce their stories; the second establishes the agenda for the remainder of the session. Below is an example of a possible opening statement providing structure for a session's start:

> Hello, Jeff, my name is Debbie Roberts and I'm one
> of the student counsellors here. We have about forty
> minutes and everything you say is confidential.
> Would you please tell me why you're here?

After the client has had a chance to state why he has come for helping, the following statement might establish structure for the rest of the session:

> You've given me some idea why you've come. What
> I'd like to do is to ask some more questions to help us
> understand more fully your problem(s) [specify].
> Then depending on what we find, I will review with
> you some skills to help you cope better. Once we
> agree on what skills might be useful, then we can look
> at ways to develop them. Does this way of
> proceeding sound all right?

One reason for not amalgamating both parts of the structuring in your opening statement is that the second part may be inappropriate for certain clients: for example those requiring either information or referral. Furthermore, lengthy opening statements may show lack of empathy to clients' immediate need to say why they have come. Some clients may seek emotonal release and feel blocked by your talking too much too soon. Sometimes, when sessions start, you may notice from body language that clients are experiencing strong emotions, for instance distress or anxiety. You can reflect such feelings and give clients permission to discuss them.

When structuring, helpers can incorporate statements indicating a rationale for the lifeskills approach. The following are examples:

> It can be useful to think of problems in terms of the
> skills you need to cope better. This way you get some
> 'handles' or leverage to work for change.

> In the past you have probably learned some
> ineffective along with some effective ways of thinking
> and acting. This approach aims to improve how you
> think and act so that you can manage your
> problem(s) [specify] better.

> The approach I take assumes that most of how people behave is learned. Ineffective skills of thinking and acting can be unlearned, and effective skills learned.
>
> My approach heavily emphasizes developing self-helping skills. You will probably need to work hard to acquire and maintain them. Also, it may speed matters up if you listen to a cassette recording of each session before you come to the next. What do you think about this?

The following are some guidelines for initial session structuring.

- Be flexible. Considerations include: your clients' expectations and problems; their emotional state; their age and intelligence level; at what stage of the initial session you are; how much time you have; and the helping context in which you work.

- Consider breaking your structuring down into more than one statement.

- Pay attention to timing.

- Use simple language.

- Use skills language.

- Be clear and relatively brief.

- Be consistent. Your remarks should be consistent with a lifeskills helping theoretical position.

- Emphasize helper–client collaboration.

- Emphasize work. Helping is not magic. Clients need to work to acquire and maintain skills.

- Check for questions and reservations. Do not assume that what you say is understood and agreed upon by clients.

VOICE AND BODY MESSAGES How you send voice and body messages is important when you structure. Your voice messages should indicate your commitment to what you do. Good voice message skills include easy audibility, comfortable speech rate, firm voice, clear articulation, and appropriate variations in emphasis. Your body messages should support your verbal and voice messages: for example by appropriate gaze, eye contact and use of gestures. A theme throughout this book is the importance of helpers' paying great attention to their voice and body messages. Structuring is a clear instance where ineffective voice and body messages can countermand verbal messages.

QUESTIONING SKILLS
Objectives of questioning

Viktor Frankl tells the following psychiatrist joke:

> 'Are you a psychiatrist?'
> 'Why do you ask?'
> 'You're a psychiatrist.' (Frankl, 1975, p.94)

Here, instead of unmasking, the psychiatrist has been unmasked. Often, as in this instance, helpers ask questions inappropriately. A major reservation about using questions is that they take clients out of their internal viewpoints. Some questions are asked more to make helpers feel secure than to help clients. However, judicious questioning can help clients better explore, clarify and understand their internal viewpoints. Furthermore, questions assist helpers to identify what clients' problems are and to break them down into component parts. Then you both possess more information for developing hypotheses about how problems are sustained. In this chapter the primary focus is on the use of questions to identify, clarify and break problems down into their component parts.

The iceberg provides a good analogy for understanding the role of questioning in lifeskills helping. Much relevant information lies below the surface. In general, clients responding to permission to tell their stories reveal useful information. Area A in Figure 5.1 depicts this information. However, effective helper questioning enables clients to provide much additional information for identifying, clarifying and breaking down problems. Area B depicts this further information. In addition, there may be additional information that clients may be either unaware of or unwilling to disclose. Helper questions may not tap this. Area C depicts this either highly private or unconscious information.

Another analogy for the role of questioning in initial sessions of lifeskills helping is that of plants and their root system. Helpers use questions to identify different roots of problems. For example, earlier a hypothetical client came to helping saying, 'I am depressed. Help me.' This represents the part of the plant which is above ground. However, by listening and effective questioning the helper starts identifying roots of the client's problem in five different areas (see Figure 5.2). Helpers may then ask further question to clarify each root area and its relative importance.

In the depressed client example, the roots of the problem are located in the present rather than the past. Questions concerning clients' childhoods may illustrate the origins of problems and help them work through and understand painful events. Nevertheless, the major focus of questioning in lifeskills helping is not on how clients arrived at their present problems, but on how they sustain them now and possibly in future.

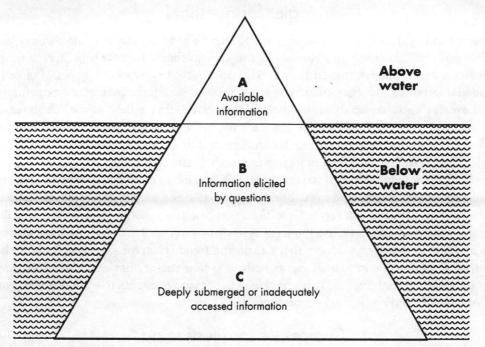

Figure 5.1 *The information about problems iceberg*

(a) **The problem**

'I am depressed.'

(b) **The root system**

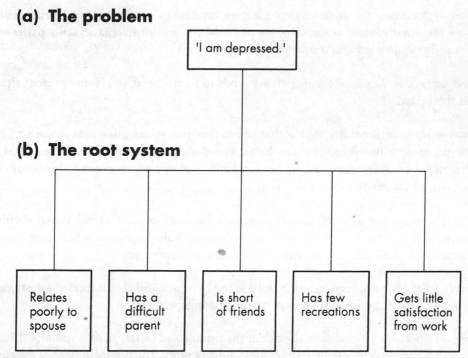

| Relates poorly to spouse | Has a difficult parent | Is short of friends | Has few recreations | Gets little satisfaction from work |

Figure 5.2 *Identifying the roots of a problem*

Strategies for questioning

Spitzer and Williams (1984) classify clinical interviewing approaches into three types: smorgasbord, checklist and canine. In the smorgasbord approach helpers sample whatever seems interesting. In the checklist approach, helpers ask a series of closed-ended questions about particular symptoms 'without giving the patient an opportunity to describe spontaneously the symptoms that are being talked about' (Spitzer & Williams, 1984, p.6). In the canine approach the helper is like a dog sniffing around for a buried bone. The helper continues to sniff around until the goal of that portion of the interview is reached and then moves on in search of another 'bone.'

In lifeskills helping, initial session questioning takes the detective approach. Helpers collaborate with clients first to ask questions that describe, clarify and break down their problems and then to ask further questions that assist in redefining problems in skills terms. Hutchins and Cole use the term systematic enquiry for collecting information in a logical and orderly fashion about a specific topic (Hutchins & Cole, 1986). The detective approach contains elements both of systematic enqury and also of sniffing around looking for bones or 'handles'. Helpers encourage clients to offfer information spontaneouly and not just when questioned.

Choices when questioning

Helpers have numerous choices when questioning, including the following:

Purpose of questions. Effective helpers ask questions that contribute to enlarging their own and their clients' understanding of problems and problematic skills patterns. They do not just ask questions for questioning's sake.

Present versus past focus. Lifeskills helping tends to focus more on clients' present than on their past.

Amount of topics covered. An issue is that of whether just to ask questions in the area of the presenting problem(s) or conduct a broader reconnaissance (Sullivan, 1954). Practical considerations, for instance what the client wants from helping, often influence how many topics you cover.

Degree of detail. How detailed should enquiries into each topic area be? When should helpers move on? Partly by intuition, effective helpers assess when areas may continue to yield valuable information and when to move on.

Intimacy level. Helpers need to be sensitive to the intimacy and threat level of questions. They still tactfully ask intimate questions, if appropiate.

Timing. Helpers require caution regarding the timing and ordering of questions. They may defer some intimate or probing questions pending the establishment of greater trust.

Number of questions. Egan admonishes, 'Do not assault clients with volleys of questions' (1990, p.142). Helpers should avoid conducting interrogations that may lead to either defensiveness or dependence, or both.

Confirmatory questions. Helpers may ask questions designed to elicit responses fitting pet theories. Sometimes they prematurely decide what are clients' problems and skills weaknesses and then ask questions only to confirm their judgements.

Types of questions

Helpers also need choose among different types of questions, including the following.

OPEN-ENDED VERSUS CLOSED-ENDED QUESTIONS Open-ended questions give clients considerable choice in how to respond, whereas closed-ended questions restrict choice. When working with new clients many helpers use open-ended questions prior to asking more focused questions.

- *Open-ended question:* 'What do you think of your previous experience in counselling?'

- *Close-ended question:* 'Was your previous counsellor good or bad?'

HOW, WHAT, WHEN, WHERE AND WHY QUESTIONS Another way of categorizing questions relates to how, what, when, where and why.

- *How questions* include: 'How do/did you think, feel or act [or a combination of these]?', 'How did he/she think, feel or act [or a combination of these]?', 'How often does it happen?', and 'How have you attempted to cope in the past?' How questions are particularly useful for eliciting details of how clients behave.

- *What questions* include: 'What happened?', 'What do you perceive as the problem?', 'What preceded your thoughts, feelings or actions?', 'What is the meaning of that for you?', 'What other ways are there of viewing it?', 'What are you afraid of?', and 'What are the likely consequences of doing that?'

- *When questions* include: 'When did it start?' and 'When is your next public speech?'

- *Where questions* include: 'Where does it happen?' and 'Where is the evidence for that perception?'

- *Why questions* include: 'Why did you behave that way?', 'Why do you think they feel that way?, and 'Why is it so important for you?' A risk of some why questions is that they may take clients into their heads rather than help them to focus on specific problematic thoughts, feelings and behaviours.

CLARIFICATION QUESTIONS Clarification questions seek information about and clarify your perception of clients' words and phrases. Examples include:

'When you say __, what do you mean?'
'Sounds to me like you're saying __ ?'

ELABORATION QUESTIONS Elaboration questions are open questions that give clients the opportunity to expand on what they have already started taking about. Examples include:

'Would you care to elaborate?'
'Is there anything more you wish to add?'

CHALLENGING QUESTIONS Challenging questions confront clients with the need to produce evidence for their perceptions. Examples include:

'Where is the evidence for __?'
'What makes you think that?'
'Are there other ways of viewing the situation?'

SPECIFIC DETAIL QUESTIONS Specific detail questions aim to collect concrete information about clients' problems and problematic skills patterns. Examples include:

'How frequent is it?'
'How do you actually behave?'
'How have you attempted to cope with it in the past?'
'What brings it on?'
'What feelings are associated with it?'
'What thoughts are associated with it?'
'When did it start?'
'Where does it happen?'

REQUEST FOR EXAMPLE QUESTIONS Request for example questions ask clients to illustrate what they talk about. Examples include:

'Tell me of a specific instance.'
'Can you give me an example?'

'SHOW ME' QUESTIONS 'Show me' questions ask clients to show the helper how they behaved. Sometimes the helper will act the other person in a role play. Examples include:

'Show me how you actually spoke to __?'
'Imagine I am your __ . Show me how you behaved to me.'

ELICITING PERSONAL MEANING QUESTIONS The information clients provide often has personal or symbolic meaning for them. For example, whenever a husband came home late without having called her, his wife would think he did not care about her (Beck, 1988). Eliciting personal meanings questions should be open and tentative since the client should, but will not always, know the answer better than anyone else. Illustrative questions include:

> 'I'm wondering what the meaning of __ is for you?'
> 'What do you make of that?'
> 'Why is it so important for you?'

Work in partnership with clients

In lifeskills helping questions are to provide information for clients as much as for helpers. Helpers try to avoid questioning in ways that create dependency, passivity and resistance. Below are some skills for collaborating with clients when asking questons.

ASK ESTABLISHING AGENDA AND TRANSITION QUESTIONS Establishing agenda and transition questions have the advantage of getting clients involved in the detective work of identifying and clarifying problems. Clients are invited to participate in working in areas important for them. Illustrative questions include:

> 'You've mentioned three areas [specify]. Which one would you like to focus on first?'
> 'Is there anything you would like to add before we move on to __ ?'

INTERSPERSE REFLECTIVE RESPONDING WITH QUESTIONS Clients feel interrogated when helpers ask a series of questions in quick succession. Helpers can greatly soften their questioning if they pause to see if clients wish to continue responding, and then reflect each response. Interspersing reflecting responding has the added advantage of ensuring that helpers check the accuracy of their understanding. The following excerpt shows what you should avoid:

> *Client:* 'I'm getting very anxious about my upcoming test.
> *Helper:* 'What makes you so anxious?
> *Client:* The fact that I may fail.
> *Helper:* Why are you so afraid of failing?
> *Client:* Because then it will be harder to get a job.
> *Helper:* What sort of job do you want?

Here is a gentler approach to the same initial statement:

> *Client:* I'm getting very anxious about my upcoming test.
> *Helper:* You're very worried about your test . . .

Would you say more about this?
Client: Yes. It's in three weeks' time and I feel overwhelmed.
Helper: So you experience this vital test as overpowering.
Client: My whole future depends on it.
Helper: You think it is make or break. Can you explain this further?

Though these are only short excerpts, in the first the helper controls and dominates the client whereas the second facilitates the client's description of his or her internal viewpoint. The emotional climate in the first excerpt is 'in the head'. The second excerpt encourages the expression of feelings as well as thoughts.

ASK FOLLOW-ON QUESTIONS Avoid jackrabbitting – quickly hopping from one topic to another (Hutchins & Cole, 1986). Always listen carefully to and respect what clients have just said. Frequently, your next question can follow on from and encourage clients to build upon their last response. Questioning that is logically linked to clients' responses creates a feeling of working together rather than of being directed by you.

ENCOURAGE CLIENTS TO DO THEIR OWN WORK Often clients can both ask and answer their own questions. Interspersing reflective responding with questions provides clients with psychological space to do their own work. If helpers establish good relationships, clients will tell them much information without being asked. Helpers may also use silences to encourage clients to engage in self-exploration and move beyond superficial answers. Furthermore, helpers can ask questions that encourage clients to think and feel for themselves. Illustrative questions are:

'What information is important for helping to understand your problem?'
'Can you just stay with the problem, try to get in touch with what you truly think and feel, and then tell me about it?'

CAREFULLY OBSERVE HOW QUESTIONS ARE ANSWERED Much of the art of qustioning lies in decoding clients' answers. Much information is conveyed by what is left unsaid or only partially said and by voice and body messages. Effective helpers are finely tuned to subtle client messages. They use tact in both asking questions and in responding to clients' answers. Clients with anxieties, confusions and vulnerabilities sensitively picked up by helpers are more likely to answer questions honestly than clients listened to clumsily.

USE GOOD VOICE AND BODY MESSAGES How you question is very important in addition to what you say. For example, clients may feel overwhelmed if your voice is loud and harsh. If you use little eye contact and have a stiff body posture, they may also feel less inclined to answer your questions. Helpers need to send questioning messages using good volume, articulation, pitch, emphasis and speech rate. Furthermore, attending and responsive body messages are conducive to clients' feeling that helpers are interested in their answers.

Example of questioning to identify and clarify problems

Below is an excerpt from the start of an initial session between a student counsellor and a client. Introductions have taken place in the waiting area. Counsellor and client are now seated in the counsellor's office.

Counsellor: We have about forty-five minutes together. Please tell me why you've come? [Open-ended opening question]

Client: I'm getting very anxious about my upcoming exam.

Counsellor: You're very worried about your exam. Would you say more about this? [Open-ended elaboration question]

Client: Yes. It's in three weeks' time and I feel overwhelmed.

Counsellor: So you experience this vital exam as overpowering.

Client: My whole future depends on it.

Counsellor: You think it is make or break. Can you explain this further? [Eliciting personal meaning question]

Client: If I fail the exam it will show on my record and make it harder for me to get a good job.

Counsellor: So failure will jeopardize your prospects of good employment.

Client: Yes. Is there anything you can do to help me?

Counsellor: I appreciate your worry. However, before answering that question I would like to become clearer regarding your problem. Perhaps we can explore it further and then I should be in a better position to suggest some skills that you might develop to cope better.

Client: Where do we start?

Counsellor: Well perhaps you can give me some basic information about what course you are on and what subject or subjects you are afraid of failing? [Specific detail questions]

Client: I'm in the final year of a business studies course and I'm afraid of failing accounting 2.

Counsellor: What specifically about accounting 2

bothers you? [Specific details question]

Client: I got very nervous about my accounting 1 exam and nearly failed the subject. My marks are generally above average, but I just scraped through. If it hadn't been for the marks on my take-home assisgnments I would have failed.

Counsellor: You're wondering whether history may repeat itself and you'll do badly in your accountancy 2 exam. How much of your marks does the exam account for? [Specific detail question]

Client: Fifty per cent. I think I'm doing okay on my homework assignments. I just don't want to mess up the exam.

Counsellor: You're worried about messing the exam up. I'm wondering if you're more concerned with how well you actually take the exam, your exam-taking skills, or how well you prepare for it, your revision skills, or both? [Establishing agenda question]

Client: What I'm most afraid of is that I will go to pieces during the exam.

Counsellor: So you're worried about falling apart during the exam. What precisely are you afraid you might do during the exam? [Specific detail question]

Client: Well in my last accountancy exam I could scarcely hold my pen. My hand was shaking and my heart was pounding. At times I felt faint, as though I might pass out.

Counsellor: Last time you had numerous distressing physical symptoms – hand shaking, difficulty holding your pen, heart pounding, feeling faint. In what ways did these feelings affect how you actually behaved during the exam? [Specific detail question]

Client: I couldn't think clearly and I didn't leave enough time to answer all the questions.

Counsellor: When you say you couldn't think clearly, what do you mean? [Clarification question]

Client: At times my head felt like cotton wool. I had to struggle to concentrate. These feelings of panic kept coming. I can't work with numbers under pressure.

In this brief excerpt, the counsellor has identified that a major concern of the client relates to being unable to handle the accountancy 2 exam-taking situation. The counsellor is still in the early stages of discovering both the dimensions of the client's accountancy exam-taking difficulties and whether there are other roots to the problem outside the exam-taking situation. The counsellor uses questions not only to discover the client's surface feelings and behaviours, but also to probe for the roots of the problem. Sometimes, when questioning, counsellors store away information for future use without responding to it directly. For example, they might note that the client perceived his/her whole future resting on this exam as an example of black-and-white or polarized thinking (Beck, 1988). This observation might form the basis for questions in stage 2 of the lifeskills model as the counsellor gathers more information to redefine the problem in skills terms.

SUMMARIZING SKILLS
Purposes of summaries

Summaries are brief statements of longer excerpts from helping sessions. Summaries can pull together different parts of extended communications and may take place at any stage of the helping process. Much of the time helpers summarize what clients communicate. However, since lifeskills helping has didactic as well as relationship emphases, some helper summaries relate to previously communicated educational content. Clients also use summaries: sometimes of their own accord and sometimes at the request of helpers. For example, clients can be asked to summarize the main points in a skills sequence they learn.

Here the focus is on helper summaries in initial sessions. Such summaries serve numerous purposes. If clients have had a lengthy period of talking, helpers summarize to establish their presence and make the interaction more two-way. Furthermore, if clients are telling their stories very rapidly, helpers may deliver summaries at a measured speech rate to calm clients down. Where possible, helper summaries serve to move the session forward. Such summaries may clarify what clients have communicated, identify themes and problem areas, and form the basis for establishing session agendas.

Types of summary

The following are different types of summary, albeit interrelated.

BASIC REFLECTIVE SUMMARY These can take place at any stage of helping. They are short summaries that helpers make after clients have spoken for more than a few sentences. Such summaries pull together the main feelings and content of what clients say. Basic reflective summaries serve a bridging function for clients, enabling them to continue with the same topic or move on to another. Other functions include making sure helpers listen actively, rewarding clients for talking, showing understanding, checking your own understanding and possibly clarifying clients' understanding. Sometimes summaries highlight each of feelings, thoughts and actions.

Helper: You feel very unhappy with your boss. You think he does not appreciate you and manipulates people all the time to get his way. Your relationship has got to the point where you only speak to each other when absolutely necessary.

REFLECTING FEELINGS AND REASONS SUMMARY Clients may convey one or more central feelings. At the same time they may either directly or indirectly suggest reasons for their feelings. Clients do not always speak in tidy and logically sequenced sentences. You may be faced with making order out of client statements varying in length and coherence. A reflecting feelings and reasons summary can usefully link emotions with their perceived sources.

> *Helper:* You feel tense and anxious all the time because you have your divorce coming up in three weeks' time and there is still considerable acrimony between you and Nick in many areas: child custody, division of property and even who gets the dog.

CLARIFICATION SUMMARY In clarification summaries, helpers seek to ensure that they understand clients' internal viewpoints correctly. These summaries are stated tentatively and allow clients to correct or add to what helpers say.

> *Helper:* Can I run what you have been telling me back to check that I understand you correctly? You have a drinking problem, but much of the time find this hard to admit. Your wife has told you that if you keep up your present level of drinking she will leave you. You feel guilty about sometimes coming home drunk and abusing her. You find her both emotionally and sexually unresponsive. You're unsure of whether you want to stay in the marriage. Is that about right?

THEME SUMMARY Theme summaries are reflections in which helpers fit together pieces of what clients communicate to identify themes. You may note recurring patterns of thoughts, feelings and behaviours: for instance fear of intimacy, preoccupation with homosexuality, avoidance of decisions, or need for approval. A theme summary puts together the different pieces of information that constitute a theme.

> *Helper:* As you've been talking I've noticed a number of occasions where you have emphasized how important it is to you that others like you. At times it comes over so strongly that it is almost as though your psychological survival depends on it. You've mentioned how vital it is for you to be popular with the other girls at school, how upset you were when you thought your history teacher was not interested

in you, and how you always make a big effort to please your parents and be nice to their friends.

IDENTIFICATION OF PROBLEM AREAS SUMMARY Imagine that a client comes to helping and starts describing a number of different problems. Summaries that overview or identify different problem areas mentioned can provide clients with clearer statements than they managed on their own. Furthermore, such summaries can provide a basis for asking clients to prioritize which problems are most important, or which ones they want to work on first.

> *Helper:* You started by talking about your problems with your housemate over keeping the place tidy, you then moved on to discuss your problems with your mother, whom you perceive as excessively controlling and interfering even though you have moved out of home. You then talked about your mixed feelings about whether or not to stay in your relationship with Keith. You also expressed some dissatisfaction with your nursing studies and wonder if it is the right career for you. Which of these areas would you like to focus on first?

DETAILS OF PROBLEM SUMMARY In the initial session many questions seek to 'flesh out' details of clients' problems. For instance, a client who reports difficulty sleeping may have difficulty either first going to sleep, or spend the night tossing and turning, or wake up early and not be able to get back to sleep, or a mixture of these. This pattern may happen every night or less frequently. Numerous different possibilities require checking to arrive at an accurate descriptive definition. The same holds true for most other problems: for instance marital conflict, job indecision, exam anxiety, and specific phobias, for example spiders. The following is an illustrative details of problem summary. Helpers may take notes to assist their memories; they may also collect further descriptive information later.

> *Helper:* We've now spent some time exploring your sleep problem and these seem to be some of its main characteristics. Your problems with sleep started three months ago when you moved out of home and into a flat at the time you took up your first social work position. You have difficulty getting to sleep practically every night. You like to get eight hours' sleep a night, but currently get about six hours. When you can't get to sleep your brain becomes very active. You start worrying about everything that has happened during the day. You also worry about not being on top form the next day. You just lie there

feeling uncomfortable, angry with yourself and somewhat depressed until exhaustion takes over. A consequence of not sleeping properly is that you feel tired the next day. Most late afternoons when you get home you lie down for about an hour. Is there anything important that I've left out?

OTHER TYPES OF SUMMARY These include the following.

End-of-session summary. Some helpers favour end-of-session review summaries along the lines of 'Let's take a look at what we've accomplished in this interview; how does it appear to you?' (Brammer, 1985, p.75). Such summaries can include an overview of homework.

Beginning of next session summary. Helpers may summarize the previous session at the start of the next one. These summaries provide continuity. However, helpers need to be careful to allow space for clients to mention current as well as previous concerns.

Problems redefined in skills terms summary. As shown in the next chapter, redefining problems in terms of the thinking and action skills weaknesses sustaining them entails clearly and concisely summarizing diverse information.

Educational content summary. Even in initial sessions, helpers may start teaching skills. Summaries consolidate the main points. Furthermore, helpers may request clients to summarize and, if necessary, correct their misunderstandings.

FOCUSING SKILLS

Ivey states: 'Focusing is a skill that enables you to direct the client's conversational flow into areas you want' (1988, p.203). Helpers need to be conscious of when, why and how they choose to influence or direct the helping process. Focused responding, focusing clients on themselves and initiating focused exploration are three important focusing skills.

Focused responding

Client statements often have many parts to them. Consequently, you can choose where to focus. Ivey, in particular, has drawn attention to this skill (Ivey, 1988; Ivey *et al.*, 1987).
   Take the following statement by Cheryl.

I've just had the most terrible row with my mother-in-law. I can't seem to control my temper. Okay, there are many problems between me and the kids, but why does she have to interfere? Right now I feel as though I could kill her.

The above statement provides a challenge even for helpers trying to reflect all of it accurately. Depending upon what you wish to achieve in your interviewing, you may choose a focus from many options:

1. *Focus on the feeling.* 'You feel like murdering your mother-in-law.'

2. *Focus on the feeling and the thinking behind it.* 'You feel like murdering your mother-in-law because . . .'

3. *Focus on one or more of the problems.* For instance, focus on controlling anger, coping with interference, and/or dealing better with the kids. You may also choose to focus on problematic skills.

4. *Focus on the other person or persons.* For instance, focus on mother-in-law or the kids.

5. *Focus on the helper.* The helper might share a reaction to Cheryl's statement: for instance 'What do you want from me?'

6. *Focus on the environmental context.* There may be broader social, cultural, racial, sex-role and economic issues that might provide an insight into the problem (Ivey, 1988).

You need to approach focused responding with caution. You may block clients from exploring and experiencing material that is important for them rather than for you. You may also get in the way of clients doing their own work. For instance, an excessive focus on Cheryl's mother-in-law's behaviour might block Cheryl from looking at her own behaviour. However, Cheryl might better examine her own behaviour if assisted to focus on her mother-in-law's perspective. A further danger is that helpers focus on areas of special interest to them: for example paying excessive attention to sexual material. A reverse problem is that helpers may not focus sufficiently on some topic areas.

Focusing clients on themselves

Frequently clients require help in speaking for themselves. By failing to send 'I' messages, clients may distance themselves from their feelings, thoughts and actions (Gordon, 1970). 'I' messages involve the use of the first person singular. Ways in which clients avoid speaking for themselves include making statements starting with words like 'You', 'People', 'We', and 'It'. Sometimes clients avoid sending 'I' messages by asking questions in the hope that they can agree with the answer.

Here are examples of non-'I' messages transposed into 'I' messages.

*   *Owning a feeling*
    Client's non-'I' message   'He is impossible when he behaves like that.'
    Client's 'I' message   'I feel hurt and frustrated by his behaviour'.

- *Owning a thought*
  Client's non-'I' message   'What do you think about women serving in the forces in combat roles?'
  Client's 'I' message   'I think women should/should not serve in the forces in combat roles.'
- *Owning an action*
  Client's non-'I' message   'The car crashed into the garage door.'
  Client's 'I' message   'I crashed the car into the garage door.'

Helpers need to develop skills in assisting clients to focus on and speak for themselves. The following are three ways to encourage your clients to send 'I' messages.

- *Respond as though clients send 'I' messages.* You can respond to clients in ways that use the word 'You' as though they had sent an 'I' message, even when they have not. For instance, to a client who says 'He is impossible when he behaves like that', you might respond 'You feel hurt and frustrated by his behaviour'. Your response implicitly encourages the client to express feelings directly.

- *Request the use of the first person singular.* If clients repeatedly fail to send 'I' messages, you might consider openly drawing this to their attention. However, you have to judge whether this intervention does not threaten clients prematurely. You may then have the further decision of how to handle clients' behaviour if they revert to their old ways.

- *Model sending 'I' messages.* If you are open in your own behaviour and use 'I' messages to own your feelings, thoughts and behaviour, your example may help clients to do likewise.

Initiating focused exploration

One way to establish focus is to ask clients to prioritize areas for exploration. However, helpers may also wish to initiate explorations of specific areas, and may also wish to focus further when exploring specific areas. For example, when attempting to clarify John's stress difficulties, the helper may initiate focused exploration of related areas such as John's recreational activities and attention to keeping fit. Within the area of recreational activities, the helper may explore why John no longer participates in a specific activity, say cycling, that previously he enjoyed. Helpers use their focusing skills to collect information on parts of problems not mentioned by clients. Helpers also need to realize when they reach diminishing returns and then shift the focus to another topic.

CONFRONTING SKILLS

The word confrontation may conjure up images of clients sitting in hot seats while helpers psychologically attack them and strip them of their defences. I do not advocate such hot seat confrontation. I use confrontations to expand clients' awareness of thoughts, feelings and actions. Confrontations may stimulate clients to provide additional information about problems and problematic skills.

Challenging is an alternative word for confronting. The skill dealt with here is that of challenging clients' existing perceptions so that together you can work with more and better information. Sometimes a challenge or confrontation from the helper's external viewpoint can broaden and deepen clients' perceptions. Egan observes: 'if challenge is successful, clients are helped to replace blind spots with new perspectives' (1990, p.186). Helpers can use confronting skills to challenge inconsistencies, possible distortions of reality, and inadequately acknowledging choice.

Confronting inconsistencies

You may experience inconsistencies in messages your clients send, including the following:

- *Inconsistency between verbal, voice and body messages.* 'On the one hand you say that you are nervous, but you smile.'

- *Inconsistency within verbal messages.* 'You say you are doing poorly, but report being in the top 10 per cent of your class.'

- *Inconsistency between words and actions.* 'You say you love your children from your former marriage, but you are behind on your maintenance payments.'

- *Inconsistency between past and present statements.* 'You now say you hate her, but about ten minutes ago you were saying how much you loved her.'

How you confront involves verbal, voice and body messages. A common helper response when confronting inconsistencies is: 'On the one hand you say __, but on the other hand __' – for example: 'On the one hand you say you are fine, but on the other hand I catch a note of pain in your voice.' This way of confronting is often shortened to 'You say __, but __' – for example: 'You say that you are fine, but I catch a note of pain in your voice.'

Confronting possible distortions of reality

When clients talk to helpers they may make statements like the following.

'They are all out to get me.'
'I have no friends.'
'I'm a terrible mother.'
'I'm no good with women (or men).'
'She (or he) doesn't love me any more.'

All of these may be examples of unrealistic perceptions that harm rather than help clients. Clients' perceptions are of varying degrees of accuracy. Sometimes helpers need to challenge perceptions directly, or to assist clients to test their own reality (Beck, 1976, 1988; Beck & Weishaar, 1989). Clients often jump to conclusions on insufficient evidence ('I have no friends'), and use polarized thinking ('Either I'm perfect or no good at all'). They may also fail to own responsibility for their thoughts, feelings and actions ('They made me do it'). You need to judge whether to continue listening within their internal viewpoints or to confront possible distortions of reality.

A good form for confronting possible distortions of reality is 'You say __, but where's the evidence?' An example is: 'You say that you have no friends, but where's the evidence?' Such a response reflects the client's internal viewpoint and then invites him or her to produce evidence to support it. The client may then make a remark like, 'Well, Roberta never calls me any more.' Then the helper may confront the client again with a question like, 'Is there any other way of looking at that?' With the questions, 'Where's the evidence?' and 'Is there any other way of looking at that?' you invite speakers to produce their own evidence or provide different perceptions to confirm or negate their version of reality. On other occasions you may suggest some evidence from your external viewpoint.

Confronting not acknowledging choice

Lifeskills helping heavily emphasizes personal responsibility. You can confront clients with their role as choosers in their lives. One way to do this is to highlight their choice processes. For example, clients who say, 'I must send my children to private schools' might be confronted with the fact that they have some choice in the matter. Another example is that of Serena, aged 37, who says of her father, 'I resent having to visit him every weekend.' Here the helper responds by both reflecting her resentment and confronting her seeming failure to assume responsibility for being a chooser: 'You feel resentful, but I wonder whether you sufficiently acknowledge that you *choose* to visit him every weekend.' Such a confrontation might open the way to exploring both how Serena thinks, for instance not always acknowledging that she has choices, and how she acts, possibly not asserting herself enough with her father. Yet another way of confronting clients with their choices is to focus on the verbs that they use. For example, if a client says 'I *can't* do that', the helper may ask 'Can you say "I *won't* do that"?'

Confronting by reframing

Helpers may also challenge clients' existing perceptions by offering new perspectives. Geldard observes: 'Sometimes a skillful counsellor can change the way a client perceives events or situations by "reframing" the picture which the client has described' (1989, p.58). Though the facts may remain the same, the picture may look different in a new frame. Beck observes of relationships going downhill that partners begin to see each other through negative frames: for instance, 'He's mean and manipulative' or 'She's irresponsible'. He states: 'Reframing consists of seeing these negative qualities in a different light' (Beck, 1988, p.267).

Below is an example of a helper confronting a client with a reframe.

Tim, 16, perceived his mother as disliking him
because she was always nagging him about doing

> household chores. The helper acknowledged his
> anger, but offered the reframe that his mother was a
> single parent who had to go to work to support the
> family and got very tired because she had more on
> her plate than she could handle. When she felt
> exhausted, she became irritable.

In this example 'the nagging mother who dislikes me' gets reframed as 'the over-tired and overwhelmed single parent'. Reframing is integral to the lifeskills helping model. Most clients do not perceive their thinking and behaviour in skills terms. Stage 2 of the model in which problems are redefined in skills terms reframes the pictures provided by clients' problems by stating them in skills rather than in descriptive language.

How to confront

The following are some guidelines on how to confront.

1. *Start with reflective responding.* Always start your response by showing that you have heard and understood clients' messages. Then build on this understanding with your confronting response. This way you are more likely to keep clients' ears open to your viewpoint.

2. *Where possible, help clients to confront themselves.* By reflecting inconsistency, you allow clients to choose their own conclusions about it. Similarly, by asking clients to search for evidence to back up their statements, you help them to confront themselves. Assisting clients in self-confrontation often leads to less resistance than directly confronting them from your external viewpoint.

3. *Do not talk down.* Keep your confrontations at a democratic level. They are invitations for exploration. Avoid 'You' messages. A major risk in confronting clients is that they perceive what you say as put-downs.

4. *Use a minimum amount of 'muscle'.* Only confront as strongly as your goal requires. Strong confrontations can create resistances. Although sometimes necessary, such confrontations are generally best avoided – especially in initial sessions where trust is not yet established.

5. *Avoid threatening voice and body messages.* Try to avoid threatening voice and body messages like raising your voice and pointing your finger.

6. *Leave the ultimate responsibility with clients.* Allow clients to decide whether your confrontations actually help them to move forward in their explorations. Many of your confrontations will involve slight challenges. If well timed and tactfully worded, such challenges are unlikely to elicit a high degree of defensiveness.

7. *Do not overdo it*. Nobody likes being persistently challenged. With constant confrontations you create an unsafe emotional climate. You can help clients move forward with skilled confronting responses, but you can block them and harm your relationship if you confront too often and too clumsily.

SELF-DISCLOSING SKILLS

Helper self-disclosure relates to the ways in which you let yourself be known to clients. Usually the term refers to intentional verbal disclosure. However, there are numerous other ways in which helpers send messages including voice and body messages, availability, office décor, written communications, and size of fees! Though the following discussion mainly focuses on intentional verbal disclosure in initial sessions, it has much relevance to later sessions.

A useful distinction exists between self-involving responses and self-disclosing responses. McCarthy observes: 'Self-disclosure responses are statements referring to the past history or personal experiences of the counselor, and self-involving responses are direct present expressions of a counselor's feelings about or reactions to client statements and/or behaviors' (1982, p.125). Another way of stating this is that there are at least two major dimensions of helper self-disclosure: showing involvement and disclosing personal information.

Showing involvement

Appropriate helper disclosures that show involvement assist in forming a working alliance. In particular, self-involving statements expressing positive rather than negative feelings about clients draw favourable reactions (Watkins, 1990). Self-involving disclosures can personalize the helping process so that clients feel they relate to real people. Even negative reactions can be used constructively as invitations for exploration. There is a 'here and now' quality about reacting to clients. The following are three areas for self-involving statements:

- *Responding to specific disclosures*. Such comments include 'I'm delighted', 'That's great', and 'That's terrible'.

- *Responding to clients as people*. Illustrative positive comments are: 'I admire your courage', 'I appreciate your honesty', and 'I like your sense of humour'.

- *Responding to the helping relationship*. Illustrative comments are: 'I'm uneasy because I sense that you want to put me on a pedestal', 'I find my attention wavering and wonder why', 'I'm pleased at your willingness to cooperate and work hard'.

Disclosing personal information

Research has yet to offer any definite conclusions on helpers' sharing personal information (Watkins, 1990). Disclosing personal information and experiences may help clients feel that you understand what they go through. For instance, unemployed clients may not only feel more positively about helpers who share past unemployment experiences, but may also talk more readily. In some types of helping, disclosure of shared experiences forms part of the helping process: for instance, disclosure of experiences by ex-alcoholics and ex-addicts in Alcoholics Anonymous and in certain drug treatment programmes.

Helpers have many choices in disclosing personal information. First, whether to mention it or not. Second, how honest to be. Third, whether to go beyond disclosing facts to disclosing feelings: for instance, not only being unemployed but also having to struggle against depression and feelings of uselessness. Fourth, how you coped with your experience. Fifth, how you feel about it now.

Below are some tentative guidelines for appropriate disclosure of personal information and experiences.

- *Be self-referent.* Do not disclose other people's experiences.

- *Be to the point.* Do not slow down or defocus the interview through irrelevance or talking too much.

- *Use good voice and body messages.* Be congruent. Your voice and body messages should match what you say.

- *Be sensitive to clients.* Have sufficient sensitivity to realize when your disclosures may help clients and when they may be unwelcome or a burden. For instance, if you are currently heavily emotionally involved in getting divorced, you must judge whether you have sufficient detachment to disclose the experience constructively. Also be sensitive to how clients receive your disclosures and decide whether to continue accordingly.

- *Be sensitive to helper–client differences.* Expectations for helpers differ across cultures, social class, race and gender and so do expectations regarding appropriateness of helper self-disclosure.

- *Do not do it too often.* Helpers who keep talking about themselves risk switching the focus of their work from their clients to themselves.

- *Beware of countertransference.* Countertransference refers to negative and positive feelings towards clients based on unresolved areas in helpers' lives. Intentionally or unintentionally, some helpers may use both involving and information self-disclosures to manipulate clients to meet needs for approval, intimacy and sex. This highlights the importance both of awareness of your motivation and also of behaving ethically.

UNDERSTANDING CONTEXT SKILLS
Viewing problems in context

Helpers require skills in eliciting information about and understanding the contexts of problems. Problems and problematic skills do not exist in a vacuum; they exist in networks of contextual variables whose relevance differs in each instance. Below are just some of the possible contexts pertinent to clarifying and understanding clients' problems (see Figure 5.3). These contexts ar also relevant to negotiating areas of difference between helpers and clients.

CULTURAL CONTEXT The values and communication patterns of clients' cultures. Exposure of clients to mainstream cultures and wishes for assimilation. Issues of culture shock, alienation, mistrust and loneliness. Cultural issues can be relevant to native-born, immigrant and overseas visitor clients.

RACIAL CONTEXT The extent of clients' racial identity and pride. Exposure to racial discrimination, and skills in handling it. Values, communication patterns and family structures that differ from the culture of the racial majority.

SOCIAL CLASS CONTEXT Rules for behaviour differ widely between social classes. Helpers need to understand many client behaviours – for instance, manners, dress and language – in the context of the clients' social classes.

FAMILY OF ORIGIN CONTEXT Here family of origin refers to parents and step-parents. The family of origin context may be direct or indirect. Take the example of Julian and Nancy, a couple in their twenties who have an unhappy marriage. Up to four natural parents, and possibly some step-parents too, may directly tell them how to behave. They may also receive advice from relatives. In addition, families of origin indirectly influence Julian and Nancy's relationship through parental 'voices in the head', many of which go unrecognized. In multicultural societies, such as America and Britain, cultural and family of origin contexts intermingle: at the extreme, all four of a couple's natural parents might be culturally different.

WORK/STUDY CONTEXT The work/study context can be relevant both to work-related problems and to non-work problems. For instance, workers whose companies are being rationalized after take-overs may experience additional work stress. This stress may manifest itself in increased irritability at home, creating problems there too.

HEALTH/MEDICAL CONTEXT Clients' states of physical health can in varying degrees contribute to psychological problems; for example glandular problems causing apathy. Furthermore, clients may behave differently when on medication. Helpers often need to explore the past and current medical contexts of clients' problems; opinions from medical practitioners are often essential. A related area meriting exploration is that of clients' prior experiences of seeking and receiving psychiatric and psychological help.

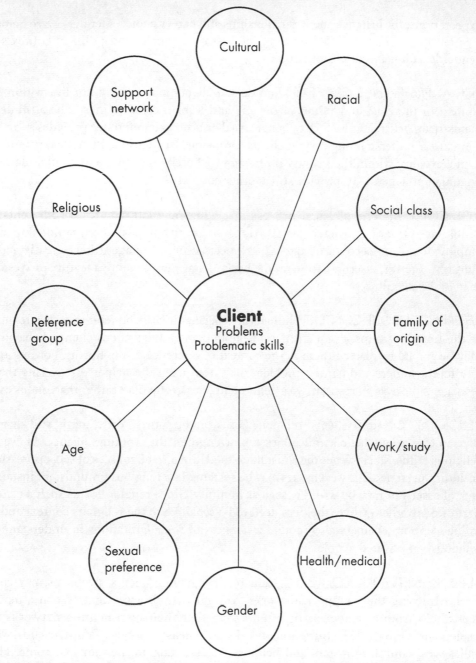

Figure 5.3 *Some relevant contexts for identifying and clarifying clients' problems and problematic skills*

GENDER CONTEXT Feminist helpers and gender-aware helpers (Good *et al.*, 1990) consider that most, if not all, problems need to be understood within gender perspectives. Helpers require sensitivity to differences in biological functioning and experiencing, for instance with regard to menstruation and the menopause. However, the main area of gender sensitivity relates to learned sex-role behaviour and expectations, for instance about relationships and career choice. Gender-aware helpers frequently emphasize understanding the historical, social and political contexts of gender learning and discrimination.

SEXUAL PREFERENCE CONTEXT Homosexual clients may or may not live within the context of the rules and values of the gay and lesbian communities. The attitude of mainstream or straight culture to homosexual or bisexual preference provides a further context for understanding certain clients' problems. In addition, changing attitudes to homosexuality within the helping professions, whereby the stigma of mental illness is no longer attached to it, provide still another context.

AGE CONTEXT The physical process of ageing may contribute to some clients' problems. Others may face deprivations – for instance in companionship and employment – on account of age. The respect accorded to age differs greatly across cultures. Ageism, discrimination on the basis of age, may be more a feature of Western than of Asian cultures.

REFERENCE GROUP CONTEXT Humans are social animals who tend to associate much of the time in groups. Frequently, valuable understandings about clients' behaviours may be gained by placing them in the context of reference group norms. For example, a different understanding of a problem may stem from the helper discovering that a teenager stole a car in response to a delinquent peer group dare rather than on his own.

RELIGIOUS CONTEXT Clients' religious faiths can be sources of strength, and sharing the same religious beliefs and ethics can strengthen the working alliance. However, religious faiths, albeit sometimes misunderstood, can also be sources of self-oppression. In addition, some skills weaknesses may be sustained on religious grounds: for instance, lack of assertion may be wrongly seen as humility. Since religion forms such a central part of many clients' lives, helpers need to be sensitive to the religious context and its influence. Some helpers also require awareness of their limitations in understanding religiously motivated people.

SUPPORT NETWORK CONTEXT A valuable insight into clients' problems may come from exploring their support networks. Murgatroyd observes that 'When a person seeks help from a stranger it is often a sign that their own helping networks are inadequate' (1985, p.151). Support networks can consist of spouse, family, friends, work colleagues, church ministers and helping professionals, to mention but some. How isolated are clients? Who is available to offer support and how useful is or might their support be? What are the clients' skills of accessing and using a support network?

Possess understanding context skills

Clients vary in the number of contextual considerations relevant to identifying and clarifying their problems. Helpers also vary in the range of clients they see. Most helpers require a range of understanding context skills, some of which are presented below.

POSSESS CONTEXTUAL KNOWLEDGE If helpers work with specific groups, for instance immigrants from a certain country, or gay and lesbian clients, they should be familiar with the assumptions, values and shared experiences of these groups. If not in possession of such knowledge, they should seek it out. Even those with a good understanding of specific cultures and minority groups always need to update their knowledge. For example, helpers working with homosexual groups need up-to-date information about legislation concerning homosexual behaviour and about the transmission and treatment of AIDS.

DEMONSTRATE CONTEXTUAL EMPATHY Helpers can show contextual empathy with their voice, body, verbal and action messages. Take demonstrating cultural empathy as an example. British people tend to speak more softly than North Americans. Japanese do not use eye contact so much as people from Western cultures (Pease, 1981). In the Arctic, 'it may be best to sit side by side rather than opposing with a forward trunk lean' (Ivey, 1987, p.169). Helpers dealing with people from different cultures need to take into account the different ways that their voice and body messages will be perceived, and also accurately perceive clients' voice and body messages. They should not assume that good intentions lead to good cross-cultural results. Furthermore, in responding to verbal messages, helpers must be sensitive to topics that may have particular meaning to people from different cultures. For instance, a desire for harmonious family relationships contains a much stronger cultural message when expressed by Asians than Anglo-Saxons. Sometimes high levels of empathy can only be offered by people who speak clients' primary language.

GIVE PERMISSION TO DISCUSS HELPER–CLIENT DIFFERENCES Helpers and clients come from different contexts. Helpers may quickly become aware that they differ on significant characteristics from clients. One possibility is to acknowledge the difference – for instance racial or cultural – and ask what clients think and feel about this. A possible advantage of being direct is that it provides clients with opportunities to air and work through mistrust. A risk is that such questions may reflect helpers' concerns more than clients' and, hence, may defocus clients.

GIVE PERMISSION TO DISCUSS PROBLEMS IN TERMS OF THEIR BROADER CONTEXTS Often a high degree of helper–client matching on significant contextual characteristics is not possible. Nevertheless, helpers can show sensitivity to contextual issues in clients' problems. One way to do this is to acknowledge a possible deficiency in understanding the context of clients' problems and ask them to fill in gaps (Poon *et al.*, 1991). The following is a simplified illustration.

> *Asian student:* My father wants me to go into the family building business and I feel under a lot of pressure to continue on my building course to please him.
> *Helper:* It sounds as though you have mixed feelings. You have reservations about continuing your building

course, yet don't want to go against your father's wishes. Cultural considerations are often important in understanding such problems and if you feel they are relevant to your case, please feel free to share them.

FOCUS QUESTIONS ON BROADER CONTEXTS As part of their attempts to elicit relevant information, helpers may use questions focusing on broader contexts of clients' problems. Depending on what seems potentially relevant, helpers may ask questions focused on one or more of the contexts depicted in Figure 5.3.

MANAGING INITIAL RESISTANCES SKILLS
What are resistances?

Resistance may be broadly defined as anything that gets in the way of helping. Clients can bring resistances to helping and also have them activated during it. Resistances can be present at any stage of the helping process. At best most clients are ambivalent when they come to helping. At the same time as wanting change, they may have anxieties both about changing and also about the helping process, for instance the need to disclose weaknesses. Some clients may come reluctantly, for example 'problem' children sent to school counsellors for disrupting class.

Sullivan (1954) observed that there were cultural handicaps to the work of the psychiatrist. These 'antipsychiatric' elements in the culture can also lead to resistances in non-medical helping. Such culturally handicapping norms include the following: people ought not to need help; people should know themselves; and people 'should have "good natural instincts" and "good intuition" which ought to govern them in choosing the "right" way to act and think' (Sullivan, 1954, p.37). Other cultural thinking errors contributing to resistances are that people who need helping are 'sick' and that you should be able to solve all problems by 'common sense'.

Helpers may wrongly attribute the sources of clients' resistances by being too quick to blame them for lack of cooperation and progress. Clients' resistances may be the consequence of poor helping skills, for instance unrewarding listening. Furthermore, some helping models, especially if incompetently applied, may engender resistances: for instance the lack of structure of the person-centred approach or the didactic nature of the rational-emotive approach. Helpers may also bring resistances to their work: for example fatigue, burnout and prejudices. Yalom mentions his difficulty, when faced with a huge female client, in overcoming his resistance to fat ladies (Yalom, 1989). Helper resistances may also interact with client resistances to slow down or stop progress.

Dealing with initial resistances

The following are skills for dealing with initial resistances. Since there are so many variations and reasons for resistances, it is impossible to cover all contingencies.

USE REWARDING LISTENING SKILLS Beginning and even more experienced helpers may both sustain and create clients' resistances through poor skills. Resistances are a normal part of initial sessions. If you listen rewardingly, you do much to build trust for lowering resistances. Some clients' resistances manifest themselves in aggression. Rather than justify yourself or allow yourself to be drawn into a competitive contest, one approach to handling such aggression is to reflect it back, locating the feelings clearly in the client but indicating that you have picked it up loud and clear. Where clients provide reasons for their hostility, you can reflect these too. Just showing clients that you understand their internal viewpoint, especially if done consistently, may diminish resistances.

JOIN WITH CLIENTS Sometimes helpers can lower clients' resistances by helping them feel that they have a friend at court. For instance, helpers can initially listen and offer support to children expressing resentment about parents.

> *Client:* I think coming here is a waste of time. My
> parents keep picking on me and they are the ones
> who need help.
> *Helper:* You feel angry about coming here because
> your parents are the people with problems.

In this instance you could focus on parental deficiencies prior to focusing back on the client. You use your client's need to talk about parental injustices as a means of building a working relationship.

Another example is that of a pupil referred to the school counsellor by the principal. Here the helper responds more to voice and body than to verbal messages.

> *Pupil:* [Looks down and sighs]
> *Counsellor:* I sense that you are uncomfortable about
> being here [Pause. If no response] Would you care
> to tell me your side of the story?

GIVE PERMISSION TO DISCUSS RELUCTANCE AND FEARS If you receive overt or subtle messages from clients that they have reservations about being in helping, you can bring the agenda out into the open and give clients permission to elaborate. In the following example, a parole officer responds to a juvenile delinquent's seeming reluctance to disclose anything significant.

> *Parole officer:* I detect an unwillingness to talk much
> to me because I'm your parole officer. I'm wondering
> what specifically are your reservations?

In the previous section, mention was made of giving permission to discuss differences in helper–client characteristics, for instance culture and race, that may create reluctance to participate in helping.

INVITE COLLABORATION The collaborative nature of the working relationship in the lifeskills helping approach both prevents and also overcomes many client resistances.

Helper initial structuring aims to create the idea of a partnership, a shared endeavour in which clients and helpers perform the detective work of finding out how clients can better attain goals.

ENLIST CLIENT SELF-INTEREST Help clients identify reasons for participating in the helping process. For instance, Simon, a client who perceives his parents as picking on him and having problems, could be helped to see that he might be happier with better 'coping with parents' skills. Questions that challenge clients with the adequacy of their own behaviour may also enlist self-interest. Such questions include, 'Where is your current behaviour getting you?' and 'How is that behaviour helping you?' Questions that encourage clients to think about goals are also useful. For example, 'What are your goals in the situation?' and 'Wouldn't you like to be more in control of your life?'

REWARD SILENT CLIENTS FOR TALKING Some clients find it difficult to talk, whether in or out of helping. Others may find it particularly difficult to talk to helpers. Without being overpowering, helpers may have to respond more frequently and more obviously. For example, helpers may use more small rewards when clients talk; they may also encourage clients by reflectively responding to most statements. Helpers may also reflectively respond to the difficulty certain clients have in talking, even though they may not have said this.

The above are just some ways of working with resistances and reluctance. Helpers need to be sensitive to the pace at which different clients work. Clients who feel pressured by helpers may become even more resistant. Furthermore, if attacked prematurely and clumsily, clients may reinforce their defences. When dealing with client resistances helpers require sensitivity, realism, flexibility and tact.

THINKING SKILLS

I deal briefly here with the important topic of helper thinking skills for stage 1. This is because I discuss assessing clients' thinking skills in the next chapter and interventions focused on clients' thinking in Chapter 10. All of this material is relevant to how helpers think too. The following are areas of helper thinking skills relevant to stage 1 of the lifeskills model and, frequently, to later stages as well.

Own responsibility for choosing

Helpers always need to be conscious that they are choosers (Nelson-Jones, 1984, 1988). They make choices in regard to their verbal, voice, body, touch and action messages. They choose how they think and how they feel. Throughout helping they continually make decisions about how to respond to clients' communications. In initial sessions there is a heavy emphasis on choosing how best to identify, clarify and break down problems. Helpers should own responsibility not only for choosing, but also for the consequences of choices. Helping choices are best viewed as hypotheses modifiable in the light of feedback.

Use self-talk

In initial sessions helpers can use self-talk in ways that create anxiety in themselves and their clients. Trish is a beginning helper. After a term-long practical skills course, she is about to see her first client and record the session for her supervisor. Trish is highly nervous and worsens matters with the following self-talk:

> Help. I've got this important interview coming up. I wonder whether I'm going to do all right. I'm scared the client will notice that I'm anxious and lacking in skills. What if the client has a problem that is out of my depth. How will I manage then? Also, my supervisor will listen and hear all my mistakes.

A more constructive way for Trish to approach her first real session would be to use coping self-talk. This consists of calming and coaching self-statements: calming statements to relax herself and coaching statements to stay focused on how best to proceed. Trish could use the following coping self-talk:

> Help. I'm feeling anxious because this is my first time with a real client. Now calm down and take a few deep breaths. I'm pretty certain I can cope with the situation. I've done a lot of practising and received good feedback. My supervisor just wants me to do as best I can and does not expect me to be perfect. I can start the interview with a good opening statement and speak calmly and clearly. Then I can use my rewarding listening skills. I do not have to control everything that happens. Already I'm starting to feel better by using my coping self-talk skills.

Helpers can also use coping self-talk during and after their sessions. For instance, they can calm themselves down and think how best to act if clients become hostile during sessions. They can talk to themselves constructively after sessions: for instance by acknowledging what went right and not overly focusing on what went wrong.

Choose realistic personal rules

Helpers can place unnecessary pressures on themselves by their unrealistic personal rules (Nelson-Jones, 1989), irrational beliefs or 'mustabations' (Ellis, 1962, 1989). Helpers can place demands on themselves: 'I *must* be perfect'; on their clients: 'My clients *must* always appreciate me'; on the helping process: 'Helping *must* always go smoothly'; and on the environment: 'Other people *must* always understand and support my helping endeavours.'

Helpers need to identify unrealistic personal rules and reformulate them into more realistic or rational rules.

Unrealistic rule: 'I must be perfect.'
Realistic rule: 'I would like to perform as competently as I can.'

Unrealistic rule: 'My clients must always appreciate me.'
Realistic rule: 'Though it is pleasant to have clients' approval, my main focus is on helping them to the best of my ability.'

Unrealistic rule: 'Helping must always go smoothly.'
Realistic rule: 'Helping is somewhat unpredictable and I can tolerate mistakes and setbacks.'

Unrealistic rule: 'Other people must always support and understand my endeavours.'
Realistic rule: 'I can try my best to explain what I do as a helper, but ultimately I can only influence other people and not control what they think.'

Choose to perceive accurately

Helpers perceive themselves, others, their clients and events with varying degrees of accuracy. It is important not to jump to conclusions when attempting to identify and clarify problems. You need to carefully sift fact from inference and, if appropriate, accumulate more information to build and test your inferences. Below are some specific perceptual errors to avoid (Beck 1976, 1988; Beck & Weishaar, 1989).

- *Tunnel vision.* Focusing on only a portion of the available information regarding a problem rather than taking into account all significant data.

- *Magnifying and minimizing.* Magnifying or exaggerating the qualities and significance of other people and events, or minimizing them.

- *Negativeness.* Overemphasizing negative aspects of clients and yourself and minimizing the positive aspects. Always searching for weaknesses rather than for strengths. Applying negative labels to yourself and others: for example, 'I'm a loser' or 'That client is impossible.'

- *Selective inattention.* Overlooking or being inattentive to material that may cause you anxiety (Sullivan, 1954). Denying and distorting information through defensive thinking.

- *Overgeneralizing.* Making sweeping generalizations unsupported by evidence: 'All my initial sessions go well'; 'My clients never stick to the point'; 'She failed in one relationship therefore she has failed in all her previous relationships.'

- *Catastrophizing.* Making highly negative predictions unsupported by evidence: 'My first session this afternoon did not go well, so all my other sessions will go badly too.'

- *Polarized thinking.* Perceiving in either/or and black-and-white terms: 'Either clients are very cooperative or very uncooperative'; 'Clients either continue having problems or are cured.'

- *Self-rating.* Going beyond functional ratings of specific characteristics to devaluing yourself as a whole person: 'I'm having difficulty learning helping skills, therefore I am a rotten person.'

- *Mind reading.* Believing you can tell what clients think, without having collected adequate evidence or checked your conclusions.

Attribute cause and responsibility accurately

Helpers may err either in the direction of attributing too much or too little cause and responsibility to themselves. Here are some helpers' statements attributing *too much* responsibility to themselves:

'I'm responsible for everything that happens in my helping sessions.'
'I'm solely responsible for the outcomes of helping.'
'Everything that goes wrong in helping is my fault.'

Below are helper statements attributing *too little* responsibility to themselves:

'Jennie is not saying much because she is a shy person.' [Jennie may be shy but the helper also has poor rewarding listening skills.]
'Boris has a lot of resistances to being helped.' [The helper may also have contributed to these resistances.]

CHAPTER HIGHLIGHTS

- Four objectives of initial helping sessions are to develop a supportive working relationship; a working model; a working definition; and working goals and interventions.

- Structuring describes the behaviours by which helpers let clients know their respective roles at various stages of the helping process.

- Structuring statements in initial sessions may be made more than once: voice and body as well as verbal messages are important.

- Questions can help identify and clarify the roots of problems.

- Helper choices when questioning include its purpose, past or present focus, amount of topics covered, degree of detail, intimacy level and timing.

- Types of questions include open-ended versus closed-ended; how, what, when, where and why; clarification; elaboration; challenging; specific detail; request for example; 'show me'; and eliciting personal meaning.

- Questioning skills for working in partnership with clients include establish agenda and transition questions; intersperse reflective responding; ask follow-on questions; and encourage clients' work.

- Summarizing skills entail making brief statements of longer excerpts from helping sessions.

- The functions of summaries include clarifying, identifying themes, identifying problem areas and feeding back details of problems.

- Focusing entails directing and influencing the helping conversation into specific areas.

- Focusing skills include focused responding to parts of clients' communications; focusing clients on themselves; and initiating focused exploration.

- Confrontations are challenges that expand clients' existing perceptions so that together you can work with new and better information.

- Helpers use confronting skills for challenging inconsistencies, possible distortions of reality and not acknowledging choice. Confronting skills include reframing problems by offering new perspectives.

- Showing involvement and disclosing personal information are two important areas of helper self-disclosure.

- Self-involving disclosures can be in response to specific disclosures, clients as people, and the helping relationship.

- Often helpers need to clarify and understand the contexts of clients' problems. Relevant contexts for problems include: cultural, racial, social class, family of origin, work/study, health/medical, gender, sexual preference, age, reference group, religious and support network.

- Understanding context skills include obtaining knowledge, demonstrating contextual empathy, permission to discuss helper–client differences, and permission to discuss problems in terms of broader contexts.

- Skills for managing initial session resistances include rewarding listening, joining, inviting collaboration, and enlisting client self-interest.

- Thinking skills for identifying and clarifying problems include owning responsibility for choosing, coping self-talk, realistic personal rules, perceiving accurately, and accurately attributing cause and responsibility.

STAGE 2

ASSESS PROBLEM(S) AND REDEFINE IN SKILLS TERMS

Chapter 6 presents helper skills for assessing clients' feelings, thoughts and actions. The chapter ends by reviewing skills for redefining clients' problems in skills terms.

Stage 1
DEVELOP the relationship, identify and clarify problem(s)

Stage 2
ASSESS problem(s) and redefine in skills terms

Stage 3
STATE working goals and plan interventions

Stage 4
INTERVENE to develop self-helping skills

Stage 5
END and consolidate self-helping skills

SIX

How to Assess Problems and Redefine in Skills Terms

We remain shackled to a scientifically outmoded conceptual framework and its terminology.

Thomas Szasz

CHAPTER QUESTIONS

What is the role of assessment in lifeskills helping?

How can helpers and clients assess feelings?

How can helpers and clients assess thinking skills?

How can helpers and clients assess action skills?

What are helper skills for redefining clients' problems in skills terms?

ROLE OF ASSESSMENT

Assessment in lifeskills helping is performed both with clients and for clients. Assessment also aims to develop clients' self-assessment skills for after helping. During stage 1 you develop working models of clients' problems and problematic skills. Clients come to helping with hypotheses, albeit inadequate, of what their problems are and how they are sustained. During the identifying and clarifying problems process, clients may start revising their models. Often the process of systematically eliciting descriptive information about clients' problems loosens their existing conceptualizations.

Stage 2 continues the loosening of clients' existing conceptualizations of problems. However, the process does not stop there. The desired outcome of stage 2 is to reconceptualize problems so that clients now have 'handles' for change; what Egan (1990) calls 'leverage'. Helpers use their skills not only to elicit basic descriptive information but also to explore the adequacy of hypotheses about problematic skills that sustain problems. Helpers work with clients to assess information, both volunteered and elicited. Together helpers and clients reform descriptive definitions of problems into skills redefinitions.

The helper's role

Helpers should always offer supportive relationships when assessing and redefining clients' problems in skills terms. Rewarding listening skills are fundamental. Furthermore, many skills used for identifying and clarifying problems – for instance focusing and summarizing – are relevant for assessing and redefining problems. In stage 2, you move beyond offering accurate *responsive* empathy based on understanding clients' internal viewpoints to offering accurate *active* empathy in which you expand clients' internal viewpoints to provide a fuller understanding of problems and problematic skills.

Helpers are practitioner-researchers who formulate hypotheses about how clients sustain problems. Sources of such hypotheses are descriptive information provided by clients, information elicited as helpers 'try on' initial hypotheses, helping theory, knowledge of relevant research, and previous experience of clients. Where possible you attempt to work openly with clients. You treat clients as intelligent people who, despite defences and anxieties, wish to help themselves through greater self-understanding. You assist clients to do much of their own assessing rather than do all of it for them. You never lose sight of the fact that helping is temporary. Especially where client contact extends over a number of sessions, helpers teach clients how to redefine problems in skills terms.

Can assessment be overdone? The answer is a resounding 'yes'. You need to be sensitive to the amount of information required for assessing problems. Furthermore, you need to take into account clients' perceptions of when 'enough is enough'. Though an ideal, you should collect information and redefine problems in skills terms as parsimoniously as possible.

The client's role

Like helpers clients are also hypothesis makers and testers. To date, their hypotheses about how to solve their problems are inadequate. Frequently, they are stuck in faulty definitions of problems. Clients can actively collaborate with helpers to generate hypotheses, provide information for assessing hypotheses, and evaluate conceptualizations of problems. They can participate in various attempts to assess their feelings, thoughts and actions. For example, they can strive for honesty in experiencing and expressing feelings. They can be open about how they think, even if in socially undesirable ways. They can assist in exploring and evaluating hypotheses about how they think. In addition, they can share specific details of how they have acted in the past, monitor their current actions, and participate in role plays.

Assessment is for clients' even more than for helpers' benefits. Clients can engage in testing the adequacy of original conceptions of problems and make corrections. They can provide confirmatory, corrective or negative feedback about helpers' hypotheses. Clients can cooperate with helpers to develop more accurate and parsimonious skills redefinitions of problems. Often, if active in assessing and redefining problems, clients acquire good motivation for change. Active participation in assessing and redefining problems fosters acquisition of these skills for later self-helping.

ASSESS FEELINGS
Why assess feelings?

The following examples are of clients who make feelings statements:

'I get panic attacks.'
'I have suicidal thoughts.'
'I have high blood pressure.'
'I can't control my temper.'
'I never know what I want.'
'I lack energy.'
'I'm sexually unresponsive.'

Helpers assess feelings for numerous reasons, some of which are mentioned below.

PROTECT CLIENTS Helpers have an ethical duty to protect clients. At the back of most helpers' minds when meeting new clients is the question: 'Is this client a suicide risk?' Helpers also seek to understand the intensity and nature of clients' pain. Such understanding is needed partly to protect clients, but also to make appropriate skills definitions of problems.

EVALUATE EMOTIONAL RESPONSIVENESS Helpers always need to be mindful of clients' ability to experience feelings. Feelings may be viewed as the core of human identity. Helpers seek to assess how responsive clients are both to themselves and to others. To what extent are clients in touch with their valuing process? Are clients in touch with significant feelings or do they deny and distort such feelings? To what extent are clients in touch with wants and wishes?

CLARIFY REAL AGENDAS Paying close attention to feelings may assist helpers to clarify clients' real agendas. Sometimes clients give feelings clues that more substantial problems underlie their 'calling card' explanations for coming. For example, by voice and body messages a woman who presents wanting to discuss a 'problem' child may indicate that her real agenda is marital dissatisfaction. Sometimes helpers also need to allow clients space to clarify feelings prior to knowing which problem to work on in skills terms.

Dave, 50, had been divorced for five years and had custody of three children Jan, 15; Beth, 17; and

Marty, 13. For the last year, Dave had been seeing Maria, 45, a divorcée who also had three children with ages ranging from 6 to 17. Dave came to helping confused about whether or not he wanted to develop his relationship with Maria further or get out of it. Dave's helper, Mel, spent much of the initial session assisting Dave to get in touch with and explore his feelings concerning his past, present and possible future with Maria; his fears of commitment after the pain of his divorce; his anxieties about how good he was at communicating in close relation-ships; his needs for companionship; and his fears of being lonely for the remainder of his life. As the session progressed Dave became clearer regarding his wish to work on his skills at relating to Maria.

OBTAIN LEADS ABOUT THINKING AND ACTION SKILLS WEAKNESSES Another reason for assessing feelings is to assist clients in regulating unwanted feelings and in expressing appropriate feelings. Since feelings reflect humans' animal nature they are not in themselves skills. Nevertheless, assessing feelings accurately can be a major route to identifying thinking and action skills weaknesses. For example, clients admitting their anger, hurt and guilt have a better starting-point for developing the thinking and action skills to manage these feelings than clients denying or distorting them. You also need to assess clients' skills at expressing feelings. For example, Liz knows what she feels about her boyfriend Rajiv, but is too inhibited to reveal it.

BE AWARE OF MEDICAL AND PSYCHIATRIC CONSIDERATIONS A simple mind–body split is erroneous, yet you should be aware that 'medical considerations' can influence how clients feel. Non-medically trained helpers should acknowledge their limitations and seek appropriate medical or psychiatric advice. Occasions where you need to take medical and psychiatric considerations into account include where clients are on medication (Burns, 1989; Ponterotto, 1985); have a physical illness, for instance cancer, that affects how they feel; show psychophysiologic symptoms, for instance peptic ulcers and migraine headaches; exhibit the effects of substance abuse; and suffer from schizophrenia, delusional disorders and mood disorders (American Psychiatric Association, 1987).

DEVELOP CLIENTS' SELF-ASSESSMENT SKILLS Helpers work together with clients to assess feelings. In their past many clients have had their feelings invalidated. Skilled assessment can both affirm the importance of awareness of feelings and help clients to experience, identify and explore significant feelings. Clients' feelings may take time to emerge and be shared with you. Revealing and assessing feelings occurs throughout helping. Also, where possible, you can assist clients to develop skills at assessing feelings for after helping.

Dimensions of feelings

In the section on reflecting feelings (Chapter 4), I discussed some ways of identifying feelings by picking up feelings words and by attending to voice and body messages. Now I review dimensions of feelings more from the viewpoint of assessing problems than making rewarding listening responses.

CAPACITY TO FEEL Helpers need to be aware of clients' abilities to experience feelings (Rogers, 1951, 1959, 1961, 1975). Some clients lack emotional responsiveness across a wide range of feelings. Other clients may have difficulty experiencing specific feelings, for example sexuality or anger. Clients' difficulties in experiencing feelings can be at different levels. An extensive and long-standing incapacity to experience feelings may have different implications for how helping might proceed than a more focused and less severe problem of experiencing feelings. One of the outcomes of any extended helping contact is that clients should become better at experiencing and expressing feelings.

ENERGY LEVEL Related to clients' ability to experience feelings is their energy level. How much mental and physical energy do they have? To what degree do they possess vitality, or seem apathetic? If clients' energy levels are very low helpers should ask them to check with their doctors whether there are medical explanations.

SELF-ESTEEM Helpers need to be aware of clients' confidence levels. Clients with very low self-esteem are potential suicide risks. Clients with reasonable self-esteem possess a useful asset for working on problems and problematic skills. Words to describe low self-esteem include worthlessness, hopelessness, helplessness (Seligman, 1975) and despair. Self-statements indicating lack of self-esteem include 'I'm no good', 'I never do anything right' and 'I can't cope'. Adjectives to describe high self-esteem include confident, strong, self-accepting, worthwhile and emotionally resilient.

ANXIETY AND DEFENSIVENESS Helpers need to assess how anxious clients are and in what areas of life anxiety occurs. Is their anxiety a pervasive trait or is it a state attached to specific situations? Helpers also need to assess how clients show anxiety, both in obvious ways and also in terms of their less obvious defensive processes or security operations (Clark, 1991; Sullivan, 1953, 1954). Pay attention to ways in which clients' anxieties – and yours too – can distort the helping process.

MOOD A mood is a state of mind or feeling. The American Psychiatric Association's *Diagnostic and Statistical Manual of Mental Disorders (DSM-III-R)* way of defining mood is, 'prolonged emotion that colors the whole psychic life; it generally involves either depression or elation' (American Psychiatric Association, 1987, p. 213). However, moods are often relatively transient: for instance a few moments, a day, or a week (McNair *et al.*, 1981). Helpers can assess severity, direction, duration and fluctuations in clients' moods.

PSYCHOLOGICAL PAIN Effective helpers are skilled at locating areas of psychological pain and assessing their severity. Sometimes, during helping, clients acknowledge major areas of psychological pain which they have hitherto either repressed or suppressed. Helpers also need to be conscious of the pain that clients may experience when discussing certain material, for instance rape or sexual abuse.

PHYSICAL REACTIONS Physical reactions both represent and accompany feelings. For example, physical reactions associated with shyness include: dry mouth, blushing, nausea, feeling faint, perspiring, knotted stomach, pounding heart, shaking, mind going blank and shallow, and rapid breathing. Sometimes clients react to their physical reactions. For example, in anxiety and panic attacks clients may experience feeling tense and anxious and then become even more tense and anxious because of this. Helpers need to develop skills in empathically describing physical reactions with appropriate words.

PSYCHOPHYSIOLOGIC DISORDERS Psychophysiologic or psychosomatic disorders are caused and maintained primarily by psychological and emotional rather than physical or organic factors. Psychophysiologic disorders can affect the skin, for instance acne, and the body's musculoskeletal, respiratory, cardiovascular, blood and lymphatic, gastrointestinal, and endocrine systems. The more common psychophysiologic disorders include peptic ulcers, migraine headaches, asthma, and high blood pressure. Psychophysiologic disorders may be distinguished from somatoform disorders, the latter being phoney or imitative rather than actual physical disorders.

PREDOMINANT FEELINGS Sometimes clients present with a specific feeling that they wish to handle better, for example anxiety in test or public speaking situations. In other instances a predominant feeling may emerge as helping processes: for instance self-pity, resentment, anger or wariness. Teyber uses the term 'characterological feeling' to describe these central feelings that clients experience as their fate because they have 'always been there and it seems like they always will be' (1989, p.84). Helpers need to keep an eye or ear out for repetitive and central feelings that clients handle with difficulty. Prior to and even during helping clients may find it hard to acknowledge such feelings.

COMPLEX AND CONFLICTED FEELINGS Clients' feelings are frequently complex. Helpers require skills at eliciting, clarifying and articulating the different elements of what may be multiple and mixed feelings. Clients may need to learn to avoid thinking about their feelings in static, rigid and simplistic terms. Feelings often come in twos and threes. For example, anger may be accompanied by hurt and guilt or depression by anxiety and sadness. Though not always with the same intensity, feelings are frequently accompanied by their opposites. Ambivalent feelings include: happy–sad, love–hate, pleased–displeased and approach–avoidance. Sometimes clients experience ambivalent feelings simultaneously, and sometimes sequentially.

ANTECEDENTS AND CONSEQUENCES OF FEELINGS When assessing feelings, helpers may assess their antecedents and consequences. The antecedents of feelings can stretch back into clients' childhoods. For example, the pain of a present loss may reactivate the pain of an earlier loss. Anger may be hard to express now because such feelings were suppressed in clients' families of origin. Frequently, helpers explore current antecedents and consequences of feelings: for example thoughts prior to experiencing feelings, and positive and negative consequences after expressing feelings.

STRENGTH AND PERSISTENCE OF FEELINGS Often feeling intensity is described by words like 'mild', 'moderate' or 'severe'. For example, clients may be mildly depressed, moderately depressed or severely depressed. There can be different perceptions of what is mild, moderate or severe both among helpers and between helpers and clients. Persistence of feelings may be described by words like chronic and acute. Chronic implies persistent; acute implies sharp and short. In addition, disorders like schizophrenia may be in partial remission or full remission (American Psychiatric Association, 1987).

APPROPRIATENESS OF FEELINGS Often helpers and clients attempt to assess appropriateness of feelings. Did the client experience an appropriate quantity of an appropriate feeling and was this appropriately expressed? Helpers and clients must take into account clients' unique styles of expressing feelings and numerous situational, contextual and cultural considerations. One way of assessing appropriateness of feelings is to assess their consequences for clients and others. To what extent and in what ways were there positive or negative emotional and behavioural consequences (Ellis, 1962, 1989)? Another way is to assess certain feelings in terms of psychiatric classification.

UNCLEAR FEELINGS Clients may be either unclear about feelings or communicate feelings unclearly, or both. Sometimes feelings are masked: for instance depression may mask anger. On other occasions feelings are displaced: anger at failing a test may be 'taken out' on a room-mate, spouse or parent. Sometimes the real agenda is unclear. For instance, married couples may argue over little things and avoid confronting more serious differences and relationship fears. Frequently, expression of feelings is inhibited or diluted. Some clients obscure feelings by going to the other extreme: they dramatize and magnify feelings. Social desirability considerations pervade the early stages of helping: clients may play out social roles to please helpers. Clients may also have acquired poor skills at using feelings words and framing their verbal feelings messages with appropriate voice and body messages. Many feelings take time to emerge. Helpers require sensitivity to the pace at which clients both can and wish to reveal their emotional selves.

FEELINGS ABOUT HELPING AND HELPERS Clients invariably have feelings both about helping and helpers. Clients may resist or cooperate in the helping process. They may feel pleased or frustrated with their progress. In addition, they may have a range of feelings about helpers, on dimensions such as like/dislike, trust/mistrust, competent/incompetent and dependent/independent. Sometimes clients express feelings that helpers find difficult to handle: for example liking, sexual attraction, anger and sadness. Often there is a reciprocity of feeling between helpers and clients: for example, mutual like or dislike.

Skills for eliciting and assessing feelings

Helpers need to realize the importance of feelings both for human functioning and for helping clients to change. Many skills for assessing feelings entail enlisting clients' cooperation in sharing feelings. Below are some skills useful for eliciting and assessing feelings.

BE A REWARDING LISTENER In supportive and trusting relationships, clients assist helpers to understand how they feel. Rewarding listening provides a safe emotional climate for clients to experience and share feelings. Helpers sensitive to clients' feelings and feeling nuances legitimize the importance of experiencing and discussing feelings. You require good skills at picking up and reflecting back feelings messages. Receiver skills include paying attention to feelings words, observing voice and body messages, and being keenly attuned to any mismatch between voice, body and verbal messages. Sometimes you can infer feelings from what is left unsaid or partially said. Sender skills that you can use to help clients share feelings include showing attention with voice and body messages, reflecting feelings, reflecting feelings and reasons and offering companionship as clients explore new and sometimes unexpected feelings.

Helpers need to be sensitive when clients encounter feelings difficult either to experience or to share. Always you require awareness of the pace at which clients wish to reveal feelings. Often a box of Kleenex helps! You can make the following remarks to encourage but not pressure clients to share feelings.

'I realize that this may be a painful area for you to discuss.'
'You seem upset. Just take your time in sharing what you feel.'

OBSERVE BODY MESSAGES AND LISTEN FOR VOICE MESSAGES Probably clients' voice and body messages provide the most valid source of information about how they feel. From the moment of first contact, skilled helpers closely watch out for body messages and listen for voice messages. Clients differ in how clearly they send messages. However, both consciously and intuitively, skilled helpers listen 'with the third ear' and observe 'with the third eye' for deviations, omissions and discrepancies in communications. They look out for feeling fragments or glimpses that are clues to more substantial and as yet unshared feelings. Skilled helpers have highly developed capacities for sensing what seems false. Their ability to tune in to their own feelings, as well as experience of numerous previous clients, provides a base for formulating feelings hypotheses.

USE ADVANCED REFLECTION OF FEELINGS As a result of observing and listening, you may sense what clients 'only half see and hint at' (Egan, 1990, p.214). Frequently clients repress, suppress or otherwise inhibit feelings. Advanced reflection of feelings entails making exploratory responses that help clients articulate more personally relevant, emotionally tinged and threatening areas of their experiencing. You require sensitivity to reflect partially hidden agendas. Sometimes you may choose not to mention such agendas for fear of upsetting clients. Advanced reflctions of feelings check out your 'hunches' or feelings hypotheses. Such responses generally require humility and tentativeness. Inaccurate, clumsily worded and badly timed responses can do more harm than good.

Example A. The helper gets the impression that the client talks around the area of lesbian feelings:

> *Helper:* You've mentioned a couple of people you know who do not find lesbian life easy. I'm wondering whether lesbianism may be an issue for you too?

Example B. The helper senses that the client is very taken with a woman he has recently met, yet keeps expressing reservations about her:

> *Helper:* You seem to be stating numerous reasons why you should be careful about starting a relationship with Brenda. However, the overriding feeling I get is that you're swept off your feet by her and can't get her out of your mind . . . nor do you want to.

Example C. The helper has a hunch that a client who recently had a blazing row with her mother earlier is or soon will feel guilty about how she behaved:

> *Helper:* On the one hand you have a sense of triumph at giving Mum a piece of your mind, but I catch an undercurrent of guilt and sorrow at how you behaved. Am I correct?

USE FOCUSING ON FEELINGS QUESTIONS Questions can assist clients in being specific about feelings and physical reactions. Frequently, since you cannot assume common meaning, you need to clarify labels clients attach to feelings. For instance, follow-up questions to a client who says 'I am very depressed' might be: 'When you say you are very depressed, what exactly do you mean?' or, 'When you say you are very depressed what are your specific feelings and physical reactions?' or, 'You feel very depressed. Tell me more about that feeling?' Then you assist the client in pinpointing feelings and physical reactions. Sometimes helpers check out feelings or physical reactions, for instance, 'Do you feel suicidal sometimes?' or 'How is your appetite?' However, most often questions elicit feelings and physical reactions rather than put them into words.

Helpers assist clients to distinguish between feelings and thoughts. If clients respond to focusing on feelings questions with how they think, you may choose to keep them focused on feelings.

> *Client:* I feel very depressed
> *Helper:* When you say you feel very depressed what exactly do you mean?

> *Client:* I'm having problems in my job and in my marriage.
> *Helper:* You're having problems at work and at home. These are thoughts or reasons why you may be very depressed. However, could you tell me more about the actual depressed feelings you experience?

Helpers may need to assist clients in expanding and elaborating their feelings (Teyber, 1989). Open-ended focusing on feelings questions can be helpful: 'Describe the feeling more fully?' Further questions that helpers may use to elicit and clarify feelings include the following.

'Tell me more about the feeling?'
'Describe how your body experiences the feeling.'
'In which part of your body do you experience the feeling?'
'Do you have any visual images that capture the feeling?'
'Are there any metaphors that illustrate the feeling?'
'How has your mood been and how is it today?'
'How confident a person are you?'
'Are there any other feelings that accompany that feeling?'
'How do you feel here and now?'

Helpers may need to ask follow-up questions that encourage clients to expand on their feelings. For example, 'You say you experience tension in your stomach. Can you describe the experience more fully?' Depending on how clients respond to such open-ended questions, helpers may then ask specific questions: for example, 'How persistent?' and 'How intense?'

USE EMOTION-ELICITING TECHNIQUES Sometimes helpers consciously attempt to induce feelings so that both they and clients can acknowledge and assess them.

Live observation. Helpers can take clients into difficult situations, observe their reactions and listen to what they say about how they feel.

Visualizing. Clients can be asked to shut their eyes and visualize how they saw and experienced the emotions attached to a particular scene.

Role play. Helpers may role-play scenes with clients, for example an argument with a parent. The helper may then process the emotions elicited by the role play.

Task assignment. Helpers and clients may agree on between-session tasks for clients. Clients are asked to monitor and record feelings before, during and after these tasks.

ENCOURAGE CLIENTS TO MONITOR FEELINGS Without setting specific tasks, helpers can encourage clients to monitor their feelings and physical reactions. Such monitoring

can raise self-awareness as well as help clients to learn a valuable skill: listening closely
to their feelings.

Daily rating forms. Clients can be asked to rate themselves daily on feelings such as
mood (very happy to very depressed), anxiety level (not anxious at all to very anxious),
feelings of stress (very relaxed to very stressed) and so on. Ratings may be on scales
ranging from 1 to 3,5,7,9 or 10. In the example below clients are asked to give
themselves a mood score for each day using the following scale.

Very happy   1   2   3   4   5   6   7   Very depressed

Specific incident logs. Clients can keep logs of how they feel in relation to specific
difficulties they experience. For example, shy clients can keep logs that record their
feelings before, during and after being in company. Below is a possible format for such
a log.

Date and time	What happened	My feelings and physical reactions

CONSIDER USING QUESTIONNAIRES Though not advocated for most clients, helpers
can use questionnaires to assess feelings. Some questionnaires focus exclusively on
assessing feelings: for example the Beck Depression Inventory (Beck, 1978; Kendall *et
al.*, 1987); the State-Trait Anxiety Inventory (Spielberger, 1983); and the Profile of
Mood States (POMS) (McNair *et al.*, 1981). POMS asks subjects how they have been
feeling during the past week including today and provides scores on six identifiable
mood states: tension–anxiety, depression–dejection, anger–hostility, vigour–activity,
fatigue–inertia, and confusion–bewilderment. Other questionnaires have sections on
feelings: for example, Lazarus's Multimodal Life History Questionnaire (Lazarus,
1981). Questionnaires may also focus on the stimuli that elicit feelings. For example.
Wolpe's Fear Inventory asks respondents to indicate how disturbed they are by each of
a range of 'things and experiences that may cause fear or other unpleasant feelings'
(Wolpe, 1973, p.283). Helpers may also devise their own questionnaires focused on
feelings.

BE SENSITIVE TO CULTURAL DIFFERENCES Cultures differ greatly in the ways in which
they express emotions. In addition, somatic symptoms associated with distress differ
across cultures. Helpers working with people from different cultures should approach
their task with 'open-mindedness to the presence of distinctive cultural patterns and
sensitivity to the possibility of unintended bias because of such differences' (American
Psychiatric Association, 1987, p.xxvi). Western helpers should be particularly careful
in assessing feelings of people from non-Western cultures. In addition to cultural
considerations, helpers need to take sex-role and social class considerations into
account. You should also be aware that clients' perceptions of you as dissimilar on
cultural, racial, sex and social class variables may also influence whether and how they
reveal feelings.

BE PREPARED TO WAIT AND SEE Even with skilled helpers, clients' feelings may take time to unfold. Clients brought up to deny feelings may change slowly. You require sensitivity to the pace at which clients are comfortable with experiencing and sharing feelings. Invariably initial session assessments of feelings require updating. Sometimes such assessments require substantial modification as you get to know more about clients, and clients more about themselves.

FORM FEELING HYPOTHESES When assessing feelings, helpers form hypotheses both to guide collection of information and also to state conclusions. Feelings hypotheses are open to modification as helping progresses. Below is a case study of a company executive who sees a counsellor after being fired. Initially, this case study illustrates forming feelings hypotheses. Later I use the same case study to illustrate forming thinking skills hypotheses, forming action skills hypotheses, and redefining problems in skills terms.

Case study: Jim Blake

Part One: Introduction

Jim Blake, 45, was a Divisional Finance Controller of a large conglomerate before being fired a week ago when his division was closed down. Jim is married with two teenage children, both at private school. He was earning a salary of over £100,000 and has a substantial mortgage. Jim's wife Lyn is not in the workforce. Jim had twenty years of service with the one company and has received a six-month severance package to tide him over while he finds another job. In addition, Jim's company has arranged for him to have the services of an external outplacement counsellor, Sam Rushton. The initial counselling session is held on company premises immediately after Jim receives the news of his severance, which is effective immediately. Jim expresses shock, disbelief and anger at being fired. He is also highly anxious about his future prospects, dreads a long period of unemployment, and is worried that his family's standard of living may be drastically curtailed. Sam allows Jim to share these feelings, discusses strategies for breaking the news to his family, and makes an appointment for him to meet next day in Sam's external office.

In this second session, Jim reports that he spent a sleepless night with worry and feels very depressed. He feels in crisis and overwhelmed at his misfortune. He still feels extremely bitter at his rejection after so many years of loyal service and fantasizes gving those responsible for his firing a sharp piece of his mind. Sam accepts Jim's feelings and then assists him in identifying and clarifying the main areas of his problem. To some extent, the *financial* area is dealt with by Jim's expertise in the area. However, Jim still has catastrophic predictions of financial disaster and inability to cope with this.

Regarding *getting another job,* Jim swears he never wants to go through the experience of being fired again. He thinks of setting up his own business, though is vague about the nature of this. Jim admits to great indecision regarding what he wants to do for the rest of his life. He feels that all his life he has been doing the 'right' thing, first for his parents and then later as a male wage slave for his wife and family. Having worked for the same company for twenty years, he has little idea about how to get another job. Part of him wants to rush back into the workforce to ease the anxiety of unemployment. Jim wonders how good he will be at presenting himself in interviews, and worries about what kind of references his former employers will give him.

Jim's *work difficulties* emerge during the session. Jim sees himself as better with figures than with people. He finds it difficult to tell people working under him what to do and even more difficult to confront them with their mistakes. Frequently, because of his financial knowledge and analytical skills, he would have good ideas for directions the company might take. However, often he is inhibited in sharing his ideas, or they have beeen discounted because of his poor presentation skills and inadequate persuasive powers.

Jim acknowledges *family difficulties* and fears that these will worsen with his unemployment especially if, as probable, his job search lasts for more than three months. His wife, Lyn, has very mixed feelings about him. On the one hand she respects his reliability, industry and obvious concern for the children. On the other hand, she feels that he is emotionally inexpressive, avoids rather than confronts marital issues and is no longer fun to be around. Apparently there are no third parties in the relationship. Jim cares for Lyn, but does not find her nearly as supportive as before. At times he thinks that, after the children, Lyn cares for her horses more than him. She stays with him partly as a means to maintain her lifestyle. Jim said he loves his children, Chris, 14, and Mark aged 17, but that they see him as too ready to pick on wrongdoings rather than prize them for themselves. Jim also mentions that he is the only son of an elderly widowed mother, who lives nearby. He visits her regularly and feels responsible for her well-being.

Jim's *health and stress difficulties* are uncovered when identifying and clarifying problems. Jim is a compulsive worker, often staying late at the office and working at weekends. He suffers from tension headaches when overworked. A recent medical examination showed that his blood pressure was too high. Jim mentions that he was becoming increasingly aware how stressed his body feels much of the time. He finds it hard to switch off and relax. Jim used to enjoy tennis and golf, but gave golf up as too time-consuming and tennis as too much effort. He has few recreational outlets, though he enjoys music and gardening. He feels he was reasonably social at the time of his marriage, but became less so after the advent of children. Now he sees himself in company as the strong, silent type. Jim observes that, without a job, he will not know what to do with his time.

Jim has never seen a counsellor before. Though desperate, he sees receiving help as a sign of weakness. He wants to stand on his own two feet as soon as possible. Sam detects Jim's resistance in talking about himself and gathers that he does not disclose much in personal and work dealings. Jim is not on medication, nor does he want to be.

Case study: Jim Blake

Part Two: Form feelings hypotheses

During the two initial sessions the counsellor, Sam Rushton, formed a series of feelings hypotheses about Jim. Sam had the advantage of observing Jim's voice and body messages. Below Sam's feelings hypotheses are presented systematically. In real life, helpers may not take these items into account in such an ordered way.

Capacity to feel   Jim is somewhat out of touch with

his capacity to feel. He does not know his wants and wishes regarding employment and has difficulty expressing emotions at home. Jim might require long-term help to develop good skills at experiencing and listening to his feelings.

Energy level   Jim's energy level seems lower than usual. Even before he was fired, he diverted too much energy into worrying. Effective helping should be able to raise both his short-term and long-term energy level and zest for life.

Self-esteem   Prior to being fired Jim's self-esteem was only moderate. Though he derived some self-esteem from family, much came from work. Jim's fragile self-esteem has taken a major knock and his confidence is very low.

Anxiety and defensiveness   Even prior to being fired, Jim was an anxious person, especially with people. He dealt with many anxiety-evoking problems by denial and avoidance. Now Jim admits to being highly anxious, though his anxiety may lessen as he comes to terms with his changed circumstances.

Mood   Immediately after being fired Jim masked the full extent of his depression. By the second session, he felt very depressed. However, in neither session did Jim appear a suicide risk.

Psychological pain   Jim is in considerable psychological pain as his work world falls apart. Other areas of psychological pain include relationship difficulties at home and work. Jim may also experience pain as he becomes aware how much of his life has been spent living other people's 'shoulds', 'oughts' and 'musts'.

Physical reactions   Jim reports spending a sleepless night. Undoubtedly he experiences other physical reactions not mentioned in the case study.

Psychophysiologic disorders   Jim suffers from tension headaches and high blood pressure. Further questioning is required to establish their severity and health risk.

Predominant feelings   In the first session, Jim's predominant feelings were shock and anger; in the second session, depression and anger. In both sessions he was very anxious.

Complex and conflicted feelings Jim's feelings about his future career are complex and conflicted. Jim also appears to have very mixed feelings about his marriage. The full complexity of his feelings in both career and marital areas has yet to emerge.

Antecedents and consequences of feelings As illustrated later, how Jim thinks contributes to the negativeness of his feelings. A possible consequence of Jim's anger towards his former company is that he may behave in self-defeating ways, for instance harming his reputation with them.

Strength and persistence of feelings Jim's anger towards his company is strong and his depression moderately severe. Though not fully revealed in the initial session, Jim may also be very angry with Lyn. Persistence of feelings remains to be seen.

Appropriateness of feelings Jim's strong initial feelings of anger, anxiety and depression at being fired may be appropriate. In fact, Sam would worry more if Jim covered up his feelings. However, if such strong feelings persist, they may be disproportionate and unhelpful to Jim.

Unclear feelings Sometimes Jim communicates feelings poorly, for instance voice and body messages are insufficiently congruent with verbal messages. Furthermore, he needs more time and psychological space to become clearer about underlying feelings.

Feelings about helping and helpers Jim is highly ambivalent about receiving help, seeing his wish for support as a sign of weakness. Also, he finds it difficult to talk about himself. Jim respects Sam's competence and sincere wish to help him. By the end of the second session Jim and Sam have established some emotional bonding.

ASSESS THINKING SKILLS

Assessing clients' thinking skills and helping clients think about how they think is central to the lifeskills helping approach. Feelings differ from thoughts. In the previous section, feelings were not referred to in skills terms. Clients' feelings reflect their animal nature. Clients can think about how they think, feel and act, but they can only feel how they feel. If clients wish to change how they experience, express and handle feelings, they need to focus on the thinking and action skills choices influencing them.

Thinking skills areas

Helpers always need to be conscious not just of what clients think, but of how they think. Lifeskills helpers help clients think about how they think, alter thinking skills weaknesses, and develop self-helping skills for working independently on their thinking. Few beginning helpers think of their own thinking in skills terms. Consequently, you may require a new way of viewing yourself as well as your clients. Assessing and working with your own thinking skills is one of the best ways to learn to work effectively with clients' thinking skills. The following is an overview of some thinking skills areas that you may assess and subsequently work on with clients. In all these areas people can make choices about how and what they think. Later in this chapter each thinking skills area is illustrated with reference to Jim Blake's thinking difficulties.

OWNING RESPONSIBILITY FOR CHOOSING In their waking hours clients are always choosers; they can make choices in relation to themselves, others and the environment. Within limits they can choose how they think, feel and act. Clients can be the authors or architects of their lives (May & Yalom, 1989; Yalom, 1980). However, clients are often unaware of the full extent of their existential responsibility to make their lives. They may also, knowingly or unknowingly, relinquish some of this responsibility. Many clients deceive themselves into thinking they own more responsibility for their choosing than is the case. They may possess an illusion of autonomy that masks a constricted approach to life.

BEING IN TOUCH WITH FEELINGS Being in touch with feelings is important since feelings are often the parents of thoughts. Furthermore, clients out of touch with their valuing process lack a firm base for assessing inner and outer information. Clients may experience difficulty sorting out what are their real feelings as contrasted with how they have been taught to feel and think. They may acknowledge specific feelings but dilute or distort their strength. Clients badly out of touch with feelings lack a firm sense of their own identity: they may experience themselves as 'leaves in the breeze' waiting to be blown around by what others think. They may be indecisive, since they lack a clear inner referent for assessing decision options.

USING SELF-TALK CONSTRUCTIVELY Here self-talk refers to how people talk to themselves before, during and after difficult situations (Meichenbaum, 1977, 1983, 1985, 1986; Meichenbaum & Deffenbacher, 1988). Clients can talk to themselves in ways that engender and worsen negative emotions and lead to self-defeating actions. The following are characteristics of self-talk likely to engender negative emotions.

- *Emphasizing mastery rather than coping.* Clients setting unrealistically high standards are prone to worrying about whether and how they can attain them.

- *Catastrophizing.* Clients can convince themselves that the worst will happen.

- *Adversely reacting to physical symptoms.* Clients can worsen their feelings of anxiety even to the extent of full-blown panic attacks by talking to themselves negatively about their bodily sensations such as tension, nausea, breathlessness, palpitations, choking, hot-and-cold flushes, and sweating.

- *Being overly self-conscious about what others think.* Clients can freeze up with anxiety by talking to themselves as though they are the centre of other people's attention.

- *Putting oneself down.* Clients can erode their confidence with statements like 'You fool', or 'I can't do anything right'.

- *Focusing on past setbacks rather than successes.* Clients can tell themselves what went wrong and ignore what went right.

Often self-talk that heightens anxiety lowers performance. In addition clients may have poor skills at coaching themselves through difficult tasks. For instance, they may not set themselves clear goals, break tasks down or concentrate on the task at hand.

POSSESSING REALISTIC PERSONAL RULES Personal rules provide the standards by which clients judge themselves and others. As mentioned earlier (p.143), Ellis (1980, 1989) coined the term 'mustabation' to refer to rigid personal rules characterized by 'musts', 'oughts' and 'shoulds'. He identifies three major clusters of irrational beliefs that create inappropriate feeling and action consequences:

1. I *must* do well and win approval for all my performances. (Ellis, 1980, p.5.)

2. Others *must* treat me considerately and kindly. (p.6.)

3. Conditions under which I live *must* be arranged so that I get practically everything I want comfortably, quickly, and easily. (p.7.)

Some of the main characteristics of unrealistic or self-oppressing personal rules include:

- *demandingness.* Clients think of wants and wishes as demands rather than preferences.

- *perfectionism.* Clients put pressure on themselves and others to be perfect. Nobody's perfect.

- *self-rating.* Clients rate themselves on their total worth as persons rather than on how functional are specific characteristics for achieving goals.

- *awfulizing.* Clients think it is absolutely awful if they, others or the environment are not as they should be.

CHOOSING TO PERCEIVE ACCURATELY Clients, like most humans, are prone to misperceive themselves and others (Beck, 1976, 1988; Beck & Weishaar, 1989). Negative self-labels are unrealistically negative perceptions either of clients' specific characteristics or of themselves as persons. More clients seem to make unrealistically negative than positive inferences about themselves. They are much better at listing what is wrong than what is right. This perceptual habit of ignoring assets and focusing on deficits perpetuates feelings such as anxiety, depression and diminished confidence and vitality.

Clients may also allow feelings to influence how they perceive others, including helpers. They make judgements without adequately taking into account available facts. Central to all marital counselling is assisting partners to perceive each other more accurately and usually much less negatively. In the preceding chapter I listed some perceptual errors for helpers to avoid. There are also perceptual errors for clients to avoid: for instance tunnel vison, magnifying and minimizing, negativeness, selective inattenton, overgeneralizing and polarized thinking.

ATTRIBUTING CAUSE ACCURATELY Clients can stay stuck in problems through wholly or in part misattributing their causes. Possible misattributions for the causes of problems include: 'It's my genes', 'It's my mental illness', 'It's my unfortunate past', 'It's my bad luck', 'It's my poor environment', 'It's all their fault', or 'It's all my fault'. Clients commonly succumb to the temptation to externalize problems: others have problems that adversely affect them. They attribute cause from outside to inside. However, change requires attribution of cause from inside to outside. Furthermore, clients can adversely affect their confidence and mood by misattributing causes of positive and negative events. For instance, depressed people may overestimate their responsibility for negative events in their own and others' lives (Beck *et al.*, 1979). In addition clients can influence their motivation to achieve by how they attribute cause for their successes and failures. For instance, they may rightly or wrongly assign the causes for their academic successes and failures to such factors as ability, effort, anxiety, task difficulty, staff competence or luck.

PREDICTING REALISTICALLY In a sense all client problems contain disorders of prediction. Many clients predict risk inaccurately by overestimating bad consequences. They may fear change, failure or success. However, some clients underestimate the risk of bad consequences, for instance in excessive gambling or grandiose business ventures. Clients can also predict reward inaccurately by either ovestimating or underestimating good consequences. Two trends are common in underestimating reward. First, clients may be poor at perceiving the potential rewards of proposed courses of action. Second, even when rewards are identified, they may not give them the weight they deserve. Predicting realistically entails accurately thinking about future consequences. Independent of notions of risk and reward, some clients are poor at consequential thinking: for instance they may remain unaware of and fail to predict how their behaviour affects others.

CLARIFYING VALUES Clients may require assistance in clarifying their values. Values are the underlying principles and priorities that guide people's lives. Another way of viewing clients' values is that they represent their philosophy of life. When clients become clearer about their values, they tend to find it easier to set goals. Illustrative values are love, friendship, religion, materialism, aesthetics, intellect, hedonism, social consciousness and self-actualization. It is important for clients to have reasonable similarity of values when entering long-term relationships, be they personal or work.

SETTING REALISTIC GOALS Some clients have difficulty articulating goals and consequently relinquish much opportunity to create their futures. Goals can be short term, medium term, or long term and in various areas: for instance relationships, study, work, recreation, health and finances. When in close relationships, clients' goals may need to be negotiated so that they become shared goals. Apart from not possessing goals, errors in goal setting include: not reflecting values, insufficient realism, inadequate specificity, and unclear time frames. Clients' goals in relation to problem areas may suffer from not being expressed in skills language. Also, clients may not focus on how to think as well as on how to act.

VISUALIZING SKILLS Lazarus observes that 'when a person's most highly valued representational system is visual, he or she is inclined to respond to the world and organize it in terms of mental images' (1989, p.514). Clients may use mental images or pictorial thinking to support or to oppress themselves. Negative images can influence feelings towards self and others. For instance, in one research study, some 90 per cent of anxious patients reported visual images prior to and concurrent to their anxiety attacks (Beck *et al.*, 1974). Absence of the capacity to visualize calming images can contribute to tension and anger. Clients who visualize themseves as socially incompetent may feel shy.

How clients visualize others influences their feelings towards them. For instance, angry clients may be poor at using visualizing to understand others' position and take a balanced view of them. Some clients are poor at communicating visual images, for instance sharing sexual fantasies. Frequently clients' negative visual images impede their performance: for example, imagining acting incompetently in either social or academic situations can be self-fulfilling prophecies. Clients may also be poor at visualizing positive and negative consequences of their behaviour; for instance clients engaged in job searches may be poor at visualizing what it is actually like working for specific employers.

REALISTIC DECISION MAKING Clients may possess decision-making styles that lessen their effectiveness. For instance, they may be hypervigilant and try too hard, taking every consideration into account. Conversely, they may be impulsive and rush into major and minor decisions. Some clients do their best to avoid decisions altogether. Sometimes decisions are best made in collaboration with others. In such instances, decision errors include being overly competitive or compliant. Rational decision making can be viewed as taking place in two main stages: first, confronting and making decisions; second, implementing and evaluating them. Clients may have weaknesses in either or both stages. An illustrative weakness when making decisions is failure to generate sufficient decision options. An illustrative weakness when implementing decisions is poor planning.

PREVENTING AND MANAGING PROBLEMS Frequently clients seek help because of poor skills at preventing and managing problems. Skills weaknesses may be in such areas as confronting problems, assessing and redefining problems in skills terms, setting goals, planning, implementing plans, and evaluating consequences. Where possible clients should develop skills for either preventing problems or catching them early: for instance, not allowing stress to endanger health.

Skills for eliciting and assessing thinking

When assessing thinking, helpers and clients work together to establish clients' thinking skills strengths and weaknesses. It is important to help clients become more aware of their thought processes (Beck & Emery, 1985). With increased self-awareness, clients may start correcting their own thinking errors. Furthermore, they are better accomplices in the detective work of uncovering faulty thinking. You aim to train clients in how to think about how they think. The following are some skills for eliciting and assessing thinking.

BUILD A KNOWLEDGE BASE It is essential that helpers wishing to work with clients' thinking skills develop their knowledge of how people think. You cannot help clients if you do not know what to look for. You may also limit your effectiveness if you focus on only one or two thinking skills. How can you develop your knowledge base? First, you can read the works of cognitive therapists such as Ellis (1962, 1980, 1989), Beck (1976, 1988; Beck & Weishaar, 1989) and of other therapists who work with clients' thinking: for instance Frankl (1959, 1967, 1969), Glasser (1965, 1984), Lazarus (1981, 1989), Meichenbaum (1977, 1983, 1985, 1986) and Yalom (1980; May & Yalom, 1989). Second, you may read secondary sources such as *Effective Thinking Skills: Preventing and Managing Personal Problems* (Nelson-Jones, 1989). Third, you can work on your own thinking skills either independently or with helpers or in training groups. Fourth, you can work with clients, preferably at first under supervision.

THINK IN SKILLS TERMS Important cognitive theorists like Beck, Ellis and Meichenbaum do not use skills language when thinking about how clients think. However, you are encouraged to do so. Failure to think in skills terms may cause you to focus on only one or two rather than on many potential thinking skills weaknesses. Stage 2 requires you to redefine clients' problems in skills terms. You will find difficulty doing this if not already assessing clients' skills. However, when eliciting and assessing thinking you may choose not to use skills language openly with clients, but leave this until your redefining statement.

COLLECT INFORMATION Rewarding listening skills are always important when collecting information about how clients think. Other ways of eliciting and collecting information about clients' thinking include the following:

- *Client self-report.* Clients may have insight into their own thought processes, for example tendencies to rigid personal rules or negative self-labelling, without knowing what to do about them.

- *Think aloud.* Think aloud involves encouraging clients to speak aloud their thought processes in relation to specific situations (Blackwell *et al.*, 1985). For instance, clients can be asked to take helpers in slow motion through their thoughts and feelings in relation to specific anxiety-evoking experiences. Additionally, clients can use think aloud when confronted with real or simulated situations.

- *Thought listing.* Clients can be asked to list, and possibly rank-order in terms of importance, thoughts in relation to specific problems. Clients can list thoughts within the ABC framework where A equals the activating event; B, the client's thoughts about the activating event; and C, the feelings and action consequences of the client's thoughts (Ellis, 1962, 1989). At B, Ellis asks clients to distinguish between rational and irrational thoughts.

- *Thought charting.* Thought charting entails clients keeping a record of the thoughts associated with specific situations involving negative feelings. Beck and Emery observe: 'The most common method by which a patient can become aware of his thinking between sessions is the thought record' (1985, pp.194–5). At its simplest, thought charting involves the double-column technique: recording situations in one column and thoughts and feelings in the other column. Thought charts may also use the ABC framework: a column each for (A) activating events, (B) thoughts, and (C) feelings and action consequences. Thought charting encourages clients to see links between how they think, feel and act.

- *Counting.* Helpers can ask clients to count the frequency of specific types of thought: for instance, negative self-labels. Clients may use index cards to make frequency records. Counting may help clients become aware of the repetitive nature of their thinking.

- *Focusing on thinking questions.* Clients can be asked what they think about themselves, their behaviour, others and specific situations. Then helpers can ask follow-up questions that encourage clients to elaborate, specify and reveal personal meanings. Before leaving an area you may ask the open-ended question: 'Can you think of anything else that might be relevant?' Such a question may elicit further information that might have been lost had you moved on prematurely. Intersperse reflective responding with focusing on thinking questions. Also, remember that sometimes focusing on feelings questions opens up the way for focusing on thinking questions.

> *Helper:* And how did you feel when that happened?
> *Client:* I felt mad as hell.
> *Helper:* You felt hopping mad? Why do you think that was?

Helpers can also use questions that challenge clients' thinking: for example, 'Where's the evidence?' However, you should resist the temptation to answer your own questions. You may also need to rephrase questions that clients do not appear to understand.

- *Thought-eliciting techniques.* Thought-eliciting techniques are similar to feelings-eliciting techniques; the same techniques may be used to elicit thoughts and feelings.

  Live observation. Helpers can accompany clients into situations that cause them difficulty, for instance returning something to a shop or driving a car after an accident, and ask them to recount their thoughts.

  Visualizing. Clients can be asked to conjure up images that elicit feelings and asked to identify the accompanying thoughts. Clients can visualize past, present or future scenes and get in touch with harmful and helpful thoughts.

  Role play. Helpers can conduct role plays with clients, for instance telephoning someone for a date, and then explore their thoughts and feelings.

  Task assignment. Helpers can encourage clients to perform feared tasks and afterwards record their thoughts and feelings. Clients can view such tasks as personal experiments to collect evidence about themslves.

- *Questionnaires.* There are numerous self-report measures to assess thinking: for example, the Anxious Self-Statements Questionnaire (Kendall & Hollon, 1989), the Attributional Style Questionnaire (Petersen *et al.*, 1982; Petersen & Villanova, 1988) and the Fear of Negative Evaluation Scale (Watson & Friend, 1969). In addition, helpers can develop their own measures of thinking.

USE A WHITEBOARD A whiteboard is an important tool for working with clients' thinking. It has many uses. First, you may use the whiteboard to help elicit thoughts: frequently clients find that the visual display of their thoughts stimulates them to generate more thoughts. However, you may need to probe to elicit less obvious thoughts. Second, the whiteboard enables thoughts to be visually stored so that clients can see linkages between them. Third, the whiteboard is useful for tracing links between stimuli or activating events (A), intervening thinking (B) and feelings and action consequences (C). Fourth, the whiteboard is useful for showing redefinitions of clients' problems in skills terms. A whiteboard is also valuable later on when intervening to develop clients' thinking skills. Fifth, correct use of the whiteboard encourages a cooperative working alliance between helpers and clients. Clients can observe their contribution going on to the whiteboard and feel that they are valued.

MAKE INFERENCES Helpers make inferences both about clients' areas of difficulty and pain and about possible thinking skills weaknesses. Inferences about thinking may stem from clients' words, feelings and actions. You may obtain clues from how clients use language. For example, use of words like 'should,', 'ought', or 'must' may indicate unrealistically rigid personal rules. Use of verbs like 'I can't' and expressions like 'I had no choice' may indicate insufficient ownership of responsibility for choosing. Use of terms like, 'What will people think of me?' and 'I wonder if I look as stupid as I feel' represent both negative self-talk and also indicate an unrealistic rule about needing others' approval.

Both helpers and clients require skills at making linkages between feelings and underlying thoughts (Beck, 1988). Often strong, persistent negative feelings indicate thinking difficulties. You require sensitivity to more subtle clues that come from voice messages, body messages or what is left unsaid. You and your clients should also make linkages between self-defeating actions and thinking. Clients need to develop skills at doing this for themselves.

FORM HYPOTHESES Helpers identify and collect evidence that helps them form hypotheses about clients' thinking skills weaknesses. Helpers may generate many more hypotheses than they eventually share with clients when redefining problems in skills terms. As part of the process of assessing thinking, you may collect further information that either supports or negates your hypotheses. Conversely, you may choose not to collect further information about some hypotheses. The following is a continuation of the Jim Blake case study, this time focusing on forming thinking skills hypotheses.

Case study: Jim Blake
Part Three: Form thinking skills hypotheses

As the counsellor, Sam Rushton, listens and probes, he develops hypotheses concerning how Jim's thinking skills weaknesses may sustain his problems. Here I list hypotheses by thinking skills rather than by problem areas: for instance, being fired, finances, getting another job, work difficulties, family difficulties and health and stress difficulties. However, when interviewing, the counsellor might have explored thinking skills hypotheses in relation to specific problem areas. Later, when offering a redefinition of Jim's problems in skills terms, the counsellor might link the main themes of Jim's thinking skills weaknesses across different problem areas.

Owning responsibility for choosing The following items might illustrate that Jim is not fully owning responsibility for being a chooser in his life.
Getting fired: Jim may have allowed himself to stay in a rut. Conceivably he might have initiated a move out of the company before being fired.
Getting another job: Jim appears not to have realized that now he has a positive opportunity to make choices, despite the pain of being fired. Jim has still to choose to accept responsibility for developing job search skills.
Family difficulties: Jim appears to have been relating

to his family on the basis of repetitive habits, some of which do not work. He can choose to think, feel and act differently.

Health and stress difficulties: Jim appears to have given up much of his capacity for choice in his leisure and recreational life. This in turn negatively affects his health, and family and work life.

Being in touch with feelings The following are some items illustrative of a possible skills weakness in acknowledging feelings:

Getting another job: Jim appears out of touch with his wants and wishes after years of doing the 'right' thing by others. He may not be fully in touch with his strengths.

Family difficulties: Jim may be emotionally inexpressive. He may not be fully in touch with either his negative feelings about his wife or his positive feelings towards his wife and children.

Health and stress: Jim seems not to listen sufficiently to his body. Also he is out of touch with his need for recreation and fun.

Using self-talk constructively Jim may both use negative self-talk and fail to use coping self-talk.

Being fired: Jim appears not to be coping using self-talk to manage his anger; rather his negative self-talk may fan his anger.

Getting another job: Jim may need to develop self-talk skills for calming himself down and coaching himself through interviews.

Work difficulties: Jim may have engaged in negative self-talk that contributed to his avoiding confrontations with subordinates.

Family difficulties: Jim may need to develop appropriate self-talk to make it easier for him to become more assertive and emotionally expressive.

Possessing realistic personal rules Jim may have some unrealistic personal rules contributing to self-defeating feelings and actions.

Being fired: 'Life must always be fair', 'People who are fired must be failures'. These rules contribute to feelings like anger, anxiety and depression.

Finances: 'I must maintain my present living standard

or else I am a failure as a person.' Such a rule puts considerable pressure on Jim, who now equates his worth as a person with his earning capacity.

Getting another job: 'I must be seen by others as successful.' This rule overemphasizes others' approval as contrasted with self-approval.

Family: 'It is not manly to show emotions.' 'Family conflict must be avoided where possible.' The first rule is a sex-role stereotype and the second ignores possibilities for constructive conflict.

Choosing to perceive accurately Jim may need to learn to discipline how he perceives himself and others.

Being fired: Jim's perceptions of his former employer may be negatively coloured by his emotions. If he does not keep his paranoia and anger in check, he may damage himself by losing existing goodwill.

Getting another job: Jim may attach all sorts of negative self-labels to himself; 'I'm no good', 'I'm a failure' and so on. He needs to engage in a search of his strengths, and must realistically appraise his abilities, interests, skills and experience.

Family: Jim's perceptions of his wife and children may be inaccurate: for instance he may overemphasize weaknesses. His perceptions of how he behaves in the family may also be inaccurate: he may be less sensitive and open to feedback than he thinks.

Attributing cause accurately Items that indicate that Jim may have difficulties in this area include the following:

Getting fired: Jim may unrealistically blame his company colleagues for their decision.

Getting another job: Jim may be passive and wait for others to help him rather than commit himself fully to managing his career transition.

Work difficulties: Jim may wrongly attribute some of his people skills weaknesses to 'That's just the way I am' rather than seeing them in terms of learned behaviour that, with appropriate assistance, he can alter.

Family difficulties: Jim may externalize the cause of any problems with Lyn and the children:

'It's their fault.' Alternatively he may blame himself, yet do nothing about it because 'That's the way I am.'
Health and stress: Jim may have blamed the company for his overwork rather than asserted himself and set limits on his workload.

Predicting realistically Items illustrative of possible problems here include the following:
Finances: Jim's catastrophic predictions of financial disaster are probably unrealistic, especially in the light of his financial expertise.
Getting another job: Jim may have unrealistic expectations of what is involved in getting another job and how long this might take.
Work difficulties: Jim may unrealistically predict negative consequences of raising issues with subordinates and insufficiently focus on gains.
Family: Jim may overemphasize the negative consequences of being more emotionally expressive and attempting to work through issues. Consequently, he remains stuck in his present behaviour.
Health and stress: Jim has been underestimating the negative consequences of overwork and under-recreation. His body gives him clear warning signals.

Clarifying values Jim seemingly needs to get much more in touch with what his true values are to provide a firmer basis for seeking meaning in the remainder of his life. The need to clarify values permeates all areas of his functioning, including work, health and family.

Setting realistic goals Though Jim may have been proficient at articulating goals for his company, this proficiency may not carry over into setting realistic goals for himself.
Getting fired: Jim appears not to have set clear goals for any future contact he may have with his previous employer.
Getting another job: Jim has now to articulate career goals, and goals for planning and implementing either his job search or the establishment of a business.
Work difficulties: Jim might consider establishing goals for developing skills to handle his work

difficulties: for instance assertion and public-speaking skills.

Family difficulties: In conjunction with Lyn, Jim might develop goals for working on his family problems. Even if Lyn does not initially cooperate, Jim can still develop goals for changing his behaviour.

Health and stress: Jim clearly needs to develop goals to protect his health and ease his stress. He might also set himself goals for developing his leisure interests.

Visualizing skills Indications that Jim may have inadequate visualizing skills include the following:

Finances: Jim may not only verbalize the worst but have graphic images as well.

Getting another job: Jim may have poor skills at visualizing life in different environments, visualizing life changing for the better, and using visualizing to rehearse interview skills.

Family difficulties: Jim may unnecessarily be feeding himself negative images about himself, his family and their future.

Health and stress: Jim may need to develop a clearer visual picture of what may happen to him unless he learns to manage his stress better.

Realistic decision making Jim may not always use realistic decision-making skills.

Getting fired: Jim may have diluted or denied the evidence that his job was at risk as a way of avoiding making the difficult decision to move on.

Getting another job: Jim may be at risk of making an impulsive decision to ease his anxiety about being unemployed. Other ways he might handle his anxiety include either avoiding decisions or being hypervigilant about every detail to the point of indecision.

Family difficulties: Jim may lack skills of making decisions in family matters collaboratively with Lyn. Many of their tensions may stem from lack of clarity over who makes which decisions and how.

Preventing and managing problems Jim clearly has a number of problem areas in his life that he either avoids or deals with inadequately.

Work difficulties: Over a period of years he appears

not to have solved his lack of assertion problems.

Family difficulties: At no stage does Jim appear to have attempted a systematic approach to breaking down and tackling his family difficulties.

Health and stress difficulties: Jim has shown insufficient skill in preventing and managing his health and stress problems.

Jim has many problem areas. His thinking skills weaknesses are also extensive. Both Jim and his counsellor may wish to narrow down both which problems they work on and also what are the most important thinking skills to focus on. However, the above analysis illustrates that the same thinking skills difficulties often occur in more than one problem area. Developing better thinking skills in one problem area can carry over into others.

ASSESS ACTION SKILLS

Action skills are observable behaviours. Helpers need to pay close attention to assessing action skills because, if clients are to manage most problems better, they must act better. Action skills interact with thinking and feeling. Improved thinking needs to be followed by effective action. Furthermore, if clients are to feel better, they frequently need to take action to achieve feelings goals: for example, clients wishing to be less lonely need to use developing friendship skills.

Generally, beginning helpers find it easier to think in terms of action skills than thinking skills. However, a common mistake is to focus only on verbal skills. Action skills involve five main message categories: verbal, voice, body, touch and action. The first four message categories usually assume face-to-face contact. The fifth category, action messages, does not require direct contact: for instance, sending flowers to someone you love.

Skills for eliciting, observing and assessing action skills

When helpers assess action skills they seek both to identify which skills are important and also to evaluate current performance in them. Below are some helper skills for assessing clients' actions and for helping clients to observe themselves.

BUILD A KNOWLEDGE BASE As with thinking, when assessing actions helpers need to think in skills terms. In addition helpers require a knowledge base of action skills for client populations they service. If you do not know what constitutes skilled behaviour in an area you cannot assess it properly. For example, helpers working with aggressive children require knowledge of action skills for managing aggression and behaving assertively. Helpers working with the unemployed require knowledge of action skills such as making career résumés (CVs), seeking employment information and handling interviews. Helpers working with sexual problem clients require knowledge of action skills for managing different sexual dysfunctions. Finally, helpers working with school and university students' study and exam-taking problems require knowledge of how to study and take exams effectively.

COLLECT INFORMATION IN INTERVIEWS Helpers can collect information about observable actions either inside or outside interviews. Here are some ways you can collect information in interviews.

Client self-report. Clients can tell you how they behave outside helping. Some limitations of client self-report are that you do not observe behaviour and that you are reliant on their versions of events. Clients may edit what they say to protect their self-pictures.

Observing clients. Depending on the areas of clients' problems, you may learn much from observing their verbal, voice and action messages as they relate to you. For example, shy clients may perform their shyness behaviours right in front of you.

Focusing on actions questions. Focusing on actions questions aim to elicit specific details of actions. 'How' questions are useful: for example, 'How did you behave?' and "When you did that [specify], how did he/she react?' You may need to direct clients to provide details of voice and body as well as action messages. Furthermore, you may need to assert yourself to ensure that clients provide you with specific behavioural information. 'How' questions go beyond the question, 'What actually happened?' to identify participants' specific skills strengths and weaknesses. 'How' questions include probing how clients avoid carrying out desired behaviours: for instance, 'When you wish to study but are unable to, how do you behave?'

Frequency is a dimension of focusing on action questions: for example, 'How many __?' or 'How many times did you __?' Duration is another dimension: for example, 'Over what period were you __?' or 'How long does it takes you to __?' or 'How many minutes/ hours do you __ each day?' Kazdin observes: 'In most behavior modification programs, the goal is to increase the frequency of a response rather than its duration. There are notable exceptions, of course' (1989, p.65).

Role play. A further focusing on action question is 'Show me?' Clients can be invited to illustrate the verbal, voice and body messages they used in an interaction either on their own or in a role play with you playing the other party. For instance, parents having difficulty disciplining children can show how they attempt this. Role play allows the possibility of an interaction that goes beyond an initial 'show me' demonstration lasting for one parental statement. You may video role plays and play them back to clients to illustrate points and develop clients' self-observing skills.

COLLECT INFORMATION IN NATURAL SETTINGS Helpers may wish to supplement interview information with that collected in clients' natural or home environments.

Helpers as observers. You can go with clients into situations in which they experience difficulty and observe how they behave: for instance, requesting a drink in a bar or relating to children at home.

Clients as observers. Always encourage clients to become more aware of how they behave in problem areas. More formally, clients can use behaviour-monitoring worksheets and thinking, feeling and action logs. Furthermore, you can set clients tasks, for instance telephoning to ask a girl out, and get them to record how they behave.

Third parties as observers. With permission, you may also collect information about how clients act from third parties: for instance, spouses, parents, siblings, peers or supervisors. Note, and possible explore, differences between third parties' and clients' observations. You may need to train third parties in what to look for and in how to observe systematically.

EXPLORE THE ANTECEDENTS AND CONSEQUENCES OF ACTIONS Helpers can encourage clients to understand inner and outer events preceding actions. For instance, how did they think and feel before they acted? What events in their outer environment influenced their actions? You can also assist clients to become much more aware that their actions always have consequences and also of what they are. Furthermore, you can assist clients to see the extent to which consequences of actions influence subsequent behaviours.

FORM ACTION SKILLS HYPOTHESES As helpers listen to clients and collect information, they form action skills hypotheses. You may feel confident about some hypotheses at the end of an initial session. You may make other hypotheses more tentatively. Still other hypotheses emerge as helping progresses. Clients may also share ideas about unhelpful actions. Such observations always merit attention, not least because clients show some responsibility for their problems and problematic skills.

Helpers may formulate many hypotheses concerning broad areas in which clients may need to develop skills. Often helpers leave detailed assessment of specific skills weaknesses until subsequent sessions when there is more time to do the job thoroughly. By then, helper and client may have prioritized which skills require detailed attention.

Case study: Jim Blake

Part Four: Form action skills hypotheses

The counsellor, Sam Rushton, formed the following hypotheses concerning Jim Blake's possible action skills weaknesses. He listed these by each of Jim's problem areas.
Getting fired: Re-establishing limited contact with former employer, for instance regarding references.

Getting another job: In conjunction with the thinking skills entailed in rigorous career decision making, Jim appears to have weaknesses in the following action skills:
– making a career résumé;
– information seeking about advertised job opportunities;
– creating and using an informal contact network to find out about unadvertised job opportunities;
– creating and implementing a marketing plan;
– interview skills;
– gathering information to assess job offers;
– establishing his own business (if he decides on this option).

In addition, Jim seems to have skills weaknesses regarding finding meaning in activity despite being unemployed. Specific action skills weaknesses include:
– managing time that has previously been highly structured;
– finding and engaging in meaningful activities, both work-related and recreational.

Finances: Given Jim's financial background, this area may be adequately covered. Nevertheless Jim possesses an action skills weakness in not discussing his affairs with another knowledgeable and trusted financial expert.

Work difficulties: Because Jim's action skills weaknesses appeared in his previous job, they may hold him back in a new job. Also, Jim's perception that he lacks people skills may create a reluctance to go for jobs he might handle well once he develops his people skills. Possible action skills Jim needs to develop include the following:
– giving instructions assertively;
– giving feedback assertively;
– disclosing more of himself so that he appears more human;
– rewarding listening skills;
– public-speaking skills;
– group discussion skills.

Family difficulties: In the family, Jim appears to have action skills weaknesses across a range of relationship skills, including the following:
– rewarding listening;
– expressing feelings;
– expressing affection;
– giving balanced feedback;
– asserting himself;
– acknowledging and managing anger;
– managing conflict;
– engaging in joint decision making;
– engaging in shared pleasant activities;
– improving social conversation skills.

Health and stress: Jim's action skills weaknesses include the following:
– inadequate muscular and mental relaxation skills;
– inadequate time spent on recreational activities, such as music, gardening, sports, and socializing. Jim may have to develop skills in specific recreational areas to gain the most from them;
– when employed, inadequate assertion skills to set limits on his workload.

REDEFINE PROBLEMS IN SKILLS TERMS

The desired outcome of the second stage of the lifeskills helping model is a clear initial statement of the skills weaknesses on which helpers and clients need to work if clients are to manage present and future problems better. Helpers and clients should arrive at mutually agreed conceptualizations of problems. Put another way, clients make poor choices which sustain problems. Good redefinitions of problems in skills terms break them down and identify specific skills areas in which clients can make better choices. During later working sessions, problems may be still further broken down into their component skills. However, such detail may be inappropriate for initial sessions. Initial skills definitions pinpoint or flag areas for later work.

Skills definitions are sets of hypotheses about skills weaknesses sustaining clients' problems. Though forming the basis for goal setting and intervening, they should be open to modification in light of feedback and new information. In short, initial redefinitions of problems in skills terms are subject to continuous testing and also to major or minor reformulations as helping progresses.

Some skills for redefining problems

Below are some helper skills for redefining clients' problems in skills terms.

PRESENT A RATIONALE In earlier structuring statements helpers may have presented rationales to clients, suggesting that their problems might be broken down and translated into thinking and action skills terms. In any event, it is probably worth re-emphasizing why problems are redefined in skills terms. Below is a possible transition statement a helper might make when starting to offer a skills redefiniton.

> Well, Jan, for the past thirty minutes or so we've been exploring in some detail the problems in your relationship with your daughter Pam. I'm now about to test out on you a way of viewing your problems in skills terms. I will try to identify and put up on the whiteboard some of the main ways your thinking and behaviour may create difficulties for you both. I present these as thinking and action skills because that allows us to work in specific areas rather than go round in circles with vague generalities. If possible, we need to agree on the main skills areas in which you experience difficulty. Your feedback is vital since you are unlikely to work on skills where you do not see the point.

Given good rationales, most clients accept a skills focus. However, some clients may express reservations about redefining problems in skills terms. They may be unused to viewing their behaviour in such terms, and take time adjusting. They may view skills redefinitions as mechanistic and be afraid that they will be treated as objects rather than people. Certain clients may be ready to own neither their problems nor their roles in sustaining them. Agreeing to skills redefinitions assumes a degree of personal responsibility for having and sustaining problems.

MAKE CLEAR AND PARSIMONIOUS REDEFINITIONS Helpers need to be mindful that redefinitions of problems in skills terms are for clients' benefit. Unless clients understand them, redefinitions are pointless. Always use simple and clear language. Aim to summarize key thinking and action skills weaknesses in areas of immediate concern to clients. Furthermore, be sensitive to the amount of material clients can absorb. It is preferable that clients be comfortable with a small amount of material than confused about a lot. In later sessions you can further redefine problems in skills terms.

Besides clarity and parsimony, the following are some other characteristics of good redefinition statements:

- They bear a clear relationship to information clients provide.

- They are formulated in conjunction with clients.

- They relate to a problem or problems of high priority to clients.

- They are stated as hypotheses.

- Clients are likely to perceive them as relevant and own them as a basis for working on their problems.

- They lend themselves to setting helpful and realistic working goals.

USE A WHITEBOARD When redefining problems in skills terms, using a whiteboard has many advantages. The discipline of writing up your T redefinition – a column each for thinking and action skills weaknesses – imposes a degree of clarity on you. The visual image may increase clients' understanding and retention of what you communicate. Furthermore, having a written definition before their eyes makes it easier for clients to provide feedback. If necessary, you can openly work together on the whiteboard to formulate more mutually agreeable redefinitions of problems.

USE CHECKING SKILLS Valid working definitions of clients' problems in skills terms are both formulated in collaboration with clients and then further checked out with them to see if they 'fit'. If clients have reservations about your working definitions, you explore these further. Assuming the reservations are not misunderstandings, you may then choose either to elaborate on how you arrived at your definitions or to modify them in light of discussion.

ATTEND TO FEELINGS Always, when redefining problems, helpers need to attend to clients' feelings. Formulating working definitions focused on thinking and action skills is not an arid intellectual exercise. The following are some of the areas in which you require sensitivity to clients' feelings. First, you should look out for any client reservations regarding taking a skills approach to their problems. If possible, work through these reservations together. Second, be aware that often you deal with highly sensitive material and that you always require tact. Often clients find it difficult to accept responsibility for their problems and not to externalize them. Do not make it harder for them by being clumsy. Third, your redefinitions in thinking and action skills terms may focus on changing clients' feelings: for instance anger or shyness. Fourth, good redefinitions deepen not just clients' thoughts about but their feelings of being understood by you. A myth of Rogers' person-centred approach is that clients feel more understood by helpers who stay within their internal viewpoint rather than actively expand their self-understanding. Fifth, good redefinitions can improve clients' morale and motivation. Whereas previously they may have been stuck, now they have 'handles' with which to work. A glimmer of light appears. Problems formerly experienced as insurmountable may now seem manageable.

ENCOURAGE BETWEEN-SESSION LEARNING From the start of lifeskills helping, you can encourage clients to take an active role in learning. Already I have mentioned working closely with clients during sessions, including using a whiteboard. You can use between-session time to build their self-assessing skills. For example, you may cassette-record sessions and ask clients to play the tapes back prior to subsequent sessions. Many clients find this useful for further exploring and assessing problems and problematic skills. They find that there is too much material to remember and absorb first time round without listening to sessions again. In addition, you may request that clients keep records of how they think, feel and behave in targeted skills areas. Clients can keep folders of their helping work. Items to go in folders include: redefinitions of problems, behaviour-monitoring records, main learnings from individual sessions, and homework worksheets and exercises. Arguably, it is more important for clients than for helpers to keep records.

Case study: Jim Blake

Part Five: Redefine problems in skills terms

The first time the counsellor, Sam Rushton, saw Jim Blake was on company premises immediately after he was fired. In this highly charged emotional atmosphere, no attempt was made to identify, clarify, assess and redefine Jim's problems in skills terms.

Towards the end of the second session, held away from company premises, Sam and Jim agreed that the two immediate areas in which Jim needed to work were handling his emotions about being fired and getting another job. Using a two-column T format on a whiteboard, one column each for thinking and action skills, Sam redefined each of these problems. Sam observed that some clients preferred the terminology of inner and outer game skills to thinking and action skills. Sam worked with handling being fired first because it was an immediate and less complex problem than getting another job. Sam wrote the skills definition in the first person singular to help Jim identify with it and checked Jim's reactions. Sam mentioned that the skills redefinition would form the basis for a statement of working goals.

Handling being fired

Thinking skills weakness hypotheses
– perceiving my former company inaccurately;
– using self-talk to heighten my anger;
– possessing unrealistic personal rules concerning being fired.

Action skills weakness hypotheses
– avoiding contact with my former employer, for instance regarding references.

After checking the accuracy and comprehensibility of this skills redefinition with Jim, Sam reformed it into a statement of working goals (see Chapter 7). Again using the T two-columns format on the whiteboard, Sam and Jim formed the following redefinition of Jim's 'getting another job' problem.

Getting another job

Thinking skills weakness hypotheses
– insufficiently owning responsibility for my choices in life;
– being insufficiently in touch with my wants and wishes;
– negative self-talk, for instance when faced with interviews;
– possessing unrealistic personal rules, for instance regarding achievement;
– perceiving myself inaccurately, for instance possessing negative self-labels;
– making unrealistic predictions about the possible length of my job search;
– insufficient clarity regarding my values;
– poor goal-setting skills, both in regard to career goals and job search goals;
– insufficiently realistic and rigorous career decision-making skills.

Action skills weakness hypotheses
– inadequate skills at making a career résumé;
– inadequate information seeking about advertised job opportunities;
– poor skills at creating and using an informal contact network to find out about unadvertised job opportunities;
– poor skills at creating and implementing a marketing plan;
– poor interview skills;
– while unemployed, poor skills at managing time and engaging in meaningful activities.

Sam and Jim discussed this redefinition in skills terms of Jim's 'getting another job' problem. Once satisfied that he and Jim agreed on a common conceptualization of the problem and problematic skills, Sam reformed them into a statement of working goals (see Chapter 7). Sam told Jim that, if he wanted, either he might work with him on his other problems, for example family difficulties, or he could refer him to another helper. Jim said he would like to think about this, but might well take up Sam's offer. He mentioned that breaking down his problems into their component skills made him feel better able to cope with them. Sam replied that Jim's other problems too could be broken down into thinking and action skill components.

CHAPTER HIGHLIGHTS

- Assessment in lifeskills helping is performed with clients and for clients. Helpers and clients are hypothesis makers and testers.

- Helpers should always offer supportive relationships when assessing and redefining clients' problems in skills terms.

- Reasons for assessing feelings include: protecting clients; evaluating emotional responsiveness; clarifying real agendas; obtaining leads about thinking and action skills weaknesses; noting medical and psychiatric considerations; and developing clients' self-assessment skills.

- Dimensions of feelings that helpers and clients assess include: capacity to feel; energy level; self-esteem; anxiety and defensiveness; mood; psychological pain; physical reactions; and psychophysiological disorders.

- Among helper skills for eliciting and assessing feelings are: rewarding listening; advanced reflection of feelings; focusing on feelings questions; and emotion-eliciting techniques such as visualizing and role play.

- Helpers and clients can assess the following thinking skills: owning responsibility for choosing; being in touch with feelings; using self-talk constructively; possessing realistic personal rules; choosing to perceive accurately; attributing cause accurately; predicting realistically; clarifying values; setting realistic goals; visualizing skills; realistic decision making; and preventing and managing problems skills.

- Skills for eliciting and assessing thinking include building a knowledge base and thinking in skills terms.

- Helpers and clients can collect information about thinking skills from: client self-report; think aloud; thought listening; thought charting; counting; focusing on thinking questions; questionnaires and thought-eliciting techniques, such as live observation, visualizing, role play and task assignment.

- Helpers make inferences and form hypotheses about clients' thinking skills strengths and weaknesses.

- Helpers and clients can collect information about action skills in interviews: for instance from client self-report, observing clients, focusing on actions questions and role plays.

- Helpers and clients can also collect action skills information from clients' natural or home settings.

- Helpers use information collected when identifying, clarifying and assessing problems to redefine them in skills terms. Redefinitions are statements about thinking and action skills weaknesses sustaining problems.

- Some skills for redefining problems include: presenting a rationale; clarity and parsimony; using a whiteboard; checking clients' reactions; and attending to feelings. Helpers can also encourage clients to observe and assess problematic skills between sessions.

STAGE 3

STATE WORKING GOALS AND PLAN INTERVENTIONS

Chapter 7 reviews how helpers and clients translate redefinitions of problems in skills terms into statements of working goals. Chapter 8 reviews skills of choosing and planning interventions to develop clients' self-helping skills.

SEVEN

How to State Working Goals

It is not enough to take steps which may some day lead to a goal; each step must be itself a goal and a step likewise.

Goethe

CHAPTER QUESTIONS

What differences are there between stating goals for problem management and for altering problematic skills?

Where are some advantages and risks of stating working goals?

What are some considerations in goals decisions?

How do helper thinking skills influence working goals?

What are some helper action skills for stating working goals?

PROBLEM MANAGEMENT AND PROBLEMATIC SKILLS GOALS

Though overlapping, a distinction exists between problem management and problematic skills goals. Short-term problems dominate much of helping. Clients want help to cope with immediate problems or crises, be they getting a job, dealing with a disruptive child, sleeping better, giving up excessive drinking, passing a test, or feeling less anxious. Statements of problem management goals can be general or specific. Often clients' *general* problem goals are obvious from their presenting concerns: for instance feeling less depressed or sleeping better. On other occasions, helpers may need to probe and spend time with clients to discover their real agendas or underlying problems. *Specific* problems management goals entail stating the outcomes by which helpers and clients can evaluate whether or not clients are adequately managing problems. Frequently, helpers need to work with clients in shaping general statements of outcome goals into more specific statements. For instance, 'I want to lose weight' needs to be translated into weight loss objectives stated in terms of pounds or kilograms. Effective helpers would also specify a period for maintaining weight loss.

Where possible, lifeskills helping goes beyond stating problem management goals to stating problematic skills goals. Even if clients are to attain problem management goals they require assistance in developing skills strengths. In Chapter 2, I mentioned that clients' problems often extend both *horizontally*, or to other current similar situations, and *vertically*, or to future similar situations. Problematic skills goals stem from redefinitions of clients' problems in skills terms. Such goals can encompass thinking and action skills for managing a specific current problem, other similar current problems, and similar future problems. Ideally lifeskills are for life, not just for managing immediate problems.

Helpers and clients can have both problem management goals and problematic skills goals. From Chapter 6 let us use the example of Jim Blake to illustrate similarities and differences between problem management goals and problematic skills goals. Getting another job is one of Jim Blake's problem areas. Jim's problem management goal of getting another job could be further specified in terms of what kind of job and by when. The various problem management steps in obtaining a job could be stated as sub-goals, each with a time frame. For instance, making a career résumé, information seeking about advertised job opportunities, creating and using an informal contact network, creating and implementing a marketing plan, and developing interview skills are all sub-goals with target dates. However, only the sub-goal of developing interview skills is stated in skills language. The other sub-goals are stated as tasks. For instance, while Jim needs to make a career résumé, he also needs to develop skills of making and updating this. The risk of only stating sub-goals as tasks is that it increases the likelihood of inadequately specifying and instructing the requisite subskills. This shortcoming may not only lead to inefficiencies in managing the current problem, but may contribute to less transfer of learning for handling future job-getting situations.

Helpers should state problematic skills goals or sub-goals not only in terms of action skills but of thinking skills as well. For instance, Jim may set himself the task sub-goal of making a career decision. He may even decide on a time frame for this. However, there is a huge difference between the task sub-goal of making a single career decision and that of developing skills for making effective career decisions, not only for now but in future. If career decision making is viewed as a single task rather than as a set of skills, helpers may play down or ignore some other thinking skills that Jim requires beyond straightforward decision-making skills. For instance, Jim may also need to work on possessing realistic personal rules about achievement.

ADVANTAGES AND RISKS OF WORKING GOALS

Establishing working goals has both advantages and risks. The following are some advantages of collaborating with clients to state working goals.

Helping clients become authors of their lives. Stating working goals helps clients assume rather than avoid personal responsibility for managing problems and problematic skills. Goals negotiated with clients enable them to become authors of their lives rather than drift aimlessly or live out other people's goals as if they were their own.

A bridge to working. A great risk in helping is that helpers and clients talk rather than work. Helping may become directionless without working goals (Cormier & Cormier, 1985). Stating working goals clearly establishes an expectancy that helpers and clients will expend effort to attain them.

Clarity of focus. Well-stated working goals clearly identify the problematic skills on which clients need to work. Where confusion and aimlessness may have reigned before, now clients have reasonably clear objectives toward which to strive. Working goals focus on what is important and, thus, economize client effort by excluding or de-emphasizing peripheral activities.

Increased motivation. Working goals can increase clients' motivation and persistence because they provide clients with something tangible to attain. Working goals may also increase helpers' motivation because they too have objectives to attain.

A basis for planning interventions. If working goals are neither stated nor clear, helpers and clients do not have an adequate basis for selecting strategies and planning interventions.

A basis for evaluation. Despite the fact that working goals differ in how easy they are to measure, statements of goals provide a basis for clients and helpers to evaluate progress and success. Clients can monitor and evaluate targeted skills at the start of, during, at the end of, and after helping.

An impetus for self-helping. Statements of working goals identify skills strengths that clients require both now and in future. After helping, clients are more likely to remember clear statements of skills strengths than if no such statements exist. They can use this knowledge to consolidate targeted skills.

There are also risks to stating goals. Such risks usually happen if goals are set and stated the wrong way or prematurely. Most risks are not inherent in setting goals.

Insufficient emphasis on feelings. Some clients require time, space and support to get in touch with their capacity to feel and their wants and wishes. A risk of stating goals is that clients are insufficiently helped to experience themselves as feeling persons. There can be an overemphasis on thinking and doing at the expense of experiencing feelings.

Premature restriction of focus. Goals stated too rigidly early on interfere with helpers' and clients' ability to deal with emerging problems and problematic skills. The die has been cast too soon. Some problems are so complex that simple statements of goals in initial sessions do not do them justice.

Inaccuracy and superficiality. Helpers may wrongly assess problems and problematic skills and this inaccuracy is reflected in statements of working goals. Furthermore, helpers may only focus on parts of problems and on less rather than more important problematic skills.

Eliciting resistances and rejection. Statements of goals may elicit resistances, 'Yes . . . but' responses and even open defiance. Working goals that may be intellectually tidy to helpers may be emotionally untidy to clients who ultimately have to implement them. Clients' resistances and reservations may be openly aired or later become manifest in lack of commitment.

Controlling and pressuring clients. Helpers may state goals more to meet their own needs for certainty and achievement than to help clients. They may have their own agendas and pet theories that they work into goal statements. In addition, helpers may state goals in ways that pressure clients: for instance setting unrealistically high goals, or stating them in a demanding manner.

CONSIDERATIONS IN GOALS DECISIONS

Besides the distinction between problem management goals and problematic skills goals, there are many other considerations when deciding on goals.

Superordinate goals

In lifeskills helping, there are two main categories of higher or superordinate goals. In Chapter 1, I distinguished between the ultimate goal of lifeskills helping, personal excellence, and mediating goals, specific lifeskills. Another category of superordinate goals is that of learning to apply the lifeskills helping model as a self-helping skill for managing problems and altering problematic skills. Instead of helpers using the model to assist clients in identifying and working on problematic skills, clients learn to do much of this work on their own. The lifeskills helping model aims to assist clients in using targeted skills in future similar situations. However, if the model itself is taught as a set of skills, clients can apply it on their own to problems and problematic skills different from those for which they originally requested help. Though my lifeskills model and Egan's problem management model differ, Egan too regards his problem management model not just as a helper tool, but also as a client self-helping tool (Egan, 1990).

Goals as hypotheses

Both helpers and clients are practitioner-researchers: helpers in how best to help, clients in how best to live. Helpers need to view problematic skills goals scientifically.

They are really a series of 'If . . . then . . .' hypotheses. For instance, '*If* I develop my career decision-making skills, *then* I will make better career decisions both now and in future.' Career decision-making skills might then be broken down into a series of sub-hypotheses contributing to the main hypothesis. Another example is that of a shy teenager wishing to be more outgoing: 'If I possess a more realistic personal rule concerning others' approval, then I am likely to become more outgoing.' Though not always using the language of research, helpers and clients hypothesize which problematic skills contribute to sustaining problems. They then state as working goals developing strengths in targeted skills. As hypotheses, such goals are open to modification in light of feedback and changing circumstances. For instance, clients and helpers may find that another problematic skill is more important to achieving desired outcomes than one initially agreed upon.

Initial and emergent goals

In initial sessions, helpers can identify, clarify and redefine some problems in skills terms and then negotiate goals that stand throughout helping. Goals are more likely to be stable where problems are relatively focused and have brief time frames, for instance passing a forthcoming driving test. However, on other occasions helpers take into account emergent goals either in addition to, as modifications of, or even instead of initial goals. Situations where helpers need to pay attention to emerging goals include the following. First, some clients may be highly anxious and badly out of touch with their valuing process. Highly vulnerable clients may require nurturing relationships to lower their defences to the point where they are prepared to accept some responsibility for working on their problems. Until they have had more time to share feelings and trust helpers, it may be premature to negotiate thinking and actions skills goals. Second, some problems, such as marital problems, may be so complex that helpers are either unwilling or unable to state a full range of goals at the end of an initial assessment. Too full a statement of problematic skills goals may only confuse clients and risks turning helping into an arid intellectual exercise. Too rigid an early skills definition of clients' problems may also exclude much valuable information that will emerge during helping. Third, both for focused and for more complex problems and problematic skills, helpers always need to be prepared to alter and fine-tune goals in light of feedback and changed client circumstances.

Imposed or negotiated goals

A basic question is 'Whose goals are these?' Goals can be helper-centred or client-centred. Ideally they are both. Helpers and clients collaborate to identify, clarify, assess and redefine problems in skills terms. When helpers sensitively and thoroughly conduct stages 1 and 2 of the lifeskills helping model, statements of working goals in stage 3 should seem the logical outcome of this earlier work. The negotiations involved in arriving at common conceptualizations of clients' problems and problematic skills essentially mean that working goals based on these conceptualizations have been negotiated too. Because the ground has been prepared, both helpers and clients subscribe to the same goals.

The risk of helpers imposing their own agendas as goals is ever present. Sometimes helpers are insufficiently thorough in redefining problems in skills terms and rush into goal statements to meet their own needs for certainty and achievement. Beginning helpers may be especially prone to this. Some helpers may work within a narrow range of thinking and action skills, and so suggest a more restricted or lop-sided range of goals than desirable. Helpers may present skills redefinitions and goals to clients in ways that leave little room for discussion. In addition, clients may be prone to acquiesce and say 'yes' to working goals when they mean 'no' or 'maybe'. Helpers may fail to recognize cues that further negotiation and explanation are necessary.

Commitment to goals

Clients can have varying degrees of commitment to goals (Janis & Mann, 1977; Watson & Tharp, 1989). Sometimes clients openly express doubts about their commitment; on other occasions they may talk commitment, but later fail to act it. It is one thing for helpers to state goals, another for clients to agree to them, and still another for clients to work to implement them both now and in future. Client ambivalence is almost always a feature of commitment to working goals. On the one hand, they wish to be problem free, yet on the other hand resist fully admitting personal responsibility for changing problematic skills. In varying degrees, they still believe in magical solutions. Fear of change, fear of failure and fear of success can all interfere with commitment (Nelson-Jones, 1991). Commitment to working goals may entail giving up the pay-offs and secondary gains of previous patterns of behaviour: for instance, blaming others, or substance abuse. In addition, clients may go back to environments that reward skills weaknesses rather than help build targeted skills strengths.

Helpers need to pay close attention to clients' degrees of commitment to goals. Clients may be more likely to commit themselves to goals that are negotiated rather than imposed. Goals expressed in skills terms may require further explanation and clarification, both initially and later. It is difficult for clients to be committed to working goals that they do not fully understand. You may need to work with clients in exploring the rewards for change as well as the losses in not changing. You need to acknowledge that there may be heavy costs to clients in giving up long-established habits of self-defeating thinking and acting. You can identify and discuss with clients potential difficulties and setbacks that may lower confidence. In addition, when planning interventions, if possible you should build in rewards. For instance, early alleviation of psychological pain or early success in achieving a sub-task may strengthen commitment to goals. Supportive helping relationships also reward clients.

Defining goals

One way of defining goals is in terms of progress in altering problematic skills rather than in coping with a specific problem. However, when focusing on problematic skills, helpers and clients need to consider criteria for progress and goal attainment. In reality, since clients have to maintain skills strengths throughout their lives, problematic skills weaknesses are never cured. Nevertheless, helpers can think in terms of how best to observe and measure changes in problematic thinking and action skills, even if somewhat imprecise. For instance, the overall goal of a stopping smoking treatment programme is in its title. However, helpers also need to think of how to measure the component skills of giving up smoking and of maintaining this change. For instance, a smoker may have a thinking skills predicting weakness that, 'Lung cancer cannot happen to me.' For a given period, the client might keep a log of how many times the thought occurred and also whether he/she disputed it and then made a more realistic predictive self-statement. The problematic skills goal might be, by the end of the period, either to have eliminated the false prediction completely or, if it occurs, always to dispute and replace it.

HELPER THINKING SKILLS

How helpers think influences how they set goals. The following are some thinking skills relevant to setting and stating goals.

USE THE LIFESKILLS CONCEPTUAL FRAMEWORK AND LANGUAGE Helpers stating goals in the lifeskills model need to assess and conceptualize problems within it. Helpers think not just about problems, but about identifying problematic skills sustaining problems. In stage 2, assess problems and redefine them in skills terms, lifeskills helpers almost invariably break problems down into their thinking and action skills components. Helpers state both overall goals and problematic skills sub-goals necessary to attain and maintain overall goals.

ATTRIBUTE ACCURATELY 'Who owns the working goals?' and 'Who owns the responsibility for attaining working goals?' If helpers and clients collaborate well in the detective work of stages 1 and 2 of the lifeskills model, then redefinitions of their problems in skills terms should be reasonably clear to clients. Statements of working goals follow easily from mutually agreed upon conceptualization of problems and problematic skills. Helpers have fulfilled their responsibilities in assisting clients to understand their problems in ways in which they can work on them. The working goals can be owned by both clients and helpers, though in different ways. Clients own the goals for themselves, whereas helpers own the goals as guides to how to help. Both helpers and clients also own responsibility for attaining working goals: the helper's being a 'professional' responsibility, the client's a 'personal' responsibility.

Helpers need to beware of attributing too much responsibility for forming working goals to themselves. Clients are more likely to feel responsible for attaining goals if they have contributed to shaping them. Goals need to be realistic for clients, perceived as important for managing their problems, consistent with their values, and comprehensible. Forming and stating working goals is a shared responsibility between helpers and clients.

POSSESS REALISTIC PERSONAL AND HELPING RULES Unrealistic personal and helping rules may negatively influence how helpers set goals. Here are some unrealistic helper rules that may contribute to faulty statements of working goals:

'I must get quick results.'
'I must always help clients set high goals.'

'I must be the person in control.'
'I must always state working goals comprehensively.'
'Clients must always be treated as though they are highly vulnerable.'
'I must always state working goals before the end of the initial session.'
'I must never revise initial statements of working goals.'
'All helping must be short term.'
'All helping must be long term.'
'I must always be liked by my clients.'
'I must never make mistakes when stating working goals.'

Helpers may need to identify, dispute and reformulate unrealistic personal rules that place unnecessary demands on themselves and clients. Unrealistic rules can rigidify the helping process as well as pressure or infantilize clients. Furthermore, helpers may be excessively vulnerable to client feedback and 'things needing to go right'. Ideally, helpers formulate and state working goals not on the basis of their own irrational thinking, but solely in clients' best interests.

PERCEIVE ACCURATELY In many ways how accurately you perceive may influence how you state working goals. First, you may have ignored or misperceived significant information when identifying, clarifying and assessing clients' problems. For instance, your perceptions of your clients' problems may be coloured by your own past struggles and present circumstances. Hence your skills redefinitions may have suffered and, in turn, your statements of working goals. Second, you may misperceive how realistic your goals are for clients. Third, you may misperceive how well your clients comprehend your statement of working goals, even though you may have checked this with them. Fourth, you may misperceive cues of resistance and lack of commitment and thus not address them. Perceiving your clients accurately is always difficult since helpers bring so much of their own 'stuff' into helping. Nevertheless, you must be aware that you are always at risk of distorting clients. You should endeavour to identify and correct the specific ways in which you do this.

PREDICT REALISTICALLY Statements of working goals assume the prediction that if clients achieve some or all of the targeted skills they will have made progress in managing problems. Helpers may overpredict or underpredict clients' capacities to develop skills strengths; they may set working goals that are unrealistically high or low. Furthermore, helpers may inaccurately predict the rewards and costs of clients' efforts to change their behaviours. In predicting reward inaccurately, helpers may overestimate or underestimate good consequences. Similarly, in predicting cost inaccurately, helpers may underestimate or overestimate bad consequences (Nelson-Jones, 1989). Predicting reward and cost accurately is relevant to predicting clients' persistence in working towards targeted goals. To counteract tendencies to inaccurate predictions when setting goals, helpers can review probability more stringently and reassess clients' coping capacities. Helpers can also plan interventions to assist clients in handling difficulties and setbacks.

HELPER ACTION SKILLS

Statements of working goals are the 'flip-side' of redefinitions of clients' problems in skills terms. Helpers take the redefinitions expressed in terms of thinking skills and action skills weakness hypotheses and turn them into statements of positive helping and self-helping objectives. Much overlap exists between the skills for redefining problems in skills terms and stating working goals.

PRESENT A RATIONALE Towards the end of stage 2, the helper presented a rationale for redefining problems in skills terms. Once helper and client have arrived at a mutually agreed conceptualization of a problem area in skills terms, the helper can make a transition statement that introduces the idea of working goals:

> Jan, we have now identified and agreed upon some possible thinking and action skills weaknesses by which you may contribute to your poor relationship with Pam. Your overall goal is to have a good mother–daughter relationship with her. By reversing your possible skills weaknesses into positive objectives, you can more easily see where you might work to develop skills strengths. Hopefully, possessing a positive statement of goals will motivate you to persist in working on them both now and in future. Also, such a statement of goals gives us a focus for discussing how best to attain them. However, if new or different goals emerge we can update or change our statement of goals.

USE A WHITEBOARD A great advantage of using a whiteboard is the ease with which two-column T redefinitions of thinking and action skills weaknesses can be edited into statements of desired skills strengths. In addition, the whiteboard makes it easier for clients to discuss goals. A further advantage of a whiteboard is that both clients and you can take down the same statement of thinking and action skills goals for each problem.

USE CHECKING SKILLS Even though you have checked your redefinition with your client and, if necessary, modified it, you should still check their reactions to seeing their problematic skills weaknesses expressed as positive working goals. Clients may require further clarification regarding some of the skills. Though you may try to clarify skills goals, you may have to defer to subsequent sessions detailed explanations of them. Furthermore, clients may not fully grasp the meaning of certain skills, especially thinking skills, until they have become proficient in using them.

ATTEND TO FEELINGS Some clients feel very positive about statements of working goals and see them as highly motivating. However, statements of working goals may threaten others. Goals connote the need for effort and change. A degree of ambivalence is inevitable in regard to working goals. Pay attention to resistances and reservations. Helpers require sensitivity to voice and body cues of inadequate commitment. Even though clients may verbalize commitment and confidence, their nonverbal messages may indicate otherwise. If possible work through with clients their reservations and commitment difficulties. Some clients feel more comfortable about goals when they become clearer about how to attain them.

BE FLEXIBLE There are many reasons why you need to be flexible in stating working goals. Always take client and problem considerations into account. Some clients may come for only one session, for instance in regard to asking for a promised pay rise, and seek more a strategy for handling their problem than a skills analysis. Children may require brief and simple statements of working goals focused more on action skills rather than thinking skills, though the latter may be relevant. With clients with complex problems, you might state working goals for the problem area of greatest priority to your client. You might then either indicate that other problem areas will be dealt with in similar fashion or mention one or two illustrative working goals for each problem area. If a specific problematic skill features in many different problem areas, for instance unrealistic personal rules, you may state developing realistic personal rules as a broad working goal. Another occasion for flexibility is that people in crisis may require goals and a plan to deal with their immediate predicament. Helping these clients think about problems in skills terms and stating working goals may come later, if at all.

Examples of stating working goals

Below are examples of stating working goals. The first example consists of statements of working goals, one brief and the other fairly detailed, for two of Jim Blake's work-related problems. The second example is a statement of working goals for a shy college student, Anita Walton.

Example 1: Case study: Jim Blake

Part Six: State working goals

Having agreed on a two-column T redefinition of Jim's handling being fired problem (see Chapter 6), the counsellor Sam Rushton told Jim that he would edit it on the whiteboard so that it became a statement of the skills strengths needed to manage the problem better.

Handling being fired
Thinking skills goals
Perceive my former company accurately.
Use self-talk to cope with my anger.
Possess realisic personal rules concerning being
   fired.

Action skills goal
Make limited contact with former employer, for instance regarding references.

Sam checked Jim's reactions to this statement of working goals. Then he and Jim wrote down the working goals to help remember them. Sam and Jim then moved on to a common conceptualization in skills terms of Jim's 'getting another job' problem. Again, Sam used the whiteboard. Once he and Jim were satisfied with the two-column T redefinition (see Chapter 6), Sam edited it so that it became a statement of working goals.

Getting another job
Thinking skills goals
Own more responsibility for my choices in life.
Become more in touch with my wants and wishes.
Use coping self-talk, for instance when faced with interviews.
Possess more realistic personal rules, for instance regarding achievement.
Perceive myself more accurately, for instance work on lessening my negative self-labels.
Make realistic predictions about the possible length of my job search.
Clarify my values.
Develop goal-setting skills, in regard to both career goals and job search goals.
Develop more realistic and rigorous career decision-making skills.

Action skills goals
Develop professional skills in making a career résumé.
Develop my skills at creating and using an informal contact network to find out about unadvertised job opportunities.
Develop my skills at creating and implementing a marketing plan.
Improve my interview skills.
Develop my skills at managing time and engaging in meaningful activities independent of full-time employment.

Sam checked Jim's reactions to the above list of goals. Sam mentioned that when Jim next came, they would discuss a plan to help Jim attain his working goals.

Example 2: Case study: Anita Walton

Anita Walton, a 19-year-old college student, came to see a helper, Maureen Perrone, because she thought she was too shy. During stages 1 and 2 of the lifeskills helping model Maureen formulated many thinking and action skills weakness hypotheses. However, Maureen only used some of the main hypotheses in her skills redefinition of Anita's shyness problem. After some discussion and minor changes, Anita agreed to Maureen's conceptualization of her problem.

Anita's *thinking skills weaknesses* included:
(a) possessing an unrealistic personal rule regarding her absolute need for others' approval;
(b) misperceiving social situations by jumping to negative conclusions about others' reactions to her;
(c) misattributing responsibility by thinking that others should always make the first move to initiate contact;
(d) using negative self-talk before, during and after social exchanges.

Anita's *action skills weaknesses* included:
(a) speaking with a very quiet and diffident voice;
(b) poor initiating contact skills;
(c) poor self-disclosure skills;
(d) poor telephone skills.

Using the two-column T format, one column for thinking skills weaknesses and the other column for action skills weaknesses, Maureen wrote her redefinition of Anita's problem on the whiteboard. Maureen then edited what she had written into the following statement of working goals. Maureen checked Anita's reactions to this statement. Afterwards both helper and client recorded it. Maureen said that she would define these skills goals more fully in subsequent sessions.

Table 7.1 Anita's overall goal and working goals

Anita's overall goal:
To feel, think and act more confidently with people my age, especially males.

Anita's working goals:

Thinking skills goals	Action skills goals
Possess a realistic personal rule about approval.	Speak with a louder, more confident voice.
Perceive others' reactions to me accurately.	Develop my initiating more contact skills.
Attribute responsibility for initiating better.	Develop my self-disclosure skills.
Use coping self-talk.	Develop my telephone skills.

CHAPTER HIGHLIGHTS

• Although they overlap, a distinction exists between problem management and problematic skills goals.

• Problem management goals can focus on both general and specific desired outcomes.

• Problematic skills goals entail targeting for development the thinking and action skills that sustain problems.

• Statements of working goals are redefinitions of clients' problems in skills terms stated as goals to be worked towards both now and in future.

• Advantages of stating working goals include: helping clients become authors of their lives; building a bridge to working; clarity of focus; increased motivation; providing a basis for evaluation; providing a basis for planning interventions; and being an impetus for self–helping.

• Risks in stating working goals include: insufficient emphasis on feelings; premature restriction of focus; inaccuracy and superficiality; eliciting resistances and rejection; and controlling and pressuring clients.

- Considerations in goal decisions include: superordinate or higher goals; goals as hypotheses; initial and emergent goals; imposed or negotiated goals; commitment to goals; and how to define goals.

- Helper thinking skills for setting and stating goals include: use the lifeskills conceptual framework and language; attribute accurately; possess realistic personal and helping rules; perceive accurately; and predict realistically.

- Helper action skills for stating goals include: present a rationale; use a whiteboard; use checking skills; attend to feelings; and be flexible.

EIGHT
How to Plan Interventions

Little by little does the trick.

Aesop

CHAPTER QUESTIONS

What do the terms interventions and plans mean?

What are some criteria for choosing interventions?

What are different kinds of plans?

What are some considerations in developing plans?

What are skills for working with clients when choosing and planning interventions?

Statements of working goals provide the bridge to choosing interventions. Helpers as practitioner-researchers hypothesize not only about goals, but also about ways to attain them. This chapter focuses on some of the many issues and skills in choosing and planning interventions. Though the focus here is on initial sessions, helpers also choose and plan interventions for working goals that emerge during helping.

Some readers may consider that this chapter on choosing and planning interventions might be better placed after the chapters on the different interventions. I start with this chapter for two main reasons. First, in helping, choosing and planning interventions comes before intervening. Second, readers may find it easier to understand the five stages of the DASIE lifeskills model if presented in the order in which they occur rather than if they have to jump forwards and then backwards. You can still choose either to read or reread this chapter after reading the subsequent chapters on interventions.

Interventions and plans

Helpers make choices both concerning specific interventions and also about interventions used in combination. An important distinction exists between interventions and plans.

INTERVENTIONS In lifeskills helping, interventions are intentional behaviours designed to help clients attain problem management and problematic skills goals. In the context of this and subsequent chapters, interventions mean 'helping strategies' (Cormier & Cormier, 1985), 'effective procedures' (Hutchins & Cole, 1986), or 'therapy techniques' (Goldfried & Davison, 1976).

Interventions or strategies for change can be either helper-centred or client-centred. Put simply, with helper-centred interventions helpers do something to or for clients: for instance helpers may give clients advice on how to behave. With client-centred interventions, helpers develop clients' capacities to intervene in their own problem and problematic skills areas: for instance, helpers may assist clients in how to monitor their thinking. Both helpers and clients can be the intervening agents. In lifeskills helping, the object of all helper interventions should be to strengthen clients' own interventions: 'I as a helper am of most use to you as a client if I help you to intervene, at first with my assistance but later on your own, to develop and maintain *your* skills to manage *your* problems.' Helpers require a repertoire of interventions or intervention skills to cover a range of clients' lifeskills weaknesses. You may need to specialize in the most useful interventions for the client populations with which you deal because the range of clients' problems and skills weaknesses is so vast.

PLANS Plans are overall statements of how to combine and sequence interventions for managing problems and attaining working goals. They are the outlines, maps or diagrams that enable helpers and clients get from where they are to where they want to be. The term 'treatment plan' is sometimes used (for instance Cormier & Cormier, 1985). A possible risk with the term 'treatment plan' is that it may connote helper-centredness rather than helpers' developing clients' skills to help themselves. The term 'working plan' may be more appropriate, since plans provide frameworks within which both helpers and clients work. Plans indicate arranging interventions beforehand. However, as the Roman writer Publilius Syrus observed in the first century BC, 'It is a bad plan that admits of no modification.'

CHOOSING INTERVENTIONS

Many beginning helpers, after stating working goals, experience a sense of emptiness about their ability to do anything useful to help clients attain these goals. Going beyond assessment to choosing and planning interventions creates added pressures for them to 'deliver the goods'. It takes time for helpers to build a repertoire of interventions and confidence in their effectiveness. Frequently even experienced helpers find that decisions about interventions are not clear-cut and involve trade-offs between conflicting considerations. Beginning helpers' anxieties about choosing interventions are not in themselves detrimental – how you handle your anxieties determines this.

Criteria for choosing interventions

This section focuses more on how to choose interventions than on choosing how to implement interventions. Once you have statements of working goals your next step is to choose appropriate interventions. You do not start from scratch in doing this. Even as you clarified, assessed and redefined clients' problems in skills terms, you were probably making intervention hypotheses. Now is the time to clarify and refine these. Below are some criteria to include in your decision making about interventions.

IMPORTANCE OF MAINTAINING A SUPPORTIVE RELATIONSHIP Whatever other interventions you choose, you always offer them within the context of supportive helping relationships. A risk for some helpers when breaking down problems, setting working goals and specifying interventions is that they become too technique oriented. The person emphasis of supportive relationships may be the major intervention for some vulnerable clients until they gain more confidence and insight. For all clients, supportive relationships can contribute to the quality of the working alliance (Kokotovic & Tracey, 1990) and facilitate clients' motivation. Furthermore, supportive relationships can assist more task-oriented interventions, for instance by providing a better emotional climate for role plays and coached performance of skills.

EMPHASIS OF INTERVENTIONS ON MANAGING PROBLEMS OR ALTERING PROBLEMATIC SKILLS You and your client may choose to focus more on managing an immediate problem than on altering problematic skills. How you intervene will be heavily influenced by such a decision. Situations where there may be more emphasis on problem management than on problematic skills interventions include the following. First, clients may be in crisis. They may feel overwhelmed by the intensity of their emotions and be in shock, disoriented, highly anxious, extremely depressed, very angry, contemplating suicide and fearing insanity or nervous breakdown. The objectives of helper interventions in crises include protecting clients, calming them down, and assisting them in here-and-now problem solving and planning so that they regain a sense of control over their lives. A clear focus on problematic skills is deferred until later, if at all. Second, clients may be faced with coping with immediate problems: for instance upcoming exams, public-speaking engagements or confrontations with difficult people. Together helpers and clients develop 'game plans' for dealing with immediate situations rather than emphasize self-helping skills for afterwards. Third, clients may have limited goals. Dealing with an immediate problem may be all that they have time or inclination for. Fourth, your own schedule as helper may be so busy that all you can offer is 'first-aid' problem management assistance.

RELEVANCE OF INTERVENTIONS FOR ATTAINING WORKING GOALS Lifeskills helping heavily emphasizes both thinking and action working goals rather than either on its own. Having taken the trouble to assess clients and negotiate working definitions, helpers have laid the basis for selecting interventions. For instance, with shy Anita (see Chapter 7, pp.199–200) who has a thinking skills goal of possessing a realistic personal rule about approval, the helper might consider a range of interventions focused on developing this personal rule skill: for instance, providing a rationale for the intervention, identifying existing unrealistic rules both inside and outside helping sessions, demonstrating disputing and reformulating rules, rehearsing and coaching the client, and setting appropriate homework. For shy Anita's action skills goal of speaking in a louder, more confident voice, the helper might consider a range of interventions: for instance, asking Anita to get feedback from significant others on how they find her voice, encouraging Anita to speak up during helping, exploring how she thinks and feels when she speaks quietly or loudly, setting her systematic speaking more loudly tasks both inside and outside helping, and possibly getting her to see a speech therapist. Your choice of working goals provides a good framework for your choice of interventions, with each intervention having many sub-choices in how you actually apply it.

HELPER COMPETENCE TO ADMINISTER INTERVENTIONS Cormier and Cormier observe that 'if your only tool is a hammer, you will probably treat everything as if it were a nail' (1985, p.297). Wise helpers know the limitations of their tools. You need to acknowledge the range of interventions within which you can work effectively. Initially beginning helpers might focus on building a repertoire of central helping interventions. For example, the intervention of helping clients build the thinking skill of identifying, disputing and reformulating unrealistic personal rules is pertinent to numerous client problem areas (Ellis, 1980, 1989). Similarly, the intervention of helping clients learn skills of delivering verbal, voice and bodily assertive messages has widespread relevance (Alberti & Emmons, 1990). Another criterion for developing your repertoire of interventions is to focus on those of most use to client populations with which you either work or are likely to work. As time goes by, most helpers acquire a fund of practical knowledge concerning what working goals and interventions are helpful for which kinds of problem and problematic skills weakness.

Beginning helpers cannot expect to perform interventions competently without adequate training, practice and supervision. A small number of interventions performed thoroughly generally help clients much more than a greater number performed superficially. You put much less pressure on yourself if aiming to achieve limited agendas well rather than attempting too much. Though some beginning helpers are overambitious, many underestimate their helping potential. This underestimation may lead beginning helpers either not to suggest interventions or not to implement them confidently. Self-consciousness and a degree of discomfort are inevitable when learning new interventions. If underconfident, you require good training and supervision coupled with realistic self-appraisal. You also need to be open to client feedback about how well you implement interventions. Experienced helpers too may doubt themselves as they take risks to develop their repertoire of interventions. Nevertheless, it is important that they continue to build their skills.

THEORETICAL AND RESEARCH SUPPORT FOR INTERVENTIONS Skilled helpers operate within theoretical frameworks. The interventions you offer should be based on psychological principles of learning, maintaining and changing behaviour. The lifeskills framework presented in Chapter 1 provides an introductory theoretical statement for assessing interventions. You should aim to know and keep abreast of the practitioner and research literature in the areas in which you help or intend helping. This way you can find out about both existing and new interventions. Also, you can assess their empirical support. Sometimes you may come across findings in the literature which indicate that interventions used in combination are more effective than interventions used in isolation. For instance, in marital work, focusing on increasing the exchange of rewarding behaviours between partners is more helpful in combination with communication training (Jacobson *et al.*, 1985). On other occasions, you may find that individual different interventions proved effective in achieving similar outcomes. For instance, Moon and Eisler (1983) conducted a study on anger control with undergraduate subjects randomly assigned to cognitive stress inoculation, problem solving, social skills, or minimal attention groups. At post-treatment, all treatment groups reported significantly fewer anger-provoking incidents and had significantly lower scores on an anger inventory than the control group. However, there were also between-group differences: the problem-solving and social skills groups displayed more socially skilled assertive behaviour in the presence of anger-provoking stimuli than did the cognitive stress inoculation group. Reasons why different interventions may lead to similar outcomes include the common contribution of the helping relationship across each intervention and the increases in clients' self-efficacy beliefs (beliefs in their ability to cope with their environments) brought about by different interventions. When reading research studies, pay particular attention to the maintenance of treatment gains. Always read the research literature critically.

CLIENT CONSIDERATIONS Numerous client considerations influence both choosing and implementing interventions. Client considerations include the following.

Anxiety level and sense of worth. Helpers always need to take into account how psychologically vulnerable clients are and how badly their anxieties interfere with how they feel, think and act. For example, marital conflict communication interventions assume clients' abilities to accept some responsibility for contributing to marital distress. Specific interventions for building career decision-making skills may be premature for clients badly out of touch with their valuing process. Action skills interventions to assist highly anxious clients initiate friendships may need to await their obtaining a sufficient sense of self-worth to implement them.

Motivation and resistances. With its emphasis on developing clients' self-helping skills, motivation is a critical issue in lifeskills helping. As with goals, clients can say 'yes' to interventions when they mean 'no' or 'maybe'. Helpers need to assess clients' motivation for implementing interventions and explore potential difficulties and resistances. Clients need to own interventions both intellectually and emotionally in order to exhibit commitment to attaining them. Interventions that bring early rewards, including relief of psychological distress, enhance motivation.

Expectations and priorities. Related to motivation is the degree to which interventions are geared to outcomes that clients want and expect from helping. You always need to take clients' priorities into account. For instance, clients who enter helping wanting to manage an immediate problem may not want interventions focused on longer-term skills building. Clients seeing career issues as the main focus for helping may resist interventions focused on their personal lives.

Age and maturity. Helpers need to adjust interventions to the age of clients. For example, though friendship skills for adults and pre-teenage children have similarities, children and adults require somewhat different skills for relating to peer and friendship groups. You also need to take into account how much both children and adults know about relationships, and must deliver interventions according to the age and maturity of clients: for instance, by varying use of language.

Intelligence level and ability to comprehend interventions. Depending on their intelligence level, some clients may find difficulty in comprehending certain interventions, for instance the thinking skills of identifying possible misperceptions, generating alternatives and choosing best-fit perceptions. Helpers need to work with interventions that clients can comprehend. Ultimately clients have to understand the choices involved so that they can implement lifeskills on their own.

Culture. Helpers need to take into account clients' cultures when choosing and implementing interventions. For instance, the rules for work and personal relationships differ greatly across cultures (Argyle, 1986); relationship skills interventions need to take into account relevant cultural rules.

Sex and gender. Depending on their biological sex, clients may have learned different skills strengths and weaknesses. Helpers need to be careful to avoid fitting clients into masculine and feminine stereotypes. Nevertheless, they can still assess where inappropriate sex-role conditioning interferes with the development of clients' lifeskills, and choose interventions accordingly.

Support factors. Families, peer groups, friendship groups and work colleagues can support or interfere with skills acquisition. Sometimes clients can be trained to identify and use environmental supports better. As part of this process they may also learn skills of being more supporting to others. On other occasions interventions may focus on helping clients develop skills to protect themselves from environmental pressures.

Practical considerations. Practical considerations may influence choice of interventions: for instance, pressing current difficulties, threatening upcoming tasks, unexpected challenges and stresses, time available for helping, whether or not the client lives locally, financial circumstances and so on.

DEVELOPMENT OF SELF-HELPING SKILLS Where possible, select and implement interventions that develop clients' self-helping skills. Some interventions may directly address issues of clients' maintaining skills: for instance, helping clients develop realistic expectations and attributions about the difficulty of acquiring and maintaining skills. Helpers may also choose to implement interventions in ways that emphasize self-helping: an example is to ensure that clients understand and can verbalize the sequence of choices involved in specific skills: for instance self-administered relaxation as contrasted with helper-administered relaxation.

APPROPRIATENESS OF GROUP INTERVENTIONS Helpers need to consider whether clients might best attain some or all of their working goals by attending one or more lifeskills training groups (Nelson-Jones, 1991). Other clients might benefit from joining longer-term, interactional groups, if possible incorporating a skills focus (Corey, 1990; Gazda, 1989; Yalom, 1985). Considerations relevant to selecting group interventions include the nature of the clients' problems, availability of appropriate groups and clients' willingness to participate in group work instead of, concurrently with, or after individual work.

APPROPRIATENESS OF INTERVENTIONS INVOLVING THIRD PARTIES Sometimes you may choose to work with clients' environments. For instance, with depressed, aggressive or attention-seeking pupils, school counsellors may choose to work with clients' parents or families as well. You can also involve third parties as helper's aides. For instance, you can enlist parents, teachers or peers to help shy clients develop confidence and skills. In a work setting, you can enlist the help of supervisors and managers, for example in developing employees' public-speaking skills.

APPROPRIATENESS OF REFERRAL Making referrals generally implies your assessment that other helpers can deal with clients' problems and problematic skills better than you can. You may start making referral hypotheses early in stage 1 of the lifeskills model. Whether or not you implement them then or later depends on whether and when you become sufficiently clear that referral is in your clients' best interests. If problems and problematic skills emerge that would be better dealt with by others, you may make referrals at later stages of helping.

Many considerations influence decisions as to whether referral is the best intervention. Ideally, helpers build up referral networks that enable them, where appropriate, to suggest suitable alternative helpers. You may neither have such a network nor be able to locate suitable alternative helpers. Your continuing to work with clients may be better than nothing. Often beginning helpers are acutely aware of their lack of experience; your perception that clients require referral may be heavily coloured by your doubts and anxieties. Another option is to continue working with clients, but obtain suitable supervision and support. On some occasions, you might rightly decide that others can work better with clients. Considerations influencing decisions about referring clients to other helpers include training, skills, values, time, cost, convenience and availability (Shaffer, 1976).

Sometimes you can make referrals and still work with clients. For instance, you may refer a client with little energy to a doctor as part of your assessment of his or her problems and problematic skills. You can also make referrals as part of overall treatment plans. For instance, when working with unemployed clients, you can refer them to workshops on job-seeking skills.

PLANNING INTERVENTIONS

Almost invariably, helpers use interventions in combination rather than in isolation. Consequently, as well as developing hypotheses about interventions, helpers develop hypotheses about how interventions might best be used in combination. In short, they develop working plans of varying degrees of structure to attain working goals.

Kinds of plans

Clients come to helping with a wide variety of problems, expectations, motivations, priorities, time constraints and lifeskills strengths and weaknesses. In lifeskills helping, helpers tailor interventions and plans to individual clients. The following are among the kinds of working plan that lifeskills helpers might consider.

PROBLEM MANAGEMENT PLANS Problem management plans are outlines of interventions and steps required to assist clients to manage specific problematic situations. Often, in brief helping, plans emphasize managing problems rather than altering problematic skills. Helpers wishing to focus on problematic skills may make treatment compromises in the interests of practicality. All that clients may have time or motivation for is to plan for managing immediate situations: for instance, a request for a pay rise, an imminent public-speaking engagement, a statistics test or a visit from the in-laws. Even in longer-term helping, helpers and clients can develop plans to deal with specific situations. However, in longer-term helping, planning for specific situations is more likely to take place within the framework of altering problematic skills weaknesses in the direction of strengths. Below are two examples of problem management planning.

Example A: In brief helping

Alex was a part-time student specializing in medical radiation. He was referred to the student counselling service by a faculty member after failing a mid-term exam in pathology, a subject he was already repeating. During the initial assessment, the counsellor assessed Alex as having limited motivation both for study and for counselling. However, Alex wanted to obtain his medical radiation qualification, and needed to pass the pathology course to do this. Alex and the counsellor agreed that the best way to spend the remainder of the first session was to develop a plan or 'survival kit' that would assist him to pass pathology. Here, as is often the case in brief helping, the statement of working goals merged into planning interventions to attain them. Using the whiteboard, the counsellor and Alex outlined the following problem management plan.

1. Obtain accurate and specific feedback on my strengths and weaknesses in the pathology mid-term exam I failed (within the next week).
2. Do weekly essays on major topics and get teaching assistant's feedback (for remainder of term).
3. Attend *all* pathology lectures (for remainder of term).
4. Attend *all* pathology tutorials (for remainder of term).
5. Define the pathology syllabus more precisely (within the next week).
6. Review what might be possible final exam questions (within the next three weeks).
7. Take properly structured notes (starting immediately).
8. Keep in contact with full-time classmates, so as not to miss tips about important areas for study and revision (starting immediately).
9. Organize study time systematically (prioritizing and time charting to be done as homework).

At the end of the session, Alex wrote down this plan.

A month later, Alex returned for a follow-up session. He reported he had made progress in items 1–8 of his plan. Much of the second session was spent developing Alex's skills of systematic time charting.

Example B: In extended helping

Katy came for counselling with numerous presenting concerns including depression, low self-esteem, difficulty holding down relationships and anxieties about being a female engineer. Katy's working goals included thinking and action skills for being more assertive. During her fifth weekly session, Katy and her counsellor planned how best to manage a specific current problem in Katy's life. Katy's first job after graduation was with a leading construction engineering company. When hired, she was promised a salary review after her first year's service. The company had not conducted this review three months into her second year. Katy and her counsellor formulated her overall problem management goal which was, before the end of two weeks, to ask her boss for a salary review. They then stated thinking and action skills working goals. For instance, an illustrative thinking skills goal was to develop a more realistic personal rule about discussing money. Illustrative action skills goals focused on verbal, voice and body messages for raising the issue of her salary review and requesting that it be conducted. Katy and her counsellor then developed a plan for how to make a salary review request when face to face with her boss. This plan included strategies for handling possible counter-moves by her boss. The counsellor demonstrated, coached and rehearsed Katy in the component skills of the plan.

PROBLEMATIC SKILLS: STRUCTURED PLANS Helpers and clients may consider a highly structured approach the best way to obtain some working goals. Structured plans or programmes are step-by-step training and learning outlines of interventions for attaining specific goals. Structured plans are commonly used in lifeskills training groups, for instance in assertion or stress management groups (Hopson & Scally, 1981; Gazda, 1989; Nelson-Jones, 1991). Structured plans may also be used to train individual clients in skills where working goals are clear and specific. Three variations of structured plans are predetermined programmes, tailor-made programmes and partially structured programmes.

Predetermined programmes. Helpers may work with clients using existing or modifications of existing packages or programmes to develop skills. Such skills development programmes may be in areas like parenting, career decision making, and weight control. Below are examples of helpers and clients using predetermined programmes.

Ken suffered from hypertension. A central working goal was to develop his relaxation skills, both physical and mental. Ken's helper decided that the best way to develop Ken's relaxation skills was to use a programme based on Bernstein and Borkovec's (1973) *Progressive Relaxation Training: A Manual for the Helping Professions.*

Lucy suffered from agoraphobia. Working goals included developing Lucy's self-talk skills for coping with feelings of panic and being able to leave home and perform feared tasks, such as going on buses and into stores. Lucy's helper negotiated with her that treatment interventions would be based on Mathews, Gelder and Johnston's (1981) *Programmed Practice for Agoraphobia: Clients' Manual.*

Tailor-made programmes. Programmes of interventions can be tailor made to specific problems or to specific persons. When tailor made to specific problems, they resemble predetermined packages. For instance, when Jim Blake saw the outplacement counsellor Sam Rushton about getting another job, Sam could either fit Jim into an existing programme on getting another job skill for unemployed executives, or design a programme specifically geared to Jim's skills weaknesses and needs, or combine the two approaches. In the tailor-made approach Sam develops a step-by-step outline to attaining Jim's working goals. Here Jim can be part of the planning process, with his specific goals, wishes and circumstances taken into account. The structured plan is suggested rather than prescribed.

Partially structured programmes. Helpers and clients can design programmes to attain working goals that have elements of structure, yet fall short of step-by-step structured programmes. For instance, in the case of the unemployed executive Jim Blake, another option for his counsellor was to set aside certain sessions for testing to assess interests and aptitudes and also for developing specific action skills, such as career résumé writing and interview skills. The agendas for the remaining sessions would be open to negotiation at the start of each session. Below is another example of a partially structured programme, a continuation of the Anita Walton case study from the end of Chapter 7, pp.199–200:

> Anita Walton's main presenting concern was shyness. Her helper Maureen Perrone worked out with Anita the following working goals. Anita's thinking skills goals were to: possess a realistic personal rule about approval; perceive others' reactions to me more accurately; attribute responsibility for initiating better; and use coping self-talk. Anita's action skills goals were to: speak with a louder, more confident voice; develop my initiating contact skills; develop my self-disclosure skills; and develop my telephone skills. Maureen Perrone had an extremely heavy client load which rarely allowed her to do long-term helping. She assessed Anita as not being seriously underconfident and suggested that they work for three further sessions at fortnightly intervals. Maureen's aim was to give Anita the maximum amount of self-helping skills within a limited time span. Maureen suggested the following programme to Anita. The first session had already been spent on assessment and stating working goals; the second session would mainly focus on interventions for Anita's thinking skills; the third session would mainly focus on interventions for Anita's action skills; the fourth session would be spent

filling learning gaps and consolidating trained skills as self-helping skills. During the fourth session, Maureen and Anita would review the advisability of holding a follow-up session, say three months later. Anita agreed to the programme, which allowed her flexibility within sessions but ensured that attention was clearly paid to both thinking and action skills rather than to one set of skills at the expense of the other.

PROBLEMATIC SKILLS: OPEN PLANS Open plans allow helpers and clients without predetermined structure to choose which interventions to use to attain which working goals, when. Many considerations influence decisions to adopt open plans. Some clients may require nurturing relationships to help them get more in touch with their feelings and reduce their anxieties. They may not be able to work effectively on thinking and action skills weaknesses until they feel less vulnerable. Also, some cases are complex and difficult to understand. Helpers risk prematurely deciding on interventions if they opt for too much structure too soon. Open plans allow helpers and clients to collaborate in setting session agendas. Such session agendas can emphasize material and the skills on which clients and helpers currently want to work. Open plans have the great advantage of flexibility. Clients may be more motivated to work on skills and material that have relevance at any given time than being run through existing programmes independent of current considerations. I revert to the example of Rob, used in Chapter 2 (pp.45–50), to illustrate a helper using an open plan.

Rob's overall goal was to improve his relationship with one of his teenage daughters, Ruth, and to improve his marriage. Sue Clark, Rob's counsellor, negotiated the following statement of working goals. Rob's thinking skills goals were: (1) to acknowledge that I am a chooser and responsible for my thoughts, feelings and actions; (2) to use coping self-talk when faced with provocations; and (3) to develop realistic personal rules concerning standards of family behaviour. Rob's action skills goals included: (1) developing good listening skills; (2) developing assertion skills with specific reference to how I state my wishes about my daughter's behaviour; and (3) developing conflict negotiation skills. Sue Clark realized that Rob's objective was to develop some skills as quickly as possible rather than have a long-term helping relationship. She suggested to Rob that instead of developing a formal plan to attain his working goals, the best way to proceed was to use appropriate interventions to develop his thinking and action skills in relation to material brought into each session. This would allow both of them flexibility on what they covered in each session, yet not preclude spending additional time on training specific skills, if necessary. Sue was confident in her repertoire of interventions for working on Rob's thinking and action skills. She also required Rob to do homework, including listening to audio-cassette recordings of each helping session.

Considerations in planning

Some helpers are good at designing and executing group lifeskills programmes, but poor at planning educational or training interventions for individual clients. They find it advantageous to combine interventions sequentially and systematically for groups, but for various reasons become less disciplined with individuals. Even when adopting open plans, some effective lifeskills group leaders still fail adequately to use their training skills. In the above section I emphasized varying degrees of structure for plans. Here I focus on plans for clients likely to develop skills from structured learning sequences. Most considerations mentioned below are also relevant to plans for managing specific problem situations.

PREPARATION TIME If you decide to design treatment plans for individual clients, when do you do it? Though you may discuss with clients possible interventions for attaining working goals, you may find it difficult to develop systematic plans during the same sessions. Instead, you may need to take time to do this before the next session. Some helpers do not develop systematic plans because they are unwilling to spend out-of-session time on this task.

INVOLVEMENT OF CLIENTS AND OTHERS Helpers need to consider at what stage and how much to involve clients in planning. Helpers' prior discussions about working goals provide some protection against making unacceptable plans. In addition, you always need to check that clients understand and are comfortable with proposed plans. If necessary, you can modify plans in light of client feedback. Sometimes you may consider it helpful to involve clients early in the planning process. Advantages of such involvement include taking clients' wishes and priorities into account and the fact that clients are more likely to implement plans that they have had some say in making. With clients' permission, you may sometimes involve significant others when planning, for instance partners, care-givers or parents.

SEQUENCING OF INTERVENTIONS What is the best way to sequence activities so as to attain working goals? Sometimes the logic in sequencing interventions is clear. For instance, with most unemployed executives, there are three logically sequenced steps in assisting them to become re-employed: (1) evaluation and career planning; (2)

developing a job marketing plan; and (3) implementing a job marketing plan (Davidson, 1988). Also, within an individual intervention like perceiving more realistically, the sequence of sub-interventions is clear: namely, identifying unrealistic perceptions, generating and evaluating alternative perceptions, and choosing the 'best-fit' perception. Here the learning tasks are cumulative. In action skills interventions, helpers often use step-by-step graduated tasks to develop clients' skills and confidence.

TIME FRAME FOR PLAN Helpers, clients and the learning process may all influence time allocated for carrying out plans. For instance helpers may have restricted amounts of time to work with clients, and may also want clients to participate in learning activities offered by others, for instance workshops, that are only available on specific dates. Client considerations include varying degrees of urgency in acquiring skills and different abilities to pay, if fees are involved. Learning process considerations include the degree to which sessions and planned activities should be intensive rather than spaced out, or a combination of the two. Also, should you plan for one or more follow-up or booster sessions?

MANAGEMENT OF LEARNING CONSIDERATIONS Helpers need to consider what is the best way to put across interventions. For each intervention, when should helpers use the following training and learning methods: assessment and facilitating client self-assessment, facilitation, verbal presentation, demonstration, in-session rehearsal, coaching, and homework assignments? Helpers also need to make decisions concerning the overall balance between facilitation and didactic input. Other considerations include availability of written training materials, such as training manuals and handouts, and of audiovisual materials and equipment. A further set of learning considerations includes sensitivity to the costs and rewards for clients of carrying out plans. How difficult are the plans' various elements? Where are clients' support factors, and how supportive are their helpers? When do clients obtain rewards from implementing planned activities?

EMPHASIS ON MAINTENANCE AND DEVELOPMENT OF SKILLS Always, when initially planning interventions, consider how to help clients maintain trained skills as self-help skills for afterwards. Both structured and open plans should emphasize clients' learning to use skills on their own. You can emphasize client thinking skills relevant to maintenance. As mentioned, examples of pertinent client thinking skills are possessing realistic expectations about the difficulty of maintaining change and also understanding the sequences of choices in targeted skills well enough to instruct themselves and, if necessary, make corrections. You can also plan interventions in ways that help clients maintain action skills. Ways of doing this include emphasizing overlearning, practice in real-life settings, and anticipating and working through difficulties in applying skills.

Helpers may leave developing more formal maintenance plans to stage 5 of the lifeskills model, ending and consolidating trained skills as self-help skills. At that stage you can take clients' end-of-helping skills levels into account as well as their current estimations of obstacles to maintaining skills. In brief helping, planning interventions, intervening and ending and consolidating self-helping skills may become compressed

Table 8.1 Draft of plan to assist Jim Blake develop 'getting another job' skills

SESSION	WORKING GOALS	ILLUSTRATIVE CONTENT
Week 1 Session 3 Counselling	Greater realism about job search Own more responsibility for choices Become more in touch with wants and wishes Clarify values Possess more realistic achievement rules	Presentation and discussion of plan in context of realities of job searching Checking out current state Facilitate self-exploring Further discussion and challenging of unrealistic achievement rules **Homework** Positive asset search Reading on career planning Write own occupational history focusing on choices
Planned activity – Testing	Perceive self more accurately Collect data relevant to job search goals	Complete interest, aptitude and occupational self-evaluation measures
Week 2 Session 4 Counselling	Perceive self more accurately Get in touch with wants and wishes Further work on job search goals Possess more realistic achievement rules	Review current state and homework Feedback and discuss test results Facilitate self-exploring **Homework** Thinksheet on rules Career planning exercise
Planned activity – All-day workshop	Creating a job marketing plan Utilizing informal networks Career résumé skills	Presentation, demonstration, coaching and practice in each skills area **Homework** Further develop job marketing plan and work on career résumé
Week 3 Session 5 Counselling	Develop goal-setting skills Develop skills at creating job marketing plan Own more responsibility for choices Be more in touch with wants and wishes	Review current state and homework Develop job plan Facilitate self-exploring Assess thinking and action skills for managing non-work time and set goals

Session 5 (cont.)	Managing time when unemployed	Work on thinking skills as needed **Homework** Refine job plan Collect information for job plan Do exercise on using non-work time
Planned activity – All-day workshop	Use coping self-talk Improve interview skills Improve skills at using informal network	Presentation, demonstration, coaching and practice in thinking and action skills for interviews **Homework** Continue data collection Imaginal rehearsal of job interviews using coping self-talk
Week 4 Session 6 Counselling	Thinking and action interview skills Other thinking and action skills as needed	Review current state and homework Coach and rehearse interview skills as needed Anticipate difficulties and setbacks in implementing job plan **Homework** Implement job plan Exercise: anticipating difficulties
Session 7 Counselling	Thinking skills for maintaining behaviour Maintaining action skills	Review of current state and homework Facilitate self-exploring Develop thinking and action skills strategies for maintaining and consolidating self-helping skills **Homework** Implement job plan Monitor progress in using skills and make corrections as needed

Follow-up sessions and telephone support as needed.

into one another. In such circumstances, helpers and clients have to plan for maintenance as best they can.

EVALUATION OF OUTCOMES OF PLAN In Chapter 6 I discussed ways of assessing feelings, thoughts and actions. When making plans, keep in mind the importance of clients' developing self-assessment skills and monitoring their progress. When stating working goals in skills terms, you have defined the areas in which it is important to observe change. Plans are successful to the extent that they efficiently help clients develop and maintain self-helping skills. If plans do not produce desired results, examine closely the reasons and, if necessary, modify plans. Also be prepared to modify plans if important information emerges during helping.

Outlining plans

Especially where plans involve some detail, consider writing outlines of plans. These may guide both your and your clients' work. Table 8.1 is an outline of a structured plan by the counsellor Sam Rushton for his client Jim Blake, the recently fired executive, to develop Jim's 'getting another job' skills.

> Sam has already seen Jim twice, the first time on company premises immediately after Jim was fired and the second time in Sam's office a few days later. In this second session, Sam and Jim agreed on a statement of working goals (see Chapter 7, p.198). Sam said that at the start of their next session he would present a plan to help Jim attain these goals. Sam mentioned that this plan would have three elements: counselling sessions; planned activities both to assess Jim's aptitudes and interests and to develop specific skills; and homework. Sam and Jim agreed that, though the job search might well take longer, a month should be the time frame for developing basic effective job search skills.

SKILLS FOR WORKING WITH CLIENTS

So far this chapter has mainly explored how helpers think when making intervention and planning hypotheses. Where detailed plans are not involved, helpers tend to discuss plans for how to attain working goals immediately after agreeing on goals. Below are some working with client skills.

MAKE TRANSITION STATEMENTS You may have signalled moving on to discussing interventions as part of your rationale for presenting working goals: for instance with a sentence like, 'Also, such a statement of goals gives us a focus for discussing how best to attain them'. The following are examples of possible transition statements after you have finished presenting and checking your client's agreement to working goals:

'Now that we have agreed on working goals, let's spend more time in discussing how best to attain them.'

'I would like to move on now to discuss ways in which we might work to build your skills.'

'Having agreed on working goals, we now need to plan how best to attain them.'

ENLIST COLLABORATION AND COMMITMENT Since the purpose of any intervention or combination of interventions is to develop client self-helping skills, it is crucial that you encourage clients' collaboration. One way of doing this is to involve clients from the start in the process of choosing interventions and planning their sequencing. You may jointly develop a plan using a whiteboard. On occasions when you present plans, you can do so in ways that imply that plans are series of suggestions for discussion that, if necessary, can be modified or fine tuned. Check your clients' comprehension and feelings about proposed plans. Explore reservations and, if necessary, negotiate changes in plans. You can explore with clients the payoffs and rewards as well as the costs of implementing plans.

GIVE SIMPLE EXPLANATIONS AND ANSWERS Without insulting your clients' intelligence, offer clear and simple explanations for suggested interventions and plans. You can give clients too much information so that they feel confused rather than motivated to work. Be prepared to answer questions, but again keep your answers simple and to the point. In initial sessions, the purposes of discussing interventions and plans are as much emotional and motivational as instructional. Clients feel better if they perceive that their helpers know ways that they can work on problems and problematic skills. Often it is best if you leave describing the detail of interventions until later, when clients require information for working on the specific skills.

DISCUSS EXPECTATIONS AND CONTRACT You and your clients can discuss your expectations of yourselves and each other in implementing plans. For instance, you may indicate that you expect regular attendance over a specified number of sessions, with possibly a joint review of progress at the end of this period. You may stress the necessity of diligently carrying out homework assignments. Sometimes helpers give clients written plans. These can assume the status of contracts by varying degrees of formality.

START IMPLEMENTING PLANS After helpers state working goals and discuss plans, they can then assign homework. One type of homework assignment is for clients to observe and monitor feelings, thoughts and actions in targeted skills areas. Sometimes clients can be instructed to start developing specific skills: for instance speaking louder or taking a few gentle risks in disclosing more information about themselves. Getting clients started on implementing plans right away has many advantages. First, it reinforces the idea of working rather than talking relationships. Second, clients may feel better for working on problems and problematic skills that have worried them for some time. Third, implementing plans may lead to short-term rewards that build motivation and commitment. Fourth, getting started enables profitable use of the time between first and second sessions. Ultimately this may mean one or more fewer sessions.

CHAPTER HIGHLIGHTS

- A useful distinction exists between interventions, or helping strategies, and plans, or how to use interventions in combination.

- Criteria for choosing interventions include: importance of maintaining supportive relationships; emphasis of interventions on managing problems or altering problematic skills; relevance for attaining working goals; helper competence; theoretical and research support; client considerations, for example anxiety level; development of self-helping skills; appropriateness of group interventions; involving third parties; and referral.

- Three categories of plan are: problem management plans; structured plans for problematic skills; and open plans for problematic skills.

- Considerations in planning include: preparation time; involvement of client and others; sequencing of interventions; time frame for plan; how to manage learning; emphasizing maintenance and development of skills; and evaluation.

- Helpers may need to outline plans for their own and clients' benefits.

- Skills for working with clients when choosing and planning interventions include: make transition statements; enlist collaboration and commitment; give simple explanations and answers; discuss expectations and contract; and start implementing plans.

STAGE 4

INTERVENE TO DEVELOP SELF-HELPING SKILLS

After helpers redefine clients' problems in skills terms, state working goals and plan how to attain them, they provide interventions or strategies to build clients' self-helping skills. Chapter 9 focuses on some central training skills for most interventions. Chapters 10, 11 and 12 focus on interventions for thinking skills, action skills, and feelings, respectively.

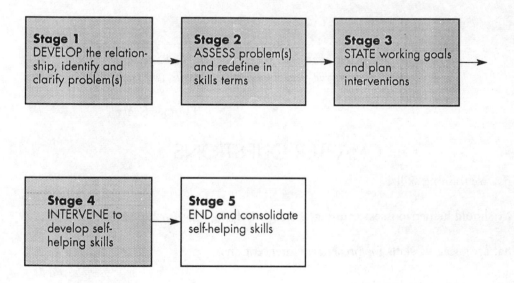

NINE

How to Use Training Skills to Deliver Interventions

The proverb warns that 'You should not bite the hand that feeds you.' But maybe you should, if it prevents you from feeding yourself.

Thomas Szasz

CHAPTER QUESTIONS

What are training skills?

Why should helpers possess training as well as helping relationship skills?

What are speaking skills for presenting interventions?

What are demonstrating skills?

What are coaching and feedback skills?

What are assigning homework skills?

THE HELPER AS TRAINER

In much of helper training the emphasis is on receiver or listening skills rather than on sender skills or training skills. Helpers as lifeskills educators also require educational or training skills. Helping is an educational process in which helpers flexibly use both relationship and training skills to assist clients to attain learning goals for now and later. This approach is consistent with Krumboltz's definition of counselling as a learning process designed to help people learn more effective ways of coping with their emotional, social and career problems (Krumboltz, 1988; Sampson & Krumboltz, 1991). Lifeskills helping encourages clients to learn for themselves and to understand, retain and use what they have learned.

What are training skills?

A broad definition of training skills includes how to facilitate, assess and design programmes as well as how to intervene (Nelson-Jones, 1991). Here I focus on the skills of how to deliver interventions, especially when first introducing clients to them. Clients as learners require helpers as trainers to guide learning. Helpers as trainers require not only knowledge of what interventions to provide, but also skills of how to intervene. The *what* of intervening needs to be supplemented by the *how* of intervening. The following are examples of helpers sabotaging effectiveness through poor training skills:

> Marie is a rehabilitation counsellor trainee on placement. She attempts to explain the thinking skill of identifying, disputing and reformulating unrealistic personal rules to a client, Robert, who devalues himself because of the after-effects of an industrial accident. Marie's presentation is muddled and she answers Robert's questions poorly. She also speaks in a monotone and keeps tugging at her hair. Robert is little the wiser about the skill Marie tries to communicate and feels frustrated both with himself and her.

> Lee is an Asian-American helper who tries to teach Tuan, a refugee from Vietnam, assertion skills. Lee spends a lot of time discussing with Tuan what he might say when he faces racial discrimination. However, at no stage does Lee demonstrate the voice and body messages that might accompany Tuan's assertive verbal messages. Consequently, Tuan does not really know how to be assertive.

> Rodney is a careers counsellor who thinks that Tracey requires better interview skills to increase her employability. Rodney talks about interview skills and demonstrates some of them. However, he never encourages and helps Tracy to rehearse and practise interview skills. Tracey tells her friends that she still goes to pieces in job interviews and devalues herself for not using the skills Rodney has shown her. Furthermore, at no stage has Rodney suggested to Tracey that she do specific homework assignments to build skills.

Helpers as trainers require good skills in three broad areas central to most interventions; namely *tell*, *show* and *do*. In Chapter 2 I mentioned that the corresponding learning modes were learning from hearing, observing and doing. In the above examples, Marie exhibited skills weaknesses in the area of tell, or helping Robert to learn from hearing; Lee, in the area of show, or helping Tuan learn from observing; and Rodney in the area of do, or helping Tracey learn from doing. You are more likely to impart lifeskills and clients are more likely to learn them if you use all three modes. When initially presenting a lifeskill, 'tell' may be accompanied by 'show' and then 'do'. On many occasions all three modes interact. For example when clients rehearse skills, 'do' may be interspersed with 'show' and 'tell'. Figure 9.1 shows the interrelationships of learning from hearing, observing and doing.

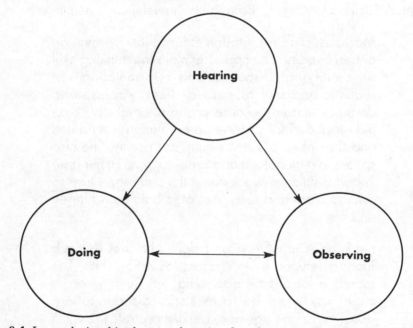

Figure 9.1 *Interrelationships between learning from hearing, observing and doing*

Helping relationship and training skills

Effective helpers require both good facilitative or relationship skills and good training skills. Helpers who only possess good relationship skills are unable to impart specific skills clearly and efficiently. They operate on the assumption that all clients have lifeskills strengths latent in their repertoires that will be unblocked by empathic helping relationships (Rogers, 1951, 1959, 1961, 1980). While such an assumption may be appropriate for some clients, it is not true for most. Imagine trying to learn how to drive a car with an instructor who only provided you with an empathic relationship. The relationship might support your learning, but in most instances it would be insufficient to help you learn the required skills, let alone learn them efficiently. Most clients do not have sufficient skills strengths latent in repertoires for you and them to rely on the quality of the helping relationship alone.

The majority of clients are stuck and require more active help to provide skills to move forward. The helping relationship is central to this learning process in many ways. Such ways include strengthening the working alliance, helping assessment and client self-assessment, assisting client self-exploration and experiencing of feelings, providing the emotional climate for clients to take risks and also look more closely at the consequences of their behaviours, and allowing clients to be open about difficulties in implementing skills. Nevertheless, central as supportive relationships may be, they are insufficient. Clients are likely to gain most from helpers who both offer good supportive relationships and also impart skills effectively. The helping relationship supports an active approach to training and learning.

SPEAKING SKILLS
Reasons for speaking skills

Whether you facilitate or train, you require effective speaking skills. For instance, when listening, you require speaking skills to communicate your reflective responses and summaries. Also, you require speaking skills when stating working definitions and goals and when negotiating plans. Here I emphasize using speaking skills when you first intervene to train clients in specific lifeskills. The following are some occasions when you might require speaking skills:

> when offering reasons for developing skills;
> when initially describing component parts of skills;
> when providing commentaries for skills demonstrations;
> when coaching clients as they rehearse skills;
> when answering client questions about skills;
> when negotiating homework.

Speaking skills for training are somewhat different to those for facilitating. Some beginning helpers find it difficult to make the switch from reflecting their clients' thoughts and feelings to imparting skills information. The latter requires you to be more active. You cannot feed off your clients' most recent utterances. Without overwhelming clients, you communicate information as clearly and as interestingly as possible. Furthermore, you are always conscious that the best learning requires that clients develop their own self-talk about how to implement skills.

Manage speech anxiety

Presenting lifeskills information to individual clients, couples, or even families, may not be as anxiety evoking as presenting the same information to training groups. Because numbers are smaller, helpers are at less risk of suffering a bad attack of MATO (My anxiety takes over). A certain amount of anxiety facilitates rather than debilitates performance (Alpert & Haber, 1960). Whether presenting to individuals or groups, beginning helpers may suffer from debilitating speech anxiety for three main reasons. First, as a beginner you still require time to become comfortable in your knowledge of the skill. Second, your outer game skills may be poorer than necessary – for instance you may possess poor delivery skills. Third, you may have inner game or thinking skills weaknesses that interfere with the relaxed concentration required to present lifeskills well.

Speech anxiety has many dimensions. Feelings that may be associated with speech anxiety include tension, insecurity, vulnerability, embarrassment and confusion. Physical reactions include nausea, a dry mouth, butterflies in your stomach and your mind going blank. Verbal messages include using confused and rambling sentences. Your vocal messages may convey anxiety; for instance too many 'ums' and 'ers', and speaking too quickly or softly. Your body messages may be inappropriate: for instance hair tugging, scratching or excessive smiling.

The following are some illustrative thinking skills weaknesses associated with speech anxiety even in individual helping:

- *Own responsibility for being a chooser.* You may inadequately own responsibility for working on presentation skills. You may pay considerable attention to developing helping relationship skills without realizing the need also to develop training skills. Consequently, albeit unwittingly, you choose to ignore an important area of your development as a helper.

- *Be in touch with your underlying feelings.* You may deny or dilute your feelings of anxiety about the training aspect of helping. This 'tuning out' may impede your working on this problem. In addition, when it comes to the more didactic aspects of helping, you may feel vulnerable and insufficiently acknowledge any feelings of strength and competence.

- *Use self-talk constructively.* You may either use negative self-talk or fail to use coping self-talk, or both. Negative self-talk statements include: 'I can't cope', 'I can't do anything right' and 'I feel totally confused' (Kendall & Hollon, 1989). You may fail to use the coaching and calming dimensions of coping self-talk (Nelson-Jones, 1989).

- *Choose realistic helping rules.* You may place unrealistic 'musts', 'oughts' and 'shoulds' on yourself and clients: for instance, 'I must be an excellent presenter of skills immediately', or 'Clients must always understand me'.

- *Perceive yourself and others accurately.* You may overemphasize your skills weaknesses in presenting skills and fail adequately to take into account your skills strengths. You may be hypersensitive to any cues of negative feedback from clients.

- *Accurately attribute cause.* You may assume too much responsibility for clients' learning. You may also misattribute the causes of your speech anxiety: for instance to your genes, or to your unfortunate previous attempts to present skills to clients. For some helpers insufficient preparation creates anxiety.

- *Make realistic predictions.* Beginning helpers may be beset by either undue pessimism, or undue optimism, or oscillate between the two regarding their abilities to present skills well.

- *Have goals that you articulate clearly.* If you suffer from anxiety when presenting skills to clients, you should make overcoming such anxiety a goal. Some helpers increase their anxiety by having unrealistic goals about what is attainable both in individual presentations and also in helping.

- *Use visualizing to best effect.* You may be visualizing the worst when you describe skills to clients. Your negative and catastrophic imaginings may interfere with competent performance. Much better is to use your imagination to rehearse and practise behaving competently (Lazarus, 1977).

The skills you require to manage your thoughts that contribute to speech anxiety are the same skills that clients require to manage their thinking skills weaknesses. In Chapter 11 I describe ways in which you and your clients can work to develop your thinking skills.

Prepare clear content

Clients cannot be expected to comprehend poorly presented skills, let alone know them well enough to instruct themselves once helping ends. Many beginning helpers experience difficulty in explaining skills clearly. Some are aware of this, others less so. In some cases, anxiety is a factor. Unfortunately, all too often neophyte helpers do not properly understand skills they present. Consequently, their explanations are either muddled or clearly inaccurate. On other occasions, beginning helpers may understand the skills, but communicate their understanding insufficiently clearly.

When leading training groups, helpers may give mini-lectures of five or ten minutes. Individual helping lends itself to a more informal and interactive approach than is sometimes possible in training groups. Nevertheless, helpers still require the skills of introducing and describing the key points of any lifeskills they impart. Systematic preparation is desirable, especially for beginners. Such preparation should not lead to rigid presentation. When they are clear in their own minds, helpers often address individual clients' needs and learning rates better.

The following are some helper skills of preparing clear content.

KNOW YOUR MATERIAL Do not overlook this seemingly obvious guideline. Most classroom teachers realize that being required to present material to others forces them to understand it more thoroughly than when they were students. It is unethical not to have a reasonable knowledge of any skill you impart. If you require more knowledge of a skill once you have stated working goals, try to obtain it prior to the next session. You lose credibility with clients if they suspect you are poorly informed.

OUTLINE YOUR PRESENTATION Though you may initially describe a skill in the first session, usually you do not present it systematically until subsequent sessions. This interval gives you time to prepare thoroughly. Especially if you have not helped clients acquire a specific skill before, consider preparing a systematic outline of how you might communicate the skill's component parts. Such an outline does not mean that you have to communicate all the skill at once. In individual helping you can adjust the pace of training to the pace of clients' learning. Below is an outline of what might end up as a series of brief presentations on identifying, disputing and reformulating personal rules for a married client with two children, Margaret, who comes to you saying she wants to learn to control her anger.

Outline of presentation(s) to develop realistic personal rules skills

Rationale for skill
- interaction of thinking, feeling and actions;
- ABC framework;
- choosing what you say to yourself at B;
- example of a client's unrealistic rules.

Identifying anger-engendering rules:
- inappropriate feelings;
- self-defeating actions;
- characteristics of mustabatory rules, for instance demandingness.

Disputing unrealistic rules:
- searching for evidence;
- looking for double standards;
- examining realism of predictions;
- questioning put-downs of self.

Reformulating unrealistic into realistic rules:
- characteristics of realistic rules;
- example of a realistic rule;
- reformulate Margaret's unrealistic rules.

Changing actions along with rules:
- 'Stop, think, act';
- alternative ways of acting;
- practice, practice, practice.

USE APPROPRIATE LANGUAGE The following are four dimensions of using appropriate language.

- *Use skills language.* Your brief presentations should clearly identify the skill or subskill you wish to describe. During your presentations, without overdoing it, help clients to think of targeted behaviours in skills terms. Also emphasize the importance of viewing trained skills as self-helping skills.

- *Use clear language.* Take the intelligence level and sociocultural background of clients into account. Use straightforward and unambiguous language: for instance *active listening* or *listening and showing understanding* may be better terms than *empathic listening* or *reflective responding*. Be concise and specific. Aim to describe skills as simply as possible so that clients can easily describe the skills to themselves. Avoid long sentences – the language of speech uses shorter sentences than written language (Bernstein, 1988). The longer your sentences, the fewer the clients who comprehend them (Goddard, 1989).

- *Use practical language.* Helper presentations of lifeskills focus on the mechanics of how to perform a skill or subskill. They are not academic discourses. To enlist motivation and interest, relate your presentations to clients' own material and experiences.

- *Use humour.* The language of lifeskills helping is not the language of boredom. If rightly used, humour can illustrate points and make learning fun. Furthermore, it can relax clients and lower defensiveness and resistances. However, if wrongly used, humour can divert both clients and helpers from goals.

CONSIDER USING AUDIOVISUAL AIDS Audiovisual aids may help you present information more clearly. You need to think carefully about how to integrate audiovisual aids into your skills presentations so they are not disruptive. The following are some audiovisual aid possibilities:

- *Whiteboard.* The structure of your presentation will be clearer if written on the whiteboard than if just spoken.

- *Flipcharts.* Especially if you have already prepared material for using with more than one client, you can integrate flipcharts into your presentation. An advantage of flipchart material is that it is reusable.

- *Training manuals and handouts.* You can help clients consolidate learning either by referral to the relevant sections in training manuals or by handouts.

- *Audio cassettes and videotapes.* You may use pre-recorded audio-cassette or videotape presentations either within sessions or for homework assignments. In addition, you may ask clients to play back a recording of your last session before coming again.

Develop delivery skills

If you prepare clear content you are only part of the way to introducing and describing skills effectively. You still need to put your message across. In Chapter 4 I emphasized sending good voice and body messages when you listen. Here I focus on sending good voice and body messages when you present material to clients. You seek to avoid client MEGO – 'My eyes glaze over' – when you describe skills (Valenti, 1982). Presenting information to individuals or couples does not require the theatrical performance skills of presenting information to larger numbers. Nevertheless, even in individual helping, your voice and body are delivery tools for holding interest, emphasizing points and enlisting motivation.

Send effective voice messages

Perhaps even more when you send messages than when you receive messages, you need to develop an awareness of your voice as a delivery tool. For better or worse, your voice messages frame your verbal messages. Let's take the VAPER acronym (Nelson-Jones, 1991) and suggest how you may use volume, articulation, pitch, emphasis and rate when you deliver content rather than respond to clients.

VOLUME When presenting skills you are under less obligation to adjust your volume to reflect that of clients than when responding as a listener. Without overwhelming clients, you need to speak reasonably loud, possibly louder than when you respond. Some helpers may be better at being gentle listeners than outgoing talkers. If this is true of you, you may need to project your voice when presenting skills in individual helping.

ARTICULATION Clear articulation may be more important when you present than when you respond. If you enunciate poorly when sending listening responses, clients at least are able to put what you say in the context of their previous utterances. They do not have this opportunity when you present information for the first time. Instead they may be struggling to understand both delivery and content. Also, the longer speakers talk, the more poor enunciation distracts.

PITCH Any pitch errors you possess – for instance uncomfortable highness, lowness or narrowness of range – may be more pronounced when you present information than when you respond. One reason is that, when responding, you may modify your pitch to match your client's. Another reason is that, when presenting information, you may be less conscious of pitch because you are thinking of what to say. Furthermore, you have more scope for pitch errors since you are likely to speak for longer when presenting material than when responding.

EMPHASIS When as a listener you use reflective responses, you emphasize the same words and phrases that clients emphasize. As a presenter of information you emphasize words and phrases highlighting your main points. Your use of emphasis should convey interest and commitment.

RATE As with responding, when describing skills speak fairly slowly. A slow, but comfortable, speech rate gives you time to think and gives clients time to comprehend. Effective use of pauses can both clarify and emphasize what you say, and also allows clients to ask questions. Pause errors include: too many, too few, too long, too short, and making extraneous sounds such as 'ums' and 'ers'.

Send effective body messages

Sending effective body messages when describing a lifeskill is partly a matter of avoiding interfering messages and partly a matter of sending good messages. Unlike presenting skills in training groups, in individual helping you are likely to be seated.

Many body messages for attending to clients when listening are still appropriate when delivering content: for instance relaxed body posture, physical openness, sensitivity to physical proximity and height, appropriate clothing and grooming, and appropriate facial expressions. The following are some additional suggestions for using effective body messages when you present.

GESTURES Use gestures economically to help explain what is being said. Fischer (1972) states that there are three main types of gesture: *emphatic* gestures, such as pointing the finger, designed to make it clear that what is being said is important; *descriptive* gestures, for instance stretching your arms out when you say that marital partners are poles apart, designed to help illustrate your point; and *symbolic* gestures to which a commonly understood meaning has been ascribed, for instance shaking your head to say no. Another broad category of gestures is that of *distracting* gestures: touching your head, scratching your nose, pulling lint off your cuff, waving your arms around, tugging your hair and so on. Learn to use gestures to work for rather than against your training messages.

GAZE AND EYE CONTACT Talkers tend to use much less gaze and eye contact than listeners (Argyle, 1983). Nevertheless, when presenting, you require an adequate gaze level to read clients' reactions. Present lifeskills as though you converse with clients rather than talk at them. Your use of gaze and eye contact is a most important way of relating directly to clients when making learning points. Gaze and eye contact errors include: looking down too much, including reading from training manuals; looking at the ceiling or out of the window; looking through clients; and keeping turned away as you write on whiteboards rather than checking client reactions.

Put content and delivery together

In the preceding discussion I focused on managing speech anxiety, preparing clear content, using audiovisual aids, and on using good voice and body message delivery skills. You may have practised long and hard to develop your responsive skills of good listening so that clients want to talk to you. Show the same conscientiousness in developing sender skills of imparting information so that clients want to hear you. An analogy may be made with effective parenting: parents not only need to listen so that their children will talk, they also need to talk so that their children will listen (Gordon, 1970). You may need to rehearse and practise gaining fluency in describing different lifeskills to clients. Furthermore, effective helpers combine talking and listening skills in such a way that clients feel valued parts of the training process and not just receptacles of others' knowledge, the so called *jug-and-mug* approach. Such helpers develop an emotional climate where clients are motivated to learn, ask questions, and take risks.

At the risk of repetition, use speaking skills to help clients develop self-instruction skills. Ideally, when learning new skills, clients start by being receptive to your voice in their heads. However, they then need to replace your voice with their voices. Your public speech becomes their private speech.

DEMONSTRATING SKILLS

By demonstrating skills, effective helpers add 'show' to 'tell'. One of the main ways in which people learn is from observational learning or learning from models (Bandura, 1969, 1977, 1986). Perry and Furukawa define modelling as 'the process of observational learning in which the behaviour of an individual or group – the model – acts as a stimulus for similar thoughts, attitudes or behaviours on the part of an individual who observes the model's performance' (1986, p.66). In real life, much modelling is unintentional. However, helpers can consciously promote observational learning of desired skills and subskills. The more everyday word *demonstrating* is used here in preference to modelling. Both model and demonstrator describe the person demonstrating.

Goals for demonstrating

Demonstrating may be used to initiate new skills strengths; develop existing skills strengths; disinhibit existing skills strengths; and inhibit and weaken existing skills weaknesses. Goals for demonstrating and observational learning can be viewed in the following categories.

THINKING SKILLS Thinking skills include possessing realistic rules, using coping self-talk and perceiving accurately. I briefly reviewed thinking skills in the previous section on speaking skills.

> Naomi, a helper, works with Vince on his public-speaking skills. As part of her plan, she aims to train Vince to use coping rather than negative self-talk before, during and after speaking situations. Naomi demonstrates coping self-talk by verbally giving examples of appropriate coping self-talk statements and also by giving Vince a handout with examples of public-speaking coping self-talk statements.

ACTION SKILLS Action skills demonstrations focus on observable behaviours. In action skills demonstrations, helpers need to pay attention to voice and body as well as to verbal messages.

> Naomi and Vince have working sub-goals to develop Vince's public-speaking delivery skills by: (a) speaking at a comfortable rather than a rapid rate; (b) being easy to hear rather than too quiet; (c) making good gaze and eye contact with his audience; and (d) using gestures to emphasize points. Naomi demonstrates one skill at a time, then coaches and rehearses Vince in it before moving on to the next skill. Ultimately she demonstrates and

coaches Vince in all four skills together. Naomi also encourages Vince either to audio-record or, if possible, to video-record his own competent performance of the skills so he can use himself as a model in future. In addition, she encourages Vince to observe good public speakers and assess how they use the targeted skills.

ACTION SKILLS WITH ACCOMPANYING SELF-TALK Here the demonstrator focuses both on action skills and on accompanying self-instructions.

To speak effectively in public, Vince needs to combine both thinking and action skills. Naomi demonstrates to Vince in slow motion how he can use calming and coaching self-instructions when speaking. Naomi's demonstration intersperses 'think-aloud' self-instructions with demonstrating action skills.

Who demonstrates?

Demonstrations can take place both inside and outside helping sessions. The following options for the person who demonstrates may be used singly or in combination.

- *Helpers*. Helpers may demonstrate skills both initially and when coaching and rehearsing clients.

- *Clients*. Clients can be asked to demonstrate skills for themselves. For instance, helpers may start by audio–cassette recording demonstrations of thinking skills, but then assist clients to make recordings using their own voices and material. Self-demonstrations of action skills may be in clients' imaginations (Kazdin, 1976) or by 'self-as-model' edited video recordings of their own performances (Cormier & Cormier, 1985; Hosford *et al.*, 1976; Hosford & Johnson, 1983).

- *Third parties*. When pre–recorded material is used, third parties may demonstrate skills.

- *Puppets and cartoon characters*. Puppets may be used as demonstrators, especially with children (Peterson & Ridley-Johnson, 1980). Cartoon characters can also be used to present lifeskills. For instance, comic strip characters with dialogue balloons can be used to demonstrate thinking skills.

Methods of demonstration

Helpers have many options when presenting demonstrations. These options, which are not mutually exclusive, are summarized in Table 9.1.

Table 9.1 Methods of demonstrating lifeskills

Methods of demonstrating lifeskills	SKILLS AREAS		
	Thinking skills	**Action skills**	**Action skills plus self-talk**
Written demonstration	✓	Difficult	Difficult
Live demonstration	✓	✓	✓
Pre-recorded demonstration	✓	✓	✓
Visualized demonstration	Less suitable	✓	✓

WRITTEN Helpers can demonstrate lifeskills through the written page – either from handouts or from passages in books and training manuals. Thinking skills in particular lend themselves to written demonstration, which can be supplemented by visual images such as cartoons. Written demonstrations can be easily stored and retrieved by helpers and clients, and can introduce subsequent written or live exercises.

Helpers need not restrict themselves to others' material; they can develop their own. Such material is especially useful where many clients have similar problems. Below is an example of a written demonstration for shy students of the skill of generating and evaluating different perceptions and choosing the 'best-fit' perception rather than jumping to negative conclusions.

Example of how shy people can perceive more accurately

Targeted skill: the skill demonstrated in this example is that of generating and evaluating different perceptions and choosing the best-fit perception.

Reason for skill: many shy people jump to negative conclusions about others' reactions without thinking realistically about the available information. They fail adequately to distinguish between fact, what actually happens, and inference, what they think about what happens. Thus they sustain their shyness by inferring negatively rather than attempting to make their inferences match the facts as closely as possible.

Example of jumping to a negative conclusion
Shirley sits with a group of her classmates in the cafeteria and observes two of them, Ben and Lynette, talking intently to each other. Shirley thinks: 'Ben and Lynette must think I'm a boring person.' The consequence of this thought is that she feels less motivated to participate in the group than before.

Example of generating and evaluating different perceptions
Alternatively, Shirley could have said to herself: 'I feel uneasy because Ben and Lynette are talking to each other. Let's stop and think what is the best way to perceive this. One possibility is that they are bored with me, however I have no evidence for this. Another possibility is that they are saying nice things about me. I also have no evidence for this. A third possibility is that they often ignore other people and just talk to each other. Again, there is no evidence that this happens all the time. A fourth possibility is that they have found something of interest that they want to share and that this does not reflect negatively on me. This seems to be the best way to perceive the situation ['best-fit' perception]. Recently, both Ben and Lynette have been friendly to me. Also, they ignore the other people at the table and not just me.'

LIVE Possibly the most individual helping demonstrations are live. Helpers may demonstrate live when initially presenting skills, when coaching clients afterwards and when working with current material that clients bring into later sessions. Live demonstrations have the advantage of here-and-now communication. Clients can receive verbal, voice and body messages as they occur. You can interact with clients and, if appropriate, show different or simpler ways to enact skills.

Live demonstrations have limitations as well as advantages. Unless demonstrations are recorded, clients have no copies to listen to or watch on their own. Though more appropriate for thinking skills than for action skills demonstrations, getting clients to listen to recordings of either all or part of helping sessions is one approach to this problem. In live demonstrations it may be difficult to portray scenes involving more than one person. However, helpers often conduct role plays with clients to overcome this limitation. Here a potential disadvantage is that clients may be absorbed in playing roles that they attend insufficiently to what helpers demonstrate.

A variation of live demonstration is Bandura's *participant modelling* intervention. This intervention has been used particularly to train those suffering from phobias (Bandura, 1976; Jeffrey, 1976). For example, clients may watch helpers performing progressively more threatening tasks in relation to feared objects, such as snakes. After each demonstration, clients are given both guidance and ample opportunities to perform demonstrated behaviours under favourable conditions. Examples of favourable conditions include both joint performance of sub-tasks with helpers and performing sub-tasks under protective conditions, for instance touching snakes while wearing gloves.

Another variation of live demonstration is to encourage clients to observe good and poor demonstrators of targeted skills in their everyday lives. For instance, clients with public-speaking problems can monitor the skills of good and poor public speakers. Clients with difficulty initating contact with others can look out for how socially skilled people do this. Clients with poor parenting skills can be asked to observe parents they admire.

PRE-RECORDED Pre-recorded demonstrations can be on films, audiotapes and videotapes. Helpers rarely if ever use films outside of group work. Disadvantages include darkened rooms, the need to purchase films, and the costs of projection equipment and, possibly, a projectionist. Audio cassettes and videotapes can either be integral parts of initial skills demonstrations or used for homework assignments. Advantages of audio-cassette and videotape demonstrations include that they can be reproduced, lent to clients, viewed repeatedly, can either be placed on 'pause' or switched on and off, and can be used with different clients.

Audio-cassette demonstration. Audio cassettes are particularly useful for demonstrating thinking skills. With audio cassettes as contrasted to videotapes, clients can be taken through the sequences of choices entailed in targeted skills without visual distractions. Initial audio-cassette demonstrations of thinking skills are best done by helpers; it is unreasonable to expect clients to demonstrate skills that they do not properly understand. However, later in the learning process, helpers can assist clients to make up their own demonstration cassettes. If clients switch to using themselves as demonstrators during helping, they may be more likely to maintain skills afterwards. Clients probably require repeated listenings to their demonstrations for the thinking skills to become part of their everyday repertoires (Ellis, 1987). Disadvantages of audio-cassette demonstrations are that they are not as spontaneous as live demonstration and that they may be insufficiently geared to individual clients' needs. Often a combination of audio-cassette, written and live demonstration is the most effective way to impart thinking skills.

Apart from recording helping sessions, the following are different ways to approach audio-cassette demonstrations. First, you may make up a tailor-made demonstration cassette targeted at a particular skill or subskill an individual client requires. Second, you may make up audio-cassette demonstrations relevant to common client problems. For instance, you could record the earlier example of a written demonstration for shy students of the skill of generating and evaluating perceptions with different voices for the commentator and Shirley, Lynette and Ben. You can build up a library of skills audio cassettes relevant to your client population. Some audio recordings may demonstrate action skills, for instance the verbal and voice message dimensions of being assertive. Others may demonstrate instructions for action skills, for instance progressive muscular relaxation (Jacobson, 1938). Third, you can use commercial self-help audio-cassette demonstrations of targeted skills (Yamauchi, 1987). Fourth, you may assist clients in making their own demonstration cassettes.

If possible, use highly sensitive recording equipment, and encourage clients to do the same. There are cassette recorders on the market that eliminate virtually all motor noise and background hiss. Clients resist having to listen to poor-quality cassettes. Be prepared to rehearse and rerecord your efforts if inadequate. If Elton John and Elaine Paige do this, why can't you?

Videotape demonstration. A major advantage of videotape demonstration over audio-cassette demonstration is that clients observe body messages. Many lifeskills training videotapes are already on the market. However, commercial videotapes may not suit your needs. If you make your own demonstration videotapes, you have the choice of whether or not to bring in outside resources. Here I assume you make your own videotapes.

When making demonstration videotapes, specify body message sub-goals as well as verbal and voice subgoals. For instance, if you were to make a videotape demonstrating how a teenager, Chrissie, might return a compact disc to a store, you might get her demonstrating the body message skills of adequate eye contact, erect posture and good use of gesture. You require many of the skills of a film director when making demonstration videotapes. For instance, you may need to coach demonstrators in how to act scripts. During rehearsing and shooting scenes, you may decide to rewrite parts of the script. Much trial and error goes into making polished demonstration videotapes.

During sessions you can use videotapes to demonstrate skills; for instance excerpts of how to make an assertive request for a behaviour change, demonstrate attention and interest when listening, or answer questions at a job interview. Clients may also self-administer demonstration videotapes without helpers present. Webster-Stratton and her colleagues assigned parents of conduct-problem children to either an individually administered videotape modelling treatment, a therapist-led group discussion videotape modelling treatment, a group discussion treatment without watching videotapes, and a waiting list control group (Webster-Stratton *et al.*, 1988). Both of the videotape modelling conditions involved parents coming for 10–12 weekly sessions and watching over 200 vignettes of parent–child interactions. One-year follow-up findings showed very few differences between the three treatment conditions. The results 'suggested the potential power of parents to learn how to change their own behaviors, as well as their children's behaviors, from self-administered videotape programs' (Webster-Stratton *et al.*, 1989, p.550).

You may want to make videotape demonstrations of action skills with accompanying self-talk. Ultimately clients have to instruct themselves through action skills sequence of choices. The following are some ways to incorporate self-talk.

- *Think aloud.* Here demonstrators pause every now and then to verbalize out loud relevant self-instructions.

- *Voice-overs.* Voice-overs of the demonstrator's self-instructions may be edited into demonstration videotapes. These are less disruptive to demonstrations than think aloud. However, a major disadvantage is that voice-overs are beyond most helpers' technical resources.

- *Subtitles.* Frequently, subtitles translate the spoken word. For demonstrations of action skills plus self-talk, subtitles demonstrate relevant inner rather than outer talk. Advantages of subtitles over voice-overs are that they do not provide added, and possibly distracting, sound and they can be left on the screen longer.

- *'Think' balloons.* 'Think' balloons containing relevant self-talk can be attached to demonstrators' heads. The technical competence required to superimpose 'think' balloons onto moving images is well beyond the scope and budgets of most helpers.

VISUALIZED Visualized demonstration is sometimes called covert modelling (Cautela, 1976; Cormier & Cormier, 1985; Kazdin, 1976). Helpers ask clients to visualize or imagine the demonstration scenes that they describe. Depending on the instructions, clients visualize either themselves or third parties demonstrating targeted action skills. Visualized demonstration has the advantage of flexibility. Different situations can be readily presented to clients' imaginations depending on their needs and how fast they learn. Clients can follow up visualized demonstration in helping sessions with visualized demonstration and rehearsal at home.

Visualized demonstration has potential disadvantages. It is only appropriate for clients who can visualize scenes adequately. Also, clients never actually see skills demonstrated: even when instructions are well given, there may be important gaps between what you describe and what clients visualize.

In general, clients visualize best when relaxed (Kazdin, 1976). Helpers may start by asking clients to visualize neutral scenes to check their visualizing capacities. For example, a client could be asked to visualize a recent conversation with a friend. Here are three guidelines for visualized demonstrations:

- *Set the scene.* Describe the situation in which targeted lifeskills are enacted in sufficient detail so that clients can easily visualize it.

- *Describe the targeted skill(s).* Describe clearly what the targeted skills are and how they are used. Remember to describe voice and body as well as verbal components of skills.

- *Depict favourable consequences.* Where appropriate, get clients to visualize demonstrator use of targeted skills receiving rewards.

Helpers can develop different visualized demonstrations around targeted skills. For instance, visualizations may be graduated by threat or difficulty. In addition, clients can visualize themselves coping with different consequences when using targeted skills.

Demonstrator skills

Beyond speaking well, the following are some demonstrator skills.

PREPARE ADEQUATELY Even live demonstrations require adequate preparation. You must know your material thoroughly to integrate good demonstrations into skills presentations. Making pre-recorded demonstrations takes time and effort. Pay attention to demonstrator characteristics. For example, in general, the greater the similarity between demonstrators and observers, the greater the effect of demonstrations on subsequent behaviours (Perry & Furukawa, 1986). Kazdin (1976) suggests that rather than being perfectly competent, there is an advantage in demonstrators showing behaviours similar to that of observers, but then overcoming problems. It is also important that demonstrators be attractive to clients (Bandura, 1977).

Pay attention to characteristics of the demonstration, not just of the demonstrator. One issue is whether to demonstrate incorrect as well as correct behaviours. You may plan briefly to demonstrate negative behaviours as a way of highlighting positive ones. However, make sure not to confuse clients and always have the major emphasis on correct rather than incorrect skills. Another consideration is that some skills may be so complex or difficult that you may need to plan a series of demonstrations. For instance, a late adolescent girl having difficulty standing up to her mother may observe her helper demonstrate how to handle a low-level confrontation before later observing more difficult confrontations. When clients should perform the demonstrated skills is a further consideration. Client performance of demonstrated skills can be simultaneous (Klingman *et al.*, 1984), interspersed between demonstrations (Bandura, 1976), follow demonstrations, or not happen at all.

PROVIDE AN INTRODUCTION Take care how you introduce demonstrations. Your initial demonstration of a skill is likely to be part of a 'tell', 'show', 'do' sequence. You can explain to clients the importance of learning from demonstration (Sarason, 1976). You may increase clients' attention by telling them what to look out for and also informing them that afterwards they will perform demonstrated behaviours (Perry & Furukawa, 1986).

PROVIDE INSTRUCTIONS AND A SUMMARY During live and pre-recorded presentations, you can intersperse breaks for instructions on what to look out for. At the end of demonstrations, you can summarize the main learning points and, possibly, give participants a handout listing them.

CHECK CLIENTS' LEARNING During and at the end you may ask clients whether they understand the points you demonstrate. Clients can summarize the main points of demonstrations. Research suggests that observers actively summarizing the main points of demonstrations are better able to learn and retain this information (Bandura *et al.*, 1966; Perry & Furukawa, 1986). Probably the best way to check clients' learning is to observe and coach them as they perform demonstrated behaviours.

EXTEND DEMONSTRATION INTO HOMEWORK Demonstrations can be integrated into homework. Clients can listen to recordings of all or part of sessions in which you demonstrate skills live. Furthermore, they can listen to and watch pre-recorded audio cassettes and videotapes. In addition, you can instruct clients to observe people in their daily lives as they demonstrate targeted skills.

COACHING SKILLS

Here I focus on coaching clients to perform skills after initial presentations. Learning from hearing and observing must be translated into learning from doing. I have listened to the supervision tapes of many beginning helpers who describe and demonstrate skills, but then omit to coach clients in how to perform them. The following are some helper skills for coaching clients in lifeskills.

BALANCE DIDACTIC AND FACILITATIVE COACHING In *didactic* coaching, helpers give a series of explicit instructions to clients on how to perform skills. The helper's comments take the form: 'First you do this, then you do that. Then you do that', and so on. The helper is the expert taking clients through a sequence of performance choices.

In *facilitative* coaching, helpers have two important objectives: to draw out and build upon clients' existing knowledge and skills; and to help them acquire the skills of self-coaching. Helpers' initial comments may include: 'Now you have listened to and observed the initial presentation and demonstration of _____ skill [specify skill], what have you learned about how to do it?', 'How do you feel about using the skill just presented?' or 'Can you describe to me the self-talk you require to use the skill?'

When coaching, helpers require both facilitative and didactic skills. For example, helpers might start with trying to build on the existing knowledge and skills of learners, but then intersperse didactic instructions when clients go badly wrong. Didactic coaching alone can produce resistances. Coaching without using facilitative skills also lessens the likelihood of targeted skills being owned and integrated into clients' daily routines.

GIVE CLEAR INSTRUCTIONS Include clear instructions for coached performance in your initial presentations and demonstrations of skills. Helper and/or client summaries at the end of demonstrations can also be ways of ensuring that instructions for performing skills are clear. When coaching, you may need to give specific instructions, tips and prompts that build targeted skills (Karoly & Harris, 1986). Coaching should always emphasize ways in which clients can help themselves, for instance by translating clear instructions into clear self-instructions.

BREAK TASKS DOWN AND CONSIDER NUMBER OF TRIALS When initially getting clients to perform them, you may decide to break skills and subskills down. You should consider how much clients can assimilate in each learning trial. For example, with a teenager wishing to return a defective compact disc to a shop, one trial might focus on verbal messages, another on voice messages, another on body messages, and another on putting it all together. Another way of breaking learning trials down is to include graded steps. Here you coach clients in using targeted skills in progressively more difficult situations. With or without graded steps, clients may require many coached attempts before performing skills competently within, let alone outside, helping sessions.

USE BEHAVIOUR REHEARSAL AND ROLE PLAY By definition, when you coach you also rehearse clients in targeted skills. Behaviour rehearsal and role play are not always the same. Clients can rehearse action skills on their own without role plays, for instance rehearsing relaxation skills. Also, they can mentally rehearse thinking skills and visually rehearse action skills plus accompanying self-talk. Role plays are especially useful for rehearsing action skills. Behaviour rehearsal and role-play skills are covered in more detail in Chapter 12.

USE FEEDBACK SKILLS When coaching, helpers are managers of feedback. The following are some feedback dimensions to bear in mind (Egan, 1990; Gazda, 1989; Gilbert, 1978; Hopson & Scally, 1981; National Training Laboratory, 1967; Osipow *et al.*, 1984).

Client self-feedback or helper feedback. Throughout, encourage clients to develop skills of monitoring and assessing their behaviour and its consequences for self and others. As a guideline, after each behaviour rehearsal, clients should be the first to comment on their learning and on reactions to their performance. Nevertheless, your feedback is still essential because of your special knowledge of targeted skills.

'I' message or 'You' message feedback. Take responsibility for your feedback and send, or at least imply, 'I' messages. For example, 'Tim, I think Sally would appreciate your request for a date more if your voice were louder' is different from 'Your voice should have been louder when asking Sally for a date.' However, Tim might still have received the latter statement as an 'I' message if you had established the ground rule that your feedback always represented perception rather than fact and was open for discussion.

Specific or non-specific feedback. Feedback should always be specific and concentrate on targeted behaviours. For instance in the previous example, suggesting to Tim that his voice might be louder is far preferable to telling him his voice quality is poor.

Verbal or demonstrated feedback. Feedback may be given largely by means of words. Often, however, you may communicate feedback even more clearly if you accompany verbal description with demonstration. For instance, in the Tim and Sally example, you could demonstrate Tim's present voice loudness and then demonstrate a more appropriate loudness.

Confirmatory or corrective feedback. Feedback can be confirmatory or corrective. Confirmatory feedback reinforces correct behaviours, whereas corrective feedback lets clients know which specific behaviours require altering and in what ways. Much feedback is both confirmatory and corrective: for example, 'Tim, when you asked Sally to go out I thought that you gave a good verbal 'I' message [confirmatory] but that your voice was too quiet [corrective].' Persistent corrective feedback, without some confirmatory feedback, can weaken clients' motivation to work and change.

Audiovisual feedback. Cassette feedback may be especially useful when helpers coach verbal messages, voice messages and thinking skills. Putting how clients think on whiteboards provides useful visual feedback. Videotape feedback is especially beneficial when helpers coach body messages. Audiovisual feedback lends itself to client self-assessment, and provides a factual basis for helper–client discussions.

Feedback or reward. You may provide feedback in the form of reward. You can say 'good' or 'well done' in response to specific behaviours that clients implement well. You can also use nonverbal forms of reward such as nods and smiles. However, beware of clients only performing targeted behaviours under conditions of external reward rather than self-reward.

Verbal or nonverbal feedback. Much feedback, for good or ill, is nonverbal. Uninterested looks and voice messages can greatly interfere with good verbal coaching messages. Conversely, good voice and body messages when giving feedback increases the likelihood of clients receiving the verbal message positively. Whether or not you speak, show interest when clients perform demonstrated skills.

Cultural feedback considerations. Helpers who are from different cultural backgrounds to clients require sensitivity to differences in cultural rules concerning giving and receiving feedback. You can ask clients how their cultures deal with feedback.

ASSIGNING HOMEWORK SKILLS

After presenting, demonstrating and coaching clients in new skills, helpers can assign relevant homework. Many reasons exist for setting homework (Cormier & Cormier, 1985; Egan, 1990; Hutchins & Cole, 1986). These include speeding up the learning process; encouraging clients to monitor, rehearse and practise skills; helping the transfer of trained skills to outside life; finding out about difficulties in using skills in real life; and increasing the client's sense of self-control and of personal responsibility for developing targeted skills.

The following are some central skills for assigning homework.

OFFER REASONS FOR HOMEWORK Helpers can often enhance clients' motivation for completing homework assignments if they explain its importance. You can introduce the idea of homework at the start of tell, show and do sequences:

> Now, Gill, first I am going to describe ____ [specify which] skill, then I am going to demonstrate it for you, then I am going to coach you in it, and then we will discuss some homework to develop your ____ [specify which] skill in real life.

Below is an example of a statement a helper might make at the conclusion of a speaking, demonstrating and coaching sequence. In this example the helper attempts both to elicit reservations and also to gain a commitment to the idea of doing homework:

TWELVE

How to Focus on Feelings

We know too much and feel too little.

Bertrand Russell

CHAPTER QUESTIONS

Why is it important to focus on feelings?

What is the helper's role when focusing on feelings?

What interventions can helpers use to assist clients to experience and explore and accurately label feelings?

What interventions can helpers use to develop clients' skills of expressing feelings?

What interventions can helpers use to develop clients' skills of managing feelings?

Focusing on feelings involves helping clients learn to live with their underlying animal nature so that it works for them rather than against them. All clients' problems involve feelings in one way or another. This chapter builds on the previous chapters by showing how to focus on clients' feelings by intervening with their thinking skills and action skills.

Reasons for focusing on feelings

Many different reasons exist for why helpers, clients and people need to pay attention to focusing on feelings. First, many clients require catharsis. Catharsis involves getting relief through purging oneself of emotions which, if allowed to persist, might interfere with fulfilment and even survival. For example, some clients have had their integrity consistently attacked by inadequate and manipulative parents, and may come to helping, either when young or later, with a backlog of insufficiently expressed hatred, resentment and self-pity. Initially, a main task of helping may be to assist clients to experience and release hatred prior to using the emotional energy invested in it for more constructive purposes.

Second, how clients experience, express and manage feelings affect physical health. Emotions that are not adequately handled may be somatized. Clients may feel stressed and fatigued. Furthermore, they may fall prey to psychophysical disorders such as eczema, muscle cramps, tension headaches, asthma, heart attacks, hypertension, peptic ulcers, chronic gastritis, and disturbances in urination and menstruation.

A third reason for focusing on feelings involves the desirability of lifting unwanted inhibitions and repressions. Clients' families of origin placed different values on which feelings it was safe for them to experience (Laing, 1969; Rogers, 1951, 1957, 1961, 1980; Satir, 1972). Cultural and sex-role conditioning further influence how people feel. Fourth, and closely related to lifting unwanted repressions, is the need for many clients to get more in touch with wants and wishes. Clients' wants and wishes stimulate both their initial motivation to act and also how persistent they are.

Developing a sense of identity is a fifth reason for focusing on feelings. In varying degrees, many clients lack a clear sense of identity. People's feelings, their unique valuing of what transpires in their lives, can allow a healthy sense of continuity and sameness. People with an effective sense of identity are centred in their unique capacity for responsiveness. They are always in the process of identity formation, yet this making and remaking of themselves is a process of renewal in accord with rather than violating the core of their beings.

Providing a base for effective relating provides a sixth reason for focusing on feelings. Clients require the ability to send and receive feelings messages accurately. Furthermore, they need to be able both to experience and express pro-social feelings. A final reason for focusing on feelings is that clients require help in managing feelings that are both self-defeating and often destructive of others: for instance, anxiety, hatred, depression and shyness. In times of crisis, clients can require assistance in handling feelings experienced as overwhelming, for instance panic.

The area of feelings is complex. I have subdivided it into three main areas: experiencing feelings; expressing feelings; and managing negative feelings. Figure 12.1 depicts the interrelationship of these areas.

Helpers as feelings educators

Broadly speaking, helpers can take two main approaches to clients' feelings. First, there is the facilitative approach. Here you use helping relationship skills to facilitate clients in experiencing, disclosing and exploring feelings. You assume that if clients truly experience their significant feelings and self-actualizing drives they think rationally and act appropriately. Second, there is the training approach. Here you use training skills to assist clients to make better choices in how they feel. The facilitative approach emphasizes experiencing feelings; the training approach emphasizes expressing and managing feelings. Rogers' person-centred therapy and cognitive-behavioural therapy are prime examples of the facilitative and training approaches, respectively.

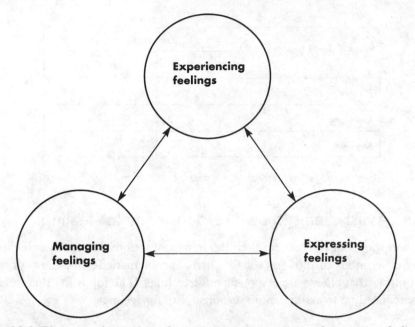

Figure 12.1 *The interrelationship of experiencing, expressing and managing feelings*

Lifeskills helping draws on both facilitative and training approaches to feelings. Helpers as psychological educators need to assist clients not only to get in touch with their animal nature, but also to use what distinguishes them from lower animals – their capacity for reason and thinking – to regulate and manage that nature. As depicted in Figure 12.2, lifeskills helpers flexibly use both helping relationship and training skills to assist clients to experience, express and manage feelings.

Areas of client's feelings	Helper skills	
	Relationship skills	Training skills
Experiencing	✓	✓
Expressing	✓	✓
Managing	✓	✓

Figure 12.2 *Helper skills to assist clients to experience, express and manage feelings*

What skills do clients require to experience, express and manage feelings? Since feelings represent humans' animal nature, I prefer not to use the term feelings skills. Instead clients require feelings–related skills to help manage problematic feelings. Figure 12.3 depicts how clients require both thinking and action skills to develop fully their potential for using their animal nature to support rather than to oppress themselves and others.

Areas of client's feelings	Client skills	
	Thinking skills	Action skills
Experiencing	✓	✓
Expressing	✓	✓
Managing	✓	✓

Figure 12.3 *Client skills for experiencing, expressing and managing feelings*

Assist clients to own responsibility for feelings

Clients are responsible not only for their thoughts and actions, but for their feelings too. Whatever other interventions you use for clients' problematic feelings, always work on the assumption that clients are responsible for feelings. The following three examples show clients needing to assume more responsibility for feelings.

> *Experiencing feelings*
> Arnold, 17, sees his school counsellor to decide what university and course he should apply for. Arnold has few ideas of his own and relies mainly on others' thoughts and feelings about what he should do.
>
> *Expressing feelings*
> Fran, 27, is in a relationship that is heading for the rocks. She has great difficulty expressing both positive and negative feelings to her boyfriend, Jim.
>
> *Managing feelings*
> Dora, 43, is the headteacher of an urban school with huge staff morale and discipline problems. Over the past few weeks, Dora has been getting increasingly tense, anxious and depressed about her work and life.

Responsibility for feelings has different dimensions: for instance, 'How can I get in touch with my feelings?', 'Who or what creates my feelings?', and 'What can I do about my feelings?' Assist clients to see that they have choices in how they feel. Though past and present circumstances may influence how clients feel, such circumstances do not create how they feel. Also assist clients to see that they have choices both in how they express feelings, and in how they react to others' feelings. However, go beyond making clients aware that they are responsible for their feelings and feelings choices. Clients need to know how to do it: they require relevant thinking and action skills for assuming effective responsibility for their feelings both now and in future.

ASSIST CLIENTS TO EXPERIENCE FEELINGS

Experiencing feelings has at least three dimensions. First, clients need the actual sensation of experiencing feelings rather than blocking them off or distorting them. Second, clients require skills to explore feelings and follow feelings trails to see where they lead. Third, clients require skills to label feelings accurately. The following interventions assist clients to experience, explore and label feelings.

Offer reasons for focusing on feelings

You may help some clients if you legitimize the importance of focusing on feelings. How you do this depends upon the needs of individual clients. Let's take the example of Arnold, the 17-year-old, whose school counsellor discovers that he relies on others' thoughts and feelings to guide his choice of university and course. Here, if you are the school counsellor you have a number of choices, albeit not mutually exclusive. First, you can keep using rewarding listening skills in the hope that Arnold becomes more inner than outer directed. Second, you can confront him along the lines of: 'Arnold, you seem to be saying a lot about what your parents and teachers want for you, but I'm wondering what *you* think and feel about *your* choice of university and course?' Note the emphasis on you and your. Third, you can suggest to Arnold that he take an occupational interest inventory to assist self–exploration. Fourth, you can offer Arnold reasons for acknowledging his own feelings more fully:

> Arnold, you seem to say a lot about what your parents and teachers want for you. However, I get the impression that you inadequately attend to *your* feelings about what *you* want to do. Though not the only source, your feelings can provide you with a rich source of information about what might be the right choices for you. Learning to acknowledge and listen to your feelings is a skill. If you inadequately listen to your feelings, you risk making choices that you may later regret. I think you need develop skills of focusing more on your feelings. What do you think?

Offering reasons for focusing on feelings may lead to a discussion with clients about how much they think they are in touch with feelings and their fears about expressing them. As an intervention for aiding emotional responsiveness, it needs to be accompanied by other interventions. However, offering reasons may accelerate some clients in taking feelings more seriously as a basis for future feelings work.

Focus on thinking skills

Helpers can assist clients to develop thinking skills conducive to expressing feelings. The following are thinking skills weaknesses blocking experiencing feelings. I refer you to Chapters 9 and 10 on how best to develop clients' thinking skills.

OWN RESPONSIBILITY FOR CHOOSING Already I have stressed the importance of helping clients to realize that they have choices in how they feel, including how they experience feelings and what feelings they experience. Emery (1982) uses the term 'choice-ability' for people's ability to choose how they feel.

USE COPING SELF-TALK Clients can talk to themselves in ways that enhance their capacity to get in touch with feelings. They may make calming self-statements like, 'Relax', 'Calm down', 'Take a deep breath'. They may also make coaching self-statements, like, 'Let's clear a space to truly get in touch with what I feel', 'Remember, my feelings are important and I need to spend time getting in touch with them', or, 'Don't rush into a decision, let's feel and think this one through'. Often clients can combine calming and coaching self-statements: 'Relax. Take my time to get in touch with how I feel about this'.

CHOOSE REALISTIC PERSONAL RULES Many clients have personal rules that get in the way of experiencing feelings. Samples of such rules are:

'I must never have strong feelings.'
'Women should not acknowledge feelings of ambition.'
'Men should be strong and silent.'
'Boys must feel competitive rather than cooperative.'
'Religious people should always pay attention to others' rather than to their own feelings.'
'People should not have strong sexual feelings because they are dirty.'
'I must never acknowledge the pro-social part of my nature and that I care for others and for the welfare of the human race.'

Helpers can assist clients to become aware of rules unhelpful to experiencing feelings and dispute and reformulate them into more realistic rules.

CHOOSE HOW YOU PERCEIVE Clients have much more choice in how they feel than most realize. Helpers can assist clients to make links between how they perceive and how they feel. Clients can develop skills of not restricting themselves to the first feeling they experience. Instead they can generate and evaluate alternative perceptions, which in turn lead to alternative feelings. Clients can then choose the 'best-fit' perceptions and feelings. Sometimes helpers can assist clients' 'choice-ability' by getting them to explore opposite feelings to how they say they feel. For instance, clients may get more in touch with what they truly feel by exploring feelings of love towards someone they say they hate. Helpers may also assist clients to feel less negatively about themselves and others. Searching for positive assets in self and others is one way to do this.

ATTRIBUTE CAUSE ACCURATELY Helpers can assist clients to attribute causes of feelings accurately. For instance, depressed clients may attribute the cause of all negative events to themselves (Beck, 1991; Beck *et al.*, 1979). Other clients may project negative feelings about themselves on to others, for instance jealous clients being hypersensitive about others' jealousy. Many clients externalize the cause of their feeling on to others, for instance, 'It's all his/her fault', or 'He/she made me feel that way'.

PREDICT REALISTICALLY Disorders of prediction permeate how people experience negative and fail to experience genuinely positive feelings. Distorted predictions play a large part in depression (Abramson *et al.*, 1978; Bandura, 1986, 1989; Beck, 1991; Beck *et al.*, 1988b). Unrealistic predictions or psychological danger are systematic biases in processing information of patients suffering from anxiety disorders (Beck & Weishaar, 1989). Many who feel shy predict that they will be rejected. Other clients require help in containing feelings of optimism, for instance manic clients or clients who do not take health risks seriously enough.

SET REALISTIC GOALS Clients with unrealistic goals set themselves up to feel anxious about attaining them and depressed if unsuccessful. Clients setting proximal or short-range goals enhance their motivation and feelings of self-efficacy (Bandura, 1986).

USE VISUALIZING SKILLS Helpers can both elicit feelings and enhance many clients' experiencing of past feelings by asking them to visualize situations in which they occurred. You can also use visualizing to help clients experience feelings about the future: for instance, with regard to getting married or moving house. Furthermore, you may enhance feelings of competence by getting clients to visualize themselves performing competently.

MAKE DECISIONS RATIONALLY Helpers can educate clients in the importance of listening to feelings when making decisions. You can assist clients' awareness of when feelings interfere with realistic decisions, for instance being impulsive or excessively vigilant. Furthermore, you can assist clients to experience and explore feelings of commitment or lack of commitment to implementing decisions.

PREVENT AND MANAGE PROBLEMS AND ALTER PROBLEMATIC SKILLS Helpers can assist clients to listen to their early warning signals that they may need either to prevent or to manage problems. For instance, tuning into feelings of stress early on may prevent more serious stress-related problems. You can also assist clients to see that experiencing and labelling feelings accurately is an important part of the process of managing problems and altering problematic skills.

Use rewarding listening

In Chapter 4 I presented ten skills for being a rewarding listener. Again I emphasize the importance of rewarding listening, particularly to help thaw clients whose experiencing of feelings is being or has been significantly frozen by adverse family of origin circumstances.

How can rewarding listening help clients get in touch with and experience feelings? Rewarding listening allows clients permission to experience their separateness and uniqueness rather than being the way others want them to be. The affirmation helpers provide with their time, attention and understanding can increase clients' sense of worth and lower anxiety and defensiveness. Being sensitively responded to, clients gain practise in listening to themselves, valuing their own experience, and increasingly identifying and labelling it accurately. Rewarding listening gives clients the psychological space to explore and delve deeper into the meanings and nuances of their feelings. It assists clients to identify wants and wishes and to distinguish what comes from them and from others. Empathic helpers provide clients with secure bases from which they can interact with the world, gain new experiences, come back and discuss them, and know that they will be understood. Though rewarding listening skills are not always sufficient or sufficiently expeditious for helping clients get in touch with feelings, they are invariably necessary. However, there are limits to the pace at which clients out of touch with feelings can work, so another facet of rewarding listening is showing sensitivity to clients' comfort zones.

Train clients in inner listening

So far I have emphasized the need for helpers to be rewarding listeners to clients, but clients also need to develop skills of being rewarding listeners to themselves. They need to experience, become aware of, explore and label their own feelings. Assuming clients have a moderate degree of insight, you can impart inner listening as a self-helping skill.
Here are some elements of inner listening training.

Offer reasons for focusing on inner listening. You can assist clients to realize that this is a useful skill for understanding both themselves and others. Clarify what you mean by experiencing feelings, exploring them, and labelling them accurately.

Stress creating sufficient time and psychological space. To practise inner listening, clients must give it sufficient priority in their lives. This may mean either that they spend a certain amount of time alone each day, or that they make sure to clear a space when something bothers them or needs deciding.

Explain and demonstrate the skill. Much of the rewarding listening material in Chapter 4 is relevant here, but with modification. For instance, the concept of internal viewpoint in this context becomes that of getting inside your own rather than another's internal viewpoint. In inner empathy, it is vital that clients tune in to feelings. They flow with them, try to understand their messages and label them accurately. You may help clients to understand the skill if you demonstrate by verbalizing your feelings and associated thoughts as you attempt to listen to yourself.

Coach and assign homework. Coach clients to ensure that they understand the skill of inner listening. Assigning homework acts as a bridge between training and clients relying on their own resources.

Eugene Gendlin and Fritz Perls are two writers who have stressed the need for inner listening and awareness. Gendlin (1962) developed a method termed *focusing* to help people change and live from deeper places than just their thoughts and feelings. In focusing people clear a space and make contact with a special kind of internal bodily awareness called a 'felt sense'. When people get in touch with this 'felt sense' there can be both a felt physical shift in their bodies and different perspectives on problems.

Perls, the founder of Gestalt therapy, developed a technique he called focal awareness. Perls observed: 'The basic sentence with which we ask our patients to begin therapy and which we retain throughout its course – not only in words, but in spirit – is the simple phrase: 'Now I am aware' (Perls, 1973, p. 65). Perls asked clients, when using focal awareness, to concentrate and become aware of their body language, breathing, voice quality and emotions as much as of any pressing thoughts. He aimed to make clients aware not only that they interrupted their contact with themselves but how they did this. Helpers may impart both focusing and focal awareness as self-helping skills.

Use feelings questions

Helpers can use feelings questions to encourage clients to experience and share feelings. Beware of getting clients talking about feelings in distant ways rather than experiencing them. Another danger of this use of questions is that clients will respond to helpers rather than get in touch with themselves. However, if skilfully used, feelings questions can give clients useful practice in listening to and becoming more aware of their feelings. Feelings questions include:

'How do you feel about that?'
'I'm wondering what the emotional impact of that is on you?'
'Could you describe your feelings more fully?'
'I'm hearing that you're feeling . . .?'
'You seem to have conflicting feelings. On the one hand ___ on the other hand ___?'

Be authentic and appropriately self-disclose

The ability of helpers to be real is very important for assisting clients to experience feelings. Rogers uses terms like congruence and genuineness (Rogers, 1957, 1975). Existential psychologists use terms like presence and authenticity (Bugental, 1981; May, 1958). Bugental views presence as consisting of an intake side called accessibility, allowing what happens in situations to affect you, and an output side called expressiveness, making available some of the content of your subjective awareness without editing. If you are alive and present in relating to clients you demonstrate experiencing feelings and create the climate for them to do so too. Some research suggests that female helpers experience and express feelings more than male helpers (Maracek & Johnson, 1980). Mintz and O'Neil observe that research studies 'suggest that female therapists may form more effective therapeutic alliances and be more affectively oriented than are male therapists' (1990, p. 384).

Clients may perceive helpers' ability to experience and express feelings as disclosing involvement. Showing such involvement may make it easier for clients to experience feelings. Helpers who appropriately disclose personal information may also help clients access their experiencing: for instance, feminist helpers with women clients, gay helpers with gay clients, and former drug addicts with substance abuse clients.

Confront inauthenticity

Helpers can use their here-and-now experiencing as guides to whether clients communicate what they really think and feel. Clients may wear masks and play roles that interfere with their experiencing and expressing what they truly feel. Such roles include playing the clown, playing stupid or playing helpless. Helpers may make clients aware of such tendencies: for example, 'I get the impression that whenever you get close to your deeper feelings, you use humour to avoid revealing them.' Helpers can also confront clients who externalize feelings on to others:

> *Client*: Judy and Joan feel pretty angry with the way
> we are taught.
> *Helper*: I'm wondering whether focusing on Judy
> and Joan's anger is a way of protecting yourself from
> acknowledging that you too feel angry with your
> teachers and are capable of angry feelings.

Helpers can confront inconsistencies between verbal, voice and body messages. For instance: 'You say you don't feel hurt by his behaviour, yet you speak in a sad tone of voice and your eyes seem weepy.'

Raise consciousness

Helpers can use consciousness raising as a means of improving clients' capacities for experiencing and expressing feelings. In Western countries few do not need to become more in tune with feelings. Mostly helpers use consciousness raising to raise awareness levels of specific subgroups: for instance, women, men, gays, and various ethnic and cultural minorities. Intervening to raise clients' consciousness of social, sex-role and cultural conditioning can beneficially affect how they experience feelings in two main ways. First, you can assist clients to overcome negative feelings, for instance low self-esteem and guilt, attached to their minority status. Second, you can encourage subgroups to respond to the range of feelings inherent in being human: for example, women to experience and express ambition and assertion, and men vulnerability and affection.

Teach sensate focus

Relatively few helpers specialize in sexual problems. Nevertheless, many have occasion to assist clients in experiencing and expressing sensuality. Insufficient sexual responsiveness takes many different forms and may have multiple causes. Often it is part of a broader pattern of inadequate relationship skills. However, some clients may have good relationship skills in other areas, yet require specific assistance in acknowledging and exploring sensuality. Such difficulties may be independent of having specific sexual dysfunctions, for instance premature ejaculation.

Masters and Johnson (1970) developed the technique of sensate focus to help couples feel and think sensuously. Sensate focus acknowledges the importance of touch in stimulating and experiencing sexual responsiveness. Partners are asked to time their periods of sensate focus for when they feel a natural sense of warmth and compatibility. They should only continue for as long as it is pleasurable. Both partners should be naked and have a minimum of physical fatigue and tension. Avoiding specifically sexual stimulation, including genitals and breasts, the 'giving' partner massages and fondles the 'getting' partner to give pleasure. The rules of sensate focus for receiving partners are that they have to protect 'pleasuring' partners from causing discomfort or initiating sex. Receiving partners need not comment either verbally or nonverbally on their experiencing, unless such expression is completely spontaneous. Giving partners are committed not only to giving pleasure, but also to acknowledging their sensations in giving pleasure, exploring another's body by touch, and receiving pleasurable reactions. After a reasonable time, partners exchange roles.

Sensate focus aims to give partners time, space and permission to respond sensually without feeling that they have to perform intercourse. Kaplan (1974) observes that, though most couples experience positive reactions to sensate focus, some individuals experience very little reaction and others negative reactions. She indicates that these negative reactions may indicate deeper inhibitions concerning sexual responsiveness and suggests how to treat them. Helpers require sensitivity in following up clients' reactions to sensate focus.

Use role-play methods

In Chapter 10 I discussed role play as a method of rehearsing action skills. Role plays can also be used to allow clients to experience and express feelings. Role-play methods can be powerful ways of releasing and exploring feelings in various kinds of personal relationship, be they past, present or future. This unburdening may in turn generate further self-exploration and deeper understandings of underlying feelings. Clients may play both people in a relationship either by visualizing with eyes closed or by switching chairs as they play each part. Alternatively, helpers may play one of the parts in the relationship, for example a parent, spouse, boyfriend or girlfriend. In role reversal, both helpers and clients switch roles. In addition, helpers may heighten clients' awareness by mirroring clients' feelings-related verbal, voice and body messages. After as well as during role plays, you can assist clients to experience, articulate and explore feelings uncovered by and associated with what happens.

Encourage action

Frequently clients cannot fully experience and explore feelings until they take the risks of acting. For example, there are limits to which clients can know how much they like or dislike any activity or person if they have no first-hand contact with them. Already I have stressed the role of rewarding listening in enabling clients to feel that helpers are secure bases from which to take the risks of exploratory behaviour and action skills experiments. In addition, Chapter 11 specified interventions for developing clients' action skills.

ASSIST CLIENTS TO EXPRESS FEELINGS

Expressing feelings well requires clients to be skilled at experiencing, exploring and accurately labelling their feelings. When clients reveal feelings they put themselves very much on the line. Some feelings are difficult for most clients to express, especially when they do not feel safe with another person: for example, worthlessness, incompetence and unattractiveness. Some feelings may be more difficult for female clients to express, though male clients may have difficulty expressing them too: for example, ambition, leadership and assertion. Some feelings may be more difficult for male than female clients to express, though again differences exist within each sex; such feelings include vulnerability, sensitivity and affection. Many clients find it difficult to express specific feelings well, for instance anger. Within the context of supportive relationships, helpers assisting clients to express feelings need to focus on both thinking skills and action skills.

Focus on thinking skills

Here I illustrate some possible thinking skills that may interfere with or assist appropriate expression of feelings. Thinking skills weaknesses blocking experiencing of feelings overlap with those hindering appropriate expression of feelings. Again, I refer you to Chapters 9 and 10 for how to work with clients' thinking skills.

OWN RESPONSIBILITY FOR CHOOSING Assist clients to know that they always have choices in how to express feelings. Also help clients to identify where their specific thinking and action skills choice points are.

USE COPING SELF-TALK As well as calming themselves down, clients can develop skills of coaching themselves through sequences of choices involved in skilled expression of feelings. For example, clients feeling strongly about obtaining a promotion might use the following self-statements before and during seeing their bosses: 'Stay calm. Remember to be polite and state my case positively. Speak firmly and make good eye contact.'

CHOOSE REALISTIC PERSONAL AND RELATIONSHIP RULES Many personal and relationship rules interfere with appropriate expression of feelings. Here are some examples:

Unrealistic personal rules

'I must have approval all the time.'
'I must always express feelings smoothly.'
'Men must not cry.'

Unrealistic relationship rules

'We must never have conflict in our relationship.'
'Wives must always be sexually available to husbands.'
'Children should be seen and not heard.'

CHOOSE HOW YOU PERCEIVE Many clients need to develop skills allowing their feelings towards others to be based on more accurate perceptions so that the feelings they express are what they truly feel. Once clients are in touch with their feelings, they still require flexibility in perceiving various action skills options for expressing them.

ATTRIBUTE CAUSE ACCURATELY Without realizing it, some clients may wait for others to make the first move in expressing feelings: for example, 'I cannot express positive feelings about him/her until he/she expresses positive feelings about me.' Helpers may need to assist clients to take an active rather than a passive stance to expressing feelings.

PREDICT REALISTICALLY Many clients do not express certain feelings either at all or well because they make false predictions. For instance, many shy clients are reluctant to initiate social contacts because of fears of rejection. Clients in relationships may be unwilling to bring up differences because of catastrophic predictions about the consequences. These predictions may also cause them either to under-react or to over-react when they eventually do discuss differences.

SET REALISTIC GOALS Clients may possess unrealistic goals about what feelings to express to whom and when. For instance, insecure teenagers with unclear or unrealistic goals may come on too strong too soon with their boyfriends or girlfriends. Another example is that of males, when learning to be more emotionally expressive, who avoid discouragement from early setbacks because they realize that developing these skills can take time.

USE VISUALIZING SKILLS Clients can use visualizing skills to rehearse how to express feelings appropriately. Furthermore, they can visualize themselves attaining their goals if they use good expressing feelings skills. Clients can also visualize the negative consequences of using poor expressing feelings skills.

Focus on action skills

Helpers can assist clients to develop action skills of expressing feelings. I refer you to Chapters 9 and 11 for how to do this. When assisting clients to express feelings, always pay attention to verbal, voice and body messages. You may also focus on touch and action messages. Let me illustrate different action messages for showing caring skills (Nelson-Jones, 1990). Needless to say, clients need to be sensitive to what others perceive as caring messages.

VERBAL MESSAGES Verbal messages of caring include statements like, 'I love you', 'I care for you' and 'I want to help you'. Clients may also pay compliments. Furthermore, clients can show caring if they use good verbal skills when listening; for instance, accurate reflective responses.

VOICE MESSAGES If clients' voice messages are wrong, they negate their verbal messages. Characteristics of caring voice messages include warmth and expressiveness. Clients' voices should convey kindness and interest rather than harshness and lack of interest.

BODY MESSAGES When clients send caring verbal messages, their gaze, eye contact, body orientation and facial expressions all need to demonstrate interest and concern for the other person. Similarly, clients need to show good attending and listening body message skills when others share problems with them.

TOUCH MESSAGES Touch can be a wonderful way to express caring. Clients can express caring by a hug, a half-embrace, an arm over the shoulder, a touch on the arm, or a hand on top of or holding a hand, among other ways. With all touch messages, clients are in another's close intimate zone, and must be very sensitive about the other person's willingness to be touched.

ACTION MESSAGES Action messages indicating caring include making the other person a cup of tea or coffee in the morning; being prepared to do your share of the household chores; giving birthday cards and presents; initiating pleasant events, such as going out to dinner; showing affection through flowers, poems and other spontaneous gifts; and being available to help out in times of need (Argyle & Henderson, 1985).

ASSIST CLIENTS TO MANAGE FEELINGS

Many clients come to help wanting release from painful and negative feelings. Often they lack confidence in themselves. In addition, they are subject to feelings like excessive anger, depression and anxiety. In reality, feelings tend to overlap: for instance, clients can be simultaneously depressed, anxious and excessively angry. Success in managing one of these feelings better is likely to enhance self-esteem and, hence, handling the others better too. Clients may use skills learned for managing one feeling for managing other feelings. Here, rather than cover a range of feelings, I use anger, depression and anxiety to show how to approach developing clients' skills of managing feelings. The discussion of pertinent thinking and action skills is illustrative rather than comprehensive. In practice, skills redefinitions of clients' managing feelings problems should be tailor-made to their particular skills weaknesses and circumstances. Always use supportive relationship skills when assisting clients to manage feelings.

Managing anger

Clients should identify and manage anger rather than attempt to rid themselves of it altogether. Anger can have positive uses. It can be a signal indicating that something is wrong and requires attention. It can be an energizer helping clients to take appropriate action. In some instances, anger may also be a purge. After expressing it, clients may calm down and be more rational. Part of managing anger is to be able to experience, explore and accurately label angry feelings. Table 12.1 shows some further skills for managing anger, each of which I discuss in turn.

Table 12.1 Illustrative thinking and action skills for managing anger

THINKING SKILLS	ACTION SKILLS
Owning responsibility for anger	Assertion
Possessing realistic personal rules	— expressing anger
Perceiving provocations accurately	— requesting behaviour changes
Using coping self-talk	Handling aggressive criticism
Using visualizing	Using relaxation
	Managing stress
	Helping one another

THINKING SKILLS

*   *Owning responsibility for anger*. Clients have choices in how they experience, express and manage anger. Until they own responsibility for their anger, they will have insufficient motivation to develop the skills to manage it effectively.

*   *Possessing realistic personal rules*. Ellis (1977) regards childish demandingness as the central thinking skills weakness in anger. Clients make 'mustabatory' demands on themselves, for instance 'I must never make mistakes', on others, for instance 'Others should always agree with me' or 'Others must never criticize me', and on the environment, for instance 'The world should always be the way I want it to be' and 'I should never have hassles'.

*   *Perceiving provocations accurately*. Clients need to develop skills of not jumping to superficial negative conclusions about others. Beck (1988) observes of relationship difficulties that much of the friction is due to misunderstandings stemming from differences in perspective and not from meanness or selfishness.

*   *Using coping self-talk*. Simple self-instructions like 'Calm down' and 'Cool it' can often give clients more time and space to get feelings under control (Goldstein & Keller, 1987). Clients can also use longer self-statements: for instance, 'I can handle this situation if I don't let my pride get in the way' (Meichenbaum, 1983; Novaco, 1977).

*   *Using visualizing*. Clients can use visualization in many ways to manage anger. They can visually rehearse how to express angry feelings appropriately. They can relax

themselves by visualizing restful scenes. They can also use visualization to perceive others' perspectives more accurately.

ACTION SKILLS

- *Assertion.* Skills for expressing anger assertively include using 'I' statements, avoiding provocative voice messages like screaming, and avoiding threatening body messages like finger-jabbing. Clients also need to develop skills of requesting others to alter their behaviour before rather than after becoming thoroughly fed up with it (Alberti & Emmons, 1990; Nelson-Jones, 1990).

- *Handling aggressive criticism.* Clients have numerous choices, other than impulsive knee-jerk reactions, in dealing with aggressive criticism. For instance, they can tell themselves to relax, calm down and breathe more slowly until they feel more under control. They can also choose from a number of verbal strategies: for example, reflecting another's anger, or partly agreeing with another's point and then putting their own, or asking another to be more specific about what they've done to upset them. Clients may back off now and react to criticism at a later date – either requesting or, on their own initiative, taking a 'cooling off' period.

- *Using relaxation.* Clients can develop skills of muscular and visual relaxation to manage anger (Deffenbacher *et al.*, 1988, 1990). I describe relaxation skills later in this chapter.

- *Managing stress.* Frequently inability to handle life's stresses makes clients prone to anger. As well as using muscular and visual relaxation, clients may manage stress better if they develop adequate recreational outlets, actively look after their health, and develop support networks. Since much stress is internally generated, helpers and clients also need to review relevant thinking skills.

- *Helping one another.* Clients can develop skills of working with their partners to help each other to manage anger. Relevant action skills for clients are: disciplining themselves to watch their tongues; expressing anger assertively; showing an awareness of what partners experience before, during and after they receive clients' expressions of anger; and using rewarding listening and questioning skills to help partners express angry feelings that they may have difficulty acknowledging or getting out into the open. When helping one another to manage anger, partners need to possess realistic relationship rules: for instance, 'When either of us expresses anger in our relationship it is a signal to explore our own thoughts, feelings, and actions, and not just those of the other person.'

Managing depression

Often helpers work with clients who feel depressed. Depressed clients can be very sensitive to the quality of the helping relationship. Experiencing difficulty affirming themselves, they seek affirmation from outside. You require good relationship skills both initially, when clients may feel dependent on you, and also later, as they develop skills for emotional independence. Table 12.2 presents some common thinking skills and action skills for managing depression.

Table 12.2 Illustrative thinking and action skills for managing depression

THINKING SKILLS	ACTION SKILLS
Possessing realistic personal rules	Relationship skills
Perceiving others and self accurately	— initiating contact
Attributing cause accurately	— self-disclosing
Predicting realistically	Assertion skills
	— setting limits and saying 'no'
	Pleasant activities skills

THINKING SKILLS
- *Possessing realistic personal rules.* Clients can create and sustain their depressed feelings when striving to attain and failing to live up to unrealistic rules (Ellis, 1989; Hewitt & Dyke, 1986). Depressogenic unrealistic rules include: 'I must be perfect', and 'I must always gain others' approval'.

- *Perceiving others and self accurately.* Beck observes of his cognitive theory of depression: 'Of all the hypotheses, pervasiveness of negative thinking in all forms of depression, symptomatic or syndromatic, has been the most uniformly supported' (1991, p. 372). Depressed clients tend to jump to negative conclusions about how others perceive them, and are skilled at blocking out positive information about themselves (Beck, 1991; Beck *et al.*, 1979)

- *Attributing cause accurately.* Depressed clients can overemphasize their responsibility for negative events (Beck *et al.*, 1979), and may attribute the causes of negative events not only as more due to themselves, but also as more due to stable and global causes than warranted (Petersen *et al.*, 1985; Seligman *et al.*, 1979).

- *Predicting realistically.* Depressed clients tend to predict the future negatively. They are more prone to feelings of hopelessness (Beck *et al.*, 1979), helplessness (Abramson *et al.*, 1978), and perceived self-inefficacy (Bandura, 1986) than non-depressed people.

ACTION SKILLS
Depressed clients may have good skills in specific areas, but underrate them. The following discussion assumes that their action skills genuinely require development.

- *Relationship skills*. Many depressed clients are lonely because they have insufficient as well as insufficiently high-quality social contacts. Initiating contact and appropriately self-disclosing are among the relationship skills such clients may need to develop.

- *Assertion skills*. Frequently depressed clients lower their self-esteem through inability to use assertion skills. For instance, clients who do not stand up for themselves may feel doubly bad. First, they have the outer negative consequences of having to do extra work, pay extra money or whatever else follows from their lack of assertion. Second, they have the inner negative consequences of feeling bad about their non-assertion.

- *Pleasant activities skills*. Lewinsohn and his colleagues state: 'If you feel depressed, it is very likely that you are not involved in many pleasant activities' (1986, p. 73). Depressed clients can develop skills of identifying activities they find rewarding (MacPhillamy & Lewinsohn, 1982). Then they can develop and implement plans to participate more in them. As the old adage says, 'A little of what you fancy does you good.'

Managing anxiety

Anxiety is a normal survival mechanism. However, many, if not most, clients suffer from excessive or debilitating anxieties that interfere with happiness and fulfilment. Again, you need to offer such clients a good helping relationship. Many anxious clients are threatened by meeting new people, including helpers. Clients can also become anxious when talking about their anxieties. Assisting clients to develop skills of managing anxiety invariably involves focusing on how they think.

Sometimes anxious clients have good action skills, but let their anxieties get in the way of manifesting them. For instance, some students perform well when tests do not count, but poorly when they do. Some otherwise adequate students have poor exam-taking skills. Here it can be important to focus on action skills as well as on thinking skills. Table 12.3 shows some common thinking skills for managing anxiety. The requisite action skills are less easy to list, since they vary with clients' problems. For example, clients require different action skills for attending job interviews than for developing intimacy.

Table 12.3 Illustrative thinking and action skills for managing anxiety

THINKING SKILLS	ACTION SKILLS
Using coping self-talk	Skills required for specific situations
Possessing realistic personal rules	Relaxation skills
Perceiving self and others accurately	
Predicting realistically	
Setting realistic goals	
Using visualizing	

THINKING SKILLS

- *Using coping self-talk*. Anxious clients engage in much anxious self-talk (Beck *et al.*, 1988a; Kendall & Hollon, 1989). Their anxiety symptoms are signals for telling themselves that they cannot cope or do anything right. In social situations, their self-talk may be about making fools of themselves. Often clients with panic disorders tell themselves that a vital system, for instance cardiovascular or nervous, may collapse (Beck & Weishaar, 1989).

- *Possessing realistic personal rules*. Anxious clients tend to have personal rules that engender both fear of failure and self-devaluation (Ellis, 1962, 1989). Making perfectionist demands on self and others is a central characteristic of such rules.

- *Perceiving self and others accurately*. Anxious clients overemphasize the degree of threat in situations. They selectively perceive what might go wrong and insufficiently perceive what might go right. In addition, anxious clients underestimate both their ability to cope and the supports available to them (Beck & Emery, 1985; Beck & Weishaar, 1989). Defensiveness, in which clients deny or distort aspects of themselves they find threatening, is another way that anxiety interferes with perception.

- *Predicting realistically*. The predictions of anxious clients exaggerate dangers and risks. Such clients worry about the future and their ability to cope with it. They live out my tongue-in-cheek definition of the future as 'anxiety about living in the context of anxiety about dying' (Nelson-Jones, 1989, p. 113).

- *Setting realistic goals*. Some anxious clients set goals that are too low to protect themselves from failure. Many set goals that are too high and become fearful about achieving them. The goals of other clients are realistically attainable, if they can manage anxiety better.

- *Using visualizing*. Most anxious clients experience negative visual images prior to and concurrent with anxiety attacks (Beck *et al.*, 1974). Clients may have poor skills for using visualizing both to relax and also to rehearse action skills.

ACTION SKILLS

- *Skills required for specific situations*. Anxiety may either be the cause of poor action skills, their consequence or a mixture of the two. Some clients may have good action skills, but experience difficulty implementing them under pressure. Other clients may need to develop specific skills: for instance, at public speaking, asking for a date, driving a car, managing a company, policing an angry crowd, and so on. Their increased competence in these skills lowers anxiety.

- *Relaxation skills*. Many anxious clients have poor relaxation skills. They engage in insufficient pleasurable and relaxing activities. In addition, they may have poor muscular and mental relaxation skills.

Table 12.4 Tensing self-instructions for progressive muscular relaxation

Muscle group	Tensing self-instructions*
Right hand and forearm	Clench my right fist and tense the muscles in my lower arm.
Right biceps	Bend my right arm at the elbow and flex my biceps by tensing the muscles of my upper right arm.
Left hand and forearm	Clench my left fist and tense the muscles in my lower arm.
Left biceps	Bend my left arm at the elbow and flex my biceps by tensing the muscles of my upper left arm.
Forehead	Lift my eyebrows as high as possible.
Eyes, nose and upper cheeks	Squeeze my eyes tightly shut and wrinkle my nose.
Jaw and lower cheeks	Clench my teeth and pull the corners of my mouth firmly back.
Neck and throat	Pull my chin down hard towards my chest yet resist having it touch my chest.
Chest and shoulders	Pull my shoulder blades together and take a deep breath.
Stomach	Tighten the muscles in my stomach as though someone were about to hit me there.
Right thigh	Tense the muscles of my right upper leg by pressing the upper muscle down and the lower muscles up.
Right calf	Stretch my right leg and pull my toes towards my head.
Right foot	Point and curl the toes of my right foot and turn it inward.
Left thigh	Tense the muscles of my left upper leg by pressing the upper muscles down and the lower muscles up.
Left calf	Stretch my left leg and pull my toes towards my head.
Left foot	Point and curl the toes of my left foot and turn it inward.

*With left-handed people, tensing instructions for the left side of the body should come before those for the right.

Relaxation skills

Helpers can train clients in muscular and mental relaxation skills (Bernstein & Borkovec, 1973; Jacobson, 1929, 1976; Wolpe, 1982). Impart these as self-helping rather than as helper-offered skills. Clients may use relaxation skills not only for managing anxiety, but for dealing with problems such as tension headaches, hypertension and insomnia. Relaxation skills may be used alone or as part of more complex skills; for instance systematic densensitization (Deffenbacher & Suinn, 1988; Goldfried & Davison, 1976; Wolpe, 1982).

PROGRESSIVE MUSCULAR RELAXATION SKILLS Progressive muscular relaxation refers to the progressive cultivation of the relaxation response (Jacobson, 1929, 1976). Tell clients that the first step in physically relaxing themselves is to find a quiet space where they will be uninterrupted. They may use a bed, a recliner chair, or a comfortable chair with a headrest. If possible, they should wear loose-fitting, comfortable clothing, and remove items such as glasses and shoes. Their arms should be either by their sides or on the arms of chairs. Their legs should be uncrossed and their eyes closed.

Progressive muscular relaxation involves clients in tensing and relaxing various muscle groups. You can demonstrate how clients should go through a five-step tension–relax cycle for each muscle group (Bernstein & Borkovec, 1973). These steps are (1) *focus* – focus attention on a particular muscle group; (2) *tense* – tense the muscle group; (3) *hold* – maintain the tension for 5–7 seconds; (4) *release* – release the tension in the muscle group; and (5) *relax* – spend 20 to 30 seconds focusing on letting go of tension and further relaxing the muscle groups.

Table 12.4, which you may give to clients as a handout, lists the various muscle groupings and self-instructions for tensing them. For their homework, either provide clients with copies of existing relaxation cassettes or make these afresh. Later encourage clients to make their own self-instructional cassettes. Having said this, it remains uncertain how much home relaxation cassettes enhance treatment outcome (Hoelscher *et al.*, 1987).

Give relaxation instructions in a calm and soothing voice. In step 5 of the cycle, use repetition to enhance relaxation: for instance: 'Your forehead feels increasingly calm and relaxed . . . calm and relaxed . . . calm and relaxed'. When relaxing clients, observe their body posture and breathing as a check on how relaxed they are. Also, ask them how relaxed they feel and whether there are any muscle groupings requiring further attention. If so, spend extra time relaxing these muscles. You can end relaxation sessions by counting backwards from five to one and, when you get to one, asking clients to wake up feeling pleasantly relaxed as though from a peaceful sleep.

Inform clients that progressive muscular relaxation requires practice to gain its full benefit. When learning, they should practise daily for at least 15 minutes. Ask clients whether they anticipate any obstacles to practice, such as finding a quiet place, and help them to devise strategies for dealing with them. Evidence exists that clients who monitor their relaxation practice are more likely to continue doing it (Tasto & Hinkle, 1973). Consequently, ask clients to keep logs monitoring homework practice. Table 12.5 shows an entry in such a log.

Table 12.5 Relaxation homework monitor log

DATE	TIME, PLACE, LENGTH	COMMENTS
3 Oct	6 p.m., living room at home 15–20 minutes	Started off feeling tense after a day at work. Tensed and relaxed sixteen muscle groups. At first thoughts about work interfered with relaxation. Ended feeling deeply relaxed.

BRIEF MUSCULAR RELAXATION SKILLS Brief muscular relaxation skills aim to induce deep relaxation with less time and effort. When clients are proficient in full progressive muscular relaxation, you can introduce such skills. Brief relaxation skills are useful both in helping sessions and in homework. Here are two examples.

- *Sequential brief relaxation.* First instruct clients and then get them to tell themselves the following instructions focused on tensing and relaxing in turn four composite muscle groupings:

> I'm going to count to ten in units of two. After each unit of two I will instruct you to tense and relax a muscle grouping. One, two . . . focus on your leg and feet muscles . . . tense and hold the tension in these muscles for five seconds . . . release . . . relax and enjoy the sensations of the tension flowing from your legs and feet. Three, four . . . take a deep breath and focus on your chest, shoulder and stomach muscles . . . tense and hold the tension in these muscles for five seconds . . . release . . . relax and enjoy the sensations of the tension flowing from your chest, shoulders and stomach. Five, six . . . focus on your face, neck and head muscles . . . tense and hold the tension in these muscles for five seconds . . . release . . . relax and enjoy the sensations of the tension flowing from your face, neck and head. Seven, eight . . . focus on your arm and hand muscles . . . tense and hold the tension in these muscles for five seconds . . . release . . . relax and enjoy the sensations of the tension flowing from your arms and hands. Nine, ten . . . focus on all the muscles in your body . . . tense all the muscles in your body together and hold for five seconds . . . release . . . relax and enjoy the sensations of the tension leaving your whole body as

your relaxation gets deeper and deeper . . . deeper
and deeper . . . deeper and deeper.

* *Simultaneous brief relaxation*. As at the end of the previous example, you instruct clients to tense all muscle groupings simultaneously. You can say:

> When I give the signal, I would like you to close your
> eyes very tightly, take a deep breath and simul-
> taneously tense your arm muscles, your face, neck
> and throat muscles, your chest, shoulder and
> stomach muscles, and your leg and foot muscles . . .
> Now take a deep breath and tense all your muscles
> . . . hold for five seconds . . . now release and relax
> as quickly and deeply as you can.

MENTAL RELAXATION SKILLS Often clients visualize restful scenes at the end of progressive muscular relaxation. Such a scene might be, 'lying in a lush green meadow on a warm, sunny day, feeling a gentle breeze, watching the clouds'. Clients can visualize such scenes independent of muscular relaxation.

Systematic desensitization

Progressive muscular relaxation forms an important part of systematic desensitization. Consider intervening with systematic desensitization when clients have specific anxieties and phobias, rather than general tension. The originator of systematic desensitization, Joseph Wolpe's version involves three elements: (1) training in deep muscular relaxation; (2) the construction around themes of hierarchies of anxiety-evoking situations; and (3) helpers asking clients, when relaxed, to imagine items from the hierarchies (Wolpe, 1958, 1982). Wolpe's 'reciprocal inhibition' or counter-conditioning explanation is that the pairing of anxiety-evoking stimuli with the relaxation response brings about a lessening of the anxiety response, in effect weakening the bond between anxiety-evoking stimuli and anxiety responses. Other explanations exist for systematic desensitization's effectiveness. Increasingly helpers present it as a self-control skill (Goldfried & Davison, 1976), thus emphasizing coping with anxiety rather than mastering it.

INTRODUCE SYSTEMATIC DESENSITIZATION Offer reasons for using systematic desensitization. Presumably, your client has some anxiety management skills weaknesses for which desensitization seems the preferred intervention. Briefly explain all three elements. Stress learning desensitization as a coping skill. Having already discussed muscular relaxation skills, I now turn to hierarchy construction skills.

CONSTRUCT HIERARCHIES Hierarchies are lists of stimuli centred around themes and ordered according to the amount of anxiety they evoke. Table 12.6 illustrates a hierarchy for a client with debilitating anxiety about maths exams.

Table 12.6 Hierarchy for client with maths exam anxiety

RANK	RATING	ITEM
1	5	Thinking about a maths exam when revising at my desk 1 month before
2	10	Thinking about a maths exam when revising at my desk 3 weeks before
3	15	Thinking about a maths exam when revising at my desk 2 weeks before
4	20	Thinking about a maths exam when revising at my desk 1 week before
5	25	Thinking about a maths exam on the night before
6	30	Waking up on the morning of the maths exam
7	40	Driving my car on the way to the maths exam
8	50	Waiting outside the exam room
9	60	Going into the exam room
10	70	Sitting down at my desk in the exam room
11	80	Looking at the maths exam paper for the first time
12	90	Sitting in the exam room looking at everybody else working hard
13	100	Having a panic attack during the maths exam

The following are hierarchy construction skills.

* *Identify suitable themes.* Precedence needs to be given to themes or areas most debilitating to clients.

* *Generate items around themes.* Assist clients to generate items around one or more themes. Items need to be described so that clients can imagine them. Sources for hierarchy items include information gathered during assessment, homework involving self-monitoring, and suggestions from clients and you. You can ask clients to write items on index cards to make for ease of ordering.

* *Rank items to make hierarchies.* Ranking items involves clients rating those for each theme on a subjective anxiety scale and ordering them accordingly. A common way to check the anxiety-evoking potential of items is to say 0 represents no anxiety and

100 is the maximum anxiety possible for that theme. In general, avoid gaps of over 10 units on the subjective anxiety scale; if necessary generate intervening items. During treatment remain flexible: you and your clients may need to reorder, reword, or generate further items.

- *Check clients' ability to imagine items.* A basic assumption of systematic desensitization is that clients are capable of imagining hierarchy items or scenes. Check your clients' ability to imagine items. Some clients imagine items better if they describe them aloud. You may provide fuller descriptions of items.

PRESENT HIERARCHY ITEMS A desensitization session starts with relaxing clients. When you are sure that clients are deeply relaxed, present items along the lines of, 'Now I want you to imagine you are sitting at your desk revising for a maths exam one month before the test . . .'. Start with the least anxiety-evoking item and ask clients to raise their index finger if experiencing anxiety. If they experience no anxiety, ask them to switch the item off and go back to feeling pleasantly relaxed. After 30–50 seconds you can ask clients to imagine the item again. If this causes no anxiety, withdraw the item, possibly spend further time relaxing clients, and move on to the next item.

If a client indicates anxiety with items, you have two main choices. First, you can withdraw the item immediately, relax the client again, and then present the item a second time. Second, and preferable for developing self-helping skills, you can both instruct the client to continue imagining the item and also encourage him or her to relax away their anxiety by calming and coaching self-talk and taking slow deep breaths (Goldfried, 1971; Goldfried & Davison, 1976; Meichenbaum, 1977). If the client repeatedly experiences anxiety with an item, intersperse less threatening items.

Systematic desensitization assumes that once a low anxiety-evoking item, for example, 10 units, ceases to stimulate anxiety, all other hierarchy items become less anxiety-evoking by 10 units. Thus the 100-unit item becomes 90 units and so on. Consequently, you only present weak anxiety-evoking items to clients.

Keep a record of all item presentations and their outcomes. Wolpe's (1982) desensitization sessions last 15–30 minutes. Initially, he may present a total of 8 to 10 items, possibly from different hierarchies. In later sessions, he may make as many as 30 to 50 presentations. Goldfried and Davison (1976) suggest covering from 2 to 5 items each session. You can also cassette-record items, and get clients to work through them as a homework assignment.

Encourage clients, when preparing for or facing anxiety-evoking situations in daily life, to develop self-helping skills of relaxing away tensions, taking slow and deep breaths and using calming and coaching self-talk. Where appropriate, give clients homework logs to monitor their use of self-helping skills.

IN VIVO DESENSITIZATION Two kinds of consideration may make *in vivo* or real-life, rather than visualized, desensitization the preferred intervention. First, clients may have difficulty imagining items. However, items for real-life desensitization need to be readily accessible. Second, where items are readily accessible, your intervention should be more powerful than if you work with visualized items. For instance, you may relax clients with public-speaking anxiety at the start of each session, then over a number of sessions have them give short talks in front of increasing numbers of people. You can introduce answering questions into the hierarchy to make for increased difficulty and real-lifeness. Many visualized desensitization considerations – such as using relaxation, constructing hierarchies, and the level of anxiety within which to present items – still apply to *in vivo* desensitization.

Use of medication

When assisting clients to manage feelings, many helpers require familiarity with psychotropic drugs – drugs that act on the mind. You find difficulty assessing how clients feel unless you take into account the effects of any medication they are on. If medication seems advisable, you need to refer clients to doctors. Furthermore, if working with clients on medication, you may need to discuss appropriate dosage and side-effects with doctors, or look these up in a reference source. Clients themselves may wish to discuss their use of medication. Though you should not go out of your depth, your clients may feel reassured if you can conduct an informed discussion.

All psychotropic drugs have possible toxic or unwanted side-effects (Burns, 1980; Ponterotto, 1985). For instance, even minor tranquillizers can affect some clients with drowsiness, lessened muscular coordination, lowered sex urge, and dependency. A drug like lithium carbonate, used for mania and depression, is highly toxic and requires close medical monitoring. The levels of dosage, both amounts and frequency, are considerations for doctors prescribing drugs and for helpers working with clients on drugs. If you require information about a drug, you can ask a doctor or look it up in the latest editions of regularly updated medical prescription reference sources, such as *The Physician's Desk Reference* in the United States or *MIMS* in Britain and Australia.

You may need to explore your own and clients' attitudes towards using drugs. Some helpers have prejudices against any use of drugs and, sometimes, also against the medical profession. Other helpers, like some clients, may treat medication as a crutch. Clients' attitudes to psychotropic drugs vary from viewing taking them as personal weakness to willing dependence on them. Though sometimes difficult to achieve, aim for clients to become psychologically self-reliant in managing feelings, including taking as little medication as possible. However, on occasion, using medication may be appropriate, for instance with seriously disturbed clients (American Psychiatric Association, 1987) or those requiring relief in crises. As helping progresses, you may be able to wean clients off drugs, possibly by smaller and less frequent dosages. For quick-acting drugs, another option is to recommend that clients use them only in emergencies.

CHAPTER HIGHLIGHTS

- Reasons for assisting clients to focus on feelings include catharsis; improved health; lifting inhibitions and repressions; getting more in touch with wants and wishes; developing a sense of identity; providing a base for effective relating; and managing unwanted feelings.

- Helpers are feelings educators who use relationship and training skills to assist clients to experience, express and manage feelings.

- Helpers should always assume that clients are responsible for their feelings and they are responsible for showing clients how to implement this responsibility.

- Helpers can assist clients to experience feelings by offering reasons for focusing on feelings; focusing on thinking skills; using rewarding listening; training clients in inner listening; using feelings questions; being authentic and appropriately self-disclosing; confronting inauthenticity; raising consciousness; teaching sensate focus; using role-play methods; and encouraging action.

- Thinking skills for expressing feelings include using coping self-talk, perceiving others accurately, and predicting realistically.

- Action skills for expressing feelings include proficiency in sending relevant verbal, voice, body, touch and action messages.

- Thinking skills for managing anger include owning responsibility for anger, possessing realistic personal rules, perceiving provocations accurately, using coping self-talk, and using visualizing.

- Action skills for managing anger include those for assertion, handling aggressive criticism, relaxing, managing stress, and helping one another.

- Thinking skills for managing depression centre on overcoming a negative outlook and include possessing realistic personal rules, perceiving self and others accurately, attributing cause accurately, and predicting realistically.

- Action skills for managing depression include relationship skills, such as initiating contact and self-disclosing; assertion skills; and pleasant activities skills.

- Thinking skills for managing anxiety centre on overcoming an excessive sense of danger and include using coping self-talk, possessing realistic personal rules, perceiving self and others accurately, predicting realistically, setting realistic goals, and using visualizing.

- Action skills for managing anxiety include relaxation and the skills required for competent performance in specific situations.

- Relaxation skills may be used on their own or as part of more complex interventions like systematic desensitization. Relaxation skills include progressive muscular relaxation, brief muscular relaxation, and mental relaxation.

- Present systematic desensitization as a self-helping coping skill. In addition to training in progressive muscular relaxation, systematic desensitization includes constructing hierarchies around anxiety-evoking themes and getting clients to imagine hierarchy items when relaxed.

- Many helpers require knowledge of psychotropic drugs, drugs that work on the mind. All such drugs have unwanted side-effects. Helpers may need to explore their own and clients' attitudes towards using medication.

STAGE 5

END AND CONSOLIDATE SELF-HELPING SKILLS

The final stage of the lifeskills helping model focuses on how to end and consolidate self-helping skills. Chapter 13 looks at different ways helpers can assist clients to maintain and develop skills after helping. The chapter also focuses on further tasks and skills in the ending stage, including evaluating helping skills.

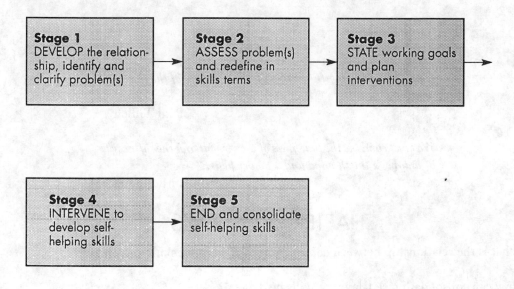

THIRTEEN

How to End and Consolidate Self-helping Skills

Courage is the self-affirmation of being in spite of the fact of nonbeing.

Paul Tillich

We must combine the toughness of the serpent and the softness of a dove, a tough mind and a tender heart.

Martin Luther King

CHAPTER QUESTIONS

What is the relationship between consolidating self-helping skills and ending?

How can consolidating self-helping skills be defined?

How can helpers focus on how clients think to consolidate self-helping skills?

What can helpers do throughout the lifeskills helping model to enhance consolidation?

What are different formats for ending helping?

When should helping end?

What are tasks and skills for the ending stage?

How can helpers evaluate their helping skills?

Stage 5 of the lifeskills helping model addresses the questions not only of how to end helping, but also of how to assist clients to continue using trained lifeskills after helping. The following examples show helping outcomes that did not last:

> Abdul, 24, sought help because he was worried about compulsively engaging in AIDS risk behaviour. Two months after helping ended, Abdul had resumed his high-risk sexual practices.
>
> Last year, after some sessions with her school counsellor, Denise, 17, was able to cope much better with test anxiety. Again, this year Denise's work suffers because she gets anxious at the thought of tests.
>
> Sharon, 39, is a single mother with two teenage boys. Two years ago, Sharon received help to improve her parent–adolescent conflict skills in relation to her oldest boy, Jude. She now experiences similar difficulties with her second son, Dave, who is three years younger than Jude.
>
> For twenty years Nancy, 43, has been smoking off and mostly on. Whenever Nancy, either in-dependently or with professional help, tries to give up smoking, she always relapses soon afterwards.
>
> With the assistance of a helper, Dan, a 51-year-old widower, started gaining confidence about going into social situations. A year after treatment, Dan is back to being an unhappy 'loner'.

A central assumption of the lifeskills helping approach is that clients require skills not just for managing current problems but also for coping with future similar problems. Problems tend to repeat themselves if clients fail to correct underlying skills weaknesses. You can approach the ending stage of the lifeskills helping model in two ways. First, throughout helping, recognize that you must not avoid its end (Teyber, 1989). Furthermore, remember that the 'Train and hope' approach to the maintenance and transfer of treatment gains is unreliable (Goldstein & Keller, 1987; Kazdin, 1989; Martin, 1990; Nemeroff & Karoly, 1991; Stokes & Osnes, 1989). Systematically attend to developing clients' lifeskills for afterwards. Second, recognize that, in addition to consolidating trained skills as self-helping skills, there are special tasks and skills attached to helping's final session or sessions.

Defining consolidating self-helping skills

Throughout this book I use the term self-helping skills in preference to self-help skills. The term self-helping, more than self-help, connotes the ongoing need for former clients to assume responsibility for maintaining and developing lifeskills worked on during helping. *Generalization, maintenance, transfer* and *development* are four terms, albeit overlapping, for understanding what consolidating trained lifeskills as self-helping skills means (Kazdin, 1989; Nemeroff & Karoly, 1991; Skinner, 1953).

Generalization. Generalization signifies that targeted thinking skills and action skills carry over or generalize to conditions other than those included in helping. Clients apply targeted lifeskills flexibly in regard to other situations and stimuli.

Maintenance. Maintenance, or resistance to extinction, refers to the extension of behaviour changes after helping. Maintenance is not always consistent. Clients can suffer lapses, but over time still maintain skills. The opposite to maintenance is going back to baseline, or worse.

Transfer. Transfer or transfer of training contains elements of both generalization and maintenance. Clients not only maintain behaviour changes but extend them to new situations and settings.

Development. When helping ends, some former clients not only maintain, but develop targeted skills to higher levels. Such people assume responsibility for shifting the balance of strengths and weaknesses in one or more skills areas still further in the direction of strengths.

WORK WITH CLIENTS' THINKING SKILLS

Though insufficiently emphasized in the helping literature (for example, Kazdin, 1989; Stokes & Osnes, 1989), assisting clients to consolidate trained skills as self-helping skills requires paying close attention to how they think. Even in brief helping, you may make it easier for clients to retain skills by influencing thinking. In longer-term helping, you have considerably more scope. For instance, your and your clients' work during helping on combating perfectionist rules is relevant to managing problems not only in the short term, but in the longer term as well. In addition, in longer-term helping you can spend more time specifically addressing issues of maintenance and preventing relapses. Last but not least, you have more opportunity to impart to clients the lifeskills helping conceptual framework.

Impart the lifeskills helping conceptual framework

Helpers can assist clients to approach specific problems and problematic skills within the context of the overall lifeskills helping conceptual framework outlined in Chapter 1. There are degrees to which this is feasible. In short-term helping, all you may be able to do is to structure the contact in skills terms, provide a skills redefinition of a main problem, and offer one or more brief interventions to develop and, hopefully, maintain skills. In longer-term helping, you can go further. For instance, you can emphasize that problems can repeat themselves both horizontally, across people and situations, and vertically, over time. Consequently, effective helping needs to be based on a psychological education conceptual framework that builds and maintains clients' skills. When working with clients in the early stages of the model, you can help them to understand not only how they initially acquired lifeskills weaknesses, but more importantly how they sustain them now. During the intervention and ending stages you can impart a psychological education viewpoint concerning the processes of developing and maintaining skills strengths. Ultimately lifeskills helping is about self-helping throughout life. If you provide truly elegant treatment, you educate clients to adopt a lifeskills approach to all situations in their lives. You move beyond treating specific problems and problematic skills weaknesses to provide them with a philosophy of living.

The following thinking skills can contribute to clients' maintaining and developing lifeskills.

Owning responsibility for choosing

A basic assumption of lifeskills helping is that clients are personally responsible for making choices conducive to their survival, happiness and fulfilment. Stress the importance for clients of choosing to maintain lifeskills. Unlike certain medical conditions, there is no concept of cure. Rather clients face choices, sometimes daily, in which they can either use or fail to use targeted lifeskills.

Self-instructing

Ensure that clients understand the sequences of choices in targeted skills well enough to instruct and coach themselves. For example, when demonstrating assertion skills, you can demonstrate self-instruction too. You can get clients to summarize self-instructions either during helping sessions or as homework, and get clients to write down self-instructions or put them on cassette. Where skills are complex, helpers can instruct clients in the main rules guiding effective enactment – for example, communication rules for couples (Stuart, 1980). Often clients need to work and practise to retain self-instructions.

Using coping self-talk

Clients can use coping self-talk before, during and after difficult situations requiring them to implement additional skills, such as when required to speak in public or attend a job interview. If necessary, they can make up cue cards to remind themselves of appropriate self-talk. Clients can also use coping self-talk to deal with 'hot' thinking connected with temptations such as food, alcohol, drugs or high-risk sex. Watson and Tharp advocate that as soon as clients become aware of high-risk situations they should say: 'Danger! This is risky. I could have a lapse here' and then tell themselves specific instructions of what to do (Watson & Tharp, 1989, p. 278). A similar approach to high-risk situations is for clients to say: 'Stop . . . think . . . calm down', and then instruct themselves what to do. Further instructions include telling themselves that cravings will pass; engaging in distracting activities or thoughts; and reminding themselves of the benefits of resisting temptation and costs of giving in. Where clients have occasional failures or lapses, they can tell themselves that these are single events, setbacks may occur, but 'hang in there' and keep working to maintain and develop skills.

Possessing realistic rules

Clients may require assistance in reformulating unrealistic rules about learning and maintaining lifeskills. Here are examples of unrealistic rules and more realistic reformulations:

> *Unrealistic rule*: 'Change must be easy.'
> *Reformulation*: 'I have not only to develop new and better skills, but also to unlearn bad habits. Consequently, I have to work hard to change and maintain changes both during and after helping.'

> *Unrealistic rule*: 'During and after helping I must improve all the time.'
> *Reformulation*: 'Developing any skill involves mistakes, uncertainty, and setbacks. All I can do is to learn from mistakes and cope with setbacks as best as possible. The important thing is to keep trying.'

> *Unrealistic rule*: 'I must have helper support to maintain my skills.'
> *Reformulation*: 'Learning new skills may entail a period of dependency on helpers. However, if I conscientiously apply what I've learned, I can be independent.'

> *Unrealistic rule*: 'Others must support and approve of my efforts to develop skills.'
> *Reformulation*: 'Though I might prefer that others approve and support me, I cannot guarantee this. What is important is that I keep my skills development goals in mind and work hard to attain them.'

These are just a few unrealistic rules that clients might possess about learning and maintaining lifeskills. You can also identify, clarify, dispute and reformulate other unrealistic rules that either you or your clients possess.

Perceiving accurately

Assist clients to monitor and perceive skills strengths and weaknesses accurately. Clients discourage themselves if they pay disproportionate attention to setbacks rather than successes. Discouragement can also result when clients exaggerate how good they are and then fail to live up to expectations. If necessary, clients can challenge their thinking by identifying possibly inaccurate perceptions, separating fact from inference, looking for alternative perceptions and choosing the 'best-fit' perception.

Clients can also discourage themselves if they fail to distinguish between a temporary lapse and a more permanent relapse (Watson & Tharp, 1989). When lapses occur, train clients not to commit the perceptual error of overgeneralizing them into relapses: 'Since I have gone back to my old behaviour once, I have permanently relapsed and can do nothing about it.' Lapses should stimulate using retrieval or 'getting back on the track' skills rather than giving up. Clients should also beware of thinking about skills in black-and-white terms – 'Either I possess a skill or I don't.' In virtually all skills areas, clients possess both strengths and weaknesses. Clients can also discourage themselves if they misperceive others' reactions. For example, they may be unnecessarily self-conscious and excessively sensitive to signs of disapproval, or they may become defensive when given constructive feedback.

Predicting realistically

Predicting realistically can assist clients to maintain skills in many ways. First, clients able to predict high-risk situations can develop strategies to deal with them. Watson and Tharp observe: 'A high risk situation is one that presents a greater than usual temptation to lapse into the unwanted behavior' (1989, p. 273). Characteristics of high-risk situations can include feeling emotionally distressed, feeling lonely, social pressure from others, and losing control under the influence of alcohol. Second, clients who predict they may have failures and lapses may feel less discouraged when they occur. Third, clients able to predict the consequences of their first post-helping failure or lapse can develop strategies for getting back on track (Marx, 1982). Fourth, clients can strengthen their resolve to maintain skills if able to predict benefits of continuing to use them, and the costs of giving them up. Fifth, clients can maintain skills if, in specific situations where realistic risk-taking is desirable, they focus on the gains of action as well as on potential losses. For example, excessively anxious clients need to develop and maintain skills of challenging and counterbalancing 'dangerous' predictions.

Using goal-setting skills

Clients should always have the goal of at least maintaining end of helping skills levels. In addition, they may have the goal of developing skills still further. Such skills development goals should be specific, realistic, and possess a time frame. Helpers and clients can make plans to assist development of skills after helping. If so, remember the importance of stating sub-goals and sequencing graded tasks. Clients who set themselves unrealistic post-helping goals may even end up losing gains made during helping. Clients should always review goals in the light of experience and feedback. In addition, helpers should always be sensitive to clients' commitment to attaining goals. If you sense that clients have insufficient commitment, you can share this observation and together explore the issue more fully.

Using visualizing

Clients can use visualizing both to strengthen skills strengths and to prevent skills weaknesses. For instance, clients can visually rehearse and practise desired skills, possibly with accompanying self-talk. In addition, they can visualize anticipated high-risk situations and develop strategies for coping with them. Clients can also visualize the negative consequences of engaging in or relapsing back to unwanted behaviours. Some clients may need to exaggerate the negative consequences to strengthen their willpower (Cautela, 1967; Lazarus, 1977).

Using self-reward

Clients can use self-reward not only to acquire, but also to maintain lifeskills. They can continue administering external rewards contingent on desired actions, for example having a cup of coffee after 50 minutes of study. In addition, clients can encourage themselves with internal rewards like 'Well done', 'I hung in there and made it', and 'I'm happy that I'm maintaining my skills'. Sometimes clients can use self-reward to help them attain 'natural' rewards. For instance, shy clients might encourage themselves as they continue working on skills that elicit the natural rewards of positive social interaction. Where possible, set up schedules of reward and self-reward that enable clients to shift from artificial treatment-based rewards to real-life rewards, such as approval, competence and money (Nemeroff & Karoly, 1991).

Managing problems

Clients can fail to maintain lifeskills because of problems in targeted skills areas. In addition, problems in other areas of clients' lives can interfere with maintaining targeted skills. For example, Jacobson's (1989) study of the maintenance of treatment gains after social learning based marital therapy found stressful life events by far the best predictor of relapse.

Helpers and clients can view maintaining a targeted lifeskill as a problem requiring managing. Accordingly, they can apply CASIE, the five-step framework for managing problems, outlined in Chapter 10, to how to maintain targeted lifeskills. The following are some considerations for each of CASIE's five steps.

C = CONFRONT, IDENTIFY AND CLARIFY MY PROBLEM You need to assist clients to confront their problem of needing to maintain and, if possible, develop targeted lifeskills. Such confrontations take place in earlier as well as in final sssions.

A = ASSESS MY PROBLEM AND REDEFINE IT IN SKILLS TERMS Maintenance redefinitions at the end of helping can be close to initial redefinitions at the start of helping. Helpers and clients predict thinking and action skills weaknesses that may interfere with retaining targeted skills. For instance, Luke, aged 16, has made considerable progress in controlling his drinking. Together Luke and his helper arrive at the skills redefinition of Luke's problem of how to maintain control of his drinking shown in Table 13.1.

Table 13.1 Luke's skills redefinition for maintaining control of his drinking

THINKING SKILLS WEAKNESSES	ACTION SKILLS WEAKNESSES
Owning responsibility for choices	Assertion skills when faced with peer pressure to drink
Coping self-talk skills in high-risk situations	Support network skills
Personal rules about needing approval and having lapses	Conversational skills
Perceiving self and progress accurately	Non-drinking-related pleasant activities skills
Preventing and managing problems	

S = STATE WORKING GOALS AND PLAN SELF-HELPING INTERVENTIONS If clients do not know how to do so already, helpers can assist them to translate skills redefinitions into statements of working goals. Clients and helpers can plan how to attain each maintenance sub–goal. Where clients decide on working goals in the penultimate session, they can bring suggestions for attaining them to the final session. Maintenance plans should in particular focus on developing and using appropriate thinking and action skills to deal with high–risk situations. Identify such situations and work out strategies for handling them. If they have not done so already, clients should keep records of how well they use skills in difficult and high–risk situations to assist their planning. Maintenance plans should also focus on retrieval skills for dealing with failures and lapses.

I = IMPLEMENT MY PLAN Since clients implement maintenance plans after final sessions, both they and you have to wait and see how they perform.

E = EVALUATE THE CONSEQUENCES OF IMPLEMENTING MY PLAN Helpers and clients can discuss how to measure success in maintaining targeted lifeskills. Important questions that clients can ask themselves are, 'How well am I maintaining and developing my targeted thinking and action skills?', 'What are the consequences for myself and others of changes in my thinking and action skills?' and, 'Do I need to modify my plan in the light of feedback and new information?'

SKILLS FOR ENHANCING CONSOLIDATION

In addition to focusing on clients' thinking skills, helpers can use other skills in each stage of the DASIE model to help them retain trained skills.

Stage 1: Develop the relationship, identify and clarify problem(s)

From the start of helping, be mindful of clients' need to consolidate trained skills as self-helping skills. For all stages of the model, if you provide a good helping relationship you will both lessen the likelihood of premature termination and increase the likelihood that clients will learn skills well and hence will continue to use them. The following stage 1 skills are relevant to clients' maintenance of trained skills.

STRUCTURE FOR MAINTENANCE You may start the first session with some open-ended structuring to encourage clients to tell their stories. Later you may make structuring comments about how you are going to work (see Chapter 5). Ideas to incorporate in structuring for maintenance include using skills language; focusing on self-helping; emphasizing work and practice to maintain skills; and letting clients know that they can sharpen and develop skills after helping. Included among such comments may be statements like:

'I would like us to collaborate in identifying thinking and action skills not just for managing this problem, but for working on future similar problems.'

'The skills you learn during helping are basically self-helping skills for you to maintain and use on your own.'

'There is no concept of cure in this approach. Even after helping, you're still going to have to work to retain your skills and their benefits.'

'You can go so far during helping, but I hope your skills are good enough by the time we end to give you a sound base for sharpening and developing them afterwards.'

DEVELOP CLIENTS' SELF-MONITORING AND CLARIFYING PROBLEMS SKILLS Accurate self-monitoring is important for maintaining and developing targeted skills. Former clients who are unaware of or misperceive how they behave lack accurate information for correcting mistakes and sharpening skills. From the start of helping, influence clients to be good observers of how they feel, think and act. If systematic in how you collaborate with clients to identify and clarify problems, you develop their skills of self-monitoring and clarifying problems. Emphasize the importance of accurate self-monitoring for learning, maintaining and sharpening targeted skills. Self-monitoring skills include both perceiving behaviour accurately and, where appropriate, recording it systematically – for instance on frequency charts and, later, by using targeted skills logs.

Stage 2: Assess problem(s) and redefine in skills terms

Helper skills for consolidating clients' self-helping skills during stage 2 include the following.

DEVELOP CLIENTS' SELF-ASSESSMENT SKILLS If you make it a joint enterprise with clients to assess how they feel, think and act, they will probably develop better self-assessment skills than if you fail to involve them in the process. Not only initial but ongoing assessment is an integral part of lifeskills helping. However, helpers should not only make assessments, but impart assessment skills as client self-helping skills. Furthermore, encourage clients to engage in self-assessment not only during, but after helping. It is insufficient for clients only to self-monitor how they think and act; they also need to make accurate assessments of the significance of this information for maintaining or altering behaviour.

DEVELOP CLIENTS' SKILLS AT REDEFINING PROBLEMS IN SKILLS TERMS How you redefine problems in skills terms influences how useful this process is for assisting clients in maintaining skills. Draw them into the process by letting them know why you break down their problems into thinking skills and action skills. Check the adequacy of your skills redefinitions with them and answer questions. Especially with longer-term clients, let them know that redefining problems in skills terms is a useful self-helping skill for understanding problems, setting working goals, assessing progress, making maintenance plans, and monitoring how well they maintain and develop skills after helping. Where possible, let clients know any characteristic thinking skills weaknesses that you perceive occurring across a range of problems – for instance, possessing perfectionist rules. This gives them a start on knowing where to look when facing future problems. Also indicate recurring action skills weaknesses – for instance, poor assertion skills are relevant to many problems.

Stage 3: State working goals and plan interventions

The following are suggestions for using stating working goals and planning interventions skills to assist clients to consolidate trained skills as self-helping skills.

DEVELOP CLIENTS' SKILLS AT STATING WORKING GOALS If you negotiate clear initial statements of working goals with clients, you make it easier for them to maintain targeted skills. Such goals are relevant for after as well as during helping. Make sure clients keep records of goals statements. During helping, clear goals assist learning – and hence maintaining skills – by providing focus and motivating clients. After helping, clear goals both remind clients of skills to retain and also provide yardsticks for assessing progress. With clients who have multiple problems, initially state working goals yourself, but later coach them as they suggest appropriate goals.

PLAN INTERVENTIONS TO ENHANCE MAINTENANCE In Chapter 8 I distinguished between structured and open plans for developing targeted skills. Helpers may write maintenance considerations into structured plans and keep them in mind when adopting open plans. Here are some ways that helpers can enhance maintenance when planning:

- *Maintain a skills focus*. Use skills language. Plans containing a clear skills focus assist clients to think in skills terms both during and after helping.

- *Focus on thinking skills*. I presented such skills earlier in this chapter.

- *Focus on self-instruction*. Plan how you can make it clear to clients how to instruct themselves through sequences of skills choices. Also plan how to make it easier for them to remember self-instructions.

- *Build in ongoing self-assessment*. Develop clients' awareness and skills of monitoring and assessing thinking and action skills.

- *Allow for overlearning*. Goldstein and Keller state: 'Overlearning involves the training of a skill beyond what is necessary to produce changes in behavior' (1987, p. 116). Where possible, train clients thoroughly in targeted skills. Strategies for overlearning include: limited goals; repeated skills demonstrations; emphasizing coaching and learning by doing; and ensuring adequate time and supervision of homework and practice.

- *Emphasize real-lifeness*. Emphasizing 'real-lifeness' means that helpers focus on practical ways of ensuring that clients can use skills in real life as contrasted with artificial settings. Plan to tailor presentations and demonstrations to clients' real-life situations. Role-play rehearsals should resemble real interactions. Plan homework that enhances transfer of skills to home settings.

- *Train diversely*. Stokes and Osnes state: 'What has frequently been documented is the fact that focused training frequently has focused effects' (1989, p. 345). Beware of narrow training that does not help clients to respond flexibly to situations. For instance, if rehearsing a client in asking for a pay rise, ensure that you have trials in which the boss responds in different ways.

- *Plan reward strategies*. Helpers can plan reward strategies that enhance maintenance (Goldstein & Keller, 1987; Nemeroff & Karoly, 1991; Stokes & Osnes, 1989). For instance, you may reward clients frequently as they initially acquire skills and then reward them intermittently as they use them. Applying reward schedules this way is called 'thinning'. Nemeroff and Karoly observe: 'it is particularly helpful if one can ensure that the behavior being trained will come to elicit *natural* reinforcers in the real world – money, competence, approval, and so on' (1991, p. 146). In addition, prompts and reminders can be gradually withdrawn or 'faded'.

- *Consider using helper's aides*. Helpers wishing to enlist third parties as aides, for instance teachers and parents, need to plan how to do this. Be systematic about creating roles for aides, contacting them, enlisting support, and offering them appropriate training.

- *Spend time on coping with difficult and high-risk situations*. Plan to work on issues of maintenance and relapse throughout your programme. Do not leave this to the end.

- *Allow adequate time for ending and consolidating skills.* Different formats for ending are covered later in this chapter. For instance, you may space out sessions towards the end of helping. Attend to ending issues before as well as during the final session. Clients need adequate time to develop maintenance plans.

Stage 4: Intervene to develop self-helping skills

Helpers who, when intervening, offer both supportive relationships and good training skills enhance clients' likelihood of maintaining skills after helping. The enhancing maintenance skills already mentioned are relevant for focusing on consolidating skills in the intervention stage. For instance, keep developing clients' self-monitoring and self-assessment skills. Also, where possible, carry out those aspects of your plans that enhance maintenance: for instance allow for overlearning, train diversely and emphasize real-lifeness. Rather than repeat myself, I bring some further enhancing maintenance skills to your attention.

EMPHASIZE HOMEWORK ASSIGNMENTS Both helpers and clients require a commitment to homework as a bridge between learning and maintaining skills. Homework should be a feature of all between-session periods. Homework tasks can give clients the opportunity to practise skills in diverse situations. In subsequent sessions, always review how clients performed and enquire about related thoughts and feelings. If appropriate, not only discuss difficulties and setbacks that clients experience, but also make them the focus of skills rehearsal role plays.

ENCOURAGE CLIENT SUMMARIES Throughout the intervention stage, check that clients understand targeted skills. In addition to providing summaries yourself, you can enhance learning and maintenance by periodically requesting client summaries of targeted skills. If clients can describe skills accurately, they have a good base for implementing and remembering them. If, however, clients misunderstand or make mistakes, correct them.

USE HANDOUTS, CASSETTES AND VIDEOTAPES Letting clients have handouts, cassettes and videotapes clearly describing and demonstrating targeted skills can enhance maintenance. First, you assist clients in initially learning skills. Second, if clients keep the material, they can use it for revising.

ENCOURAGE CLIENTS TO KEEP HELPING FILES Helpers may enhance maintenance by encouraging clients to keep a helping file. Arguably it is more important for clients than for helpers to keep records. What clients call the file is up to them. The purpose of this file is to record important information and learnings collected during and after helping. Contents can include statements of working goals; plans; self-monitoring logs; handouts describing skills; homework assignments; answers to homework assignments, and so on.

The helping file enhances maintenance in many ways. First, by making the effort to keep the file, clients show a commitment to maintaining targeted skills. Second, clients can use the file for revising. Third, they can use it for evaluating progress. Fourth, after helping ends, they can update the file as they keep working on targeted skills until firmly established in their repertoires.

DEVELOP CLIENTS' IDENTIFYING AND USING SUPPORT SKILLS In Chapter 10 I mentioned the helper skill of assisting clients to identify and use supports as they develop skills. Many of the supports clients identify during helping should be available after helping. In addition, during helping, you can encourage clients to view identifying and using supports as a useful self-helping skill. One way of using others as supports is to encourage them to give honest feedback in non-threatening ways. Open acknowledgement by others of positive behaviour changes can motivate clients to keep working. However, feedback can also be useful if corrective rather than confirmatory.

THE ENDING STAGE

The boundaries of the ending stage are imprecise. As implied in the previous discussion on consolidating self-helping skills, helping has its ending built into its beginning. In another sense, the ending of formal helping is the beginning of independent self-helping. Despite advocating countdowns to ending in earlier sessions, here, for the sake of simplicity, I define the ending stage as starting with the penultimate session and concluding when all scheduled contact between clients and helpers finishes.

Formats for ending helping

FIXED ENDING Helper and client may have a contract that they work for, say, ten sessions in one or more problem and problematic skills areas. Advantages of fixed endings include lessening the chance of dependency and motivating clients to use helping to best effect. Potential disadvantages are that it restricts coverage of problems and thoroughness of attention to problematic skills. Sometimes external factors make for fixed endings: for instance, upcoming exams or the end of term.

OPEN ENDING WHEN GOALS ARE ATTAINED With open endings, helping concludes when helpers and clients agree that clients have obtained their objectives. Such objectives include managing a specific problem, developing skills to manage current and future problems, and, in exceptional cases, staying in helping long enough to become thoroughly grounded in the lifeskills philosophy of life.

FADED ENDING Here the withdrawal of helper assistance is gradual. For example, instead of meeting weekly, the final sessions could be at fortnightly or monthly intervals.

ENDING WITH BOOSTER SESSION(S) Booster sessions, say after three months, are not to teach new skills, but to check clients' progress in consolidating skills, motivate them, and help them work through difficulties in translating trained skills into home einvironments.

ENDING WITH SCHEDULED FOLLOW-UP PHONE CALLS Helpers can schedule follow-up phone calls with clients. These perform the same functions as booster sessions. From both phone calls and booster sessions helpers obtain feedback on how successful helping was in assisting clients to maintain skills.

PREMATURE ENDING Frequently clients leave helping before helpers think they are ready. However, what may seem premature to helpers may seem different to clients. Beck and his colleagues cite as reasons for premature termination: rapid relief of symptoms; negative reactions to the therapist; and lack of sustained improvement or relapse during treatment (Beck *et al.*, 1979). Another reason why clients leave helping is that they find their helpers' theoretical approaches, rather than their personalities, uncongenial. Some clients may not like the lifeskills helping approach, but hopefully most do. Helpers who clumsily handle clients' doubts about and resistances to helping increase the likelihood of premature termination. Further reasons why clients leave prematurely include pressure from significant others, laziness, defensiveness, lack of money, moving to another location, and fear of being trapped by helpers unwilling to 'let go'.

Helpers may consider it premature if clients leave helping feeling able to cope with immediate problems but without having consolidated thinking and action skills for dealing with future problems. In such instances, helpers and clients can still have done useful work together. Ex-clients may now possess insights about skills needed to cope with future problems and be more inclined to seek further assistance, if needed.

When should helping end?

Start helper–client termination discussions before final sessions and aim for convergence either then or by the final session. Throughout helping, helpers and clients collect information relevant to termination decisions. The following are sources of and kinds of relevant information.

CLIENT SELF-REPORT Clients may perceive themselves as better able to cope with problems. They may think they have attained thinking and action skills working goals. They may feel more confident and less prone to negative emotions. They perceive that they no longer require the support of helpers and can maintain skills.

HELPER OBSERVATION Over a series of sessions, helpers may notice improvements in how well clients use targeted thinking skills and action skills. These observations come from various sources: the helping conversation, role plays and other structured activities, and from probes about how clients use skills outside helping. You may observe clients feeling happier and more relaxed. They no longer have symptoms that brought them to helping: for instance excessive anxiety. Problems that previously seemed insurmountable now seem manageable. Clients use better skills in responding to such problems, and seem to understand and use targeted skills well enough to maintain them.

FEEDBACK FROM SIGNIFICANT OTHERS Another set of reasons for considering ending helping is 'when significant others in clients' lives give clients feedback that they are different, or have changed, or make comments such as "you never used to do that before" ' (Teyber, 1989, p. 190). Sometimes feedback may come directly to you: for instance, from helper's aides, spouses, bosses or parents.

ATTAINMENT OF MEASURABLE GOALS Clients can have easily measurable goals. For example, they may pass a driving test or fly in an aeroplane. Other examples of measurable goals include: losing a stipulated amount of weight and maintaining the loss over a given period; cutting down on smoking and maintaining the reduction; keeping off alcohol; and only spending a certain amount of money each week. Clients' goals can be both objective and subjective: for instance making a given number of friends in a set period of time. The given number and set period are objective, whereas the definition of friends is more subjective.

If you and your clients consistently obtain positive information from all four of the above sources, your decision about when to end is easy. However, if positive changes are recent, it may pay to 'wait and see' if clients maintain them. Inconsistent information, either from within or between different sources, merits further exploration.

Consolidating self-helping skills in the ending stage

The main task of the ending stage is 'the consolidation of what has been achieved in terms of some durable benefit for the interviewee' (Sullivan, 1954, p. 41). Many skills that you use in this stage build on skills you have used earlier. With clients who come for brief, focused helping, you trade off and compromise in what you can achieve in the ending stage. The following are some skills for enhancing consolidation in the ending stage.

MAKE TRANSITION STATEMENTS During helping, you may make statements indicating its finiteness: for instance comments about developing self-helping skills for after helping. Such comments may encourage clients to make the most of sessions. You can introduce the ending stage with one or more transition statements:

> 'Our next session is the final session. I think we should discuss how we can use the time we have left to help you retain and build on the skills you've learned for managing your problem. We could even develop a maintenance plan for you.'

> 'I think the agenda for this final session should mainly be how to help you use the skills you've learned here for afterwards. For instance, we can review how much you've changed, where you still need to change, how you might go about it, and how you can deal with high-risk situations.'

SUMMARIZE Already I have stressed the need throughout helping for helper and client summaries. In the ending stage summaries can review both main learnings and perceptions of progress. Formulating personal summaries can be a homework assignment prior to final sessions. You can also ask clients to cassette-record their summaries as reminders. Another idea is for clients to keep cassette recordings of final sessions.

FACILITATE SELF-ASSESSMENT AND DEVELOP MAINTENANCE PLANS During the ending stage, continue to develop clients' self-monitoring and self-assessment skills. Helpers and clients can take a systematic approach to the problem of maintaining skills. Because you assume that clients maintain skills on their own, use the client-centred CASIE self-helping framework rather than the more helper-centred DASIE framework. I refer you to the earlier discussion on how to use the CASIE framework for maintaining targeted lifeskills.

REHEARSE COPING WITH HIGH-RISK SITUATIONS AND WITH LAPSES Rehearsing coping with high-risk situations and lapses should be part of structured activities during helping, and not an afterthought. Helpers and clients can rehearse thinking and action skills for implementing maintenance plans. For example, clients can role-play how to use appropriate thinking and action skills in specific high-risk situations. In addition, they can rehearse and write down appropriate self-talk for handling lapses, underachievement and failure.

Helpers can re-emphasize clients' responsibility for their lives. When clients are in difficulty, looking at the adequacy of their own thinking, acting and use of targeted skills is the best place to start. Clients can ask themselves questions like 'What are my goals and how is my behaviour blocking me from attaining them?'; 'What are my characteristic thinking and action skills weaknesses in relation to this problem?'; and 'How well am I using the skills I have learned and how can I improve?' Stress the importance of clients' developing good retrieval skills and realizing that maintaining gains requires continuing effort.

REINFORCE EFFECTIVE THINKING SKILLS Helpers can use the ending stage to reinforce the importance of clients continuing to focus on their inner game, how they think, as well as on their outer game, how they act. You can also reinforce specific thinking skills conducive to maintaining targeted lifeskills. Where possible, introduce such thinking skills prior to the final session. During final sessions, helpers and clients can review previously presented thinking skills and rehearse thinking skills for coping with specific difficult or high-risk situations.

WORK WITH HELPER'S AIDES During the ending stage, helpers can contact their aides to receive assessments of clients' progress outside helping. Helpers can also work with aides to identify ways in which they can continue supporting clients once helping ends. Sometimes three-way meetings between helpers, clients and aides are desirable. For example, at the end of a series of helping sessions designed to help a primary school child become more outgoing, teacher, child and school counsellor might together plan how the teacher could continue supporting the child.

EXPLORE ARRANGEMENTS FOR CONTINUING SUPPORT Self-support is the main way that clients can receive continuing support. However, given the high probability of some degree of lapse in using targeted skills, think through how clients might receive ongoing support. The following are some options:

- *Further contact with helper.* Possibilities for further contact with helpers include: scheduled booster sessions: follow-up sessions at clients' request; and either scheduled or unscheduled phone calls. You can discuss with clients how you view further contact with them.

- *Referral for further individual helping.* Though clients may have made considerable progress with the problems and problematic skills for which they came to helping, they may still require further professional assistance. For many reasons you may decide to refer such clients to other helpers: for instance, your time may be limited or another helper may have special expertise in an emerging problem area.

- *Using outside supports.* At the end of helping you can assist clients to identify and use supports for maintaining and developing targeted skills.

- *Group helping.* Some clients might gain from joining groups in which they can practise and develop targeted skills. Peer self-help groups provide an alternative to professionally led groups. Helpers can also discuss opportunities for participating in courses or workshops run by themselves or others.

- *Further reading and audiovisual material.* Some clients appreciate the support provided by further reading, audio cassettes and videotapes. On your own initiative or by request, you can suggest appropriate books, training manuals, audio cassettes and videotapes.

Further ending stage tasks and skills

In addition to the major task of consolidating self-helping skills, there are other tasks for the ending stage. How you handle them varies with length of helping, nature of problem(s) and problematic skills, and the helper–client relationship.

DEAL WITH FEELINGS Most lifeskills helping contacts are focused and short to medium term: though the helping relationship is important, it is not the central feature of lifeskills helping. Consequently, there is less likelihood of clients feeling angry, sad, anxious and abandoned than in longer-term relationship-oriented therapy. Clients should feel better able to cope with problems and problematic skills as a result of helping. Ideally, they have a sense of accomplishment and optimism.

Clients' feelings at the end of helping fall into two main categories: feelings about how they are going to fare without helpers and feelings towards helpers and the helping process. Many clients have feelings of ambivalence about how they will cope after helping. On the one hand, they feel more competent; on the other hand they still have doubts about their abilities to implement skills. Helpers can facilitate open discussion of clients' feelings about the future. Looking at how best to maintain skills also addresses the issue of clients' lingering doubts. Other clients will feel that they can cope very well without you – hopefully, a sign that together you have done a good job!

Clients may also wish to share feelings about you and the helping process. Since the helping relationship is not the main agenda, do not get sidetracked into lengthy discussions of unfinished emotional business. Nevertheless, allow clients the opportunity to share feelings about their contact with you: you may obtain valuable feedback about how you come across. You may also share feelings with clients, for instance, 'I enjoyed working with you' or, 'I admire the courage with which you face your situation'.

SAY GOODBYE Saying goodbye or the formal leave-taking 'should be a clean-cut, respectful finish that does not confuse that which has been done' (Sullivan, 1954, p. 216). Last impressions as well as first impressions are important. Aim to say goodbye in a businesslike, yet friendly way, appropriate to a professional rather than a personal relationship. By ending helping sloppily, you may undo some of your influence in helping clients to maintain skills. In addition, getting your personal and professional wires with clients crossed is not only unethical, but can make it more difficult to help if future need arises.

END ETHICALLY A number of important ethical issues surround ending helping. For example, helpers need to think through their responsibilities to clients after helping. Too much support may engender dependency, too little may fail to carry out professional obligations. Each case must be judged on its merits. Another ethical issue is what to do when you think clients have other problems on which they need to work. I suggest bringing your views tactfully to their attention. A further set of ethical issues surrounds the boundaries between personal and professional relationships. Most professional associations have ethical codes covering issues in providing helping services (for instance, American Association for Counseling and Development, 1988; American Psychological Association, 1981, 1987, 1990; Australian Psychological Society, 1986; British Association for Counselling, 1990; British Psychological Society, 1991; National Association of Social Workers, 1979; National Board of Certified Counselors, 1987).

EVALUATE YOUR HELPING SKILLS By the ending stage, helpers have many sources of information for evaluating their helping skills. These include attendance; client feedback, both intentional and unintentional; perceptions of client progress; session notes; possibly videotape or audio-cassette feedback; feedback from third parties; and compliance with homework tasks. Effective helpers, like good clients, evaluate their skills throughout helping. You need to make a final evaluation of your work with each client soon after helping ends, otherwise you risk forgetting valuable information. Beware of perceptual distortions when evaluating helping skills – you may be too hard or too easy on yourself. What you seek is a balanced appraisal of strengths and weaknesses. Here are some questions that you might ask yourself:

1. To what extent did the client achieve his/her goals in relation to managing the problem(s) that brought him/her to helping?

2. To what extent did the client achieve his/her thinking skills working goals?

3. To what extent did the client achieve his/her action skills working goals?

4. What is the client's likelihood of maintaining and developing targeted skills?

5. What were my strengths and weaknesses in offering a supportive helping relationship?

6. What were my strengths and weaknesses in identifying and clarifying the client's problem(s)?

7. What were my strengths and weaknesses in assessing the client's feelings, thinking skills and action skills?

8 What were my strengths and weaknesses in redefining the client's problem(s) in skills terms?

9. What were my strengths and weaknesses in stating working goals?

10. What were my strengths and weaknesses in planning interventions?

11. What were my strengths and weaknesses in using speaking skills to deliver interventions?

12. What were my strengths and weaknesses in using demonstration skills to deliver interventions?

13. What were my strengths and weaknesses in using structured activities to deliver interventions?

14. How satisfied am I with the way I assigned and monitored homework?

15. How well did I deliver each intervention that I attempted?

16. Was I sufficiently flexible in responding to emerging problems and issues during the intervention stage?

17. How satisfied am I with the way I planned and handled individual sessions during the intervention stage?

18. What strategies did I use for consolidating trained skills as self-helping skills and how effective did they seem?

19. What were my skills strengths and weaknesses in handling the ending stage?

20. How satisfied am I with the way I identified and handled ethical issues arising during helping?

21. When working with this client, did I have adequate professional support and supervision?

22. What specifically did I learn about my helping style and skills?

23. What, if any, are my goals for improving my helping skills?

24. How can I implement any goals I have for improving my helping skills?

POSTSCRIPT

Congratulations: you have now reached the last part of the ending stage of this book. In it I presented a systematic model for assisting clients to develop and maintain lifeskills. As a helper, you have a twofold challenge: to maintain and develop both your lifeskills and your helping skills. I hope this book, with its accompanying training manual, provides a useful conceptual framework and set of skills for both tasks. May you enjoy good thinking and action skills in your personal and helping lives.

CHAPTER HIGHLIGHTS

- Helpers need systematically to attend to developing clients' lifeskills for after helping.

- Generalization, maintenance, transfer and development are important considerations for consolidating clients' self-helping skills.

- Helpers need to work with clients' thinking skills to enhance consolidation. This includes imparting the lifeskills conceptual framework.

- Stage 1 skills for enhancing consolidation of trained skills as self-helping skills include structuring for maintenance and developing clients' self-monitoring and clarifying problems skills.

- Stage 2 skills for enhancing consolidation include developing clients' skills of self-assessment and of redefining problems in skills terms.

- Stage 3 skills for enhancing consolidation focus both on developing clients' skills at stating working goals and on how to plan interventions for maintaining skills.

- Considerations in planning for consolidation include: maintain a skills focus; focus on thinking skills and self-instructing; build in ongoing self-assessment;

allow for overlearning; emphasize real-lifeness; train diversely; plan reward strategies; consider using helper's aides; spend time on coping with difficult and high-risk situations; and allow adequate time for ending and consolidating skills.

- When intervening in stage 4, skills for enhancing consolidation include: emphasizing homework assignments; encouraging client summaries; using handouts, cassettes and videotapes; encouraging clients to keep helping files; and developing clients' identifying and using supports skills.

- Formats for the ending stage include: fixed ending; open ending when goals are attained; faded ending; and ending with booster session(s) or scheduled follow-up phone calls. In addition, from the helpers' viewpoint, clients may end helping prematurely.

- Helpers should raise the issue of ending before the final session.

- Sources of information for when to end include client self-report, helper observation, feedback from significant others, and attainment of measurable goals.

- Stage 5 skills for enhancing consolidation include: making transition statements; summarising; facilitating self-assessment and the development of maintenance plans; rehearsing coping with high-risk situations and with lapses; reinforcing effective thinking skills; working with helper's aides; and exploring arrangements for continuing support.

- Further ending stage tasks and skills include: dealing with feelings, saying goodbye, ending ethically, and evaluating your helping skills.

- As a helper you have a twofold challenge: to maintain and develop both your lifeskills and your helping skills.

Bibliography

Abramson, L. Y., Seligman, M. E. P. & Teasdale, J. D. (1978) Learned helplessness in humans: critique and reformulation. *Journal of Abnormal Psychology*, **87**, 49–74.

Albee, G. W. (1984) A competency model must replace a defect model. In J. M. Joffe, G. W. Albee & L. D. Kelly (eds) *Readings in Primary Prevention of Psychopathology: Basic Concepts.* Hanover, NH: University Press of New England, pp.228–46.

Alberti, R. E. & Emmons, M. L. (1990) *Your Perfect Right: A Guide to Assertive Living* (6th edn). San Luis Obispo, CA: Impact Publishers.

Allport, G. W. (1955) *Becoming: Basic Considerations for a Psychology of Personality.* New Haven: Yale University Press.

Allport, G. W., Vernon, P. E. & Lindzey, G. (1960) *A Study of Values.* Boston: Houghton Mifflin.

Alpert, R. & Haber, R. N. (1960) Anxiety in academic achievement situations. *Journal of Abnormal and Social Psychology,* **61**, 204–15.

Amatea, E. S., Clark, J. E. & Cross, E. C. (1984) Life-styles: evaluating a life role planning program for high school students. *Vocational Guidance Quarterly,* **32**, 249–59.

American Association for Counseling and Development (1988) *Ethical Standards.* Alexandria, VA: AACD.

American Psychiatric Association (1987) *Diagnostic and Statistical Manual of Mental Disorders* (3rd edn, revised). Washington, DC: APA.

American Psychological Association (1981) Ethical principles of psychologists. *American Psychologist,* **36**, 633–8.

American Psychological Association (1987) General guidelines for providers of psychological services. *American Psychologist,* **42**, 724–9.

American Psychological Association (1990) Ethical principles of psychologists. *American Psychologist,* **45**, 390–5.

Argyle, M. (1983) *The Psychology of Interpersonal Behaviour* (4th edn). Harmondsworth, Middlesex: Penguin Books.

Argyle, M. (1984) Some new developments in social skills training. *Bulletin of the British Psychological Society,* **37**, 405–10.

Argyle, M. (1986) Rules for social relationships in four cultures. *Australian Journal of Psychology,* **38**, 309–18.

Argyle, M. & Henderson, M. (1985) *The Anatomy of Relationships.* Harmondsworth, Middlesex: Penguin Books.

Arlow, J.A. (1989) Psychoanalysis. In R. J. Corsini & D. Wedding (eds) *Current Psychotherapies* (4th edn). Itasca, IL: Peacock, pp. 19–62.

Arroba, T. (1977) Styles of decision making and their use: an empirical study. *British Journal of Guidance and Counselling,* **5**, 149–58.

Australian Psychological Society (1986) *Code of Professional Conduct.* Melbourne: APS.

Axelson, J. A. (1985) *Counseling and Development in a Multicultural Society.* Pacific Grove, CA: Brooks/Cole.

Bacorn, C. N. & Dixon, D. N. (1984) The effects of touch on depressed and vocationally undecided clients. *Journal of Counseling Psychology,* **31**, 488–96.

Bandura, A. (1969) *Principles of Behavior Modification.* New York: Holt, Rinehart & Winston.

Bandura, A. (1976) Effecting change through participant modelling. In J. D. Krumboltz & C. E. Thoresen (eds) *Counseling Methods.* New York: Holt, Rinehart & Winston, pp. 248–65.

Bandura, A. (1977) *Social Learning Theory*. Englewood Cliffs, NJ: Prentice-Hall.

Bandura, A. (1986) *Social Foundations of Thought and Action: A Social Cognitive Theory*. Englewood Cliffs, NJ: Prentice-Hall.

Bandura, A. (1989) Human agency in social cognitive theory. *American Psychologist*, **44**, 1175–84.

Bandura, A., Grusec, J. E. & Menlove, F. L. (1966) Observational learning as a function of symbolization and incentive set. *Child Development*, **37**, 499-506.

Barrett-Lennard, G. T. (1962) Dimensions of therapeutic response as causal factors in therapeutic change. *Psychological Monographs*, **76** (whole no. 562).

Barrett-Lennard, G. T. (1981) The empathy cycle: refinement of a nuclear concept. *Journal of Counseling Psychology*, **28**, 91–100.

Barrow, J. C. & Moore, C. A. (1983) Group interventions with perfectionist thinking. *Personnel and Guidance Journal*, **61**, 612–15.

Batson, C. D. (1990) How social an animal? The human capacity for caring. *American Psychologist*, **45**, 336–46.

Beck, A. T. (1976) *Cognitive Therapy and the Emotional Disorders*. New York: New American Library.

Beck, A. T. (1978) *Depression Inventory*. Philadelphia: Center for Cognitive Therapy.

Beck, A. T. (1988) *Love Is Never Enough: How Couples Can Overcome Misunderstandings, Resolve Conflicts, and Solve Relationship Problems through Cognitive Therapy*. New York: Harper & Row.

Beck, A. T. (1991) Cognitive therapy: a 10-year retrospective. *American Psychologist*, **46**, 368–75.

Beck, A. T. & Emery, G. (1985) *Anxiety Disorders and Phobias: A Cognitive Perspective*. New York: Basic Books.

Beck, A. T. & Weishaar, M. E. (1989) Cognitive therapy. In R. J. Corsini & D. Wedding (eds) *Current Psychotherapies* (4th edn). Itasca, IL: Peacock, pp. 285–320.

Beck, A. T., Laude, R. & Bohnert, M. (1974) Ideational components of anxiety neurosis. *Archives of General Psychiatry*, **31**, 319–25.

Beck, A. T., Rush, A. J., Shaw, B. F. & Emery, G. (1979) *Cognitive Therapy of Depression*. New York: John Wiley.

Beck, A. T., Epstein, N., Brown, G. & Steer, R. A. (1988a) An inventory for measuring clinical anxiety: psychometric properties. *Journal of Consulting and Clinical Psychology*, **56**, 893–7.

Beck, A. T., Riskind, J. H., Brown, G. & Steer, R. A. (1988b) Levels of hopelessness in DSM-111 disorders: a partial test of content specificity in depression.*Cognitive Therapy and Research*, **12**, 459–69.

Bem, S. L. (1974) The measurement of psychological androgyny. *Journal of Consulting and Clinical Psychology*, **42**, 155–62.

Bem, S. L. (1981) Gender schema theory: a cognitive account of sex typing. *Psychological Review*, **88**, 354–64.

Berne, E. (1961) *Transactional Analysis in Psychotherapy*. New York: Grove Press.

Berne, E. (1964) *Games People Play*. New York: Grove Press.

Berne, E. (1972) *What Do You Say After You Say Hello?* New York: Grove Press.

Bernstein, D. (1988) *Put It Together, Put It Across: The Craft of Business Presentation*. London: Cassell.

Bernstein, D. A. & Borkovec, T. D. (1973) *Progressive Relaxation Training: A Manual for the Helping Professions*. Champaign, IL: Research Press.

Blackwell, R. T., Galassi, J. P., Galassi, M. D. & Watson, T. E. (1985) Are cognitive assessment methods equal? A comparison of think aloud and thought listing. *Cognitive Therapy and Research*, **9**, 399–413.

Blatner, A. (1989) Psychodrama. In R. J. Corsini & D. Wedding (eds) *Current Psychotherapies*

(4th edn). Itasca, IL: Peacock, pp. 561–71.

Bordin, E. S. (1979) The generalizability of the psychoanalytic concept of the working alliance. *Psychotherapy: Theory, Research and Practice*, **16**, 252–60.

Bowlby, J. (1979) *The Making and Breaking of Affectional Bonds*. London: Tavistock.

Brammer, L. M. (1985) *The Helping Relationship: Process and Skills* (3rd edn). Englewood Cliffs, NJ: Prentice-Hall.

British Association for Counselling (1990) *Code of Ethics and Practice for Counsellors*. Rugby: BAC.

British Psychological Society (1991) *Code of Conduct, Ethical Principles and Guidelines*. Leicester: BPS.

Bugental, J. F. T. (1981) *The Search for Authenticity*. New York: Irvington Publishers.

Burns, D. D. (1980) *Feeling Good: The New Mood Therapy*. New York: New American Library.

Burns, D. D. (1989) *The Feeling Good Handbook: Using the New Mood Therapy in Daily Life*. New York: Willian Morrow.

Carkhuff, R. R. (1983) *The Art of Helping* (5th edn). Amherst, MA: Human Resource Development Press.

Cautela, J. R. (1967) Covert sensitization. *Psychological Reports*, **20**, 459–68.

Cautela, J. R. (1976) The present status of covert modeling. *Journal of Behavior Therapy and Experimenal Psychiatry*, **6**, 323–6.

Christensen, C. P. (1989) Cross-cultural awareness development: a conceptual model. *Counselor Education and Supervision*, **28**, 270–87.

Clark, A. J. (1991) The identification and modification of defense mechanisms in counseling. *Journal of Counseling and Development*, **69**, 231–6.

Corey, G. (1990) *Theory and Practice of Group Counseling* (3rd edn). Pacific Grove, CA: Brooks/Cole.

Corey, G., Corey. M. S. & Callanan, P. (1988) *Issues and Ethics in the Helping Professions* (3rd edn). Pacific Grove, CA: Brooks/Cole.

Cormier, W. H. & Cormier, L. S. (1985) *Interviewing Strategies for Helpers: Fundamental Skills and Cognitive Behavioral Interventions* (2nd edn). Pacific Grove, CA: Brooks/Cole.

Corsini, R. J. (1989) Introduction. In R. J. Corsini & D. Wedding (eds) *Current Psychotherapies* (4th edn). Itasca, IL: Peacock, pp. 1–16.

Daley, M. F. (1969) The 'reinforcement menu': finding effective reinforcers. In J. D. Krumboltz & C. E. Thoresen (eds) *Behavioral Counseling: Cases and Techniques*. New York: Holt, Rinehart & Winston, pp. 42–5.

Davidson, F. (1988) *The Art of Executive Firing*. Melbourne: Information Australia.

Deffenbacher, J. L. & Suinn, R. M. (1988) Systematic desensitization and the reduction of anxiety. *The Counseling Psychologist*, **16**, 9–30.

Deffenbacher, J. L., McNamara, K., Stark, R. S. & Sabadell, P. M. (1990) A comparison of cognitive-behavioral and process-oriented group counseling for general anger reduction. *Journal of Counseling and Development*, **69**, 167–72.

Deffenbacher, J. L., Story, D. A., Brandon, A. D., Hogg, J. A. & Hazaleus, S. I. (1988) Cognitive and cognitive-relaxation treatments of anger. *Cognitive Therapy and Research*, **12**, 167–84.

DeVoe, D. (1990) Feminist and nonsexist counseling: implications for the male counselor. *Journal of Counseling and Development*, **69**, 33–6.

Dorn, N. & South, N. (1986) Developing work-related education on alcohol and drugs. *British Journal of Guidance and Counselling*, **14**, 88–96.

Dusay, J. M. & Dusay, K. M. (1989) Transactional analysis. In R. J. Corsini & D. Wedding (eds) *Current Psychotherapies* (4th edn). Itasca, IL: Peacock, pp. 405–53.

Egan, G. (1977) *You and Me: The Skills of Communicating and Relating to Others*. Pacific Grove, CA: Brooks/Cole.

Egan, G. (1990) *The Skilled Helper: A Systematic Approach to Effective Helping* (4th edn). Pacific Grove, CA: Brooks/Cole.

Egan, G. & Cowan, M. (1979) *People in Systems: A Model for Development in the Human-service Professions and Education*. Pacific Grove, CA: Brooks/Cole.

Ekman, P., Friesen, W. V. & Ellsworth, P. (1972) *Emotions in the Human Face*. New York: Pergamon Press.

Elliott, R. (1985) Helpful and nonhelpful events in brief counseling interviews: an empirical taxonomy. *Journal of Counseling Psychology*, **32**, 307–22.

Ellis, A. (1962) *Reason and Emotion in Psychotherapy*. New York: Lyle Stuart.

Ellis. A. (1977) *Anger: How to Live with and without It*. New York: Lyle Stuart.

Ellis, A. (1980) Overview of the clinical theory of rational-emotive therapy. In R. Grieger & J. Boyd (eds) *Rational-emotive Therapy: A Skills-based Approach*. New York: Van Nostrand Reinhold, pp. 1–31.

Ellis, A. (1985) *Overcoming Resistance: Rational-emotive Therapy with Difficult Clients*. New York: Springer.

Ellis, A. (1987) The impossibility of achieving consistently good mental health. *American Psychologist*, **42**, 364–75.

Ellis, A. (1989) Rational-emotive therapy. In R. J. Corsini & D. Wedding (eds) *Current Psychotherapies* (4th edn). Itasca, IL: Peacock, pp. 197–238.

Ellis, A. & Harper, R. A. (1975) *A New Guide to Rational Living*. North Hollywood, CA: Wilshire Books.

Emery, G. (1982) *Own Your Own Life*. New York: New American Library.

Enns, C. Z. & Hackett, G. (1990) Comparison of feminist and nonfeminist women's reactions to variants of nonsexist and feminist counseling. *Journal of Counseling Psychology*, **37**, 33–40.

Erikson, E. H. (1963) *Childhood and Society* (2nd edn). New York: W. W. Norton.

Feifel, H. (1990) Psychology and death: meaningful rediscovery. *American Psychologist*, **45**, 537–43.

Fischer, R. L. (1972) *Speak to Communicate: An Introduction to Speech*. Encino, CA: Dickenson.

Frankl, V. E. (1959) *Man's Search for Meaning*. New York: Washington Square Press.

Frankl, V. E. (1967) *Psychotherapy and Existentialism*. Harmondsworth, Middlesex: Penguin Books.

Frankl, V. E. (1969) *The Doctor and the Soul*. Harmondsworth, Middlesex: Penguin Books.

Frankl, V. E. (1975) *The Unconscious God: Psychotherapy and Theology*. New York: Simon & Schuster.

Freud, S. (1936) *The Problem of Anxiety*. New York: W. W. Norton.

Freudenberger, H. J. (1980) *Burnout: The High Cost of High Achievement*. London: Arrow Books.

Gallwey, W. T. (1974) *The Inner Game of Tennis*. London: Pan Books.

Gazda, G. M. (1989) *Group Counseling: A Developmental Approach* (4th edn). Boston: Allyn & Bacon.

Geldard, D. (1989) *Basic Personal Counselling: A Training Manual for Counsellors*. Sydney: Prentice-Hall.

Gendlin, E. T. (1962) *Experiencing and the Creation of Meaning*. New York: The Free Press of Glencoe.

Gendlin, E. T. (1981) *Focusing* (2nd edn). New York: Bantam Books.

Gilbert, T. F. (1978) *Human Competence: Engineering Worthy Performance*. New York: McGraw-Hill.

Glasser, W. (1965) *Reality Therapy: A New Approach to Psychiatry*. New York: Harper & Row.

Glasser, W. (1984) *Control Theory: A New Explanation of How We Control Our Lives*. New York: Harper & Row.

Gill, we have now been through a tell, show and do sequence in relation to ____ [specify which] skill. However, learning any new skill can require much work and practice until you are comfortable using it in real life. Throughout helping, I am likely to negotiate homework assignments with you so that we can use the time between sessions to best effect. I would now like to discuss activities to do before next session. Do you have any problems with the idea of doing homework?

NEGOTIATE REALISTIC HOMEWORK I use the word 'negotiate' to highlight the importance of client participation in homework decisions. I assume that clients are more likely to comply with homework assignments that they have had a say in designing. Here are three aspects of realistic homework:

- *Consolidates earlier learning.* The homework is a logical extension of the speaking, demonstrating and coaching sequence which has just taken place. Do not introduce any new skills and ideas that clients will have insufficient time to assimilate before the session ends.

- *Appropriate difficulty level.* The tasks take into account clients' understanding of and readiness to perform targeted skills. Where appropriate, suggest graded steps.

- *Realistic amount.* Work out with clients what constitutes a realistic amount of homework. It is preferable for clients to make a definite commitment to a small amount of homework than a vague commitment to a larger amount. Encourage clients to view homework in terms of learning contracts not just to you but, more importantly, to themselves (Wehrenberg, 1988).

GIVE CLEAR INSTRUCTIONS IN TAKE-AWAY FORM How can clients know precisely what homework you expect? What?, when?, how often? and how recorded? are all pertinent questions. Sometimes clients have already received handouts summarizing the main learning points of a skill. Where possible, give homework instructions in take-away form. At the very least you can use a standard instructional form (Figure 9.2). You may either fill out the form yourself or supervise clients as they do this.

If you require clients to fill out forms such as monitoring logs, specific worksheets and thinksheets, and homework record logs, provide these forms yourself. This practice ensures clear instructions and saves clients' writing out homework forms before filling them in.

ANTICIPATE DIFFICULTIES AND SETBACKS Explore with clients their motivation for completing homework tasks. Where possible, identify and help clients to work through

resistances. Also, identify rewards for completing homework. If you have negotiated realistic amounts, hopefully clients will complete homework. Sometimes, implementing a skill requires asking clients to give up long-established habits. Here, it can be especially important not to assign too difficult a homework task too soon. Some clients return to unsupportive, if not downright hostile, environments. Here you may need to prepare clients more thoroughly prior to suggesting they implement targeted skills in real-life settings. Such preparation is likely to include devising strategies for coping with negative feedback. In Chapter 13 I discuss more thoroughly how to prevent clients' relapses.

Homework assignment instructions

For _____ (client's name)

During the period _____

Targeted skill(s)

1. _____

2. _____

3. _____

4. _____

5. _____

Instructions

_____
_____
_____
_____
_____
_____
_____
_____
_____
_____
_____
_____

Figure 9.2 *Homework assignment instructions form*

SIGNAL A JOINT PROGRESS REVIEW Let clients know that at or around the start of the next session, together you will review their homework progress. Your declared interest should motivate them to do homework.

CONCLUDING COMMENT

This chapter focused on basic training skills, somewhat in isolation from each other. When intervening, you put helping relationship, speaking, demonstrating, coaching and setting homework skills together. You start from where clients are and use training skills to help them get to where they want to be. Always remember that, after helping, clients need to retain and develop trained skills as self-helping skills. Beginning helpers need to rehearse and practise hard to develop good training as well as good helping relationship skills. Obtain training and also train yourself in training skills.

CHAPTER HIGHLIGHTS

- Helpers require training skills in three broad areas central to delivering most interventions: speaking, demonstrating and coaching, or 'tell', 'show' and 'do'.

- Speaking skills include: managing speech anxiety; preparing clear content; and the delivery skills of sending good voice and body messages.

- Observational learning is extremely important for acquiring and developing applied lifeskills.

- Demonstrations can focus on thinking skills, action skills, and action skills with accompanying self-talk.

- Methods of demonstration include written, live, pre-recorded – for instance audio cassettes or videotapes – and visualized.

- Demonstrator skills include: preparing adequately; providing an introduction; providing instructions and a summary; checking clients' learning; and, where appropriate, including demonstrations in homework assignments.

- Learning from hearing and observing must be translated into learning from doing.

- Assist clients to become their own coaches for acquiring, maintaining and developing targeted skills.

- Coaching skills include: balancing didactic and facilitative coaching; giving clear instructions; breaking tasks down and paying attention to the number of learning trials; using behaviour rehearsal and role play; and using feedback skills.

- Consolidate initial learning from hearing, observing and doing by assigning relevant homework.

- Assigning homework skills include: offer reasons for homework; negotiate realistic homework; give clear instructions in take-away form; anticipate difficulties and setbacks; and signal a joint progress review.

- Beginning helpers need to rehearse and practise hard to develop good training as well as good helping relationship skills.

TEN
How to Focus on Thinking Skills

There is nothing either good or bad, but thinking makes it so.
William Shakespeare

CHAPTER QUESTIONS

Why is it important that clients think about how they think?

How are thinking skills related to feelings and actions?

Why is it important that helpers attend to feelings when focusing on thinking?

What are the PTC and STC frameworks?

What reasons can helpers offer for working with clients' thinking?

What is a desirable helping relationship when focusing on thinking skills?

What are helper interventions for ten different thinking skills?

The importance of focusing on how both helpers and their clients think is a major theme of this book. In Chapter 2 I used the analogy of the inner game, or how you think, and the outer game, or how you act. Most often people feel and think before they act. Then their subsequent actions influence how they think and feel. I refer you back to Chapter 6 for details on how to assess thinking skills in initial sessions. Problems redefined in skills terms almost invariably include one or more thinking skills weaknesses which, in turn, become working goals. This chapter looks at skills for working with clients' thinking. Most of the skills are relevant to working with your thinking too. Unless you develop skills

at understanding and working with how you think, you risk ineffectiveness when focusing on how clients think. To paraphrase the old adage 'Physician, heal thyself', 'Helper, learn thinking skills by working with your own as well as clients' material'.

Thinking about thinking

Both helpers and clients are hypothesis makers and testers who have the reflective capacity to think about how they think. Why do both helpers and clients need to develop such skills? Unless clients can think about how they think they risk condemning themselves to repetitive patterns of thinking skills weaknesses. They do not have the tools to take responsibility for how they think. Unless they develop a language categorizing different thinking skills, they cannot target specific skills for development. Furthermore, helpers and clients capable of thinking about how they think are better able to define themselves and make their lives. For example, those capable of understanding how their thinking has been affected by parental and cultural rules are in a stronger position to free themselves from unwanted 'voices in the head' than are those unable to analyse how they think. Helpers and clients can also use skills of thinking about how they think to increase their sense of self-efficacy, or belief in their capabilities to exercise control over events that affect their lives (Bandura, 1977, 1986, 1989). In addition, those able to think about how they think are capable of learning and instructing themselves in how to think more effectively. Ideally what Martin (1987) terms cognitive instructional counselling leads to cognitive instructional self-helping.

How helpers and clients think about how they think gives them the capacity to influence how they feel and act. For example, good use of thinking skills can help you and your clients get in touch with your feelings, wants and wishes, your valuing process and your sexuality. Effective thinking skills contribute to releasing desirable feelings and regulating debilitating feelings. Thoughts and feelings tend to be the precursors of action. Developing the capacity for thinking about thinking can help remove blocks and inhibitions to action. Without losing spontaneity, effective thinking skills can help people think before they act, including identifying action skills for managing specific situations.

Attend to feelings

Working with clients' thinking skills should not be an arid intellectual exercise. Always, you require sensitivity to their and to your feelings. The following are some reasons why, when focusing on thinking, it is important to attend to feelings.

- *Assess readiness and motivation*. Helpers need to take into account client readiness to work on thinking skills. For instance, vulnerable clients may wish to use the early phases of helping to discharge and discuss feelings of hurt and pain. Some clients may be so anxious and distort information so badly that they have insufficient insight to explore thinking difficulties until they are less anxious. Clients take differing lengths of time to trust helpers. Until trust is established, they may be neither willing nor able to deal with their faulty thinking choices.

- *Elicit thoughts and feelings*. Working with clients' thinking can be a delicate process in which helpers create the emotional climate for clients' thoughts and feelings to

emerge. Helpers and clients collaborate in unearthing and detecting both dysfunctional feelings and the thoughts and thinking skills weaknesses that sustain them. Helper lack of empathy blocks clients' experiencing, identifying and exploring of feelings and associated thoughts.

- *Distinguish clients' own thoughts.* Helpers need to attend closely to feelings to help clients distinguish what they think from what they have been taught to think. You may need to give clients permission to articulate their thoughts and support them through the pain and guilt of going against significant others' ways of thinking.

- *Acknowledge defences and resistances.* Helpers require awareness of barriers and resistances to acknowledging and working with specific thoughts and thinking skills weaknesses. Frequently, clients do not bare their souls. You require sensitivity to the degree of threat in focusing on certain areas of clients' lives. Then you have various options: for example, helping clients acknowledge and work through resistances or backing off temporarily or permanently.

- *Check emotional validity of thinking skills hypotheses.* Hypotheses about clients' dysfunctional thoughts and thinking skills weaknesses must have emotional validity if they are to work for change. It is possible, while overtly agreeing with helper-offered thinking skills hypotheses, for clients to disagree covertly. You require skills in checking the emotional validity for clients of how they think about their thinking. Furthermore, you require skill in helping clients do their own work. Conclusions that clients reach for themselves about their thinking are more likely to feel right for them.

- *Offer support during learning, rehearsal and practice.* Helpers need to pay attention to clients' feelings as they train clients in thinking skills. Feelings requiring attention include: confusion about understanding a skill properly; insecurity about being asked to demonstrate it in a helping session; and disappointment when unsuccessfully practising the skill outside helping.

Rewarding listening skills are central when working to develop clients' thinking skills. The desirable helper–client relationship is one of mutual collaboration in pursuit of working goals. Helpers support clients in many ways: emotionally, facilitating exploration of thoughts and feelings, and helping clients check out and analyse the information they generate, and encouraging clients as they learn. At all times helpers attempt to listen to the information provided by their own feelings as well as showing sensitivity to the feelings and personal meanings of clients.

PRESENT A RATIONALE
The PTC and STC frameworks

Ellis (1962, 1980, 1989) developed a simple ABC framework for thinking about thinking: A represents the activating event; B, a person's rational and/or irrational beliefs about the activating event; and C, the emotional and behavioural consequences

of both A and B. Ellis considers that much of the time people are only aware of what happens at points A and C. However, what happens at point C is mediated by beliefs at point B.

The PTC and STC frameworks extend Ellis's ABC framework by (a) distinguishing between problems and specific problematic situations; (b) allowing more room for thoughts other than beliefs, for instance attributions and perceptions; and (c) incorporating skills language.

The PTC framework applies to overall problems:

P   Your overall problem
T   Your thoughts and thinking skills relating to the overall problem
C   Your feelings and actions that are the consequences of P and T

The STC framework applies to specific situations within overall problems:

S   The situation
T   Your thoughts and thinking skills relating to the situation
C   Your feelings and actions that are the consequences of S and T

When helpers redefine problems into their thinking and action skills components, the thinking part represents an analysis within the PTC framework. Sometimes, where problems are specific, the PTC and STC frameworks overlap. However, on other occasions, helpers may focus on how clients think in relation to a specific situation within an overall problem area. For instance, Jason is the manager of a building supplies sales yard. His overall problem area is managing anger at work and at home. A specific situation he wants to work on is managing his anger towards one good but difficult customer.

Offer a rationale

Before the intervention stage, helpers may present rationales for focusing on thinking skills. For example, you might state such a rationale when redefining problems. You may also offer reasons when you intervene. You can use the PTC or STC framework to highlight the importance of how clients think in relation to managing either overall problems or specific situations. Some clients react favourably to analogies: for example, the inner game and outer game analogy. Also you may use humour: for example encouraging clients to avoid 'Stinkin thinkin'. Some clients may find the distinction between 'thinking smart' and 'thinking dumb' useful. Another way of emphasizing the importance of effective thinking is to make the distinction between self-support and self-oppression (Nelson-Jones, 1989). When offering reasons for focusing on thinking, incorporate clients' own material to heighten interest. Below is an example of a brief rationale given to a shy male college student for developing the skill of coping self-talk when asking girls out.

> Tony, we agreed to spend part of this session in
> looking at how you can use self-talk to feel more

confident and skilled when asking girls out. Let's look at what happens in a simple STC framework where S is a situation in which you want to ask a girl for a date, T represents what you think or how you talk to yourself about asking a girl out, and C represents how you feel and act or the consequences of the situation and how you think about it. At the moment it seems as if you are talking to yourself in ways that increase your anxiety and lower your performance. To attain your working goal of developing coping self-talk, you need to become more aware of your negative self-talk at T, for instance 'I'm going to screw up', and develop the skills of substituting self-talk that calms you down and focuses on how you can best achieve your task. Does this make sense to you?

THINKING-FOCUSED INTERVENTIONS

Below I describe interventions for ten thinking skills. These interventions are in addition to offering a supportive relationship, presenting skills clearly, demonstrating, coaching and setting homework. This listing of thinking skills is not exhaustive. Some of the skills overlap and are interrelated. The numbering of the skills does not reflect any order of importance. Which skills you and clients focus on depends on your working definition and goals. At all times, remember that you are imparting self-helping skills. Clients need to understand the thinking skills well enough to instruct themselves outside helping. Interventions are suggested for the following thinking skills.

Skill 1   Own responsibility for choosing
Skill 2   Use coping self-talk
Skill 3   Choose realistic personal rules
Skill 4   Choose how you perceive
Skill 5   Attribute cause accurately
Skill 6   Predict realistically
Skill 7   Set realistic goals
Skill 8   Use visualizing skills
Skill 9   Make decisions rationally
Skill 10   Prevent and manage problems and alter problematic skills

SKILL 1: OWN RESPONSIBILITY FOR CHOOSING

How can helpers assist clients to attain the working goal of owning more responsibility for being choosers in their lives? Four dimensions of owning responsibility for choosing are choice awareness; responsibility awareness; existential awareness and feelings awareness (Nelson–Jones, 1989). Choice awareness consists of awareness of the fact that people are always choosers in their lives, even in relation to suffering and genuinely

adverse external circumstances, for instance poverty, racial discrimination, or concentration camp internment (Frankl, 1959). Responsibility awareness entails awareness that people are responsible for making their lives through their choices. Thus clients may need to become more effective authors or architects of their lives (May & Yalom, 1989). Existential awareness consists of awareness of the existential parameters in which all humans lead their lives, for example death, fate and isolation. Feelings awareness entails the capacity to listen to your bodily sensations and to your inner valuing process.

Assisting clients to make better choices permeates helping. Clients may resist owning responsibility for choosing. Sometimes these resistances are very deep-rooted. Below are some suggestions for helping clients become more responsible for their choices.

RAISE CONSCIOUSNESS Some clients may need to be told in simple language that they are responsible for their choices. They may require help in seeing that they can choose not only how they act, but also how they think and feel. In the past they may have taken a passive stance to life, waiting for things to happen to them. You can encourage them to see that they can be active agents in shaping their lives.

ENCOURAGE CHOICE LANGUAGE Helpers can assist clients to become more aware of how their use of language restricts their choices. You can encourage: using 'I' statements; using verbs that acknowledge choice, for example, 'I won't rather than I can't'; and avoiding static self-labelling, for example, 'I am a poor correspondent' rather than 'I choose to be a poor correspondent'.

FACILITATE EXPLORING CHOICES Skilled helpers assist clients in exploring choices and their consequences. Clients are always choosers. Spending time exploring choices is valuable to developing their skills of owning responsibility for their choices. You do not make clients' choices for them, but assist them in learning to choose for themselves.

EXPLORE OPPOSITES You may help some clients become more aware of their capacity for choice by getting them to explore opposite ways of thinking and behaving. For example, 'Think of someone who makes you feel angry. Now imagine yourself going out of your way to do something to make that person happy. How might he or she react?' Often clients can gain insight into their choices in sustaining problems by exploring opposite ways of viewing them.

CONFRONT NOT ACKNOWLEDGING CHOICE Clients may make statements like 'I had no choice but to __'. You can either challenge such statements or help clients challenge themselves. You can not only confront clients with how they restrict choice, but also help them explore the consequences for themselves and others of this behaviour. Sometimes clients insufficiently acknowledge choices. Here you may need to strengthen clients' perceptions and will to be choosers, for instance with regard to resisting peer group pressure.

CONFRONT EXTERNALIZING All clients and helpers in varying degrees externalize thoughts, feelings, actions and responsibility for problems on to others. Looking at others' shortcomings is easier than looking at our own. Skilled helpers resist colluding with clients who consistently see themselves as the victims of others' persecution. You require both confronting and facilitative skills in assisting clients to look at their own behaviour and choices.

EXPLORE DEFENCES Helpers can assist clients to acknowledge and become aware of the impact of any characteristic 'security operations' or 'defensive processes' they possess (Arlow, 1989; Clark, 1991; Freud, 1936; Sullivan, 1953). Defensive processes diminish choice awareness in the interest of making life more psychologically comfortable in the short term. Illustrative defensive processes include denying or distorting information, rationalizing or making excuses while unawares, and projecting unwanted aspects of yourself on to others. You need to assist exploration of defences with skill and caution: clients' defences alleviate their anxiety and may protect highly sensitive areas.

RAISE CONSCIOUSNESS CONCERNING DEATH, DYING AND FINITENESS Helpers may assist some clients by increasing their death awareness (Feifel, 1990; Yalom, 1980). Relevant interventions include: (1) assisting clients in imagining the process of dying and their own death; (2) encouraging clients to write their own obituaries; (3) facilitating clients in reminiscing about their contacts with dying people and with death; and (4) encouraging clients to make contact with dying people, for instance by visiting hospices.

SKILL 2: USE COPING SELF-TALK

Meichenbaum and others have trained many different clienteles in coping self-talk. Targeted problems include: managing anger, managing stress, being creative, curbing impulsiveness, managing pain, and controlling weight (Meichenbaum, 1977, 1983, 1985; Meichenbaum & Deffenbacher, 1988). One way to help clients understand that they engage in self-talk is to ask them to close their eyes for thirty seconds and think of nothing. Most become highly aware that they cannot rid themselves of self-talk.

Help clients to distinguish coping self-talk

Below is an example of the kind of content a helper might use in instructing a shy client in coping self-talk (Nelson-Jones, 1991). Needless to say, there would be opportunity for comments, feedback, checking understanding and relating the content of the presentation to the client's own material.

> Coping self-talk is a useful thinking skill for managing feelings of shyness. The idea is that during your waking hours you continuously engage in an internal dialogue, or perform self-talk. The goals of coping self-talk are to calm your anxieties and to help you deal effectively with the task at hand. Thus, coping

self-talk contains two major elements: calming self-talk and coaching self-talk. Coping self-talk is about coping or 'doing as well as I can' rather than about mastery or 'being perfect' and 'having no anxiety'. Coping is a much more realistic goal than mastery.

Coping self-talk involves replacing negative self-talk statements with helpful ones. Let's take the example of Anne and Mary at a party. Note how Anne's self-talk oppresses her, while Mary's self-talk supports her.

Anne: 'I know that I am going to find this party difficult. Everybody is looking at me. I feel unattractive. I don't want to make a mistake. I'm feeling tense and, when this happens, I know it will only get worse.'

Mary: 'I enjoy parties and meeting new people. Although I get a little anxious with strangers, I know I can overcome it. I have developed some good party skills and these usually work. All I have to do is my best.'

Calming and coaching statements tend to be interspersed in coping self-talk.

Two important aspects of *calming* self-talk are as follows.

- *Tell yourself to stay calm.* Simple self-statements include: 'Keep calm', 'Relax' and 'Take it easy'. In addition, you can instruct yourself to 'take a deep breath' or 'breathe slowly and regularly'.

- *Tell yourself you can cope.* Sample self-statements include 'I can handle this situation', or 'My anxiety is a signal for me to use my coping skills'.

Coaching self-talk can help you to cope with shyness in the following ways:

- *Specify your goals.* An example could be: 'I will go up and talk to a minimum of three new people at a party.'

- *Break tasks down*. Think through the steps needed to attain your goal.

- *Concentrate on the task at hand*. Instruct yourself in the specific elements of competent behaviour.

You may use coping self-talk before, during and after stressful social situations – for example, going to a party full of strangers or out with a new date.
  Examples of possible coping self-talk statements *before* stressful social situations include:

- 'This anxiety is a sign for me to use my coping skills.'

- 'Calm down. Develop a plan to manage the situation.'

- 'I know if I use my coping skills I can manage.'

Examples of possible coping self-talk statements *during* stressful social situations include:

- 'Take my time. Breathe slowly and regularly.'

- 'Relax. I can manage if I just take one step at a time.'

- 'I don't have to be liked by everyone. All I can do is the best I can.'

Examples of possible coping self-talk statements *after* stressful social situations include:

- 'Each time I cope it seems to get easier.'

- 'I'm proud of the way I'm learning to manage my fears.'

- 'I've shown myself that I can do it now.'

Relate coping self-talk to action

The above presentation represents one of the many skills helpers need to impart the thinking skill of coping self-talk. Helpers also require assessing thinking, rewarding

listening and coaching skills. Both helpers and clients should view coping self-talk along with taking appropriate action. For instance, a shy person requires not only the thinking skill of coping self-talk, but also the action skills of performing competently in social situations. Consequently, often in the same session you are likely to work with both thinking and action skills. You can encourage clients to write their coping self-talk statements on cue cards for rehearsing and using before difficult situations.

SKILL 3: CHOOSE REALISTIC PERSONAL RULES

Albert Ellis has been particularly prominent in highlighting the importance of realistic personal rules, or what he terms rational as contrasted with irrational beliefs (Ellis, 1962, 1980, 1989). Personal rules represent a form of self-talk, much of which goes on below conscious awareness. Personal rules provide standards for judging our own and others' behaviour. Many clients possess rules representing the internalization of others' standards rather than rules thought through by themselves. Such rules can be benign and realistic so long as they help clients meet their needs. However, unrealistic rules can cause clients to be tyrannized by their 'shoulds'. Such unrealistic rules contribute to negative emotions, for instance anger and anxiety, and self-defeating actions, for instance withdrawal and temper tantrums.

Assist clients to identify unrealistic personal rules

Helpers can assist clients to develop the skills of identifying danger signals that they may possess one or more unrealistic personal rules.

- *Attend to inappropriate feelings*. Persistent inappropriate feelings are one signal alerting clients to unrealistic personal rules. Clients can ask themselves questions like, 'Is this feeling appropriate for the situation?' and, 'To what extent does this feeling have unnecessary negative consequences for me?'

- *Attend to inappropriate actions*. Inappropriate feelings and actions are interrelated. Clients can ask themselves questions like, 'Are my actions helping or harming me and others?', 'Am I overreacting?', and, 'Is my behaviour self-defeating?'

- *Attend to inappropriate language*. Words such as 'should', 'ought', or 'must' may signal irrational beliefs or rules.

- *Look for linkages between stressors*. You can assist clients in the skills of identifying which rules are most important. For example, it may be more important for clients whose anger at home is related to self-induced stress at work to focus on stress rules than anger rules.

Help clients put unrealistic rules into the STC framework

Assuming adequate initial explanation, helpers should encourage clients to do their own work rather than spoon-feed them. Below are two examples of clients' rules put

into the S, situation, T, thoughts, and C, feelings and action consequences, framework. The first example focuses on an unrealistic *personal* rule and the second on an unrealistic *relationship* rule.

Jeff is a family man with two children.

S   His children do not overtly show appreciation for how hard he works to support them.
T   I must always have my kids' approval or else I am less of a person.
C   Hurt, self-pity and anger. Curtness with children that creates emotional distance.

Anna and David are a newly married couple.

S   Anna and David disagree over how much time to spend with the in-laws.
T   We must never have conflict in our marriage.
C   Both Anna's and David's negative feelings persist. The in-law issue in their relationship is not openly worked through.

Assist clients to dispute unrealistic rules

Ellis (1980) considers disputing to be the most typical and often-used method of his rational-emotive therapy (RET). Disputing means challenging unrealistic rules. An issue for helpers is whether to dispute clients' rules or assist clients in doing their own disputing. One approach is to demonstrate the skill first, then coach clients in developing disputing skills. Take the earlier example of Jeff whose personal rule was 'I must always have my kids' approval or else I am less of a person'. Here are questions that Jeff might ask himself or be asked:

'What evidence exists that I cannot survive without my kids' approval?'
'Does the fact that my kids do not overtly show approval for what I do mean that they do not notice it?'
'Is it realistic to expect children to be aware of what their father does for them outside the home, let alone to always appreciate it?'
'Would I expect the children of my friends to show approval in the same way that I expect my kids to, or do I have a double standard?'
'Did I use to show appreciation always for what my parents did for me?'
'What is it about me that may make me vulnerable to not having shows of appreciation from my kids?'
'How exactly does not having constant appreciation from my kids make me less of a person?'

Clients need to become aware that they may need to dispute the same unrealistic rule again and again. They may possess well-established habits of re-indoctrinating and recontaminating themselves.

Assist clients to reformulate unrealistic into realistic rules

Reformulating means substituting realistic for unrealistic characteristics in specific personal or relationship rules. Assist clients in understanding some of the main characteristics of realistic personal rules.

- expressing preferences rather than demands: for example, 'I'd PREFER to do very well but I don't HAVE TO' (Sichel & Ellis, 1984, p. 1);

- emphasizing coping rather than mastery or being perfect;

- being based on clients' own valuing process rather than rigid internalizations of others' rules;

- flexibility or, where appropriate, being amenable to change and updating;

- Absence of self-rating: for example, 'I am a PERSON WHO acted badly, not a BAD PERSON' (Sichel & Ellis, 1984, p. 1).

Then assist clients in reformulating unhelpful into helpful rules. Get them to do much of the work. Make sure the reformulations are in clients' own language, since they have to live with their new rules. I illustrate reformulating with the examples of Jeff's unrealistic personal rule and Anna and David's unrealistic relationship rule.

JEFF

Unrealistic personal rule:	'I must always have my kids' approval or else I am less of a person.'
Realistic personal rule:	'I would prefer to have my kids' approval much of the time. However, it is more important that I take responsibility for how well I behave to them and approve of what I do.'

ANNA AND DAVID

Unrealistic relationship rule:	'We must never have conflict in our marriage.'
Realistic relationship rule:	'We would prefer not to have serious conflicts in our marriage. However, differences and conflict are part of all close relationships. We need to develop skills of working through rather than avoiding conflicts.'

It is important that clients take away, remember and practise reformulated rules. Encourage either cassette-recording them or writing them down. Such records should be used for homework and reminder purposes – playing back the recording or displaying the reformulated rules in an obvious place. Emphasize that maintaining reformulated rules requires practice, practice, practice.

Encourage clients to change actions along with reformulated rules

Effective thinking should lead to effective action. Psychologists differ over whether practice is best approached gradually, from the less to more difficult tasks, or 'floodingly', going straight to a difficult assignment. With either approach, encourage clients to develop relevant action skills; for instance unappreciated Jeff might need to improve his showing affection skills. Ellis asks clients to do practice assignments repetitively and floodingly (1980, 1989). He believes that, by jumping in at the deep end over and over, clients find that their worst fears rarely materialize. Other psychologists advocate a more gradual approach. For instance, they would ask a woman afraid of saying 'no' to people to say 'no' to less threatening people before repeating the behaviour with more threatening ones. Often clients do not have much choice: a difficult encounter or an imminent exam is the reality they face.

SKILL 4: CHOOSE HOW YOU PERCEIVE

Aaron Beck of the University of Pennsylvania is a prime advocate of helping clients influence their feelings by choosing more realistic perceptions. In particular Beck has focused on the thoughts that precede depression (Beck, 1976; Beck *et al.*, 1979), anxieties and phobias (Beck & Emery, 1985), and anger in relationships (Beck, 1988). You can assist numerous clients with a wide range of problems to develop skills of challenging and altering their distorted perceptions and perceptual processes.

Help clients become aware of the influence of perception on feelings

You can let clients know that they may have tendencies to jump to unhelpful conclusions that contribute to negative feelings. You may illustrate this point through stories. For example, you can ask clients to imagine that someone has trodden on their toe. Realistically they might experience some pain. If they perceived the toe-treading as accidental they might also feel mild irritation, but this should not persist. However, if they perceived the toe-treading as intentional, they might feel very angry. In each instance, how they perceive influences how they feel.

Clients can be encouraged to monitor upsetting perceptions. Ideally, they should monitor them as they happen. Clients need to develop the skills of becoming aware of the thinking that accompanies inappropriate feelings. You can get clients to set aside some time each day to monitor and record upsetting perceptions. Clients can fill in a thinksheet with the following three column headings.

A. The situation (inc. date and time)	B. My feelings	C. My thoughts (perceptions)

Ensure clients know the difference between fact and inference

Clients' perceptions of themselves, others and the world are their subjective 'facts'. Often, however, they fail to realize that these perceptions may be based on inference rather than fact. A favourite illustration of this point by one of my Stanford University professors was: 'All Indians walk in single file: at least the one I saw did.' That one Indian was seen is a fact; that they all walk in single file is inference. Facts are the true data of experience; inferences are deductions and conclusions drawn from the data. Inferences are both necessary and useful so long as their assumptions are recognized and accurately evaluated. All too often, however, clients treat their inferences as facts. This deprives them of accurate information on which to base further thoughts, feelings and actions. Below is an example:

Fact: Husband comes home very late from work three nights in a row.
Wife's inference: He does not love me any more and has a girlfriend.

Assuming the husband had genuine reasons for staying late, which he may even have explained to her, his wife was making an erroneous inference that could have serious repercussions for their relationship. However, we don't know the husband's previous track record: this may have supported his wife's inference!

Help clients identify characteristic perceptual distortions

Helpers can assist clients to become aware of characteristic ways in which they distort how they perceive. In regard to distressed couples Beck observes: 'These cognitive distortions occur automatically, often in a fraction of a second, and the number of distortions that can take place in that short period is considerable' (1988, p. 159). Especially under stress, clients are likely to activitate their perceptual 'fault lines'. Awareness of characteristic distortions provides clients with information with which to check specific perceptions. They have a start in knowing where to look and what to avoid.

Using the STC framework, the following are some perceptual distortions that clients may have at T that lead to negative feelings and action consequences at C.

- *Tunnel vision*. Focusing on only a portion of the available information in a situation rather than taking into account all significant data.

- *Polarized thinking*. Perceiving in black-and-white terms. For example, 'Either I am a total success or a total failure.'

- *Negative labelling*. Attaching negative and critical labels to yourself, and others. Overemphasizing the negative at the expense of the positive or neutral. Going beyond a functional rating of a specific characteristic to devaluing your whole personhood.

- *Personalizing*. Perceiving yourself as the centre of attention more than is warranted. For instance, 'Everybody in the office is aware of how well or poorly I perform.'

- *Overgeneralizing*. Making global comments that are probably untenable if the evidence is checked. For example, 'My daughter *never* does anything for me', and 'I *always* try to understand my employees' viewpoints.'

- *Misattributing*. Failing to accurately assign cause and responsibility for your own and others' behaviour. Giving biased explanations of others' behaviour and intentions: for instance 'He is not good at showing affection because he has a poor personality.'

Help clients to stop, think, generate, evaluate and choose the 'best-fit' perception

Helpers can assist clients to realize that they have choices in how they perceive. Help clients to check the accuracy of their information base when they become aware that they either feel and act, or are at risk of feeling and acting, in inappropriate ways. Clients can ask themselves the following kinds of question:

'Stop . . . think . . . am I jumping to conclusions in how I perceive?'
'Are my perceptions based on fact or inference?'
'If based on inference, are there other ways of perceiving the situation more closely related to the facts?'
'What further information might I need to collect?'
'Does my way of perceiving this situation reflect any of my characteristic perceptual distortions?'
'What perception can I choose that best fits the available facts?'

GENERATE DIFFERENT PERCEPTIONS Clients are often very poor at generating alternative ways of viewing people and situations. Below is an example in the STC framework.

S   Gary has cooked a nice dinner for his girlfriend Wendy, who is 30 minutes late.
T   Gary thinks 'Wendy is very inconsiderate of my feelings.'
C   When Wendy finally arrives, Gary verbally attacks her and they have a row.

You need tactfully to inform Gary that he requires the skill of perceiving accurately rather than jumping to conclusions. One element of this skill is acknowledging that you have choices in how you perceive and looking for alternative explanations. You could help him to generate alternative perceptions at T. For example: 'Wendy may have had a flat tyre'; 'Wendy may have been forced to stay late at work'; 'Wendy may have stopped off to buy me a present'; and 'Wendy and I may not have made our arrangement clearly enough.'

EVALUATE DIFFERENT PERCEPTIONS Another element of the skill of perceiving accurately is evaluating different perceptions and choosing the 'best-fit' perception. For instance, you might assist Gary in evaluating the perception, 'Wendy is very inconsiderate of my feelings'. How closely does the inference fit the facts? Then you encourage Gary to evaluate the other perceptions generated. Gary decided that the

'best-fit' perception in this case is 'Wendy and I may not have made our arrangements clearly enough.' The feelings consequence of this perception is that Gary is not angry with Wendy. The action consequence is that Gary welcomes Wendy and they calmly talk over what went wrong.

Reframing

Reframing is a variation of the skill of generating and evaluating different perceptions and choosing the best-fit perception. Either the helper or the client places a situation, feeling or behaviour within a different frame. Reframes should not be rationalizations. Often reframing focuses on one alternative perception rather than generating and evaluating a series of different perceptions. Helper-offered reframes confront clients with new ways of perceiving events. However, clients can also develop skills of generating and evaluating their own reframes. Below is an example of a helper-offered reframe.

> *Client*: I feel guilty that, since returning from being off work with stress problems, I'm not performing my supervising job to my full ability. I like to do as well as I can by the company.
> *Helper*: I get the impression that what you do is really important to your company and that, even though you don't feel 100 per cent, your being back at work has saved them from a lot of problems.

How can helpers assist clients develop reframing skills? First identify reframing as a useful self-helping skill. The concept of reframing may be easier for certain clients to grasp than that of generating and evaluating different perceptions. Second, as in the above example, use the client's material to demonstrate how to reframe. Third, where appropriate, encourage clients to suggest their own reframes: for instance by questions such as: 'Can you think of a way to reframe that?' Fourth, encourage clients to practise the skill of reframing in their daily lives. Fifth, assist clients to assess not only the consequences of individual reframes on how they feel and act, but also the longer-term consequences for developing reframing as a self-helping skill.

SKILL 5: ATTRIBUTE CAUSE ACCURATELY

Earlier I mentioned the skill of owning responsibility for choosing. Here I elaborate on how to assist clients' motivation by working with them on how they attribute cause for what happens in their lives. Attributions are the explanations, interpretations or reasons that clients give themselves for what happens. They influence how clients think about the future as well as how they feel and act. Clients often make attributional errors that interfere with their motivation and effectiveness. Let's take the example of the women's movement. When women attributed their lack of status to male dominance, they were relatively powerless. However, when women also attributed their lack of status to insufficient assertion, they empowered themselves.

Help clients become aware of inaccurate attributions

Frequently clients' attributions of cause are partly rather than totally inaccurate. A partial truth gets converted into a whole truth. For instance, a partial cause of Rosemary's difficulties may be that she was rejected by her father when growing up. However, Rosemary can immobilize herself from working for change if she attributes the whole cause of her difficulties to her father's past behaviour. The following are some attributional errors for different areas.

CAUSES OF PROBLEMS Many misattributions can cause clients to remain unnecessarily stuck with problems. Here are some examples:

- *It's my genes.* Though genetic endowment does limit capacities, clients also limit themselves. For instance, clients who say that they are 'naturally' lazy obscure their own roles in sustaining their laziness.

- *It's my mental illness.* The medical profession has done psychology a huge disservice by fostering the concept of mental illness. For most psychological problems, the attribution of mental illness overemphasizes the role of heredity and physical factors and underemphasizes the role of learning and choice.

- *It's my unfortunate past.* As shown in the example of Rosemary, unfortunate pasts may contribute to problems and skills weaknesses. However, clients are unlikely to change unless they assume responsibility for how they sustain their problems.

- *It's my poor environment.* Adverse social, economic and psychological environments may make it more difficult for clients to fulfil themselves. However, even in Nazi concentration camps, people can change and grow (Frankl, 1959).

FEELINGS OF DEPRESSION Clients' attributions of cause for positive and negative events in their lives affect their self-esteem. Here are some inaccurate attributions that may contribute to depression:

- *I am the cause of all negative events.* Clients can overemphasize their role in negative events in their own and others' lives (Beck *et al.*, 1979).

- *I am never the cause of positive events.* Clients may deny and distort their roles in positive events in their own and others' lives.

- *I am unable to act on my own environment in such a way as to produce desired results.* Frequently depressed people think of themselves as powerless or helpless to influence their environments (Schulman *et al.*, 1987; Seligman *et al.*, 1979).

RELATIONSHIP CONFLICTS Often clients require help in acknowledging their contributions to sustaining problems. The following are some common attributional errors:

- *It's all your fault.* Instead of looking at conflicts from the inside to the outside, clients view them from the outside to inside. Disliking what they see outside provides a convenient excuse for not looking at their own behaviour.

- *You must change first.* Here clients allow their feeling, thinking and actions to be dependent on their partner's behaviour. Unwittingly clients give up some control over their lives.

BECOMING AND STAYING UNEMPLOYED Depending on clients' specific situations, the following attributions may be inaccurate:

- *It was my fault.* Numerous external reasons contribute to unemployment: for instance, recessions, company take-overs and technological changes. Clients may genuinely not be responsible for their job loss.

- *It was their fault.* Some clients may fail to acknowledge that they have personal and work-related skills weaknesses that increase the chance of their being fired.

- *The state should provide for me.* Whatever clients' political persuasion, the reality is that they are likely to receive limited welfare payments.

- *My work skills are adequate.* Clients may need to review the accuracy of this assumption. For example, their work skills may be in demand, but they perform them poorly. Alternatively, their work skills may be obsolete.

ACADEMIC SUCCESSES AND FAILURES Helpers may assist both underachieving and overstriving students to be more realistic about the attributions they make for their academic successes and failures. The following are some causes to which students may attribute academic success and failure (Nelson-Jones, 1989; Weiner & Kukla, 1970). Needless to say, there is a subjective element in what students perceive as success or failure.

- *Aptitude.* Aptitude is an internal and stable attribute.

- *Effort.* Effort is an internal attribute largely within a client's control.

- *Task difficulty.* Task difficulty is composed of the task's realistic level of difficulty and any of the client's perceptual distortions that magnify or minimize it.

- *Luck.* Academic results due to chance are outside clients' control.

- *Anxiety.* Anxiety can both help and hinder academic performance (Alpert & Haber, 1960). The effects of debilitating anxiety may be inadequately recognized.

- *Staff competence.* Good or poor teaching may help or hinder achievement.

- *Socioeconomic considerations.* Some students need to take outside work to support themselves. Some live in inadequate housing and so on.

- *Peer group pressure.* The peer group either values or does not value academic success.

Alter inaccurate attributions

Helpers can use some of the skills already described for helping clients alter unrealistic attributions. For example you can encourage clients to examine the evidence for their attributions and see how closely they fit the facts. Then clients can generate and evaluate alternative attributions. In addition, clients can dispute attributions and reformulate them into more realistic attributions. For example, the attribution in a relationship conflict that 'It's all my partner's fault' can be reformulated as 'Even though I may not like how my partner behaves, I need to look at how I behave to my partner and, where possible, change my behaviour to achieve both my and our goals.' You can also assist clients to conduct behavioural experiments in which they act on altered attributions. For example, a husband's 'It's all my partner's fault' attribution is disproved if he acts differently towards his wife, who in turns acts better towards him.

Helpers can both provide new information and encourage clients to collect additional information that confirms existing attributions. For instance, you can inform clients wrongly diagnosing themselves as schizophrenic that they do not possess any of its key symptoms, or you can encourage clients attributing their maths problems to insufficient aptitude to collect additional information by taking a maths aptitude test.

SKILL 6: PREDICT REALISTICALLY

Clients lead their lives into the future rather than into the past. Predictions are thoughts and images forecasting the future. George Kelly took a rational approach to prediction when he wrote: 'The two factors from which predictions are made are the number of replications already observed and the amount of similarity which can be abstracted among the replications' (1955, p. 53). Invariably clients experience disorders of prediction of varying degrees of intensity. Anxiety is a disorder of prediction (Beck & Emery, 1985). Distorted predictions also play a large part in depression, for instance hopelessness (Beck *et al.*, 1988b), helplessness (Abramson *et al.*, 1978) and perceived self-inefficacy (Bandura, 1989).

Help clients to become aware of their predictive style

Helpers can assist clients to become more aware of their predictive styles and their consequences, both in general and in relation to specific problems. Predicting risks and rewards are interrelated. However, clients can become more aware of where specific skills weaknesses lie. The following are the four main options.

PREDICT RISK INACCURATELY
- *Underestimate bad consequences.* For example, some research in the health area indicates that people tend to underestimate their own, relative to others', risk of

various illness and negative life events (Weinstein, 1980, 1984). Compulsive gamblers and stock market speculators have a similar tendency.

- *Overestimate bad consequences.* Fear of change, failure and success can be powerful motivators for clients to overestimate negative consequences of actions. Many clients engage in catastrophic predictions.

PREDICT REWARD INACCURATELY

- *Overestimate good consequences.* Overestimating good consequences frequently accompanies underestimating bad consequences, for instance in compulsive gambling.

- *Underestimate good consequences.* Many helping clients underestimate good consequences. They have a predictive style that focuses far more on risk then reward. Two trends are common in underestimating reward. First, clients are poor at identifying rewards. Second, even when clients identify rewards, they minimize their significance.

Help clients to become aware of current predictions and their consequences

A simple two-column technique can be useful for eliciting clients' assessments of risks and rewards in specific situations. For example, using the STC framework, the S (situation) is that Sean is a shy 30-year-old bachelor wondering whether to ask Suzanne for a date. Sean's helper places the following two column headings on the whiteboard to elicit Sean's thoughts or predictions at T.

Risks (–s)	Rewards (+s)

Then the helper assists Sean to articulate his fears about asking Suzanne out: for instance, 'This might contribute to keeping me depressed', and 'I could get hurt'. At this stage, Sean has difficulty predicting that there will be rewards from his actions.

Helpers can go beyond pinpointing predictions to exploring their consequences at C. Exploration can focus on consequences for clients; for instance, Sean's overemphasis on the risks rather than the gains may lead to persistent loneliness. You can also assist clients to become better at predicting consequences for others: for instance, drug addict Jean may need to see more clearly the dangers for others of sharing her needles.

Help clients generate and evaluate additional risks or rewards

If clients' predictive errors lean towards underestimating risks, helpers may need to assist them to develop the skill of generating what other risks there may be. Most clients

tend to overestimate risks. Frequently, they need to develop skills of generating and evaluating potential rewards.

> Sean started by mentioning items to go in the risks column in regard to asking Suzanne for a date, but had difficulty generating items for the rewards column. Sean's helper worked with him to generate some potential rewards for asking Suzanne out, including the following: 'I might have a chance of a strong relationship'; 'I might gain more experience in developing relationships'; and 'I might gain confidence and a more positive self-image'. Working to generate rewards enabled Sean to obtain a more balanced picture about asking Suzanne out. Sean decided the rewards outweighed the risks, acted on his changed predictions, and Suzanne later became his first steady girlfriend.

Help clients to assess probability

Helpers can assist clients to review their assumptions about their likelihood of risks or rewards actually occurring. Clients may wrongly assign high probability to low-probability events or low probability to high-probability events.

> Fifteen years ago, when a senior lecturer, Daniel had an extremely painful nervous breakdown. Now Daniel is a professor. Recently, on doctor's orders, he took sick leave for a 'holiday' because he had started experiencing his pre-breakdown symptoms of fifteen years ago. A few days before returning to his university, he experienced chronic anxiety. A major contributor to his anxiety was his prediction that he might have another breakdown. Daniel's helper assisted him to assess the evidence for his prediction. Once Daniel faced the facts, he realized that this time he had taken preventive action and had the skills to monitor his load and seek further assistance, if necessary. Consequently, Daniel recognized that the chances of having another full-blown breakdown were close to nil. This realization lowered his anxiety, thus further reducing the likelihood of another breakdown.

Questions that clients might ask themselves in assessing probability fall into two categories. First, what *rational* basis do I have for making a particular prediction? Here,

clients need to assess the connections between facts and inferences. Second, what *irrational* considerations might interfere with the accuracy of my prediction? The perceptual distortions mentioned earlier, clients' states of emotional arousal, and their physical condition might all interefere with their ability to predict.

Help clients to assess their coping capacity and support factors

Clients may predict on the basis of inaccurate assessments of their skills at coping with particular situations. They may engage in focusing on their weaknesses and need to counteract this by searching for and affirming their resources. Additionally, clients may possess many support factors that they inadequately acknowledge: for example people who can help them prepare for upcoming tasks, friends and relatives to provide emotional support, and opportunities to repeat failed tasks. Encourage clients to identify, acknowledge, use and develop appropriate supports (Emery, 1982).

Encourage clients to reality-test predictions

The most conclusive way for clients to test the accuracy of their predictions is to reality-test them. Here are two examples of clients whom helpers might encourage to reality-test predictions.

Maureen, age 27, is afraid to tell her husband how she would like him to make love to her. She predicts, 'If I tell him, he'll be furious.'

Wayne, a widower, is reluctant to throw a party to mark his sixtieth birthday. He predicts, 'No one will want to come.'

In these examples, each client needs to set a specific goal. For example, Maureen's goal might be to tell her husband how to pleasure her better within the next month. Wayne's goal might be to throw a moderate-sized party on or within two weeks of his sixtieth birthday. You may need to assist clients to think through and develop the action skills for attaining their goals. For example, Maureen requires verbal, voice and body message action skills to make an assertive request for her husband to change his behaviour.

SKILL 7: SET REALISTIC GOALS

Clients may bring to helping different errors in setting goals. Some clients may possess goals, but these may be unrealistically high or low. Furthermore, their goals may be based on how others think they should be rather than on their own valuing process. Other clients may lack clear goals. Still more may require assistance in stating their goals clearly. Some of the rewards for clients of setting realistic goals include increased authorship of their lives, clarity of focus, finding increased meaning, and gaining increased motivation. Risks to clients' setting themselves unrealistic goals include self-alienation, overemphasizing doing as contrasted with being, putting too much pressure on themselves, and compromising their health.

Assisting vulnerable clients to formulate clear goals may entail long-term helping. Such clients lack a clear sense of their identity. You may need to assist these clients in getting more in touch with their feelings, wants and wishes. Furthermore, you may need to caution clients against making major decisions until they are less anxious.

Many other thinking skills are relevant to assisting clients in setting realistic goals. Clients' goals need to be based on realistic personal rules. Furthermore, where clients' goals involve others, for instance if they aim to get engaged or married, they need to perceive them accurately. In addition, clients can use visualizing skills to formulate goals, and when setting goals, clients can engage in the steps of rational decision making.

Assist clients to state goals clearly

Clients are more likely to attain goals that they state clearly. You can make clients aware of the following critera for effective goals:

- *Do your goals reflect your values?* Clients' goals should reflect what they consider to be worthwhile in life.

- *Are your goals realistic?* Clients' goals are realistic when they adequately acknowledge both external and personal constraints. Encourage clients to set goals reflecting potentially attainable standards.

- *Are your goals specific?* Assist clients in stating goals as specifically as possible. Ideally, clients' goals should be stated so that they can easily measure the success of attempts to attain them. For instance, 'I will introduce myself to three new people in my ballroom dancing class' is much preferable to 'I want to meet some new people.'

- *Do your goals have a time frame?* Goals can be short term, medium term, or long term. Vague intentions are insufficient. Assist clients in stating a realistic time frame for attaining goals: for instance, 'By the end of this month, I will introduce myself to three new people in my ballroom dancing class.'

Once goals are stated, you may need to work with clients to identify the thinking and action skills required to attain them. In the above example, you might assist the client in articulating the thinking and action skills helpful for meeting three new people in the ballroom dancing class. Sometimes assist clients in breaking tasks down into more easily attainable sub-goals: for example, an initial goal of meeting one new person, a second goal of meeting two new people, and a third goal of meeting three new people.

SKILL 8: USE VISUALIZING SKILLS

Visual images play a large part in everyone's lives. Glasser (1984) asserts that 80 per cent of the perceptions people store in their memory albums are visual. Visual images interact with feelings: in one research study, some 90 per cent of anxious patients

reported visual images prior to and concurrent with their anxiety attacks (Beck *et al.*, 1974). Lazarus observes that a tendency to react with visual images is particularly strong in certain clients: 'When a person's most highly valued representational system is visual, he or she is inclined to respond to the world and organize it in terms of mental images' (Lazarus, 1989, p. 514).

Help clients develop an awareness of visualizing

Some clients may need to become more aware of the role of visual things in sustaining their problems. The following are a few ways that helpers can highlight the importance of visualizing.

QUESTIONS Helpers who ask questions about clients' visual imagery are more likely to assist clients to recognize its importance than are helpers who avoid the area. Sample questions might be: 'Were you aware of any visual images that accompanied the anxiety attack?' and 'To what extent do you use imagery to help cope with the situation?' As clients answer questions, helpers can attempt to assess their visualizing powers. Clients can also be asked to close their eyes and recount specific instances as though they were describing a slow-motion replay of a movie. In general, the more clients can experience sensations and feelings attached to images, the greater their potential for using visualizing as a self-helping skill.

EXPLANATIONS You can incorporate visual images into the PTC or STC framework used to explain problems or problematic situations. For instance, the STC framework requires elaboration to:

S   the situation;
T   your thoughts and *visual images*;
C   your feeling and action consequences.

EXERCISES You can use exercises to illustrate various aspects of visualizing. A simple exercise to highlight the presence of visualizing is to ask clients to think of someone they love. Almost invariably they will get a visual image. You can show the relationship between visualizing and feelings by getting clients first to visualize something that 'makes' them feel happy and then something that 'makes' them feel afraid.

Helpers can assist clients to develop visualizing skills for numerous purposes (Lazarus, 1977; Nelson-Jones, 1989). Visualizing skills are most effective when used in conjunction with other thinking and action skills. Here I illustrate visualizing by focusing on three of its uses: becoming more relaxed, performing better, and breaking bad habits.

Help clients use visualizing to relax

When clients visualize, it is best if they are relaxed. Relaxation can be a useful skill for clients to develop if they suffer from such problems as tension headaches, hypertension and feelings of excessive stress. It is also a useful skill for helping manage such feelings as anxiety (Deffenbacher & Suinn, 1988; Wolpe, 1973) and anger (Deffenbacher *et al.*,

1988). The most common helping approach to relaxation is probably the Jacobson progressive muscular relaxation technique (Jacobson, 1938), more fully described in Chapter 12. Visual imagery may be used independently of as well as in conjunction with muscular relaxation. You may assist clients in the following elements of visual relaxation.

IDENTIFYING RELAXING SCENES You can encourage clients to identify one or more favourite scenes conducive to their feeling relaxed, for instance looking at a valley with lush green meadows or sitting in a comfortable chair at home.

DEVELOPING SELF-INSTRUCTIONS Though helpers may initially relax clients, the idea is for clients to develop visual relaxation as a self-helping skill. First, you can demonstrate how clients can instruct themselves in visual relaxation. Then you rehearse clients as they use their own instructions. Clients may wish to record their self-instructions for playback outside of helping sessions. Here is a brief example:

> I'm lying on an uncrowded beach on a pleasant, sunny day, enjoying the sensations of warmth on my body. There is a gentle breeze. I can hear the peaceful noise of the sea steadily lapping against the nearby shore. I haven't a care in the world, and enjoy my feelings of peace, calm relaxation, and well-being.

USING VISUAL RELAXATION IN DAILY LIFE You can assist clients in identifying opportunities for taking 'time out' in their daily lives to use visual relaxation. You can encourage clients to keep visual relaxation monitoring logs of their daily practice and use of the skill. Clients can also record the consequences of using visual relaxation skills.

Help clients use visualizing to perform better

Visualized rehearsal and practice and visualizing attaining goals are two main ways in which clients may use visualizing to enhance how they perform tasks.

VISUALIZED REHEARSAL AND PRACTICE Clients may have limited opportunity to rehearse and practise skills in real life, for instance going for a job interview or speaking in public. However, they have virtually unlimited opportunity to use visualized rehearsal and practice. While no substitute for the real thing, visualized rehearsal has many advantages. These include assisting clients to break tasks down and focus on the processes of skilled performance; identify potential setbacks and ways of coping with them; and rehearse and practise coping self-talk along with their visualizing skills.

The following are instances of clients using visual rehearsal and practice:

Wendy, 61, a recently retired widow, has a goal of asking her friend, Louise, if she can join her bridge group. Wendy visually rehearses the best way to do this, including how she might respond if Louise says 'no'.

Bruce, 41, a car factory foreman, visualizes different ways he can assertively tell workers when their work is not up to standard.

Duncan, 23, a police officer, visualizes how he can calmly yet firmly react to people who call him a 'pig' when he is on crowd control duty.

VISUALIZING ATTAINING GOALS Visualized rehearsal and practice focuses on the processes of skilled performance. However, clients may enhance their performance if they visualize themselves being successful in attaining goals (Lazarus, 1977; Woolfolk *et al.*, 1985). For example, if clients rehearse hard and then visualize that they are going to perform very competently when speaking in public, they are more likely to do so than if they visualize lack of success. Often clients are far too good at visualizing the worst. They need to be able to counteract this tendency by visualizing success experiences. Helpers can also encourage clients, even when imagining the worst possibility, to visualize how they can cope successfully in such adverse circumstances (Emery, 1982).

Help clients to use visualizing to break bad habits

There is an Oscar Wilde aphorism: 'I couldn't help it. I can resist everything except temptation.' Visualizing can be a helpful skill when trying to overcome bad habits. Clients with bad habits, instead of dwelling on negative consequences, often switch to dwelling on short-term rewards. If clients sincerely wish to break bad habits, the time to reward themselves is when they have resisted temptation, not when they have given in to it. Visualizing realistic negative consequences and visualizing exaggerated negative consequences are two ways in which helpers can assist clients to break bad habits.

VISUALIZE REALISTIC NEGATIVE CONSEQUENCES How can you assist clients to visualize realistic negative consequences from such activities as smoking and engaging in unsafe gay sex? One way is to encourage clients to collect visual images of negative consequences, for instance coloured medical photographs of the effects of smoking on lung tissue or of AIDS-related symptoms, such as Kaposi's sarcoma and malignant lymphomas. In addition, clients can be encouraged to develop visualizations, possibly including photographic images, of negative consequences of bad habits. Clients can also develop the following self-helping skills. When tempted, they can instruct themselves, 'Stop!', and then intensely visualize the negative consequences of giving in to the temptation. Clients may then engage in substitute rewarding activities involving little or no risk.

VISUALIZE EXAGGERATED NEGATIVE CONSEQUENCES Cautela (1967) developed what he termed a 'covert sensitization' approach to undermining the resisting temptations. Clients are encouraged to visualize exaggerated negative consequences whenever an unwanted temptation is anticipated or experienced. For instance, if clients wish to break overeating, and they have targeted rich cakes as a food to avoid, they might practise visualizing the following sequence:

> I am at home, sitting at the table at dinner, and a rich cake is being served. As I see it I start getting nauseous. I accept a piece. As I take my first bite, I vomit all over the table and my clothes. I throw up all my dinner in a disgusting smelly mess. Seeing and smelling my vomit makes me retch even more violently. I feel very weak and faint. Everybody is looking at me in disgust. As I get up from the table, having made up my mind to eat no more, I feel better. I wash, change and feel great to have stopped eating rich food.

I prefer encouraging clients to visualize realistic rather than exaggerated negative consequences. Realistic consequences can be horrific enough. However, some clients may find that exaggeration increases the power of their negative imagery, with a beneficial effect on their willpower.

SKILL 9: MAKE DECISIONS RATIONALLY

Frequently clients are faced with decisions. Such decisions include making choices about jobs and career, major areas of study, college and further education, getting married or divorced, and whether or not to give up a bad habit. Decisions produce varying degrees of conflict and anxiety. Clients may fear the consequences of making the wrong decision, and may be under stress at the time of making the decision: for instance, about leaving college. How can you assist clients to make better decisions and, even more important, to become better decision makers? Basically the main thrust of all helping interventions is to assist clients to make better choices. Here I discuss two areas, decision-making styles and rational decision making, in which you specifically focus on clients' decision-making processes.

Help clients to become aware of their decision-making styles

Clients have styles of decision that may be helpful or harmful (Arroba, 1977). In reality, each client possesses a profile of decision-making styles. Furthermore, they may make different decisions in different ways, and their styles may alter when making decisions in conjunction with other people.

You can assist clients to become more aware of their decision-making styles and their positive or negative consequences. Though far from an exhaustive listing, below are eight styles that describe how people make individual decisions.

- *Rational.* You dispassionately and logically appraise all important information and then select the best option in light of your criteria.

- *Feelings-based.* Though you may generate and appraise different options, the basis for choice is what intuitively feels right. This style emphasizes getting in touch with what you truly feel.

- *Impulsive*. You make decisions rapidly, based on sudden impulses. You act on initial and surface feelings rather than explore and evaluate options.

- *Hypervigilant*. You try too hard. You become so anxious and aroused by the conflict and stress triggered by the decision that your decision-making efficiency decreases. You may become indecisive and fail to see the wood for the trees.

- *Avoidant*. You can cope with decisions by refusing to confront them, hoping they will go away, and procrastinating over them.

- *Conformist*. You conform to what others expect of you. You allow your decisions to be heavily influenced, if not made, by others.

- *Rebellious*. You rebel against what others expect of you. Your decisions are dependent on what others think, though in an oppositional way.

- *Ethical*. The framework for your choice is a code of ethics, be it religious or secular.

Sometimes helpers need to assist clients to become more aware of their styles of joint decision making. Frequently, clients are in situations where they have differences and potential conflicts of interest with others, for instance their partners. The following are three main styles of joint decision making:

- *Competitive*. You operate on an 'I win – you lose' basis and view decisions as competition for scarce resources. You think, and very likely behave, aggressively.

- *Compliant*. You are non-assertive and go along with or give in to the other person. This can be an 'I lose – you win' style.

- *Collaborative*. You both assertively search for a solution that best meets each person's needs. You search for an 'I win – you win too' solution. If necessary, you make rational compromises in the interest of the relationship.

You can assist clients in identifying their decision-making styles and exploring their strengths and weaknesses. Some clients may need to think through the consequences of their decision-making styles more thoroughly: for instance, impulsively choosing friends or buying goods on credit. You require skills such as reflective listening and confrontation when clients explore decision-making styles and their consequences. You may need to challenge clients who distance themselves from responsibility for decisions and who do not perceive their consequences accurately.

Help clients develop rational decision-making skills

Some clients require assistance in learning to make decisions in a systematic fashion. Rational decision making can be viewed as taking place in two main stages: first,

confronting and making the decision; second, implementing and evaluating it. The following is a seven-step framework for rational decision making within the context of these two main stages.

STAGE ONE: CONFRONTING AND MAKING THE DECISION

Step one: confront the decision. Component skills include acknowledging the need for decisions and clearly stating what is the decison to be made.

Step two: generate options and gather information about them. Some clients may be poor at generating options and thus restrict their decision effectiveness. Other skills weaknesses include inability to identify and gather relevant information.

Step three: assess the predicted consequences of options. Clients need accurately to perceive and evaluate positive and negative short-term and long-term consequences of options, both for themselves and for others.

Step four: commit yourself to a decision. Clients need to go beyond making rational decisions to committing themselves to implement them. Clients may have various barriers to commitment, including post-decisional anxieties and conflict (Janis & Mann, 1977).

STAGE TWO: IMPLEMENTING AND EVALUATING THE DECISION

Step five: plan how to implement the decision. Component skills of planning include: stating goals and sub-goals clearly; breaking down tasks; generating and assessing alternative courses of action; anticipating difficulties and setbacks; and identifying sources of support.

Step six: implement the decision. Clients need to consider when best to implement decisions and be open to feedback during implementation. Clients may require skills of rewarding themselves for performing targeted behaviours: for instance by positive self-talk or more tangible rewards, such as a new item of clothing or some special entertainment.

Step seven: assess the actual consequences of implementation. Rational decision making requires accurate perception of feedback and a willingness to act on it. Clients may stick with original decisions or modify or discard them.

Especially if you work in a decision-related area, for instance as a career counsellor, you can make clients more aware of the steps of rational decision making. One approach is to go through the steps, preferably using a whiteboard and then giving clients a handout. In addition, you can request clients to identify decision-making strengths and weaknesses. Take into account previous skills weaknesses when assisting clients to deal with current decisions. Clients can also work through current decisions in terms of the steps of rational decision making. Here focus on developing clients' skills rather than doing the work for

them. For example, rather than saying 'Your options seem to be . . .', you might ask 'What are your options and what information do you require to assess them adequately?'

SKILL 10: PREVENT AND MANAGE PROBLEMS AND ALTER PROBLEMATIC SKILLS

Decision making and problem management overlap. The previous section focused on making decisions at major and minor turning points, where clients needed to decide between different options. Here the focus is on helping clients to use thinking skills to prevent and manage thoughts, feelings and behaviours that are problematic for them.

Help clients to prevent problems

Helpers can assist clients to recognize the preventive function of using good thinking skills in their daily lives. When thinking effectively, clients may be less disposed to a range of problems. Good thinking skills make them more confident persons, less prone to be threatened by imaginery, as opposed to real, difficulties. Clients can also acquire skills of anticipating problems and 'nipping them in the bud'. For example, clients able to anticipate when they are at risk of excessive stress are in a better position to take preventive action than those less aware. Given awareness of the risk of allowing themselves to be excessively stressed, clients may still need to use a range of thinking skills to prevent them from giving in to bad habits, for instance possessing realistic rules about achievement. Also, clients who have come to helping with stress-related problems are never totally cured. They still need to use their thinking skills to prevent recurrences.

Help clients to manage problems and alter problematic skills

Managing problems effectively requires clients to use many of the same skills as for making decisions. Nevertheless, there are important differences, for instance in how problems are assessed and redefined. The lifeskills helping model is basically a self-helping model. Helpers can train clients in how to use the model to manage future problems and problematic skills. The five-stage DASIE model can be modified to CASIE when used for client self-helping purposes.

C *Confront* identify and clarify my problem
A *Assess* my problem and redefine it in skills terms
S *State* working goals and plan self-helping interventions
I *Implement* my plan
E *Evaluate* the consequences of implementing my plan

Because of limited exposure, clients in brief helping are unlikely to learn how to apply the lifeskills helping model to future problems. Clients in longer-term helping will acquire some knowledge of the model as they and their helpers work with the problematic skills underlying their problems. Furthermore, helpers may identify characteristic thinking skills weaknesses. Consequently, longer-term clients have a start in knowing where to look when assessing future problems. In addition, helpers can

systematically train clients in how to prevent and manage problems. Such training may form part of stage 5 of the DASIE helper–client model, end and consolidate self-helping skills. Here helpers may use clients' anticipated future problems as case material for developing preventing and managing problems skills. Helpers require both good relationship and good training skills to impart the DASIE model effectively in its CASIE client self-helping format.

CHAPTER HIGHLIGHTS

- Developing your own thinking skills is a good way to learn how to work with clients' thinking skills.

- When focusing on how clients think, you always require sensitivity to how they feel.

- Helpers and clients can usefully view thinking skills within the PTC (problem, thinking, consequences) and STC (situation, thinking, consequences) frameworks.

- Clients may work better if helpers present them with easily comprehensible rationales for focusing on how they think.

- Interventions for helping clients own responsibility for choosing include: raising consciousness about being a chooser; encouraging choice language; facilitating exploring choices; exploring opposites; confronting clients when they do not acknowledge choice and externalize; exploring defences; and raising consciousness concerning death, dying and finiteness.

- Helpers can both train clients in the calming and coaching dimensions of coping self-talk and also help them to combine self-talk with action.

- Interventions for choosing realistic personal rules emphasize assisting clients to: identify unrealistic rules; put unrealistic rules into the STC framework; dispute unrealistic rules; reformulate unrealistic into realistic rules; and change actions along with reformulated rules.

- Interventions for helping clients choose how they perceive include assisting them to: become aware of the influence of perception on feelings; know the difference between fact and inference; identify their characteristic perceptual distortions; learn to stop, think, generate, evaluate and choose the 'best-fit' perception; and develop reframing skills.

- Helpers can assist clients to develop skills of identifying inaccurate attributions and altering them to more accurate attributions. The skills for perceiving accurately are relevant to attributing accurately.

- Clients may predict risk, reward, or both inaccurately. You can assist clients to become aware of their predictive styles; become aware of current predictions and their consequences; generate and evaluate additional risks or rewards; assess probability; assess their coping capacity and support factors; and reality-test predictions.

- Helpers can assist clients to develop goal-setting skills. Criteria for effective goals include reflecting values, realism, being specific, and having a time frame.

- Helpers may need to develop clients' awareness of visualizing. Areas in which clients can develop visualizing skills include how to relax, perform better, and break bad habits.

- With assistance, clients can become more aware of their decision-making styles and their consequences. In addition, clients can learn to apply the steps of rational decision making.

- The five-stage DASIE lifeskills helping model can be modified to CASIE when used for client self-helping purposes. CASIE's five stages are: (1) confront, identify and clarify my problem; (2) assess my problem and redefine it in skills terms; (3) state working goals and plan self-helping interventions; (4) implement my plan; and (5) evaluate the consequences of using my plan.

ELEVEN

How to Focus on Action Skills

Activity is the only road to knowledge.
George Bernard Shaw

CHAPTER QUESTIONS

Why is it always important to focus on action skills?

Why do helpers need helping relationship skills when developing clients' action skills?

What are some skills for handling resistances to focusing on action skills?

How can helpers develop client self-monitoring skills?

How can helpers assist clients to rehearse action skills?

How can helpers and clients timetable desired activities?

How can helpers and clients plan sub-goals and sequence graded tasks?

How can helpers assist clients to generate and evaluate alternative actions and action skills?

How can helpers and clients design changing action skills experiments?

How can helpers and clients design and use exercises and games?

How can helpers assist clients to use self-reward?

How can helpers use aides?

How can helpers assist clients to identify and use supports?

However well clients feel and think, unless they act more effectively they are unlikely to attain personal goals. Action skills provide the link from the inner to the outer world, from self to others and the environment. Helpers and clients cannot afford to ignore action skills. Whereas the last chapter focused on how to develop clients' thinking skills, their inner game, this chapter focuses on how to develop clients' action skills, their outer game. Action skills entail verbal, voice, body and touch messages. They relate to how clients act when on their own and also with others. Though interrelated, here I focus more on learning new action skills and on developing existing action skills strengths rather than on lessening and extinguishing action skills weaknesses.

Helpers who have inadequately assessed clients may fail to or inadequately intervene on action skills. The following are two examples of inadequate assessment.

Lucy was a beginning helper who brought a cassette of an initial interview to a supervision session. Lucy's client was Katrina, who spent much of the session talking with great intensity about her relationship with Carl, a student in her home economics class. Lucy never asked questions that established how Katrina and Carl actually related. At the end of the session, it emerged that Katrina and Carl had never spent any time outside class on their own. The so-called relationship took place largely within Katrina's head. Lucy had failed to elicit relevant information about how Katrina behaved to enable her to set appropriate action skills goals for subsequent interventions.

Andrew was a beginning helper who brought a cassette of an initial interview with Georgia, aged 17, to a supervison session. Andrew allowed Georgia to talk at great length about how angry she was with her parents' behaviour towards her. Every now and then Georgia would make remarks about how she behaved towards her parents, for instance when she came home from school spending most of her time in her room, and also not making the effort to socialize with her parents' friends. By allowing Georgia's main focus to be on how her parents treated her and never focusing on how Georgia behaved towards her parents, Andrew lost the opportunity to assess Georgia's action skills properly. Indeed, he probably

colluded in keeping Georgia stuck in her present pattern of unproductive behaviour.

When to intervene on action skills

Basically, there are three main options for when to intervene on clients' action skills: action skills before thinking skills; thinking skills before action skills; thinking and action skills together.

ACTION SKILLS BEFORE THINKING SKILLS Without necessarily using skills language, you may early on focus on getting clients to change how they act. A reason for intervening on action skills first is that many clients understand the need to change how they act more easily than the need to change how they think. Throughout helping, some clients work better with an approach focused on overt actions rather than on covert thoughts. Furthermore, some helpers consider that 'It is much easier to change concrete actions, or to introduce new ones, than it is to change patterns of thinking' (Beck, 1988, p. 208). Early successes in changing action can instil confidence. For example, when working with severely depressed patients, Beck initially attempts to restore their functioning to pre-morbid levels through interventions such as scheduling activities (Beck *et al.*, 1979). Early changes in actions can also engender goodwill in others. For instance, distressed couples who see some immediate positive changes in each other's behaviour may create a better emotional climate to work on deeper issues (Beck, 1988; Stuart, 1980).

THINKING SKILLS BEFORE ACTION SKILLS Sometimes both helpers and clients may wish to intervene on thinking skills prior to action skills. For example, clients may have numerous fears about changing their outer behaviour. Changing private thoughts may seem less risky than altering outer behaviour, which is mostly public. You may have to work with clients' fears about performing skills adequately; coping with the consequences of failure; coping with the consequences of success; and reluctance to give up rewarding 'secondary gains'. Often in relationship conflicts, clients may externalize their problems on to partners. You can assist them to see their need for change prior to working with relevant action skills.

THINKING AND ACTION SKILLS TOGETHER Frequently you can simultaneously intervene on thinking and action skills. For example, with clients whose fears about change are not excessive, you can work to overcome such fears when you train relevant action skills. You can focus on thinking and action skills when targeting distressing feelings such as anxiety, anger, shyness and stress. Sometimes a thinking skill forms part of learning an action skill; for example using visualized rehearsal of assertion skills. Thinking skills invariably form part of maintaining action skills: for instance, having a realistic expectation about taking responsibility for maintaining and developing skills after helping. Clients also need to develop the capacity for self-instruction through the sequences of choices entailed in implementing action skills. Then action skills more clearly become self-helping skills.

IMPORTANCE OF THE HELPING RELATIONSHIP AND SUPPORT

Helpers need to create safe and constructive emotional climates for clients to develop action skills. You require helping relationship skills to support client learning both within and outside helping sessions. Also, when focusing on action skills, helpers always require sensitivity to clients' feelings.

Support in-session learning

Why is it important that you remember to use helping relationship skills to develop clients' action skills? The temptation for some helpers is to emphasize the didactive mode at the expense of facilitation. The following are reasons why clients require emotional support as they develop action skills. First, you avoid creating resistances in clients who feel they are taking part in a mechanical 'teacher knows best' process. Second, if feeling supported and understood, clients are more likely to engage in honest initial assessments of their skills strengths and weaknesses. Third, clients can air and work through their reservations about change. Fourth, they may feel freer to take part in decisions about learning goals and processes. Fifth, clients are more likely to motivate themselves and take risks in various learning activities: for instance role plays. Sixth, after structured learning experiences, clients require debriefing. If feeling supported and understood, they may feel freer to give you and themselves honest feedback about progress. Furthermore, they may feel better able to make links between in-session learning and out-of-session reality.

Support out-of-session learning

You can also use helping relationship skills to support out-of-session learning. For example, towards the end of sessions, you can discuss with clients appropriate homework goals and activities. If in a good helping relationship, clients can be more honest about which activities appeal to them and why. They may share fears and anxieties about carrying out tasks, and discuss ways of overcoming anticipated difficulties. Helping relationship skills are also useful when you debrief clients about homework. You can help clients to be honest and accurate in assessing how they acted and its consequences.

Attempts to implement targeted skills in real life can generate strong feelings. Clients may feel discouraged at real or imagined setbacks or elated at real or imagined successes. Effective helpers support clients in their sorrows and joys as they struggle to acquire and apply action skills in their daily lives. Often clients both require and show considerable courage as they use skills outside helping.

MANAGE RESISTANCES TO WORKING ON ACTION SKILLS

Assuming you have thoroughly conducted the first three lifeskills helping stages, you run less risk of eliciting client resistances in the fourth stage, when intervening to

develop action skills. By now clients should have agreed to develop specific action skills. Nevertheless, they may still have resistances of varying degrees of strength: for instance residual resistances about change; resistances about the learning process; and also resistances to applying skills outside helping.

In Chapter 5 I reviewed some helper skills for dealing with initial resistances. These skills were: rewarding listening, joining with clients, giving permission to discuss reluctance and fears, inviting collaboration, enlisting client self-interest, and rewarding silent clients for talking. Most of these skills are relevant to dealing with resistances in the intervention stage. Here I focus on some additional managing resistances skills.

WORK THROUGH CLIENTS' THINKING BLOCKS Go beyond allowing clients to discuss their reluctance and fears to pinpoint the specific thoughts contributing to resistances. You may need to use a mixture of assessment, rewarding listening and questioning skills. (Beck (1988) lists four main 'beliefs' that interfere with partners in distressed relationships changing their behaviour: defeatist beliefs; self-justifying beliefs; reciprocity arguments; and the problem is my partner. Helpers can assist clients to identify such beliefs, challenge the thinking skills weaknesses involved in them – for instance unrealistic prediction and inaccurate attribution – and help them choose more realistic ways of thinking.

BE CLEAR AND SPECIFIC WHEN PRESENTING SKILLS Sometimes clients resist learning action skills because they do not understand them properly. In order to minimize this possibility, develop good presentation and demonstration skills, and check how well clients understand skills.

USE REWARD SKILLS Your genuine interest in helping clients achieve action skills goals should reward their efforts. In addition, you can send verbal and nonverbal positive feedback messages, such as 'Well done', and a smile. You can encourage clients to give themselves positive feedback when they attain goals and sub-goals.

ARRANGE FOR EARLY SUCCESS Where possible, build in an easily attainable goal or sub-goal to allow clients to experience early success. Such success should strengthen their motivation.

UNDERSTAND AND ANTICIPATE DIFFICULTIES Where clients resist using skills in outside settings, find out their reasons for this. Often clients feel that they cannot cope with real or imagined difficulties. Help clients be specific about what might go wrong. Once such fears are out in the open, helpers and clients can develop strategies to deal with them.

USE CONFRONTING SKILLS Reward skills are the carrot, confronting skills are the stick. You can confront clients who state action skills goals and then make little effort to attain them. A possible response to a discrepancy between goal and effort is: 'On the one hand you agreed to _____ [specify] as an action skills goal, yet I experience little enthusiasm or effort on your part to attain it. What do you think of this observation?' In addition,

you can either confront clients or assist clients to confront themselves with the consequences for self and others of not working hard enough on action skills.

ENCOURAGE CLIENTS TO VIEW THEMSELVES AS RESEARCHERS Clients may be more willing to attempt to use action skills outside helping if they do not feel that their whole personhood is at stake. One way of lessening this threat is to encourage them to view attempts to change behaviour as personal experiments in which they try out different behaviours and evaluate what happens. An extreme example of such an approach is Kelly's fixed role therapy, where clients adopt a changed role for a specified period of time to see how it suits them (Kelly, 1955).

DEVELOP CLIENT SELF-MONITORING SKILLS

Here are some examples of clients engaging in systematic self-monitoring:

> Hanif, 17, is trying to stop smoking. As part of his programme, he not only keeps a daily tally of how many cigarettes he smokes, but also keeps a log of the time, antecedents and consequences of each time he smokes.

> Joanna, 53, is receiving help for depression. Joanna has a goal of increasing the number of times she engages in pleasant activities. She keeps a daily chart of each time she engages in a number of specific pleasant activities (Lewinshon *et al.*, 1986).

> Seiji, 39, has had heart problems and is on a weight-loss programme. He keeps a chart listing his daily weight. Each time he eats between meals, he records the time, what happened immediately before, what he eats, and the consequences of his behaviour.

> Theo, 26, is an unemployed client searching for a job. Theo keeps a daily record of each time he engages in a range of specific job-search activities: for instance, making phone calls and written applications.

Systematic self-monitoring or self-observation enables clients to become more aware of their thoughts, feelings and actions. Here the main focus is on self-monitoring of actions. Systematic self-monitoring can be important at the start of, during and after interventions focused on developing specific action skills. Initially, it establishes a baseline and increases awareness. During an intervention, it acts as a reminder, a motivator and a check on progress. Afterwards, self-monitoring is relevant to

maintaining gains, though information may not be collected so systematically as during helping. Self-monitoring is best thought of as an adjunct to other interventions. The effects of self-monitoring as a treatment intervention alone are often short-lived (Thoresen & Mahoney, 1974).

Methods of self-monitoring

DIARIES AND JOURNALS Keeping a diary or journal is one way of monitoring action skills. Clients may pay special attention to writing up critical incidents where skills have been used well or poorly. Although diaries and journals may be useful, some clients find this approach too easy to ignore and too unsystematic.

FREQUENCY CHARTS Frequency charts focus on how many times clients enact a specific behaviour in a given period of time, be it daily, weekly or monthly. For example, clients may add up how many cigarettes they smoke in a day and then transfer this information to a monthly chart broken down by days. Take the earlier example of unemployed Theo recording his job-search behaviours. Theo's helper gives him a Job-Search Activity Self-monitoring Chart and suggests that he fill it in over the next two weeks. The chart lists various job-search activities which can be recorded for each day (Figure 11.1). Where clients are monitoring only single actions, they may use wrist counters or pocket counters (Thoresen & Mahoney, 1974). However, they still need to transfer the information gathered by such methods to frequency charts.

STIMULUS, RESPONSE AND CONSEQUENCES LOGS To become more aware of their behaviour and its consequences, clients can fill in three-column stimulus, response, consequences logs.

Stimulus (What happened?)	Response (How I acted)	Consequences (What resulted?)

For example, clients who work on anger management skills might record each time they feel angry in the stimulus column, what they did in the response column, and the consequences for themselves and others in the consequences column.

SITUATION, THOUGHTS AND CONSEQUENCES LOGS Filling in three-column situations, thoughts and consequences logs can help clients to see the connections between how they think and how they act.

Situation (What happened and when?)	Thoughts (What you thought)	Consequences (How you felt and acted)

Activity	1 M	2 T	3 W	4 Th	5 F	6 Sa	7 Su	8 M	9 T	10 W	11 Th	12 F	13 Sa	14 Su	15 M
Written application															
Phone application															
Letter enquiry															
Phone enquiry															
Cold canvass															
Approach to contact															
Employment centre visit															
Interview attended															

Figure 11.1 *Theo's self-monitoring chart for recording job-search activities*

USE OF TARGETED SKILLS LOGS Helpers and clients need to go beyond monitoring actions to monitoring action skills. During the intervention stage, clients can usefully monitor and evaluate use of targeted skills. For instance, a helper works with a teenager, Lori, on how to make assertive requests to her parents. Together, helper and client agree on the following verbal, voice and body message subskills for each time Lori makes such a request: verbal messages: make 'I' statements and say 'please'; voice messages: speak with a calm, yet firm voice; body messages: use good eye contact and avoid threatening gestures such as finger pointing. Lori's helper asks her to complete an assertive request self-monitoring log after each request to her parents (see Figure 11.2). In particular, the helper asks Lori to record how she uses targeted subskills.

Lori's targeted assertive request skills
Verbal messages: make 'I' statements, say 'please'.
Voice messages: speak calmly and firmly.
Body messages: use good eye contact, avoid threatening gestures.

Date and situation	How I acted		
	Verbal skills	Voice skills	Body skills
1.			
2.			
3.			
4.			
5.			
6.			
7.			
8.			

Figure 11.2 *Lori's log for monitoring assertive request skills*

Helper skills for assisting self-monitoring

Since self-monitoring tends to take place outside sessions, helper skills for assisting clients' self-monitoring overlap with those for assigning homework. Below are some ways helpers can assist clients to monitor themselves and to develop self-monitoring skills.

OFFER REASONS FOR SELF-MONITORING Clients are not in the habit of systematically recording observations about how they act. You need to motivate them to do so. You may make explanatory remarks like, 'Counting how many times you perform a behaviour daily not only indicates how severe your problem is but also gives us a baseline against which to measure your progress in dealing with it', or 'Systematically writing down how you send verbal, voice and action messages each time you make a behaviour change request provides us with information we need to build your skills.'

TRAIN CLIENTS IN DISCRIMINATION AND RECORDING Thoresen and Mahoney observe: 'Individuals are not naturally accurate self-observers. Training in the discrimination and recording of behavior is essential' (1974, p. 63). Clients require clarity not only about what to record, but about how to record it. In addition, they need to

become aware of any tendencies they have to misperceive or selectively perceive their actions: for instance, being more inclined to notice skills weaknesses than skills strengths.

DESIGN SIMPLE AND CLEAR RECORDING LOGS Always supply the log yourself; do not expect clients to make up their own. They may not do so in the first place and, if they do, they may get it wrong. Simple recording systems enhance comprehension and recording accuracy.

USE REWARD SKILLS Reward clients with interest and praise when they fill in logs. This guideline is based on the basic behavioural principle that actions that are rewarding are more likely to be repeated. Furthermore, always reward clients by debriefing when they finish self-monitoring tasks.

ENCOURAGE CLIENTS TO EVALUATE SELF-MONITORING INFORMATION When clients share self-monitoring logs with you, use this as a basis for self-exploration and evaluation. When debriefing, assist them to understand the meaning of the information they have collected. However, do not do their work for them. After helping ends you are not going to be around to assess the implications of their frequency counts and self-monitoring logs. You need to train them in how to do this for themselves.

USE OTHER SKILLS-BUILDING STRATEGIES Do not expect clients to develop action skills on the basis of self-observation alone. They are likely to require other interventions, for example behaviour rehearsals, to develop action skills. Furthermore, they must work and practise to acquire and maintain skills.

CONDUCT ACTION SKILLS REHEARSALS AND ROLE PLAYS

Learning any skill generally requires repeated performances of targeted behaviours. Rehearsals may take place immediately after initial coached performance of skills or later, as clients apply targeted skills in their daily lives and as they seek further assistance during helping.

Methods of rehearsal

Different methods of rehearsing action skills include the following.

LIVE REHEARSAL Live rehearsals can take place both within and outside helping sessions. For instance, the skills of progressive muscular relaxation can be rehearsed within and outside interviews. Bandura's participant modelling approach is an example of live rehearsal within helping sessions. Here helpers use rehearsal and practice with clients who have repeated trials in graded steps with such stimuli as snakes (Bandura, 1976; Jeffrey, 1976). Helpers assist clients to perform and rehearse feared actions by allowing them to use response aids, for instance gloves for those afraid of snakes or furry animals.

Live rehearsals can take place outside helpers' offices, with or without helpers present. For instance, in working with agoraphobic clients, helpers might rehearse targeted skills by taking them into real-life anxiety-evoking settings. Much live rehearsal takes place without helpers. Sometimes such rehearsal takes place in private: for instance practising public speaking with a cassette recorder or in front of a mirror. On other occasions, clients may rehearse skills in 'sheltered environments', for example with cooperative friends or relatives. Or clients may rehearse skills by using them in real-life situations. Here using skills in less difficult situations may be a rehearsal for using them in more difficult ones.

ROLE PLAY In role plays, clients rehearse action skills in simulated or pretend situations involving one or more others. Most often helpers play the part of the other person, but sometimes clients switch roles. Examples of role-playing to rehearse action skills include rehearsing job interview skills, discussing vocational choices with parents, phoning to ask for a date, and expressing appreciation to employees.

ROLE PLAY WITH ACCOMPANYING SELF-TALK An addition to role play is to train clients in the accompanying self-talk. For instance, before Michael proceeds with action role plays on discussing vocational choices with his parents, his helper rehearses him in calming and coaching self-talk. During the role plays Michael's helper responds as a parent in different ways, for instance either being accepting or raising objections. With each variation, Michael verbalizes appropriate self-talk.

VISUALIZED REHEARSAL Visualized rehearsal, also known as imaginal or covert rehearsal, is a form of mental rehearsal involving images. The images in visualized rehearsal are usually of actual rather than role-played scenes. As such, visualized rehearsals are often stepping stones to transferring skills to live situations. Clients imagine themselves actually asking girls for dates or discussing their vocational choices with parents. Clients can also imagine themselves using calming and coaching self-talk. Often helpers assign visualized rehearsal as homework.

Skills for assisting rehearsal

Many helper skills for assisting clients in rehearsing action skills overlap with those of coaching: for example giving clear instructions, breaking tasks down and using feedback skills. Here my focus is on action role plays of outside helping situations where clients require the targeted skills. The following are some helper skills for role-play rehearsals.

PRESENT A RATIONALE Some clients may find the idea of role-playing offputting. For example, they may be self-conscious about their acting skills. You may need to offer a rationale to clients to ease anxieties and help motivate them. Here is a rationale for using role-play rehearsal with a client, Darren, who gets excessively angry when his teenage daughter, Virginia, comes home late.

> Darren, I think it would be helpful if we role-played
> how you might use your new skills to cope better with

Virginia next time she comes home late. I realize that it may seem artificial acting the scene here. However, role-playing gives us the chance to rehearse different ways you might behave – your words, voice messages, and body messages – so that you are better prepared for the real event. It is safer to make mistakes here where it doesn't count. There is no substitute for learning by doing. What do you think about this approach?

SET THE SCENE Elicit information about the physical setting of proposed scenes, what other characters are involved, and how they behave. If you are to role-play someone, for instance Virginia, collect sufficient information about Virginia's verbal, voice and body messages for you to get into the role. Depending on what sort of office you have, you may be able to move the furniture around to create a 'stage', for instance a family living room.

ASSESS CURRENT ACTION SKILLS Usually, you spend time well if you conduct assessment role plays in which clients demonstrate how they currently act in problem situations. You can elicit much relevant information about nonverbal communication that may not be apparent if clients only talk about how they act. Assessment role plays can also review how clients think in the situations.

FORMULATE CHANGED ACTIONS Collaborate with clients to formulate new and better ways of acting that use targeted lifeskills, yet feel 'comfortable' for clients. Facilitate clients' suggestions prior to making your own. You may ask, 'How do you think you might use your new skills to behave differently in the situation?' Together with clients, you can generate and review alternative scripts, and review appropriate voice and body messages. As part of this process you may demonstrate appropriate action skills. In addition, review with clients how to cope with different responses by others.

REHEARSE CHANGED ACTIONS Once clients are reasonably clear about their new roles and helpers understand their 'parts', trial enactments or rehearsals take place. Avoid trying to do too much or anything too difficult too soon. You may allow role plays to run their course. Alternatively, you may intervene at one or more points along the way to provide feedback and coach. Rehearsal role plays are dry runs of how to use action skills in specific situations. Video feedback may be used as part of coaching both during and after role plays. You may need a number of rehearsals to build clients' skills. Some of these may involve responding in different ways to clients. For example, clients asking for dates by phone may get accepted, postponed or rejected in separate role plays.

Role reversal and mirroring are psychodrama techniques that you may use (Blatner, 1989; Moreno, 1959). In role reversal, you get clients to play the other person in interactions. Role reversals force clients to get some way into another's internal viewpoint. With mirroring, you 'mirror back' clients' verbal, voice and body messages. Clients see themselves as others experience them.

REHEARSE THINKING SKILLS You may rehearse clients' thinking skills alongside action skills. For example, you can rehearse clients in the calming and coaching dimensions of appropriate self-talk to accompany new action skills, and in other thinking skills relevant to targeted action skills. For instance, rehearsing visualizing restful scenes can accompany rehearsing relaxing by means of progressive muscular relaxation.

PROCESS ROLE PLAYS Processing involves spending time dealing with clients' thoughts and feelings generated by role plays. Together you can discuss learnings from them, and make plans to transfer rehearsed skills outside. You can ask clients processing questions like, 'How were you feeling in that role play?', 'How well do you think you used your skills in that rehearsal?', 'What have you learned in that role play to use outside?', and, 'What difficulties do you anticipate in implementing your changed behaviour and how can you overcome them?' After processing the previous role play, helpers and clients may move on to the next, either with the same or with another problem situation.

TIMETABLE ACTIVITIES

Helpers can work with clients to timetable desired activities and to build clients' skills in this area. How helpers assist in timetabling activities varies according to clients' needs.

Areas for timetabling

The following are some areas in which timetabling may assist clients to perform desired activities and to build action skills. Figure 11.3 shows a blank weekly timetable that can serve numerous purposes.

TIMETABLING DAILY ACTIVITIES Beck and his colleagues (Beck & Emery, 1985; Beck *et al.*, 1979) stress the usefulness of developing daily activity schedules for clients who are immobilized by depression and anxiety. Helpers and clients collaborate to plan specific activities for one day at a time. These planned activities are recorded on a weekly timetable, with days represented by columns and hours represented by rows. As clients develop skills and confidence, they can do their own activity scheduling, with the last activity for one day being the scheduling of the following day. To ease pressure, you can instruct clients to state what rather than how much they will accomplish and to realize that it is okay not to complete all activities – the important thing is to try.

TIMETABLING MINIMUM GOALS Some clients get extremely anxious over performing certain tasks and then engage in avoidance behaviour. For instance, Alison is a college student who is very distressed because she is not studying. She has lost all sense of control over her work. One approach to Alison is to assist her to timetable some minimum goals that she feels prepared to commit herself to keeping before the next session. Her minimum goals may be as little as three half-hour study periods during the week. For each study period, Alison needs to write down time, task and place. This does not mean that she cannot spend more time studying if she wishes. With certain highly anxious clients, helpers need to be very sensitive to avoid becoming just another source

of pressure. The idea of timetabling minimum goals is to show clients that they can succeed in achieving modest targets instead of having to achieve large targets. Later on Alison may increase her study periods.

Date							
Time	Monday	Tuesday	Wednesday	Thursday	Friday	Saturday	Sunday
6.00							
7.00							
8.00							
9.00							
10.00							
11.00							
12.00							
1.00							
2.00							
3.00							
4.00							
5.00							
6.00							
7.00							
8.00							
9.00							
10.00							

Figure 11.3 *Weekly timetable*

TIMETABLING TO CREATE PERSONAL SPACE Many clients need timetabling skills to prioritize and create personal space. Such clients include housewives trying to stop being at everyone's beck and call; stressed executives needing to create family and relaxation time; depressed people needing to timetable more pleasant activities; and students needing to plan their study time so that they know when they can say 'yes' rather than 'no' to requests to go out. Helpers can assist clients to define personal space goals and to allocate time accordingly.

TIMETABLING TO KEEP CONTRACTS Clients make commitments to perform certain activities to themselves, to helpers and to third parties, for instance their spouses. You

can assist clients to develop skills of keeping commitments by getting them to timetable when they are going to carry out these activities. For instance, Alan is a teenager who has been resisting doing any of the household chores. He finally decides he is prepared to mow the lawn each week. Alan may be more likely to keep this commitment if he timetables when he is going to perform the task.

TIMETABLING HOMEWORK Certain homework activities lend themselves to being timetabled at regular times: for instance, practising progressive muscular relaxation or planning an activity schedule for the next day. Other homework activities do not lend themselves so easily to regular scheduling, but are more likely to be performed if clients timetable them. For instance, homework for Jim, an unemployed executive, includes developing an effective career résumé, a task he has avoided. Jim is more likely to complete this task and to develop career-résumé-making skills if he sets aside specific periods of time to do it properly.

Some skills for timetabling

As shown above, many reasons exist why helpers and clients use timetabling. Below are some helper skills for using timetabling to develop action skills.

Provide timetables. Give clients timetables. Do not expect them to have easy access to made-up timetables or to make the effort to develop their own.

Offer reasons for timetabling. For some clients the need to timetable activities and goals is obvious. Other clients require an explanation. You may need to confront certain clients who insufficiently acknowledge the negative consequences of their failure to timetable.

Be sensitive to anxieties and resistances. Timetabling can be very threatening to highly anxious clients – they feel failures if they do not do as agreed. Be very sensitive how much pressure timetabling creates for vulnerable clients. Some clients may play timetabling games – either consciously or unconsciously they have little intention of achieving goals.

Do not overdo timetabling. Even with less vulnerable clients, helpers may overdo timetabling. Clients can spend too much time scheduling activities and too little time carrying them out.

Review progress. At the next session, check with clients on progress in adhering to timetabled activities and on any difficulties experienced.

Work with thinking skills. Often the reasons why clients do not adhere to timetables reflect faulty thinking skills, for instance perfectionist rules about achievement. Identify and work with interfering thinking skills weaknesses.

Help clients to develop timetabling skills. Always work closely with clients regarding what goes in the timetable. Aim to help them develop timetabling skills so that you can 'fade' away from assisting them.

PLAN SUB-GOALS AND SEQUENCE GRADED TASKS

When helpers attempt to develop clients' action skills, planning sub-goals and sequencing graded tasks overlap. Helpers may plan sub-goals in two main ways.

Sequencing subskills

When assisting clients to learn complex skills, you can break the skills down into their component parts. Then decide in what order they wish to train each component. For example, Lori and her helper have the overall goal of being able to make assertive requests to her parents. However, Lori's helper decided during their sessions to focus on verbal messages first, voice messages second, and body messages third. To date, there appears to have been little research on how helpers can best sequence subskills.

Sequencing graded tasks

Sequencing graded tasks is sometimes called graded task assignment (Beck *et al.*, 1979) or setting proximal sub-goals (Bandura, 1986). A useful distinction is that between setting distant and proximal, or nearer, goals. The research evidence is equivocal regarding the effectiveness of setting distant goals (Bandura, 1986; Whelan *et al.*, 1991). More certain appears the desirability of setting proximal goals or sub-goals (Bandura, 1986; Stock & Cervone, 1990). Bandura observes that, 'Subgoals provide present guides and inducements for action, while subgoal attainments produce efficacy information and self-satisfactions that sustain one's efforts along the way' (1986, p. 475).

The following is an example of sequencing graded tasks to develop action skills.

Ron is a shy college student with an action skills goal of developing his dating skills. Together Ron and his helper draw up a sequence of graded tasks that Ron thinks he can complete before their next session.

1. Say 'hello' to the girls in my class when I see them on campus.
2. Sit down in the student union with a group of classmates of both sexes and join in the conversation.
3. Sit next to a girl in my class and initiate a very brief conversation in which I ask her what she thinks about the class.
4. Sit next to a girl in class and hold a slightly longer conversation in which I make a personal disclosure at least once.

Near the start of the next session, Ron and his helper review progress in attaining each task. The helper facilitates Ron in sharing thoughts and feelings about progress. The helper emphasizes that Ron is achieving his sub-goals as a result of his willingness to take risks, his effort and his skill. As a result of feedback Ron gets from others and gives himself about his growing skills, the helper and he develop further graded tasks for the next between-session period. At progress reviews the helper rewards Ron for working to develop his skills whether or not he is successful. For instance, when Ron eventually asks a girl for a date, the helper rewards him for effort, even if she refuses. The helper encourages Ron to view as learning experiences all attempts to attain graded tasks.

Skills for sequencing and reviewing graded tasks

RELATE GRADED TASKS TO TARGETED SKILLS Always make links between tasks and skills. The purpose of graded tasks is not only to assist clients to manage specific problems, but also to help them develop specific skills. You can encourage clients to view graded tasks as ways of developing their skills for handling not just immediate but future problems.

SEQUENCE GRADED TASKS IN COLLABORATION WITH CLIENTS Work with clients to assess whether they feel willing and able to work on graded tasks. Discuss with them the tasks that are important to them. When sequencing tasks, go at a comfortable pace. Start with small steps which clients think they can achieve. Be prepared to build in intermediate steps if clients think the progression of tasks is too steep. As depicted in Figure 11.4, graded tasks should be stepping-stones for clients to develop skills and confidence.

ENCOURAGE REALISTIC EVALUATION OF SKILLS Before they attempt graded tasks, encourage clients to assess what skills they need to attain them. Also. when reviewing progress, assist clients to evaluate use of targeted skills.

ENCOURAGE CLIENTS TO VIEW THEMSELVES AS PRACTITIONER-RESEARCHERS To avoid connotations of failure, encourage clients to view attempting each graded task as an experiment in which they gain valuable information about themselves. Even if unsuccessful, attempting tasks provides useful learning experiences about how clients think, feel and act.

PAY ATTENTION TO FEELINGS AND THOUGHTS Facilitate clients in sharing their feelings and thoughts about attempting graded tasks. Work with clients' thinking skills weaknesses as necessary.

Figure 11.4 *Graded tasks as stepping-stones for developing skills and confidence*

ASSIST CLIENTS TO OWN SUCCESSES Encourage clients not only to acknowledge their successes, but also help them to realize that success results from willingness to take risks, and from skills and effort.

SEQUENCE NEW AND DIFFERENT TASKS AS APPROPRIATE In collaboration with clients, sequence either easier or more difficult tasks as necessary.

ENCOURAGE HOMEWORK AND PRACTICE Though some graded tasks are performed within helping sessions, most are performed outside. Where feasible, encourage clients to rehearse and practise graded tasks before trying them. Repeated success experiences with specific tasks consolidate clients' skills and confidence.

ASSIST CLIENTS TO GENERATE AND EVALUATE ALTERNATIVE ACTIONS AND ACTION SKILLS

Many clients act in repetitive ways as if they had no choice. In Chapter 10 I discussed helping clients to stop, think, generate, evaluate and choose the best-fit perception. Here I shift the focus to helping clients generate and assess alternative actions and action skills. Clients' thinking skills weaknesses provide many blocks to adequately considering alternative actions: for instance, spouses continually externalizing blame to partners are likely not only to think but to act rigidly. In such instances, helpers need to work with relevant thinking skills as well as with action skills. On other occasions, clients may simply have developed a style of acting where they either do not consider

alternatives at all, do not consider enough of them, or do not consider them in skills terms. Below are some examples:

Khalid, 11, thinks that the only way to act when he feels angry with another boy is to punch him.

Harriet, 32, criticizes her children vehemently whenever they leave their rooms untidy.

Frances, 58, longs for a phone call from her son Ben. When Ben finally calls, Frances starts complaining that he did not call sooner.

Helper skills for assisting clients to generate and assess alternative actions and action skills

ASSIST CLIENTS TO DEFINE GOALS In the above examples, you could work with Khalid, Harriet and Frances to clarify what they wanted from their overall relationships with peers, children and son, respectively. Then you could assist them in stating appropriate goals for specific situations: for example, feeling provoked by another boy, getting frustrated over untidy rooms, and feeling hurt by the lack of a phone call.

TRAIN CLIENTS IN APPROPRIATE SELF-TALK Assist clients to become aware that they always have choices in how they act. They do not have to act out their first idea of how to behave. Instead they instruct themselves to say, 'Stop, think, what are my goals? What are alternative ways to attain them and what action skills do I need?'

MAINTAIN A SKILLS FOCUS Help clients to analyse their behaviour in skills terms. It is insufficient to think of alternative actions without also thinking of the skills entailed in such actions. For instance, if Harriet decides that her best course of action is to sit down and talk to her children, she still needs to work on the verbal, voice and body message skills of doing this effectively.

ASSIST CLIENTS TO GENERATE ALTERNATIVES In addition to rewarding listening, here are some helper skills for assisting clients to generate alternatives:

- *Use questions*. Some questions that helpers might ask: 'What are your options for how you act?', and 'What action skills do you need to attain your goal?'

- *Confront*. Helpers can ask questions that encourage clients to confront themselves: for example, 'Is your present way of acting likely to help you attain your goals?' or 'How is your current behaviour helping you?' Helpers may also confront directly: 'The course of action you propose seems contrary to your goals. Are there any other approaches?'

- *Assist brainstorming*. Helpers can loosen clients' thinking by getting them to brainstorm options. Two rules for brainstorming are: quantity is good, and suspend

evaluation of ideas until later. Encourage clients to generate options before suggesting options yourself.

- *Assist exploring opposite ways of acting.* Sometimes, though not always, clients gain valuable insights by exploring the opposite ways of acting to current intentions. For instance, the spouse who is going to give her husband a piece of her angry mind might explore being nice and taking a conciliatory approach to him.

ASSIST CLIENTS TO EVALUATE ALTERNATIVES Assist clients to evaluate the consequences for themselves and others of alternative actions. When evaluating different courses of action, helpers and clients need to pay close attention not only to what is done, but also to how it is done. As a result of evaluating alternatives, clients should choose the 'best-fit' course of action that is most likely to help them attain their goals.

SUPPORT CLIENTS IN IMPLEMENTING 'BEST-FIT' ACTIONS AND ACTION SKILLS Support clients as they implement their chosen actions in real life. For instance, you can work with them to identify and develop relevant skills for their 'best-fit' actions. Offer support and encouragement to clients who are developing skills for generating and evaluating alternative actions outside helping.

USE ACTION SKILLS EXPERIMENTS

A major concern of all effective helpers is how best to help clients take the risks in changing their behaviours. Another major concern is how best to help them transfer trained skills to outside helping. Action skills experiments provide an excellent way to approach both concerns. Clients in conjunction with helpers develop hypotheses about the consequences of using outside helping the skills they learn inside. Then clients implement the skills and evaluate the consequences of their changed behaviour. An advantage of viewing changing action skills in experimental terms is that it helps clients to be detached about what they do and its results. When experiments do not work out quite as planned, clients do not have to think they have failed; each experiment is a learning experience that gathers information useful for developing action skills.

Often experiments simultaneously focus on changing both thinking and action skills. For instance, Kevin wants to increase his skills at showing affection to his girlfriend Tanya. An experiment focused solely on action skills might target Kevin's skills at sending verbal, voice and body messages of affection. An experiment focused solely on thinking skills might target Kevin's skills of coping self-talk before, during and after he sends affection messages. An experiment focused on both action and thinking skills would target both how Kevin sends affection messages to Tanya and his use of coping self-talk. In this section, for the sake of simplicity, I focus on changing action skills experiments.

Steps in action skills experiments

Experiments focus on the use of targeted skills in specific situations or relationships. There are six main steps in designing, conducting and evaluating action skills experiments.

1. *Assess*. Helpers and clients assess clients' action skills strengths and weaknesses in problem situations.

2. *Formulate changed action skills*. Helpers and clients work out how to behave differently in situations by using better action skills. They pay attention to voice and body messages as well as to verbal messages.

3. *Make an 'If . . . then . . .' statement*. The 'If' part of the statement relates to clients rehearsing, practising and then using their changed action skills. The 'then . . .' part indicates the specific consequences they predict will follow from using their changed skills.

4. *Rehearse and practise*. Possibly with assistance from helpers, clients need to rehearse and practise changed action skills to have a reasonable chance of implementing them properly.

5. *Try out changed action skills*. Clients implement changed action skills in actual problem situations.

6. *Evaluate*. Initially clients should evaluate their use of changed action skills on their own. This evaluation should focus on questions like, 'How well did I use my changed action skills?', 'What were the positive and negative consequences for using the targeted skills for myself and for others?', 'Have my predictions been confirmed or negated?', and 'Do I want to use my changed action skills in future?' Afterwards helpers can assist clients in processing the learnings from their experiments.

Example of designing an action skills experiment

The following is an illustrative outline for an experiment in which Kevin uses targeted action skills in how he expresses appreciation to Tanya.

WHAT HAPPENS WHEN I USE MY ACTION SKILLS FOR EXPRESSING APPRECIATION TO TANYA

PART A: ASSESSMENT
1. For a period of a week, monitor on a worksheet how I send expressing affection messages to Tanya. Focus strengths and weaknesses in each of the following subskills of expressing affection: verbal, voice, body, touch and action messages. Use the following column headings on my worksheet:

Date and situation	Expressing affection messages

2. List all the positive thoughts and feelings that I either fail to or inadequately convey in our relationship.

_____

_____

_____

_____

3. Based on the answers to questions 1 and 2 above, assess my action skills strengths and weaknesses in sending affection messages to Tanya. Use the following column headings:

Expressing affection skills strengths	Expressing affection skills weaknesses

PART B: MAKE AN 'IF . . . THEN . . .' STATEMENT

Make an 'If . . . then' statement along the lines of:
'*If* I use the following changed action skills [specify] to express affection to Tanya during the next week, *then* these specific consequences [for instance, (a) I will feel better about myself for being honest, and (b) Tanya will feel and act more positively towards me] are likely to follow.'

If _____

_____

then

a) _____
b) _____
c) _____
d) _____

PART C: TRY OUT AND EVALUATE USING MY ACTION SKILLS

During the next week, try out using my changed action skills in expressing affection to Tanya. What are the positive and negative consequences for myself and Tanya? Have my predictions been confirmed or negated? Have I learned anything useful from this experiment? If so, what?

_____

_____

_____

_____

USE EXERCISES AND GAMES

Exercises are structured activities designed with a specific learning purpose. The training manual that accompanies this book contains numerous exercises that I designed to build your lifeskills helping skills. Whether for children or adults, exercises involving play are called games. Helpers may assist clients to develop action skills, thinking skills and action skills with accompanying self-talk by using exercises and games. Clients may use these materials both within sessions and also as homework assignments.

There are two main sources of exercises and games: using other people's or making up your own. Using the relationship skills area as an example, existing sources of exercices include those in Egan's *You and Me* (Egan, 1977), Johnson's *Reaching Out* (Johnson, 1990), the present writer's *Human Relationship Skills* (Nelson-Jones, 1990) and Pfeiffer and his associates' series *The (date) Annual Developing Human Resources* (Pfeiffer *et al.*, 1972–92).

Other people's material may not be appropriate either for the clientele or for specific individuals with whom you work. If so you may need to construct some exercises. Such exercises are particularly cost-effective if they can be used repeatedly. For instance, helpers who work with clients, many of whom have relationship difficulties, might often use exercises on making assertive requests to change others' behaviours. I encourage you not only to use existing material, but also to tap your creativity in designing learning material tailor-made to your clients and needs.

Designing exercises

The following are guidelines in designing exercises and games.

Set clear, specific and relevant goals. Clients should be clear about the targeted skills they are expected to work on in the exercise. Helpers should present and demonstrate these skills prior to asking clients to do exercises in them.

Emphasize take-away skills. Exercises should be highly practical and focused on learning by doing. Avoid vague exercises unrelated to the development of specific take-away skills. Many beginning trainees have difficulty putting sufficient practical emphasis into their exercises.

Make written instructions available. Ensure that clients are clear about and remember an exercise's instructions. Written instructions, as contrasted with verbal instructions, lessen the chance of slippage when clients perform exercises.

Demonstrate the exercise. Demonstrate exercises between giving instructions and asking clients to perform them. Such demonstrations go beyond demonstrating skills or subskills to show how to do the exercise.

Coach and provide feedback. Where necessary, coach clients on how to do the exercise.

Process the experience. When clients have completed the exercise, give them the opportunity to share their thoughts and feelings about it. Ensure that clients understand the main learnings from the exercise.

Pilot the exercise. If possible, pilot your exercise to see if it works. If necessary, refine the exercise or even discard it and try again.

ASSIST CLIENTS TO USE SELF-REWARD

Helpers may choose to use reinforcement or reward to help develop action skills. Helper-administered rewards include praise, encouragement, smiles and nods. However, ultimately clients have to learn to perform targeted action skills independent of your rewards. They may also influence and administer their own rewards. Approaches using helper-administered and client-administered rewards as based on operant conditioning (Skinner, 1953, 1969). The word 'operant' emphasizes the fact that behaviour operates on the environment to produce consequences as well as being influenced by or contingent upon the responses produced by that environment. Where clients find responses rewarding, the probability of their using the action skills again increases, and vice versa.

Basic concepts

Here I use the everyday word 'reward' in preference to the more technical term 'reinforcement', because reward better suits the language of self-helping. Some basic reward concepts are as follows:

- *Positive reward*. Providing positive rewards entails presenting stimuli that increase the probability of responses occurring: for example, money increases the probability of work responses. Positive rewards can be verbal, material and imaginal.

- *Negative reward*. Negative reward also increases the probability of a response occurring through removing something from the situation: for example, removing teachers from classrooms increases the probability of pupils talking.

- *Contingencies of reward*. To consider adequately the contingencies or circumstances involved in the provision of rewards, take into account: (1) the occasion upon which a response occurs; (2) the response itself; (3) the rewarding consequences.

- *Schedules of reward*. Basically there are three reward schedules: reward each response; do not reward any response; and intermittently reward responses. Intermittent rewards can be very powerful: for instance, in sustaining gambling behaviour.

- *Self-reward*. Here clients influence how they act by administering their own rewards.

- *Prompting and fading.* Prompts are verbal, physical or environmental cues that direct clients' attention to desired actions. Fading entails progressively eliminating prompts.

- *Shaping.* Action skills may be shaped by rewarding successive approximations to targeted goals.

- *Covert conditioning.* Using clients' imaginations to provide consequences of varying degrees of reward.

Assist clients to identify suitable rewards

In many instances, clients find that using targeted action skills is both intrinsically rewarding and brings about rewards from others. For instance, clients developing appreciation skills may enjoy using paying compliments skills, give pleasure and also receive it. On other occasions clients may need to strengthen their motivation by self-administering rewards. The basic idea in using self-reward to develop action skills is that clients make the administration of rewards contingent upon occurrence of target behaviours (Watson & Tharp, 1989). Rewards should be accessible and potent (Cormier & Cormier, 1985). Consequently, you may need to assist clients in identifying suitable rewards. There are several ways of helping clients identify rewards, including asking them; getting them to monitor what they find rewarding; asking others who know them, though here you must be sensitive to confidentiality; observing them; and asking them to fill out reward questionnaires.

MacPhillamy and Lewinsohn's Pleasant Events Schedule is an example of an identifying rewards questionnaire (Lewinsohn *et al.*, 1986; MacPhillamy & Lewinsohn, 1982). The questionnaire consists of 320 'pleasing events'. Respondents rate each item on 3-point scales for frequency and pleasantness during the previous month. The authors believe that one way to combat clients' feelings of depression is to encourage them to participate in more rewarding activities. Illustrative pleasant events include: being with happy people; thinking about friends; breathing clean air; listening to music; reading a good book; petting and necking; eating good meals; being seen as sexually attractive; seeing beautiful scenery; and visiting friends.

For children, pictures may portray rewards. An example is Daley's 'reinforcement menu' for finding effective rewards for 8–11-year-old mentally retarded children (Daley, 1969). Daley enclosed twenty-two high probability rewarding activities drawn in colour in a single book or 'menu' with one activity per page. Children identified rewarding activities from the 'menu' book.

Assist clients to deliver self-rewards

Helpers can assist clients in knowing how to deliver positive self-rewards. There are two main categories of reward that clients can self-administer: external and internal.

- *External reward.* External reward includes: (1) self-administration of new rewards that are outside the client's everyday life, such as a new item of clothing or a special

event; and (2) initial denial of some pleasant everyday experience and later administration of it contingent upon a desired action. Kanfer and Gaelick (1986) observe that wherever possible a positive self-reward should be relevant to the target behaviour: for instance clients who achieve weight-loss goals might buy slimmer-fitting clothes.

- *Internal reward.* Internal reward includes self-talk statements like 'That's great', 'I did it', or 'Well done' that clearly indicate the client's satisfaction at performing a sub-goal or goal. Clients can use their imaginations to visualize significant others praising their efforts.

Work with clients to determine the precise conditions for self-administering rewards. In making positive self-reward plans, several considerations may be pertinent: identification of rewards; sequencing of graded steps in developing action skills; and clear connections between achievement and reward. It is best for clients to reward themselves immediately after performing targeted action skills or subskills.

Helpers may encourage clients to draw up personal contracts that specify the relationship between administering positive self-rewards and developing targeted action skills. Alternatively, you and your clients may draw up contracts between yourselves. Such bilateral contracts are a transitional phase in plans aimed at developing clients' self-helping skills.

Not all clients like self-reward plans or follow them. Some consider the use of self-reward too mechanical. Also, you may introduce self-reward ideas too soon, before clients are sufficiently motivated to change. You need to assess how clients accept the idea of self-reward, and their motivation for change. Often you need to intervene with clients' thinking skills weaknesses that hinder change.

Assist clients to modify their environments

In addition to helping clients use self-reward, you can assist them in modifying their environments to overcome action skills weaknesses and develop action skills strengths. Clients can modify environments to influence action skills prior to their execution. Often self-reward plans entail clients using both positive self-reward skills and also modifying environment skills.

Helpers can assist clients to develop *stimulus control* skills (Thoresen & Mahoney, 1974). With stimulus control, clients learn to use presence or absence of environmental prompts to influence behaviour. It can be used both to develop strengths and modify weaknesses. An example of the use of stimulus control to enhance an action skills strength is that of students who specify a place that they use only for study. An example of stimulus control to help overcome an action skills weakness is that of Terry who has a goal of losing 25 lb by the end of the next three months. Ways in which Terry modifies her environment to influence her eating skills weakness include putting food out of sight and easy reach; equipping her refrigerator with a time lock; and only keeping as much food in the house as can be consumed in a short period of time. In addition, Terry tries to control her environment by associating with people who are counting calories and interested in exercise.

Terry's helper also encourages her to engage in *stimulus narrowing*. This involves reducing the number of stimuli associated with her eating skills weaknesses. Terry agrees it is a good idea to eat only in the dining room and, where feasible, only in the presence of certain family members.

USE HELPER'S AIDES AND HELP CLIENTS TO OBTAIN SUPPORT

As a helper you may both use third parties to develop clients' action skills and also assist clients to identify and use third parties to support change attempts.

Using helper's aides

Reasons why helpers enlist others as aides include pressure of work and the opportunity to extend interventions into clients' home environments. Helpers may use a variety of people as aides: teachers, parents, paraprofessionals, supervisors and friends. Here are two examples:

> Janie, aged 8, is referred by her teacher, Felicity, to Dorothy, the school counsellor, because she is very shy and does not participate in class. As part of Janie's treatment plan, Dorothy enlists Felicity's help both to ask questions that draw Janie out and also to reward her when she participates in class. In addition, Dorothy asks Felicity to monitor any changes in how well Janie relates to the other children in the playground.

> Rachel, 21, volunteers to be a student paraprofessional 'companion therapist' in a programme to support anorexic and bulimic fellow students undergoing professional treatment at the university counselling service (Lenihan & Kirk, 1990). Rachel undergoes a 25-hour training programme. She then maintains daily personal or phone contact with her allocated client. In addition, she engages in such activities as joint exercise, walking and lunching. Rachel also helps her client monitor nutrition and assists with meal planning and shopping.

The following are skills in selecting and using helper's aides:

Identify suitable aides. Carefully select and screen helpers' aides. They have the potential to do both harm and good.

Obtain client permission. With adults, helpers always need to obtain clients' permissions to discuss their behaviour with 'non-professional' third parties. Clients need to accept the potential usefulness of helpers' aides if they are to work with them. It is sometimes inappropriate to obtain children's permission: for instance, in the above example of Janie's teacher helping her.

Involve aides in planning interventions. Helper's aides such as teachers, parents and supervisors may have special knowledge of how best to support clients in developing action skills. Furthermore, if consulted, aides may be more motivated to participate in treatment plans than if they think plans are imposed on them.

Train aides. Some helper's aides work with many different clients. Where this is the case, effort put into training them may reap rich rewards. Even where aides work with single clients, it is essential that they understand their roles and can competently carry them out.

Support and debrief aides. Keep in touch with aides and make sure that they perform their functions as agreed. Give aides the opportunity to share thoughts and feelings about clients and about their contribution to helping. Where necessary, revise agreements on how your aides should assist.

Withdraw or fade out helper's aide assistance Clients need to learn how to perform action skills without others' assistance. Consider how best to withdraw your aides' assistance. One option is to withdraw all assistance at once. Another option is to progressively withdraw or fade out assistance.

Help clients identify and use supports

Helpers may need to raise some clients' awareness about the importance of identifying and using supports and of lessening contact with unsupportive people. Helpers and clients can work together to identify people in home environments who can support their efforts to develop targeted skills. For example, university students with study skills weaknesses can seek out sympathetic faculty members to help them develop specific skills, for instance how to write essays or prepare for exams. Unemployed people can approach friends and relatives, who may not only offer them emotional support but also be sources for job leads. Women working on developing assertion skills can seek out women's groups where they may find other women with similar objectives. Teachers who feel burned out can associate with colleagues relatively happy with their lot rather than those who are perpetually complaining. Furthermore, they can develop self-care skills by engaging in pleasant activities with people unconnected with education.

An inverse approach to support is for helpers and clients to identify unsympathetic or counterproductive people. Clients are then left with various choices: getting such people to accept, if not support, their efforts to change; seeing less of them; or stopping seeing them. If these people are family members, avoiding them altogether may be difficult, especially if clients are financially dependent on them. Here, helpers and

clients may discuss damage-control strategies. However, often clients can choose their friendship and membership groups. For example, if juvenile delinquents want to develop action skillls that integrate them into the wider community, they may need to change the company they keep (Sarason, 1976).

CHAPTER HIGHLIGHTS

- Action skills interventions require adequate assessment of clients' action skills weaknesses.

- Helpers and clients may focus on action skills before, after or simultaneously with thinking skills.

- Helpers require relationship skills to support inside-session and outside-session development of action skills.

- Skills for managing clients' resistances to working on action skills include: working through thinking blocks; presenting skills clearly; using reward; arranging for early success; understanding and anticipating difficulties; confronting; and encouraging clients to view themselves as practitioner-researchers.

- Diaries and journals, frequency charts and recording logs are methods of client self-monitoring.

- Skills for assisting client self-monitoring include: offering reasons; training clients in discrimination and recording; designing simple and clear logs; using reward; and encouraging clients to evaluate information.

- Methods for rehearsing action skills include live, role play, role play with accompanying self-talk, and visualized.

- Skills for conducting role-play rehearsals include: presenting rationales; setting scenes; assessment; formulating changed actions; rehearsing; and processing.

- Helpers and clients may use timetables to schedule daily activities; set minimum goals; create personal space; keep contracts; and perform homework.

- When assisting timetabling, always provide the timetables and be sensitive to clients' anxieties and resistances.

- Helpers may plan sub-goals either by sequencing subskills or by sequencing graded tasks. Where possible, sequence graded tasks with clients.

- Helpers can assist clients to be more flexible in how they act by helping them develop skills of generating and evaluating alternatives and choosing the 'best-fit' actions and action skills.

- Action skills experiments encourage clients to try out new skills. Six steps in action skills experiments are: (1) assess; (2) formulate changed action skills; (3) make an 'If . . . then . . .' statement; (4) rehearse and practise; (5) try out changed actions; and (6) evaluate.

- Helpers may either use other people's exercises and games or design their own. Exercises and games should emphasize development of practical 'take-away' skills.

- Helpers can assist clients to use self-reward by helping them identify suitable rewards, and self-administer rewards contingent on performance of targeted skills.

- Stimulus control, using or discarding prompts that influence behaviour, is a useful client skill for modifying clients' environments.

- Helpers may use third parties as aides. Select aides carefully and train and support them.

- Helpers can also train clients to identify and use supports in their home environments.

Goddard, R. W. (1989) Use language effectively. *Personnel Journal*, **68**, 32–6.

Goldfried, M. R. (1971) Systematic desensitization as training in self-control. *Journal of Consulting and Clinical Psychology*, **37**, 228–34.

Goldfried, M. R. & Davison, G. C. (1976) *Clinical Behavior Therapy*. New York: Holt, Rinehart & Winston.

Goldstein, A. P. & Keller, H. (1987) *Aggressive Behavior: Assessment and Intervention*. New York: Pergamon.

Good, G. E., Dell, D. M. & Mintz, L. B. (1989) Male role and gender role conflict: relationships to help seeking in men. *Journal of Counseling Psychology*, **36**, 295–300.

Good, G. E., Gilbert, L. A. & Scher, M. (1990) Gender aware therapy: a synthesis of feminist therapy and knowledge about gender. *Journal of Counseling and Development*, **68**, 376–80.

Gordon, T. (1970) *Parent Effectiveness Training: The Tested New Way to Raise Responsible Children*. New York: Wyden.

Grieger, R. (1989) A client's guide to rational-emotive therapy (RET). In W. Dryden & P. Trower (eds) *Cognitive Psychotherapy: Stasis and Change*. London: Cassell, pp. 99–120.

Guerney, B., Stollak, G. & Guerney, L. (1971) The practicing psychologist as educator – an alternative to the medical practitioner model. *Professional Psychology*, **2**, 276–82.

Hall, E. T. (1966) *The Hidden Dimension*. New York: Doubleday.

Hatch, E. J. & Guerney, B. (1975) A pupil relationship enhancement program. *Personnel and Guidance Journal*, **54**, 103–5.

Havighurst, R. J. (1972) *Developmental Tasks and Education* (3rd edn). New York: David McKay.

Henley, N. M. (1977) *Body Politics: Power, Sex, and Nonverbal Communication*. Englewood Cliffs, NJ: Prentice-Hall.

Heppner, P. P., Neal, G. W. & Larsen, L. M. (1984a) Problem-solving training as prevention with college students. *Personnel and Guidance Journal*, **62**, 514–29.

Heppner, P. P., Rogers, M. E. & Lee, L. (1984b) Carl Rogers: reflections on his life. *Journal of Counseling and Development*, **63**, 14–20.

Hewitt, P. L. & Dyke, D. G. (1986) Perfectionism, stress, and vulnerability to depression. *Cognitive Therapy and Research*, **10**, 137–42.

Ho, D. Y. F. (1985) Cultural values and professional issues in clinical psychology: implications from the Hong Kong experience. *American Psychologist*, **40**, 1212–18.

Hoelscher, T. J., Lichstein, K. L., Fischer, S. & Hegerty, T. B. (1987) Relaxation treatment of hypertension: do home relaxation tapes enhance treatment outcome? *Behavior Therapy*, **18**, 33–7.

Holland, J. L. (1973) *Making Vocational Choices: A Theory of Careers*. Englewood Cliffs, NJ: Prentice-Hall.

Hopson, B. & Scally, M. (1981) *Lifeskills Teaching*. London: McGraw-Hill.

Hosford, R. E. & Johnson, M. E. (1983) A comparison of self-observation, self-modeling, and practice without video feedback for improving counselor interview behaviors. *Counselor Education and Supervision*, **23**, 62–70.

Hosford, R. E., Moss, C. S. & Morell, G. (1976) The self-as-a-model technique: helping prison inmates change. In J. D. Krumboltz & C. E. Thoresen (eds) *Counseling Methods*. New York: Holt, Rinehart & Winston, pp. 487–95.

Hutchins, D. E. & Cole, C. G. (1986) *Helping Relationships and Strategies*. Pacific Grove, CA: Brooks/Cole.

Ivey, A. E. (1976) Counseling psychology, the psychoedmentor model and the future. *The Counseling Psychologist*, **6**, 72–5.

Ivey, A. E. (1987) Cultural intentionality: the core of effective helping. *Counselor Education and Supervision*, **26**, 168–72.

Ivey, A. E. (1988) *Intentional Interviewing and Counseling: Facilitating Client Development* (2nd edn). Pacific Grove, CA: Brooks/Cole.

Ivey, A. E., Ivey, M. B. & Simek-Downing, L. (1987) *Counseling and Psychotherapy: Integrating Skills, Theory and Practice* (2nd edn). Englewood Cliffs, NJ: Prentice-Hall.

Jacobson, E. (1929) *Progressive Relaxation.* Chicago: University of Chicago Press.

Jacobson, E. (1938) *Progressive Relaxation* (2nd edn). Chicago: University of Chicago Press.

Jacobson, E. (1976) *You Must Relax.* Boston: Unwin Paperbacks.

Jacobson, N. S. (1989) The maintenance of treatment gains following social learning-based marital therapy. *Behavior Therapy*, **20**, 325–36.

Jacobson, N. S., Follette, V. M., Follette, W. C., Holtzworth-Munroe, A., Katt, J. L. & Schmaling, K. B. (1985) A component analysis of behavioural marital therapy: 1 year follow-up. *Behaviour Research and Therapy*, **23**, 549–55.

Janis, I. L. & Mann, L. (1977) *Decision Making: A Psychological Analysis of Conflict, Choice, and Commitment.* New York: The Free Press.

Jeffrey, R. W. (1976) Reducing fears through participant modeling and self-directed practice. In J. D. Krumboltz & C. E. Thoresen (eds) *Counseling Methods.* New York: Holt, Rinehart & Winston, pp. 301–12.

Johnson, D. (1990) *Reaching Out: Interpersonal Effectiveness and Self-actualization* (4th edn). Englewood Cliffs, NJ: Prentice-Hall.

Jones, J. M. (1990) Correspondence from Associate Professor J. M. Jones, Classics Department, University of Western Australia, dated 2 June.

Kanfer, F. H. & Gaelick, L. (1986) Self-management methods. In F. H. Kanfer & A. P. Goldstein (eds) *Helping People Change: A Textbook of Methods* (3rd edn). New York: Pergamon Press, pp. 283–345.

Kaplan, H. S. (1974) *The New Sex Therapy: Active Treatment of Sexual Dysfunctions.* Harmondsworth, Middlesex: Penguin Books.

Karoly, P. & Harris, A. (1986) Operant methods. In F. H. Kanfer and A. P. Goldstein (eds) *Helping People Change: A Textbook of Methods* (3rd edn). New York: Pergamon Press, pp. 283–345.

Kazdin, A. E. (1976) Developing assertive behaviors through covert modeling. In J. D. Krumboltz & C. E. Thoreson (eds) *Counseling Methods.* New York: Holt, Rinehart & Winston, pp. 475–86.

Kazdin, A. E. (1989) *Behavior Modification in Applied Settings* (4th edn). Pacific Grove, CA: Brooks/Cole.

Kelly, G. A. (1955) *A Theory of Personality: The Psychology of Personal Constructs.* New York: W. W. Norton.

Kendall, P. C. & Hollon, S. D. (1989) Anxious self-talk: development of the anxious self-statements questionnaire (ASSQ). *Cognitive Therapy and Research*, **13**, 81–93.

Kendall, P. C., Hollon, S. D., Beck, A. T., Hammen, C. L. & Ingram, R. E. (1987) Issues and recommendations regarding use of the Beck Depression Inventory. *Cognitive Therapy and Research*, **11**, 289–99.

King, M. L. (1963) *Strength to Love.* Philadelphia, PA: Fortress Press.

Kinsey, A. C., Pomeroy, W. B. & Martin, C. E. (1948) *Sexual Behavior in the Human Male.* Philadelphia, PA: W. B. Saunders.

Kinsey, A. C., Pomeroy, W. B., Martin, C. E. & Gebhard, P. H. (1953) *Sexual Behavior in the Human Female.* Philadephia, PA: W.B. Saunders.

Klingman, A., Melamed, B. G., Cuthbert, M. I. & Hermecz, D. A. (1984) Effects of participant modeling on information acquisition and skill utilization. *Journal of Consulting and Clinical Psychology*, **52**, 414–22.

Kluckhohn, C. (1951) Values and value orientations in the theory of action. In T. Parsons & E.

A. Shils (eds) *Toward a General Theory of Action*. Cambridge, MA: Harvard University Press.

Kohlberg, L. & Gilligan, C. (1971) The adolescent as philosopher: the discovery of the self in a postconventional world. *Daedalus*, **100**, 1051–86.

Kokotovic, A. M. & Tracey, T. J. (1990) Working alliance in the early phase of counseling. *Journal of Counseling Psychology*, **37**, 16–21.

Kruger, A. H. (1970) *Effective Speaking: A Complete Course*. New York: Van Nostrand Reinhold.

Krumboltz, J. D. (1988) The key to achievement: learning to love learning. In G. R. Waltz (ed.) *Building Strong School Counseling Programs*. Alexandria, VA: American Association for Counseling and Development, pp. 1–39.

LaFromboise, T. D., Trimble, J. E. & Mohatt, G. V. (1990) Counseling intervention and American Indian tradition: an integrative approach. *The Counseling Psychologist*, **18**, 628–54.

Laing, R. D. (1969) *The Politics of the Family*. London: Tavistock Publications.

Lazarus, A. A. (1977) *In the Mind's Eye*. New York: The Guildford Press.

Lazarus, A. A. (1981) *The Practice of Multimodal Therapy*. New York: McGraw-Hill.

Lazarus, A. A. (1989) Multimodal therapy. In R. J. Corsini & D. Wedding (eds) *Current Psychotherapies* (4th edn). Itasca, IL: Peacock, pp. 503–44.

Lee, D. Y. & Uhlemann, M. R. (1984) Comparison of verbal responses of Rogers, Shostrum and Lazarus. *Journal of Counseling Psychology*, **31**, 91–4.

Lenihan, G. & Kirk, W. G. (1990) Using student paraprofessionals in the treatment of eating disorders. *Journal of Counseling and Development*, **68**, 332–5.

Lewinsohn, P. M., Munoz, R. F., Youngren, M. A. & Zeiss, A. M. (1986) *Control Your Depression* (rev. edn). New York: Prentice-Hall.

MacPhillamy. D. J. & Lewinsohn, P. M. (1982) The Pleasant Events Schedule: studies on reliability, validity and scale intercorrelation. *Journal of Consulting and Clinical Psychology*, **50**, 363–80.

Maracek, J. & Johnson, M. (1980) Gender and the process of therapy. In A. M. Brodsky & R. Hare-Mustin (eds) *Women and Psychotherapy: An Assessment of Research and Practice*. New York: Guildford Press, pp. 67–93.

Martin, J. (1987) Cognitive change in clients: cognitive-mediational models. *Counselor Education and Supervision*, **26**, 192–203.

Martin, J. (1990) Confusion in psychological skills training. *Journal of Counseling and Development*, **68**, 402–7.

Marx, R. (1982) Relapse prevention for managerial training: a model for maintenance of behavior change. *Academy of Management Review*, **7**, 433–41.

Maslow, A. H. (1962) *Towards a Psychology of Being*. New York: Van Nostrand.

Maslow, A. H. (1970) *Motivation and Personality* (2nd edn). New York: Harper & Row.

Maslow, A. H. (1971) *The Farther Reaches of Human Nature*. Harmondsworth, Middlesex: Penguin Books.

Masterpasqua, F. (1989) A competence paradigm for psychological practice. *American Psychologist*, **44**, 1366–71.

Masters, W. H. & Johnson, V. E. (1970) *Human Sexual Inadequacy*. London: J. A. Churchill.

Mathews, A. M., Gelder, M. G. & Johnston, D. W. (1981) *Programmed Practice for Agoraphobia: Clients' Manual*. London and New York: Tavistock Publications.

May, R. (1958) Contributions of existential psychotherapy. In R. May, E. Angel & H. F. Ellenberger (eds) *Existence*. New York: Basic Books, pp. 37–91.

May, R. & Yalom, I. D. (1989) Existential psychotherapy. In R. J. Corsini & D. Wedding (eds) *Current Psychotherapies* (4th edn). Itasca, IL: Peacock, pp. 363–402.

McCarthy, P. R. (1982) Differential effects of counselor self-referent responses and counselor status. *Journal of Counseling Psychology*, **29**, 125–31.

McNair, D. M., Lorr, M. & Droppleman, L. F. (1981) *EITS Manual for the Profile of Mood States*. San Diego, CA: Educational and Industrial Testing Service.

Meichenbaum, D. H. (1977) *Cognitive-behavior Modification: An Integrative Approach*. New York: Plenum.

Meichenbaum, D. H. (1983) *Coping with Stress*. London: Century Publishing.

Meichenbaum, D. H. (1985) *Stress Inoculation Training*. New York: Pergamon Press.

Meichenbaum, D. H. (1986) Cognitive-behavior modification. In F. H. Kanfer & A. P. Goldstein (eds) *Helping People Change: A Textbook of Methods* (3rd edn). New York: Pergamon Press, pp. 346–80.

Meichenbaum, D. H. & Deffenbacher, J. L. (1988) Stress inoculation training. *The Counseling Psychologist*, **16**, 69-90.

MIMS (latest edition) Middlesex, England: Haymarket Publishing.

Mintz, L. B. & O'Neil, J. M. (1990). Gender roles, sex and the process of psychotherapy: many questions and few answers. *Journal of Counseling and Development*, **68**, 381–7.

Moon, J. R. & Eisler, R. M. (1983) Anger control: an experimental comparison of three behavioural treatments. *Behavior Therapy*, **14**, 493–505.

Morawetz, D. (1989) Behavioral self-help treatment for insomnia: a controlled evaluation. *Behavior Therapy*, **20**, 365–79.

Moreno, Z. T. (1959) A survey of psychodramatic techniques. *Group Psychotherapy*, **12**, 5–14.

Morgan, C. (1984) A curricular approach to primary prevention. *Personnel and Guidance Journal*, **53**, 467–9.

Mosak, H. H. (1989) Adlerian psychotherapy. In R. Corsini & D. Wedding (eds) *Current Psychotherapies* (4th edn). Itasca, IL: Peacock, pp. 65–116.

Murgatroyd, S. (1985) *Counselling and Helping*. London: Methuen.

National Association of Social Workers (1979) Code of ethics. In G. Corey, M. S. Corey & P. Callanan (1988) *Issues of Ethics in the Helping Professions* (3rd edn). Pacific Grove, CA: Brooks/Cole, pp. 397–401.

National Board for Certified Counselors (1987) *Code of Ethics*. Alexandria, VA: NBCC.

National Training Laboratory (1967) *Feedback and the Helping Relationship*. Washington DC: NTL Institute for Applied Behavioral Sciences (mimeo).

Nelson-Jones, R. (1984) *Personal Responsibility Counselling and Therapy: An Integrative Approach*. Milton Keynes: Open University Press.

Nelson-Jones, R. (1986) Toward a people centred language for counselling psychology. *The Australian Counselling Psychologist*, **2**, 18–23.

Nelson-Jones, R. (1988) Choice therapy. *Counselling Psychology Quarterly*, **1**, 41–53.

Nelson-Jones, R. (1989) *Effective Thinking Skills: Preventing and Managing Personal Problems*. London: Cassell.

Nelson-Jones, R. (1990) *Human Relationship Skills* (2nd edn).London: Cassell.

Nelson-Jones, R. (1991) *Lifeskills: A Handbook*. London: Cassell.

Nemeroff, C. J. & Karoly. P. (1991) Operant methods. In F. H. Kanfer & A. P. Goldstein (eds) *Helping People Change: A Textbook of Methods* (4th edn). New York: Pergamon, pp. 122–60.

Novaco, R. (1977) Stress inoculation: a cognitive therapy for anger and its application to a case of depression. *Journal of Consulting and Clinical Psychology*, **45**, 600–8.

Oakley, A. (1972) *Sex, Gender and Society*. London: Temple Smith.

Office of Population Censuses and Surveys (1991a) In brief. *Population Trends*, **63**, 1–5.

Office of Population Censuses and Surveys (1991b) A review of 1990. *Population Trends*, **66**, 1–13.

Osipow, S. H., Walsh, W. B. & Tosi, D. J. (1984) *A Survey of Counseling Methods* (rev. edn). Homewood, IL: Dorsey Press.

Parloff, M. B. (1967) Goals in psychotherapy: mediating and ultimate. In A. R. Mahrer (ed.)

The Goals of Psychotherapy. New York: Appleton-Century-Crofts, pp. 5–19.

Pease, A. (1981) *Body Language: How to Read Others' Thoughts by Their Gestures*. Sydney: Camel.

Perls, F. S. (1973) *The Gestalt Approach and Eyewitness to Therapy*. New York: Bantam Books.

Perry, M. A. & Furukawa, M. J. (1986) Modeling methods. In F. H. Kanfer & A. P. Goldstein (eds) *Helping People Change: A Textbook of Methods* (3rd edn). New York: Pergamon, pp. 66–110.

Perry, W. G. (1970) *Forms of Intellectual Development in the College Years*. New York: Holt, Rinehart & Winston.

Petersen, C. & Villanova, P. (1988) An expanded attributional style questionnaire. *Journal of Abnormal Psychology*, **97**, 87–9.

Petersen, C., Semmel, A., von Baeyer, C., Abramson, L. Y., Metalsky, G. L. & Seligman, M. E. P. (1982) The Attributional Style Questionnaire. *Cognitive Therapy and Research*, **6**, 287–99.

Petersen, C., Villanova, P. & Raps, C. S. (1985) Depression and attributions: factors responsible for inconsistent results in the published literature. *Journal of Abnormal Psychology*, **92**, 165–8.

Peterson, L. & Ridley-Johnson, R. (1980) Pediatric hospital response to survey on pre-hospital preparation of children. *Journal of Pediatric Psychology*, **5**, 1–7.

Pfeiffer, J. W., Goodstein, L. & Jones, J. E. (1972–92) *The (date) Annual Developing Human Resources*. San Diego, CA: University Associates.

Physicians Desk Reference (latest edition) Oradell, NJ: Medical Economics Co.

Pomales, J., Claiborn, C. D. & LaFromboise, T. D. (1986) Effects of black students' racial identity on perceptions of white counselors varying in cultural sensitivity. *Journal of Counseling Psychology*, **33**, 57–61.

Ponterotto, J. G. (1985) A counselor's guide to psychopharmacology. *Journal of Counseling and Development*, **64**, 109–15.

Poon, D., Nelson-Jones, R. & Caputi, P. (1991) Cross cultural sensitivity and perception of counsellor characteristics and effectiveness in a white-counselor–Asian client dyad. Symposium conducted at the Annual Conference of the Australian Psychological Society, Adelaide (October).

Raskin, N. J. & Rogers, C. R. (1989) Person-centred therapy. In R. J. Corsini and D. Wedding (eds) *Current Psychotherapies* (4th edn). Itasca, IL: Peacock, pp. 155–94.

Robertson, J. & Fitzgerald, L. F. (1990) The (mis)treatment of men: effects of client gender role and life-style on diagnosis and attribution of pathology. *Journal of Counseling Psychology*, **37**, 3–9.

Roessler, R. T. (1988) Implementing career education: barriers and potential solutions. *Career Development Quarterly*, **38**, 95–103.

Rogers, C. R. (1951) *Client-centered Therapy*. Boston: Houghton Mifflin.

Rogers, C. R. (1957) The necessary and sufficient conditions of therapeutic personality change. *Journal of Consulting Psychology*, **21**, 95–103.

Rogers, C. R. (1959) A theory of therapy, personality and interpersonal relationships as developed in the client-centered framework. In S. Koch (ed.) *Psychology: A Study of Science* (Vol. 3). New York: McGraw-Hill, Study no. 1, 184–256.

Rogers, C. R. (1961) *On Becoming a Person*. Boston: Houghton Mifflin.

Rogers, C. R. (1962) The interpersonal relationship: the core of guidance. *Harvard Educational Review*, **32**, 416–29.

Rogers, C. R. (1975) Empathic: an unappreciated way of being. *The Counseling Psychologist*, **5**(2), 2–10.

Rogers, C. R. (1980) *A Way of Being*. Boston: Houghton Mifflin.

Rogoff, B. & Morelli, G. (1989) Perspectives on children's development from cultural psychology. *American Psychologist*, **44**, 343–8.

Rokeach, M. (1967) *Value Survey*. Palo Alto, CA: Consulting Psychologists Press.

Rokeach, M. & Ball–Rokeach, S. J. (1989) Stability and change in American value priorities, 1968–1981. *American Psychologist*, **44**, 775–84.

Romano, J. L. (1984) Stress management and wellness: reaching beyond the counselor's office. *Personnel and Guidance Journal*, **62**, 533–7.

Sampson, J. P. & Krumboltz, J. D. (1991) Computer-assisted instruction: a missing link in counseling. *Journal of Counseling and Development*, **69**, 395–7.

Sarason, I. G. (1976) Using modeling to strengthen the behavioral repertory of the juvenile delinquent. In J. D. Krumboltz & C. E. Thoresen (eds) *Counseling Methods*. New York: Holt, Rinehart & Winston, pp. 56–66.

Sartre, J.-P. (1956) *Being and Nothingness*. New York: Philosophical Library.

Satir, V. (1972) *Peoplemaking*. Palo Alto, CA: Science and Behavior Books.

Schulman, R., Seligman, M. E. P. & Amsterdam, D. (1987) The attributional style questionnaire is not transparent. *Behaviour Research & Therapy*, **25**, 391–5.

Seligman, M. E. P. (1975) *Helplessness: On Depression, Development and Death*. San Francisco, CA: W. H. Freeman.

Seligman, M. E. P., Abramson, L. Y., Semmel, A. & von Baeyer, C. (1979) Depressive attributional style. *Journal of Abnormal Psychology*, **88**, 242–7.

Shaffer, W. F. (1976) *Heuristics for the Initial Diagnostic Interview*. Paper presented at the annual meeting of the American Psychological Association, Washington, DC.

Sichel, J. & Ellis, A. (1984) *RET Self-help Form*. New York: Institute for Rational-Emotive Therapy.

Skinner, B. F. (1953) *Science and Human Behavior*. New York: Macmillan.

Skinner, B. F. (1969) *Contingencies of Reinforcement*. New York: Appleton-Century-Crofts.

Skinner, B. F. (1971) *Beyond Freedom and Dignity*. Harmondsworth, Middlesex: Penguin Books.

Spielberger, C. D. (1983) *Manual for the State-Trait Anxiety Inventory (Form Y)*. Palo Alto, CA: Consulting Psychologists Press.

Spitzer, R. L. & Williams, J. B. W. (1984) *The Initial Interview: Evaluation Strategies for DSM 111 Diagnosis – Interviewer's Manual*. New York: BMA Audio Cassette Publications.

Sprinthall, N. A. (1980) Psychology for secondary schools: the saber-tooth curriculum revisited? *American Psychologist*, **35**, 336–47.

Steiner, C. M. (1974) *Scripts People Live*. New York: Bantam Books.

Stock, J. & Cervone, D. (1990) Proximal goal-setting and self-regulatory process. *Cognitive Therapy and Research*, **14**, 483–98.

Stokes, T. F. & Osnes, P. G. (1989) An operant pursuit of generalization. *Behavior Therapy*, **20**, 337–55.

Strong, S. R. (1968) Counseling: an interpersonal influence process. *Journal of Counseling Psychology*, **15**, 215–24.

Strong, S. R. (1978) Social psychological approach to psychotherapy research. In S. L. Garfield & A. E. Bergin (eds) *Handbook of Psychotherapy and Behavior Change: An Empirical Analysis* (2nd edn). New York: Wiley, pp. 101–35.

Stuart, R. B. (1980) *Helping Couples Change: A Social Learning Approach to Marital Therapy*. New York: Guilford Press.

Sue, S. & Zane, N. (1987) The role of culture and cultural techniques in psychotherapy. *American Psychologist*, **42**, 37–45.

Sugarman, L. (1986) *Life-span Development: Concepts, Theories and Interventions*. London: Methuen.

Sullivan, H. S. (1953) *The Interpersonal Theory of Psychiatry*. New York: W. W. Norton.

Sullivan, H. S. (1954) *The Psychiatric Interview*. New York: W. W. Norton.

Swain, R. (1984) Easing the transition: A career planning course for college students. *Personnel and Guidance Journal*, **62**, 529–32.

Tasto, D. L. & Hinkle, J. E. (1973) Muscle relaxation for tension headaches. *Behaviour Research and Therapy*, **11**, 347–9.

Teyber, E. (1989) *Interpersonal Process in Psychotherapy: A Guide for Clinical Training*. Pacific Grove, CA: Brooks/Cole.

Thoresen, C. E. & Mahoney, M. J. (1974) *Behavioral Self-control*. New York: Holt, Rinehart & Winston.

Tillich, P. (1952) *The Courage to Be*. New Haven: Yale University Press.

Valenti, J. (1982) *Speak up with Confidence: How to Prepare, Learn, and Deliver Effective Speeches*. New York: William Morrow.

Ward, D. E. (1984) Termination of individual counseling: concepts and strategies. *Journal of Counseling and Development*, **63**, 21–5.

Watkins, C. E. (1990) The effects of counselor self-disclosure: a research review. *The Counseling Psychologist*, **18**, 477–500.

Watson, D. & Friend, R. (1969) Measurement of social-evaluative anxiety. *Journal of Consulting and Clinical Psychology*, **33**, 448–57.

Watson, D. L. & Tharp, R. G. (1989) *Self-directed Behavior: Self-modification for Personal Adjustment* (5th edn). Pacific Grove, CA: Brooks/Cole.

Webster-Stratton, C., Kolpacoff, M. & Hollinsworth, T. (1988) Self-administered videotape therapy for families with conduct-problem children: comparison with two cost effective treatments and a control group. *Journal of Consulting and Clinical Psychology*, **56**, 558–66.

Webster-Stratton, C., Hollinsworth, T. & Kolpacoff, M. (1989) The long-term effectiveness and clinical significance of three cost-effective training programs for parents with conduct-problem children. *Journal of Consulting and Clinical Psychology*, **57**, 550–3.

Wehrenberg, S. B. (1988) Learning contracts. *Personnel Journal*, **62**, 100–2.

Weiner, B. & Kukla, A. (1970) An attributional analysis of achievement motivation. *Journal of Personality and Social Psychology*, **15**, 1–20.

Weinstein, N. D. (1980) Unrealistic optimism about future events. *Journal of Personality and Social Psychology*, **39**, 806–20.

Weinstein, N. D. (1984) Why it won't happen to me: perceptions of risk factors and susceptibility. *Health Psychology*, **3**, 431–57.

Whelan, J. P., Mahoney, M. J. & Meyers, A. W. (1991) Performance enhancement in sport: a cognitive behavioral domain. *Behavior Therapy*, **22**, 307–27.

Wolpe, J. E. (1958) *Psychotherapy by Reciprocal Inhibition*. Stanford, CA: Stanford University Press.

Wolpe, J. E. (1973) *The Practice of Behavior Therapy* (2nd edn). New York: Pergamon Press.

Wolpe, J. E. (1982) *The Practice of Behavior Therapy* (3rd edn). New York: Pergamon Press.

Woolfolk, R. L., Parish, M. W. & Murphy, S. M. (1985) The effects of positive and negative imagery on motor skill performance. *Cognitive Research and Therapy*, **9**, 335–41.

Yalom, I. D. (1980) *Existential Psychotherapy*. New York: Basic Books.

Yalom, I. D. (1985) *The Theory and Practice of Group Psychotherapy* (3rd edn). New York: Basic Books.

Yalom, I. D. (1989) *Love's Executioner: And Other Tales of Psychotherapy*. London: Bloomsbury.

Yamauchi, K. T. (1987) Self-help audiocassette tapes: adjunct to psychological counseling. *Journal of Counseling and Development*, **65**, 448–50.

Yeo, A. (1981) *A Helping Hand: Coping with Personal Problems*. Singapore: Times Books International.

Name Index

Subject Index